LIFE'S RAGIN' STORMS

LIFE'S RAGIN' STORMS

DEXTER HARRISON

CITI OF
BOOKS

CITIOFBOOKS, INC.
3736 Eubank NE Suite A1
Albuquerque, NM 87111-3579
www.citiofbooks.com
Hotline: 1 (877) 389-2759
Fax: 1 (505) 930-7244

Ordering Information:

Quantity sales. Special discounts are available on quantity purchases by corporations, associations, and others. For details, contact the publisher at the address above.

Printed in the United States of America.

ISBN-13:   Softcover   978-1-960952-75-2
                eBook   978-1-960952-76-9

Library of Congress Control Number: 2023912757

TABLE OF CONTENTS

Author Disclaimer

This is a work of creative nonfiction. All characters and other entities appearing in this work are based on real life accounts written in a fictious manner. Any resemblance to real persons, dead or alive or other real-life entities past or present is purely coincidental.

This book is dedicated to five beautiful African.

American Queens:

Lillie, Wanita, Tere, Chloe and Cristen Harrison, and also, to my wonderful dad, Lee.

A very special thank you from the depths of my heart to Momma, Daddy, Aunt Mary Cockrell, Aunt Lillie Jackson, Aunt Lorina Turner, Uncle Bryant Bartie, Jr., Uncle Walter Bartie, Aunt Ethel Dozier, Annie Laurie Miller, Momma Lillie Harrison, Son and Jeanette January.

Cliff Hudder, you're the greatest!

In loving memory of Grandma Frances January, Paw-Paw Dominic and Maw-Maw Mary Bishop, Pappa Bryant and Momma Bean Bartie, Big Momma Bartie, Uncle Jimmy "Bill" LaSalle, Sr., Pappa Simon Harrison, Aunt Beanie Avant, Mrs. Agnes "Aunt Coot" Nash, Emma Nunez and to all the victims who lost their lives during Hurricane Audrey back on June 27, 1957. Without you, there would be no Life's Ragin' Storms.

CHAPTER 1

Sheets of rain slammed down on the tin roof of a four-room, unpainted, unsealed farm shack. The rain turned the dusty, clamshell-surfaced track of The Front Ridge Road to mud. The shack and road stood out against a flat landscaping of cotton fields, pastures, and marshlands about three miles west of the Warren 'Jiggy' Miller Cotton Gin. This gin was about the most significant economic enterprise in the rustic Gulf Coast community of Creole, Louisiana.

Once the crystal white rain mixed with the dirt, it produced a smell of putrid eggs in the marsh, and in the pastures the odor of clabbered milk and fresh fertilizer. The residents of this forlorn shack, Bryant Tilman and Lovenia Bishop-Bartie, had grown accustomed to the odors, the high winds, and heavy rain. In one sense, that storm on the night of March 23, 1935 was bringing nothing unusual—just another storm to weather.

On the other hand, the night brought with it a very special fervidity for the Bartie couple and Lovenia's son Jimmy, a child she had conceived from a previous marriage to Jimmy LaSalle, Sr., who had predeceased her some time ago. Jimmy was asleep on the living room floor, without an inkling that he was soon to become a big brother, but everyone else was anxiously awaiting the arrival of Bryant and Lovenia's firstborn child. The pioneer Dr. Stephen O. Carter, a white physician had come to assist with the travailing labor process.

"Bean, how you feeling?" asked Dr. Carter. Everyone in the area called Lovenia, Bean.

"Well, I feel pretty good, but I thank this baby's about to come out right now," she sighed.

"Just relax and take it easy."

During this special moment of anticipation, Bryant was sitting in an old rocking chair near the corner of the bed with a smile on his face. He could hardly wait for the birthing process to begin. Large balls of sweat streamed down Bean's face, however her complexion changed, momentarily, and she began to take short broken grasps of breath. Bryant, startled by the commotion, hastily raised his eyes to the ceiling, and began to pray to God silently for a safe delivery of his offspring. Dr. Carter sat next to Bean on the bed and wiped her face with a cold towel. He yelled across the room to Bryant.

"Hey, fetch me some hot boiling water and pour it into this here big bowl."

"Yeah sir, Dr. Carter." Bryant replied hurriedly. "Yeah sir!"

His conversation with "the man upstairs" disrupted. Bryant rushed into the kitchen and retrieved some water from the pail on the counter top. He threw a couple of logs into the stove and poured kerosene over them, which started the water to boil briskly.

"Hurry up Bryant, I'm gonna need that water, pretty quick!" yelled Dr. Carter from the other room. Bryant heard Bean's moans and groans, as the baby prepared to make its entrance into the world.

"Push, Bean. Push" shouted Dr. Carter. "Push, Push! That a good girl. Push! Push! Okay, once more. Now give me one big push."

The shack Bryant and Lovenia Bartie called home was owned by a white widower named Jim Rutherford who lived with his son 'Tee' Rutherford, and Tee's wife Eunice in a much nicer house east of the Bartie place. Two other households lived between their two homes, and across the road from this line of four houses, pure marshland ran southward to the Gulf coast.

Bryant Tilman Bartie, born October 25, 1905, was a very proud, light-brown colored, brawny, seasonal sharecropper. He received approximately $300 annually for his share of cotton, corn, potatoes, and other vegetation harvested during the hot, humid spring and summer Louisiana months. To supplement his farm income, Bryant trapped muskrats in the winter, and raised chickens, White Chester pigs, horses and cows, which provided him and Lovenia an earnest living. Lovenia Mary Bishop-Bartie, born October 3, 1910 was a soft-spoken, neat attractive, shy, light complected lady of Indian and mulatto descent. Lovenia had a subtle air of distinction, though neither she nor her husband had obtained a formal education past the sixth grade. Often mistaken for a white woman because of her fair skin and fine, curly black hair, she never lost sight of the fact that her place in society was that of a colored lady.

Despite Lovenia and Bryant's lack of education and material possessions, they truly were a proud, God-fearing couple. They thanked the almighty Master immensely for life, for the love they shared, and for the plain living during this country's period of severe economic decline. There was always something to eat on their table. Needless to say, not the best of shelter stood above their heads, nor the sturdiest of floors below their feet, and far from the best of clothing clung to their backs, but they were grateful for what little they owned. Even though they were poor colored people, Bryant and Lovenia still managed to keep themselves and their place neat, clean and wholesome.

Creole, a small agricultural province lodged in the center of lower Cameron Parish along the deep southwest coast of Louisiana, was roughly six miles north of the Gulf of Mexico. The seashore town of Cameron, formerly Leesburg, was about ten miles west of Creole, bordered by the Calcasieu River on the west. The Gulf sat at its front door to the south. Grand Chenier, a similar community, noted for its ridges of live oak trees, marshes, and bayous, was about fifteen miles east of Creole. The Gulf adjoined that area on the south, while the Mermentau River ran in a northerly semicircular route from east to west. All three communities were within the boundaries of Cameron Parish. Cameron Parish was named in honor of Confederate soldier Robert Alexander Cameron in 1870, after being separated from Calcasieu and Vermilion Parishes. One of the largest parishes in the state, Cameron had a 75-mile coastline and well over a million acres of land, however it reported one of the smallest populations during this period. The Police Jury, seated in the town of Cameron, was the governing body. The first courthouse erected in 1874 was nothing extraordinary, though the two-story structure had several windows to capture those cool occasional Gulf breezes during Sunday morning church services.

The very first road built in 1935 ran north to south approximately 50 miles between Creole and Lake Charles, the largest city in Calcasieu Parish. The construction of that road practically did away with the Borealis Rex or "King of the North", a stern-wheeled steamboat that transported citizens up and down the Calcasieu River from downtown Cameron to Calcasieu Lake in Lake Charles; about a six hour trip each way. In addition to transporting passengers, The Rex carried the United States mail, freight, groceries, bales of cotton, cattle, firewood, building materials, articles of commerce, and trade transactions, from which the area's inhabitants bought and sold.

During this tempestuous night of thunder and lightning, Bryant and Bean's old, detached wagon, lodged in the front yard under a mulberry tree of their farm shack, swayed in the gusts of wind and rain. The interior of the hovel, eagerly referred to as "home", had been made slightly more attractive by ragged newspaper and magazine pages pasted haphazardly over large cracks in the living room's walls. Bean had used flour and water paste to glue the substitute wallpaper onto the dismal, unfinished walls. Evidence of roach and mice gnawing were present on some of the patches, which had peeled away in spots. In addition to the hideous walls, one could see the ground through a large hole in the wooden floors.

The hole allowed constant exposure to the elements, as well as access for rodents and all the types of insects who invited themselves in. Bean tried to arrange the living room furniture in a complementary fashion to enhance the gloomy room's appearance and to camouflage the unsightly hole in the floor. She had covered three old wooden benches with ruffled gingham. Several homemade pillows tossed over the seats of each bench provided added comfort and decoration. A pedestal table with two kerosene lamps sat in the center, between the benches and two, broken-down, straight-back wooden chairs.

There were two bedrooms located on the east side of the shack, each with a steel frame bed painted silver. The old, worn out, smelly mattresses on the frames were stuffed with wild duck feathers. Plain white cotton sheets had been neatly tucked under them, while homemade duck-downy pillows lay at the head of each bed. An antiquated, darkly varnished cedar chest stood tall in one room along a bare wall. In the same room sat a large tin tub on an old, worn-out, multicolored rug. In the center of the house, the kitchen had an old safe standing tall in one corner, mainly used to store dishes, cakes, and pies once they had been baked. Several shelves along the walls held pots, pans, and other kitchen utensils. In another corner, a pile of logs was neatly stacked and a pail of water sat on the edge of a countertop near the back door. The entire interior of the place released a smell of smoke and charred wood accumulated from the burning of the logs. There were no bathrooms, only an old, run down, smelly outdoor toilet accessible for nature's call. Once Bryant returned from the kitchen with the hot water, Dr. Carter reached into his black bag, pulled out a scalpel and plunged it into the steaming bowl. He continued to wipe Bean's flushed face. The poor woman was in so much pain. To make matters worse, she was also a bit shy because Bryant was looking over her half naked body. Bryant sensed his wife's uneasiness, so he grabbed her hand and tried to console her.

"Everything's gonna be all right, Bean. I know. Because I took it to the Almighty Master. Don't worry' about nothin. He gonna take good care of you and this baby."

Bean gazed at Bryant with a peculiar look, as though to say "I'm ashamed with you looking over me like this." Meanwhile, the baby's head protruded out of her birth canal. Too much blood and birth fluids surrounded its little face to determine just who it resembled. One thing was for sure, the little one had a thick head of dark hair and fair skin.

"Push! Real hard, this time Bean" shouted Dr. Carter. "Real, real, hard. Push! Push! That a gal. One more big push!" Bean released a loud yell and then screamed "Ah! Ah!" Dr. Carter shouted "One more good push. Just one more." By this time the baby's head and torso projected out. Dr. Carter pulled the rest of its helpless body free from Bean's womb. He gave the little one a spank on the bottom and then cut the cord. The precious infant merely panted a soft whimper. Bean tried to raise her impaired body, to get a quick glimpse. Bryant, on the other hand, was overly excited, so he immediately, announced the sex of the child before Dr. Carter ever had a chance to utter a single word.

"Bean, it's a pretty little ol' baby girl. Plague-take-it!" (A homemade expression that Bryant made up himself and used regularly.) "Will you look at that little angel?" he gasped, with much warmth in his eyes. "She sure is a pretty little thing," said Dr. Carter. Bean nodded approvingly and reached for her newborn child. Dr. Carter handed it to her, as soon as its fragile little body had been wiped with some old rags. The infant looked at its mother with one eye open and the other closed. Bryant fell to his knees and thanked God for a safe delivery of his first-born daughter. Bean stared deeply into its face, then held the baby close to her breast. The baby girl felt an immediate serenity and true love coming from her mother. Eventually, she went fast asleep, peacefully, without a single care in the world. Nevertheless, the baby girl had no clue that she, too, would join her parents at a standard of living far below the poverty level. Later, she would grow up to learn that material possessions were not the spice of life, but it's the simple things that really make life worthwhile. Yes, this infant would be poor; however, she shall be immersed in love, something far more valuable than wealth.

***

The next morning couldn't come quickly enough for Bryant, who had awakened earlier with a sense of urgency. He prayed; milked the cows; gathered the eggs from the chicken coop; and then fed the pigs. He pumped some fresh water into a bucket from the well behind the house. Then he cooked his tired, enervated wife a hearty breakfast of bacon, eggs, hominy, and biscuits. The little infant had not yet awakened.

"Here Bean. I cooked you something to eat" he replied.

"I don't want no ol' food right now. I ain't hungry."

"Na, Na, Na, Na, Na, Na, Bean" he responded in a short stutter,

"You got to eat something. That's the only way you gonna get your strength back."

"Thanks for the breakfast, Bryant, but I can't eat nothing right now."

Disappointed, Bryant returned to the kitchen and placed the tray of food on the table. A thought hit him from out of nowhere, causing him to rush back into the bedroom, where his wife was lying. He demanded her full attention.

"Bean, what we gonna name this baby?"

"I don't know. I ain't thought about it yet."

"Well, I did Bean. You know something, I like the name Juanita. Now that's a pretty' name. I always liked that name."

"Juanita is pretty, Bryant. But how you gonna spell a name like that?"

"Let me see." Slowly he broke the name down into its three syllables. Then he repeated the name out loud again. He spelled it the way it sounded to his ears. "W-a-n-i-t-a," he said. "Juanita."

"You sure that's how you spell it, Bryant?"

"Yep, Bean. I's sure that's the way you spell it. W-a-n-i-t-a."

"Well, that sounds right to me!"

"Yeah, me too, Bean. Me too."

"What's her middle name gonna be Bryant?"

"I like Cecilia, Bean."

"Oh! That's a pretty name, too."

"Ain't it though?"

"Well Bryant, how do you spell Cecilia?"

"I thank you spell that C-e-c-i-l."

"You sure?"

"Yeap, I'm sure."

Later, during the day Bryant recorded his first daughter's name in the family Bible. Even though he didn't have much education, he did the best he could. Although Bean had completed the sixth grade, Bryant had received only a third-grade education. He came from a large poor family. His mother, the former Matilda Hebert was born in August 1874, didn't even know the exact date of her birth. The only thing she knew was that she was born around the time the peaches ripened during the month of August. During Bryant's childhood, very little emphasis was put on educating the area's Negro children. They were lucky to go past the third grade. School only lasted approximately three months out of a year, making it very difficult for a child to obtain much learning.

Once school ended for the session, it meant going back to the cotton fields, trapping muskrats and attending to domestic chores that required their labor.

Nevertheless, Bryant printed his daughter's name proudly as "Wanita Cecil Bartie" in the family's Bible. Born on a stormy night in March, the twenty-third day of 1935 to Bryant and Lovenia Bartie in Creole, Louisiana. Most colored people kept records of births, marriages, deaths and keepsake photographs in the family Bible for safekeeping. Eventually, those very same records evolved into the only permanent chronicles of their family's lineage.

Bryant's mother, Matilda-known by that time by everyone in the region as "Big Momma"—and Bean's parents, the Bishops, would be delighted to get the news of the arrival of their new granddaughter, Wanita. Bean's folks lived approximately eight miles west of Bryant's home, which would require an hour's ride by horseback. Big Momma's house was on the back ridge, about five miles from the Bishops. He'd have to cross many stretches of marshland to bring the word to her.

Bryant saddled up his favorite old mare and off he trotted into the windy, humid, Louisiana climate to spread the good news.

CHAPTER 2

Wanita grew into a beautiful toddler. Unlike Bean's fine, silky, curly hair, her's was rich, thick, dark, and course. She wasn't a tender-headed baby. Bean had no struggle to comb her hair. She simply parted it down the middle and across the top of her head and braided it into four big plats. She conditioned Wanita's scalp daily with "Lucky Heart" hair grease. On occasion, Bean dressed up her braids with a ribbon or two. Wanita always had a smile on her face.

She was a very happy infant, although just a bit hyper at times. Wanita wore mostly blue denim coveralls. Bryant and Bean could only afford to buy her clothes and shoes, annually. Bean generally made the most of her own and Wanita's dresses. Wanita's one and only little dressy outfit was worn mainly to church, funerals and other special occasions, a rarity for the family. Outside of visiting family and friends, church was really the only form of entertainment and socializing the Barties undertook. Bryant didn't own very much clothing himself. He had one good suit and an old, beat-up pair of worn-out dress shoes for church. When he kneeled to pray, a hole through the first layer of his shoe sole was visible to other worshipers. Bean had maybe three or four decent Sunday dresses. Nothing fancy. Nevertheless, Bryant and Bean never complained about their simple lifestyle. And even though they were poor, there wasn't a single time when Wanita walked around filthy.

The Barties felt that it's one thing to be poor, to be poor and filthy was another. Cleanliness was a ritual that both Bean and Bryant swore by and lived by. It was evident by the manner in which she kept Wanita smelling fresh and clean at all times.

Wanita slept in the same room as her parents in a large makeshift bassinet, located near a window. The bassinet was simply a large rocking chair covered with a blanket and downy pillow on the seat. Nothing elegant, nothing fancy, just a practical bed for a sweet little angel to lay her precious head.

"Bean, if we don't get no rain, we gonna lose everything we planted this year."

"Don't worry about it, Bryant. Poppa said if we don't make good on the crop, he'll help us out."

"I know, Bean, but I can't take anything from your Poppa. Anyways, God put me here in charge of you and ol' Piggy-Pon-Tole sleeping right over there in that rocker. And it's my responsibility to take care both of ya'll. It ain't your Poppa's worry.

It's mine, Bean."

"Ump," sighed Bean. "Who in the world is Piggy-Pon-Tole?"

Bryant chuckled. "This here's ol' Piggy-Pon-Tole," he said pointing at Wanita.

"Bryant, you always coining up with some ol' silly mess. What kind of name is Piggy-Pon-Tole, anyways?"

"Now Bean, just let ol' Bryant be Bryant. Piggy-Pon-Tole is a nickname I give our little daughter Wanita." Bryant moved over next to the bassinet. "We ain't got much, ol' Piggy-Pon-Tole, but with God's help some day you won't have to be poor like me and your momma. You see, Piggy-Pon-Tole, you gonna make something big out of yourself, girl. Just listen to your daddy, you hear me? Because ol' Bryant knows what he's talking about." Wanita awoke with a big smile on her little face, as though she comprehended exactly what her father was saying.

"Look Bean, ol' Piggy-Pon-Tole done woke up and she look like she hungry."

"Ump, Bryant you ain't got no sense a-tall. Piggy-Pon-Tole? You always coming up with some foolishness. Give me that baby, here."

"Na-na-na-now Bean, you just let ol' Bryant be Bryant!" He laughed out loud. "This is ol' Piggy-Pon-Tole' and that's that." Several months later, Bean woke up bright and early to get an initial start before Sunday church service. Feeling a bit fatigued, she starched and ironed Bryant a shirt to wear, then gathered some eggs for a potato salad, rinsed the dirt off a fresh batch of collard greens, and wrung a yard chicken's neck. Afterwards, she plucked its feathers and fried the bird for their lunch. Bryant worked very hard every day, so he expected a good solid meal, especially on Sunday. After Bean finished her chores, she heated some well water on the stove, poured it into the big round tin tub already half-filled with water at room temperature. She took her bath first, then bathed and dressed Wanita. After Bryant finished his chores for the morning, he took a bath and got dressed, too. Ebenezer Baptist Church wasn't too far from Bean's parents; nevertheless, it would take the family about an hour and a half to get there by horse and wagon. Soon after Wanita's birth, Bean's mother convinced her to allow Jimmy to be reared by her and her husband, since Bryant was merely the young boy's stepfather. Mrs. Bishop intuitively felt this was the best solution for Jimmy and her daughter's marriage, therefore she refused to except no for an answer. So shortly thereafter, Jimmy without raising a fuss over his new living arrangements moved in with his grandparents at the Bishop place.

Wanita always enjoyed the long ride to church with her parents. Bean had to hold onto her tightly because she was such an active infant. The task had become even harder now, being that Bean was seven months pregnant with her third child. She could no longer handle Wanita in her lap, so she sat her down on the wagon seat, between herself and Bryant. Along the way, Wanita held her little arms outward so that the wind could sweep through her hands and fingers. She loved the feeling as it rushed through her hair and over her infant body. She kept those little arms extended constantly for the better part of the trip. Wanita had a bad habit of trying to crawl off the front seat to the bed of the wagon to play back there, but Bryant wouldn't allow such a thing because it was too dangerous.

She could fall off and severely injure herself since there was nothing back there to keep her contained. Sometimes her little temper flared up when she couldn't have her way. Eventually, that tantrum would require a spanking if she didn't cool it, quickly.

"Piggy-Pon-Tole, I'm gonna stop this wagon and skin them little legs, if you don't stop that whining. I mean it girl! Now sit here and act like you got some sense."

But Wanita kept struggling with her mother, determined to get back to the bed of the wagon. "Bryant, I can't do nothing with her" said Bean, out of breath. Wanita pushed and pulled, and tried to free herself from Bean.

"Plague-take-it! Now Piggy-Pon-Tole you sit down, girl and stop fussing with your momma, before I stop this wagon. And if I do, it ain't gonna be good, for you."

Wanita whined, squirmed, pulled and pushed, until she finally fell asleep in her father's lap. The hot sun helped to calm her free spirits.

"Wold, horse" yelled Bryant. "Whoa!"

They arrived at the Ebenezer Baptist Church drenched with sweat from the glistening heat. It was even hotter inside the sanctuary. Hand fans were disbursed at the door, to help circulate a cool breeze over their warm, sunburned bodies. Although Bean looked very faint, she managed to pull herself together after a while. She'd grown up Catholic, but after marrying Bryant, Bean converted in support of her husband's wishes for the family to serve God as a unit. Ebenezer Baptist had a fairly large colored congregation, patronized mostly by relatives. Once church concluded, Big Momma greeted Bryant and Bean outside on the grounds.

"Bryant, she shows is a pretty lil ol' thing. Now, I can see she got her momma's color, but she put me in the mind of you in the face.

Matilda Bartie, "Big Momma", was a straight-forward and to-the-point person, holding back few of her own notions. She was a stout, heavy-set, very light complected woman. Her husband, Miles Henry, had died many years before. One day, Miles had come in from working out in the fields and just dropped dead on the spot from an apparent heart attack. Big Momma, a devoted Protestant, attended Ebenezer Baptist every Sunday, though like her daughter-in-law, she'd been a devout Catholic before her marriage to Miles Henry. Their union changed her religious perspective. After Miles Henry passed away, Big Momma was left with several acres of fertile farmland, and a modest home.

Her parents were Noah Hebert, a Dutchman, originally from Holland, and Elizabeth, who was Negro. Bryant's father Miles Henry was the son of Sarah Jane Dozier and Miles Bartie, Sr. The couple had six other children: Jonah, Samson, Andrew, Martha, Hattie ("Pump") and Elvira. Jonah, Samson and Andrew presumably froze to death at a very early age. Matilda and Miles Henry raised thirteen children. Ten boys: Levion, Noah, Johnny, Henry, Earl, Alcy, Lester, Abram, Joe, and Bryant, along with three girls Lucinda, Sarah, and Mary. Some of Big Momma's sons continued to farm the land, while she spent most of her time doing domestic chores.

"Momma, how you feeling?" asked Bryant.

"I feel pretty good, Bryant. It's just been so hot lately. I'm afraid we gonna have a bad storm or something like that from this ol' hot weather. And Bean how you doing my girl?" Now you listen to me, you better take good care of you-self. Especially since you in the family way. Don't do too much round the house, my girl, because you might lose that baby."

Bean knew better than to challenge Big Momma's assumptions. Meanwhile, Wanita was trying to pull away from her father's arm, so that she could wander around the church's grounds being as if she was such an independent baby, always insisting on roaming some place where she had no business. Once Wanita broke loose, she took off running as fast as she could away from Bryant and the others.

"Come back here girl! Don't you go too far away, now! You hear me?" yelled Bryant.

"Look at her go!" chuckled Big Momma. "She's got so much life in her. Just like a little mystery child blowing everywhere in the wind. God's really blessed you and Bryant, Bean."

"Yes, indeed Big Momma, he sure have."

Soon after, Bryant returned with Wanita out of breath. "Don't run away from me no more" he gasped.

"Bryant, leave that child alone. She's just like a little storm, tearing up everything in sight. She'll grow out of that. Trust me! I done raised thirteen kids of my own. I art-to-know!"

CHAPTER 3

The hot summer sun and lack of rain affected Bryant's cotton and vegetation crops tremendously. At harvest time, he made little money because of the inferior production. Regardless of his sparse income, however, he still managed to tithe generously, even if it meant being indebted to a local merchant. The Lord always came first in Bryant's eyes, so making the sacrifice to the church was the natural thing to do. The owner of B. Nunez General Store understood his low production and allowed him to buy all the goods he needed for his family on credit. Bryant kept his own record of credit items purchased, listed according to their individual cost. A limited education didn't hinder his accurate account of those transactions. Whenever it came time for him to settle his bill with the merchant, there never were any discrepancies. He knew in advance exactly how much he was indebted.

"Thanks Mister Newness. I promise to make good on my credit, as soon as things get better for me. You'll see, Mister Newness. You'll see."

"By all means Bryant. I know you had a bad season this year. Everyone did. It's a shame we didn't get as much rain as we needed. But I know that you're a man of your word."

"Yea Sir, you right Mister Newness. You right Sir. But as soon as things get better for me, I'm gonna pay you. You'll see, Mister Newness.

Ol' Bryant don't believe in owing anybody no money. I's a man of my word."

"I trust you, Bryant. You are a good colored fellow. I've been doing business with you for a long time, and I've never had any trouble with you not paying your bill."

"Thank you, Sir."

"You've always been a good customer. Take care of yourself and your family. Just pay me when you can."

Bryant returned home with the goods. He unloaded them off the wagon and carried everything into the house. Lately, life had become a heap of chores. Before he headed back out into the fields, he helped Bean rub some clothes on the washboard in a tub of sudsy water. Afterward, he rinsed them thoroughly before hanging them out to dry on a wire clothesline strung between two Chinaberry trees which were aligned out back of the shack to the west. Bean couldn't do much work in those days because she was almost ready to have the baby. When Bryant wasn't calling Wanita, "Piggy-Pon-Tole", he called her "Nita" for short.

He was overwhelmed with her progress in just a very short year and a half. Nita was an obedient, inquisitive toddler to say the least. She entertained herself with makeshift toys such as empty thread spools, a rattle that Mr. Rutherford handed down to her, and a homemade rag doll that Bean sewed herself. Nita could always be found following Bryant around, mimicking his every action, such as attempting to pump water out of the well. Of course, she couldn't do it without his assistance. He had to lift the little toddler up far enough so she could reach the handle. When she tried to help him milk the cows, she got more milk on herself than in the bucket. The two of them even gathered eggs together on several occasions from the coop. However, that was only when Nita wasn't throwing them back at the chickens. If Nita wasn't getting in Bryant's way, she would be chasing the chickens and ducks around in the yard. The small infant really created more work for her father, but Bryant didn't mind the extra frustration. He was obsessed with his first-born daughter.

Later on, that afternoon, after Bryant had returned home from a tiring day out in the fields, he soaked his tired, worn body in a hot bath. Bean prepared the family's supper consisting of cornbread and milk. Bryant, a bit somber this evening, let his pride stand before him, causing some unwarranted anxiety and remorse. He kept reflecting on the fact that his crop had done so poorly that season. He also desired to provide a better living for Bean, Nita and himself, but things were looking pretty dismal. At supper time, Bryant recited the blessing out loud. Bean fed Nita, while he chewed on the large chunks of yellow cornbread sprinkled with sugar, submersed in a large bowl of milk. After everyone ate, he and Bean cleaned the kitchen. Then all three gathered together in the living room. Bryant pulled out his Bible, and Nita crawled up onto his lap. He read out loud, and very slowly, as best he could by a kerosene lantern, the 127th Psalm.

"Except the Lord build the house, they labour in vain that build it: except the Lord keep the city, the watchman waketh but in vain. It is vain for you to rise up early, to sit up late, to eat the bread of sorrows: for so he giveth his beloved sleep. Lo, children, are a heritage of the Lord: and the fruit of the womb is his reward. As arrows are in the hand of a mighty man; so are children to the youth. Happy is the man that hath his quiver full of them; they shall not be ashamed, but they shall speak with the enemies in the gate."

When he finished reading that passage a small tear formed in the corner of his eye. Bean looked at her husband with strong conviction "Bryant we gonna make it, just as long as we got each other, we'll make it. We are a family. We ain't got much, and we never had. But we do have the Lord. And that's all each one of us needs right now. It's just another storm passing over us, Bryant. But, before you know it, the Lord's gonna bring us some sunshine, after a while."

Bryant remained silent after Bean spoke those words. All three of them just sat together and stared at each other for a long moment with looks that said, "everything's gonna be all right." Nita looked at her parents with the same conviction, even though her little mind didn't quite comprehend the crisis that faced the family. The glow in her little, innocent face gave Bryant and Bean the added encouragement to push forward, regardless of the obstacles that lay ahead.

The month of September was often associated with tropical storms and bad weather. Bryant and Bean had no radio to get the forecast. The only information they received about the weather was from Mr. Jim Rutherford, and that was only when severe conditions were predicted. Most times, Bryant relied on signs taught to him as a child by his father, Miles Henry. A crescent moon in a bowl shape meant no rain. Or, a north wind blowing in early fall meant a mild winter. However, this particular September day, on the twenty-first, in 1936, came with a precious calmness. A quiet little storm blew in over the Bartie home, bringing with it a beautiful baby girl, Mary Winona. Her skin was the color of light-brown sugar. Named after Bryant's sister, and also Bean's mother, Mary had beautiful, coal-black straight hair and light brown eyes. Bryant issued her the nickname of "Toad". He had a unique way of renaming his children once their birth names were given. Bryant was hoping for a son, but thanked God immensely for the new little blessing that had arrived safely that afternoon. The spitting image of Bean, Mary was just what the doctor ordered so far as Nita was concerned. It had become a very lonely time around the farm without any other little people to relate to. Particularly, after Jimmy moved away to the Bishops. Nita had had no one else to play with. She adored her little sister. Neither Bean nor Bryant could keep the toddler away from the baby's bassinet. At first, Nita could not comprehend the delicacy of her newborn sister. She always wanted to hold her hand, foot or whatever other body part she could grasp.

At one point, Nita tried to pick Mary up and carry her around. From sun-up to sun-down, Nita gazed into her little sister's eyes with enthusiasm, and Mary stared right back with the very same energy. A match made in Heaven, like ebony and ivory keys on a piano. Instant love developed between the two little Bartie girls; a special type of love, that was sure to last a lifetime. Whenever Mary cried, Nita was right there along with Bean to help ease any discomfort. There wasn't much Nita could do but get in the way, however the mere fact that she wanted to help so willingly revealed a true bond in the making.

Even though the times were hard for the Bartie's, they loved each other unconditionally. The family always sat together at mealtimes, a ritual passed down through the generations. Bryant prayed to God from the heart. Sometimes his blessings before a meal were more like the morning prayer. He thanked and thanked and thanked God for the innocence that he, Bean, Piggy-Pon-Tole and Toad were experiencing.

Poor little Toad had no inkling of what a simple, meager, life meant. One thing's for sure though, the road ahead was bound to be a good one, with lil ol' Piggy-Pon-Tole by her side. No one had to tell Toad, for she had already sampled a taste of true love, first-hand from Nita.

One night, when Bean had finished breast-feeding Mary, she laid the infant down on its little back. Nita observed her mother's gentle rocking motion as the baby fell fast asleep. Then, all of a sudden, Nita cried out to rock the little one. Mary, awakening at the sound of Nita's shout, began to whine. Bean said "take it real easy with her, cause she's just a tiny lil baby, Nita." So, Nita listened closely to her mother's instructions and rocked the baby slowly, delivering a soft contentment. Bean left the two of them together for a moment and went into the living room where her husband was reading his Bible by a kerosene lamp. Nita got sleepy during the process, so she crawled into the big rocker, and lay alongside her little sister. When Bean returned to check on the two girls, she found them asleep in the big chair, Nita's little arm embracing Mary's infantile body in a loving fashion. Bean looked at that picture with a great deal of admiration. She called Bryant in. They smiled at each other and retired for the evening with a sense of strong family ties.

Each day had gotten better and better for Nita as time went on, simply because of her new-found responsibility. She began taking charge and doing whatever a big sister was supposed to do. Bryant even noticed how Nita grasped the role of protecting Mary. He was so proud of the way his two daughters' chemistries agreed. Some times after a hard day's work in the fields, Bryant would take a moment to become a bit sentimental as he watched their sisterly relationship flourish.

Several months zoomed by, with Toad trying to take a few steps on her own. Of course Piggy-Pon-Tole was right there to guide her each step of the way. Toad probably started taking steps early because of Piggy-Pon-Tole's influence. She watched Nita's every move and imitated her in any way she could. It didn't take long for Toad to start making complete steps by herself.

One day Nita and Toad were playing on a big quilt under a tree in the garden while their mother was washing clothes. All of a sudden, Nita got to her feet and reached for the sky, spinning around in a circle with both arms extended. Mary watched cheerfully, as though wishing she could do the same thing. All at once, Nita ran swiftly toward her mother who was scrubbing clothes on an old scrub board. As Nita ran for Bean, Mary felt abandoned. She blurted out a loud, babyish noise, stood up all by herself, and started making steps toward Bean and Nita. Once they saw what she had done, both of them ran towards her to make sure their eyes weren't playing tricks on them. Mary took a few more independent steps. Overcome with joy, Nita turned in full circles around and around, her arms extended upward. Mary raised her little arms, too, and tried the same thing. Bean and Nita were so happy to see the baby's progress, they couldn't wait for Bryant to return from the fields.

The next day Mr. Jim Rutherford brought over a box of second-hand clothes for the family. "Come here Nita", said Bean.

"Ol' Mr. Jim done give us a box of clothes for you and Mary. Stay still girl, so I can see if this is going to fit. Good, that'll fit you and that'll fit Mary."

Just about all of Nita and Mary's clothes were hand-me-downs. Every now and then Bean purchased some material when Bryant was able to save up enough money, to make them new dresses, but that was a rare occasion. Bean was very grateful for whatever the Rutherfords offered the family. Bryant was especially appreciative.

He accepted their offerings wholeheartedly, just like it was a hundred dollars. Big Momma and Miles Henry instilled in him to be accepting of whatever someone wanted to bestow. Whether the family could use the items or not was never the issue. Bryant took whatever those white folks gave him, and showed much appreciation for their generosity. Those very same values were passed on to Nita and Mary.

"Them little dresses sure looks good on you Piggy-Pon-Tole and Ol' Toad. Always thank God for whatever he blesses you with. And remember, ain't nobody in this here world owes you nothing just cause you are poor. When you get something like this from anybody, just be thankful. Because when you show a person you' thankful, God's going to bless you even more. Always be thankful!

Whether it's a penny or a hundred dollars. Somebody might even give you a ol' grass sack, but plague-take-it, you take that ol' sack just like it's gold and find something to do with it. And keep on thanking the Lord over and over and over again."

In 1937 while President Franklin Delano Roosevelt was in office, the local Cameron Parish Police Jury applied for a new courthouse under his WPA (Works Project Administration) program. When the application was received in Washington, the officials there proposed that a very small courthouse be built, instead of the larger one requested by the parish's governing body.

Congress felt that Cameron Parish's population was too small and would most likely stay that way because it was in such an isolated area of Louisiana. When President Roosevelt heard of the discrepancy, he personally took charge and demanded that Cameron get the larger building they requested. According to Senator Allen Ellender, Roosevelt said, "I know those people down there; I've hunted at Jim Bonsall's hunting camp; and he's a good friend of mine. They must have their large courthouse. They are good people and they deserve it." So Cameron Parish got it's new courthouse personally approved by President Roosevelt under the Federal Emergency Administration of Public Works No. La. 1023-D. Erected in 1937, Herman J. Duncan & Co., Inc. of Alexandria, Louisiana, were the architects, and J. Parnel Blair of Lake Charles was the contractor. The large beige courthouse became Cameron Parish's best-known landmark. The courthouse stood proudly in the middle of town square, on the same property where the original one once did. "Pop, pop, pop, pop" went the old Jiggy Miller Cotton Gin as it separated the lint from the seed. The noise was a common sound around the Bartie household, especially during cotton season. The year's crop turned out to be a fairly decent one for Bryant. A sea of pretty white cotton covered the fields. He and Bean could definitely use the additional money, since they now had four lovely little girls to support. With two new additions to the family, the portrait of a poor happy, colored kindred painted an even prettier picture for the Barties. Lillie Naomi came into the world on September 27, 1938.

Named after Bean's sister, and the biblical character, she was a very precious, proud, particular, light complected little girl. Lillie adjusted well to her older sisters, Nita and Mary, and the baby of the family

Lorina Rose, born December 22, 1939. Lorina's middle name was taken from one of Bean's father's sisters. Bryant nicknamed Lillie "Bay-Bay" and Lorina "Pole". Lillie resembled Nita most closely; the two of them could almost pass for twins. At birth, Lorina turned out to be a beautiful infant with very charming facial features, and bore the same complexion as Nita and Lillie. Lil (short for Lillie) and Lo (short for Lorina) both had coarse hair, just like Nita's. Lo, however, was a little more tender-headed than Nita and Lil. She put up a big fuss whenever Bean tried to pass a comb through her thick hair. On the other hand, Mary received the most blessings out of the bunch when it came to hair texture. She experienced fewer hassles, because her hair was much softer and finer than the three other girls.

Piggy-Pon-Tole, Toad, Bay-Bay, and Pole, made for a rowdy little bunch of girls living under the same roof. Three fair complexions and a light brown one comprised this lively, colorful quartet. Each of the precious little angels had their own unique personality and shared quite a few similarities with Bean and Bryant. The fact that they were poor never troubled the little ones, because they had never known a better lifestyle. That they were loved so dearly by their parents and each other made up for any "delusions of grandeur" that they could possibly be missing anything in their lives.

Nita had taken charge as the leader of the group. Since she was the oldest, she felt a need to keep the others in line. Then there was Mary, a subdued, shy little girl, who was most cooperative and supportive amongst the foursome, always willing to lend a hand, and rarely challenging the wishes of the other three. Lil was the wittiest, laughing continually, and constantly teasing Nita and Mary. She also developed quite a need to be seen and heard, ever since Lo had come on the scene, stealing the public's attention. Lo, however, was the cry-baby of the bunch, simply because the other three girls had spoiled her rotten. Nita, Mary, and Lil feuded constantly over any opportunity to hold and carry Lo around, and the littlest Bartie ate up the attention.

Bryant was extremely proud of his little girls, even though he had hoped Lo might be a boy. Each of them touched his life in a very special way, and they respected him to the utmost. Bryant's masculinity commanded high regard. He never hesitated to enforce discipline whenever their occasional, obstinate, demeanors flared up. Even though they were but little girls, Bryant tolerated only minimal foolishness.

Morning devotion was a daily ritual in the Bartie home. A scripture was always read first, followed by a prayer. The girls knew not to talk during this sacred family time. Bryant taught them to humble themselves, especially when God's written word was recited. He even took on an additional initiative to teach Nita how to read at the mere age of four. Bryant got the idea when Mr. Rutherford gave him some old "Primer Books" that his family no longer needed. Obsessed with learning to read. Nita vied for Bryant's attention even more. Lately, it had become quite an ordeal for her, battling the others who desired the same attention that Bryant was paying to her. So, whenever Nita could steal a few extra moments with her father, she snatched the opportunity. Mary and Lil became very irritated over Bryant's sudden partiality toward Nita, especially since she had already taken most of his available time in the first place. Nita even had nerve enough to demand their fullest attention whenever she desired to demonstrate to them her reading skills. Most times when she attempted to read from the "Primer Books", Mary and Lil dispersed in different directions.

They were so tired of hearing about "Jip running. Jack jumping high, and Sally skipping alone", it simply made them cringe.

Bean's responsibilities over the past few years had become extremely hectic. She had four heads to comb in the morning, five mouths to prepare food for, and four little bodies to dress and bathe, in addition to her own. The poor woman maintained a very tough daily regimen. Nita and Mary were helpful at times, —that's when the two of them were not playing with Lil and Lo.

One day, when Nita, Mary, and Lil were outside playing, Nita, as their ringleader, suggested to the others a brilliant idea.

"Hey ya'll, let's go out to the cow pastures."

Mary dared not challenge her big sister's proposal. Neither did Lil. So off they went excitedly—without Bean's consent. They had known beforehand that they weren't supposed to leave Bean's sight without telling her. However, Nita wanted to introduce the other two girls to some friends that Bryant had introduced her to a while ago.

The three girls walked west of the shack, past the barn and crib where Bryant stored his harvested corn and potatoes in individual bins. The crib was also used to store homemade smoked sausages and bacon. Beyond it a windmill rose up high above the pasture. It pumped water from underground, into a vat for the cows to drink. Sometimes when the water sat in the vat too long, a thick layer of green algae or "pond scum" created a slimy layer on the surface. Apparently, the "pond scum" had no effect on the cow's because they continued to drink the water, scum, and all. The vat's water well was used to cool the milk once it had been obtained from the cows. The milk was stored in a gallon jug and lowered down into the chilled well waters by means of a rope. The cool temperature kept the milk from spoiling until needed for an evening meal.

Once they arrived at the vat, Nita said "close your eyes real tight." Mary and Lil did just that, and waited for further instructions. Nita walked over to it hoping that her surprise would be available today. When she looked down into the slimy, greenish water, lying idle, there they were. The scavenger beetles were swimming around, up and under the pond scum. The bugs would come up for air momentarily, and then swim back down beneath the mush. The girls had very few toys to play with, so using their imagination on the farm made life much more fascinating.

"Okay, you can open your eyes now," said Nita. Mary and Lil opened their eyes wide and giggled.

"Whacha call them ol' things?" asked Mary.

"Whacha think they is?"

"I don't know."

"They's bugs. That's what!" answered Nita.

The girls got a big kick out of watching the beetles swim through the water covered with algae. Mischievous Lil wandered off by herself. She picked up an old stick that she saw lying on the ground. Nita ran after her. Once she caught up to Lil, she grabbed her by the arm and pulled her back to the vat. Mary stayed near the vat and continued watching the bugs. "Plague-take-it" she said, imitating her father's verbiage, "just look at them go in that water." Once Lil came back with Nita, she wouldn't turn loose of the stick. She poked it through the water, breaking up some of the pond scum into smaller pieces. Then she tried to chase the beetles around the vat with the stick. Nita grew frantic.

"Stop that Bay-Bay. You gonna kill um girl!" she said with a big frown.

"Yea, don't do that" added Mary.

Lil kept stirring the water in a circular motion, trying to surface the beetles. Next, she stuck her whole arm underneath the green slime, and tried unsuccessfully to catch some of the bugs as they swam by. The little toddler ended up drenched with the greenish, mucky water all over her body and hair.

"Don't do that Bay-Bay" Nita shouted, again.

Meanwhile, during household chores, Bean realized that the girls were nowhere in sight. She yelled out for them over and over. When she went to look for them in the barn, she could see from that vantage point the tops of Nita and Mary's head, but not Lil's.

"Ya'll get back over in that yard, right now. I mean it!" she yelled.

When Lil heard her mother's loud summons, she dropped the stick into the vat and ran behind the two older girls, who rapidly left her behind. Unable to keep up. she stopped and cried.

"Go ahead Toad, I'll go back and get her" said Nita with a huffy voice. Nita ran back to retrieve her little sister, while Mary ran toward her mother.

"Come on Bay-Bay. Momma's callin us and she gonna be real mad, if we don't hurry up and get home. Come on girl, let's go" said Nita dragging Lil by the arm.

"What ya'll doin out there in them ol' pastures? Before some old snake come along to bite you on the leg. Don't you ever let me catch ya'll back out there again" shouted Bean. Ya'll hear me?"

"Momma" Mary said. "Nita brung us over there to see the bugs in dat ol' green water the cows drank from." By that time Nita arrived with Lil.

"Look at you Lil, all wet from head to toe. Ya'll get home, right now. And you better stay out them ol' fields. I done told you before, they got snakes, rats and all kinda ol' mess runnin round out there. Mess around and fall in that ol' vat and drown. Ya'll hear me?" Don't let me catch ya'll back out there again by yourself!"

"Okay Momma," they promised.

Thirsty and sweaty, they went inside the house to get a drink of water. After each got a mason jar full, they fell onto the floor laughing loudly at the beetles and Lil. Lo woke up when she heard their commotion, and let out a big cry. Lil rushed into her parents' room to rock Lo, slowly, herself. Meanwhile, Mary was in the kitchen cleaning up the mess that the other two had made. Bean came in and said "Mary, ya'll better stay out of them ol' fields. I mean it now! You, Nita and Lil about to run me crazy. Always in to something. That ol' vat is for the cows to drink out of, and not for ya'll to be playin' around in that ol' green water. And leave them ol' nasty bugs along too. Oh Lord, have mercy Jesus!!"

All three girls slept together in one big bed. Night times were always a big production. Each of the girls had an imaginary line drawn on the mattress, and if one crossed over into another's territory, that meant an immediate eruption of teasing and fussing.

Sometimes Bryant had to go into the room and threaten the little ones with a spanking if the noise didn't cease quickly. That night was a bit different. All three girls fell fast asleep. The hot sun had drained so much energy out of them during the day, their enervated bodies rested with ease. At about twelve midnight, Nita had nightmares. She tossed, turned and shook all over in the bed screaming loudly in her sleep. Bryant heard her cries, so he got up to see what was troubling the child. When he reached the girl's room, he shook Nita slightly to wake her from the bad dream.

"Piggy-Pon-Tole, Piggy-Pon-Tole, what's wrong girl?"

"Daddy, I see a devil's head. See over there at the window?"

"Ain't no ol' devil at that window" said Bryant.

"Yea, there is Daddy. Look he right over there!"

"Over where girl?"

"Look he over there" she cried out. "On the window!"

But when Nita looked at the window again, the devil's head had disappeared, right before her eyes. The commotion awakened Mary and Lil, which frightened them into a frenzy.

"All right! All right, I said! Ya'll go back to sleep. Ain't no ol' devil in this house. If it is, Ol' Bryant'll get him out of here." He laughed. "I ain't scared of no ol devil, noways. Now go back to sleep, Piggy-Pon-Tole, Toad, and Bay-Bay!"

Finally, after much patience, Bryant settled the trio down. However, Nita couldn't fall back asleep, so she just lay in bed, still frightened over her nightmare. Not only was she afraid of the imaginary image she had seen earlier at the window, she feared losing Bean and Bryant, because she loved them so dearly.

Bean's brother, Joe Bishop, his wife Alice, and daughter Annie lived in a house west of Jim Rutherford's, and east of the Eloi Conner family, in an even smaller hovel than Bryant's. Joe, a Catholic, was also a sharecropper for the Rutherfords like Bryant. He was short, like his mother, but he definitely inherited his father's carpentry skills, which was evident throughout his place. Joe worked very hard to provide a decent living for Alice and Annie.

Alice was a shy lady, who possessed facial features which made her sort of resemble the "Virgin Mary" when taking a quick glance at her profile. Unlike Joe, she was Baptist, a bit on the plump side, but as sweet as sugar. Alice always kept her home neat and tidy. She didn't visit Bean and Bryant much, just sort of stayed to herself, mostly. Annie resembled her mother. She was a beautiful, light complected little girl with long thick, straight, black hair. Annie was a few years older than her first cousin, Nita. Occasionally, Joe brought Annie over to play with Nita and the others. They were always delighted to see her on each visit. The Bartie girls and Annie got along like sisters. The Eloi Conner Family lived between Bryant and Joe's houses. They were very nice, kind, white people, who had three sons: Joseph Euclide, William Andrew, and John Sidney. The three young men were very well mannered, and a lot older than Nita and Annie. All three of them attended the all-white Creole High School.

The Conner's shared a lot of their fruits, vegetables, slaughtered pork, and beef with both colored families. Both Bryant's girls and

Annie loved the Washington navel oranges the Conners raised. The girls found it difficult to wait all year long for the fruit to be in season, and it always turned out to be a well-deserved, sweet treat. The Charlie LaBove family was another white household on the west side of the Barties between the barn and the cow pastures.

They too were very friendly and occasionally shared some of their fruits and vegetables with Bryant and Joe.

One day, Joe butchered a pig, and took over some fresh-smoked meat to his sister Bean, who cooked it right away. Annie came along with him. The girls were delighted to see her. They played hide-and-seek and hopscotch, and then played with some of the homemade rag dolls that Bean had made. Always, when the girls were having so much fun, the evening passed in a flash, and before they knew it, it was time for Annie to go back home. The girls got a bit sentimental each time she had to leave. However, they knew that there would be plenty more fun-filled days to come, after each of them exchanged good-byes. Nightfall found Bryant and his family enjoying a hearty meal of ham hocks, potatoes, and homemade rolls. Everyone enjoyed the feast to the fullest.

"Hurry up! Let's go" shouted Bryant.

Poor Bean had the hardest job of all, trying to get four girls and herself dressed. She had to get up very early, so that she would have enough time to complete an endless list of chores before the family's departure to Ebenezer Baptist Church. Lunches needed to be packed for everyone, because the service lasted practically all day. In addition, Bean also had to make sure that she didn't forget any of Lo's things. Somehow, through her rigorous schedule, the poor woman managed to be punctual, and maintain a level head each nerve-racking Sunday morning.

Bryant installed a bench behind the front seat of the wagon for the girls to sit on. He loaded Nita on the left side, Lil in the middle, and Mary on the right. The two oldest girls were in charge of keeping Lil under control, while Bean held Lo in her arms up front.

At church, the girls were very well disciplined. No talking or acting the fool was ever tolerated. Even though the services were lengthy, the girls knew better than to challenge Bryant's disposition. All he had to do was look at them, and the girls ceased their trivial play immediately. Church was a lot of fun, despite the fact Bryant's daughters had to behave like toy soldiers. Church allowed the four sisters an opportunity to see some of their cousins and relatives that lived in other parts of Creole and Cameron. On most occasions, after the services concluded, the family visited Bean's parents Mary and Dominic.

Dominic and Mary Bishop lived approximately eight miles west of Bryant's home. Their home was a short distance off The Front Ridge Road, west of "the ole swing gate", not far from the Gulf of Mexico, at the old Bishop home place. From their front porch they could see practically all the way to the beach. Dominic, born January 26, 1881, was part mulatto and part Choctaw Indian. Dominic's father, Joseph Bishop was Choctaw and his mother the former Celeste Boudoin was part Negro and French. The union between Joseph and Celeste Bishop resulted in twelve children: Joseph, Filogene, Ezeb, Eli, Pierre, Desira, Rose, Celeste, Marshall, Melody, Alzina and Dominic. Bean's mother, Mary born August 13, 1889 was part Negro and part white. Mary's mother Louisa Bartie, a Negro lady who was as dark as the night, conceived her with a white man named John "Grandpa" Wetherill Jr., who's father ran a school on Grand Chenier prior to becoming the first Superintendent of the Cameron Parish Schools. Mr. John Wetherill, Sr. was originally from Philadelphia. His own wife Emmeline Hargrave Wetherill was one of the earliest settlers in Cameron Parish. Louisa, a former slave, worked as a servant for the Welch family with whom Mr. John Wetherill, Jr. visited frequently. "Grandma Louisa" later married Alcede "Grandpa Seedy" Andrews, a colored man and from this marriage gave birth to her two other daughters, Lucille and Marthy.

Dominic and Mary were a very fair-complected couple. In addition to Bean, they had three boys: Harry (Jack), Joseph and Robert, and one other daughter, Lillie. The Bishops attended the St. Hubert Catholic Church, a congregation of mostly colored parishioners, located on The Front Ridge Road not far from their home. Mary sported a bit of an attitude, being that she was part white. Her mother Louisa, however, was a constant reminder of her African American ancestry. Whenever Mary tended to ignore her colored heritage, all she had to do was look at Louisa's dark skin to realize that she was no different from the rest of the colored humanity in the area.

The Bishops owned a modest two-story home and the land on which it sat. The house had a large front porch, shaded by several huge live oak trees. The second level contained a large open living area, with various antiques, moderate furniture and several types of carpentry books. Three bedrooms surrounded that section of the home. The place had a unique architectural design, in that Dominic and his brothers were master carpenters. Mary, on the other hand, was simply a full-time housewife who loved to bake and cook.

By 1940, Mary-who was generally known by then as "Maw-Maw",— and Dominic—who was called "Paw-Paw"-had matured gracefully. Paw-Paw was a lot taller than his wife. He could easily eat a bowl of soup on top of her head. Paw-Paw was a very attractive, soft-spoken man, with high cheek bones and beautiful fine, dark hair. Sort of a shy gentleman, he was rarely confrontational. The most unusual thing about him was his soft, quack-like laugh. Maw-Maw had beautiful, long silky straight hair which she usually wore rolled up in a bun. She was a very pretty lady who loved and adored her grandchildren. It wasn't hard to determine why Bean was such a pretty lady. Maw-Maw and Paw-Paw were both very fond of Bryant, and they treated him with the utmost respect. He also admired and respected them.

The girls couldn't wait to get to their grandparent's home after church each Sunday, simply because Maw-Maw was an excellent cook who always had something good on the stove. Her fresh, homemade rolls melted in their mouths, right from the start. As soon as everyone walked through the front door, they could smell those good rolls baking. She would fix each girl a hot, fresh-buttered roll, and slice it down the middle with their choice of thick cane syrup or honey. Afterward, the girls went outside and played with their older brother Jimmy, on the huge front porch. Jimmy had become a shy, good-looking boy, who kept pretty much to himself. He always enjoyed seeing his sisters and mother Bean, but as soon as he had his stay with them Jimmy was back off to himself, being "Bill", a nickname he acquired from Maw-Maw and Paw-Paw. Besides, Bill had outgrown child's play being that he was gainfully employed in the town of Cameron at a very early age. His laboring caused him to mature fast and playing trivial games was simply not one of his favorite pass-times.

Meanwhile, the girls chased the chickens and guineas round and round in the yard. They played upstairs in the large living area, and looked through page after page of Paw-Paw's carpentry books. Nita tried her best to read a few of the sentences, but they were too difficult for her to comprehend. Mary and Lil were delighted to no end because they didn't want to be caught in the middle of another one of Nita's renditions.

After playing upstairs, the girls went back outside again to play in Paw-Paw's beautiful big car. The Model-T Ford was a real treat for them, especially since their mode of transportation was still a horse-drawn wagon. Nita, of course, sat at the steering wheel, and designated herself as the driver, while Mary and Lil usually wound up as passengers. The girls played in the car for hours imagining themselves riding all around Creole. Lorina was too young to join in the fun, so she slept peacefully in one of the bedrooms upstairs. Paw-Paw didn't mind them playing in his car the least bit. He knew that the girls looked forward to it each time they came by for a visit, so he was more than happy to let them enjoy themselves. Bean, however did mind.

"Ya'll get out of Poppa's car, right now! Ya'll know better than that, Nita." "That's okay Bean," said Paw-Paw. "Them kids just playin a little bit. Leave them alone."

"No Poppa, I don't want them playin in your car. Mess around-n-break something in there. And Lord know's me and Bryant ain't got no money to get it fixed." Bean loved her mother and father to death, but she did prefer to rear her kids the way she and Bryant thought best.

"Git out of that car, right now! I mean it!" shouted Bean.

The girls obeyed their mother and dispersed from the car in different directions. Bean continued her conversation with Paw-Paw.

"Poppa, how you been feelin?"

"Oh, I feel pretty good, Bean."

"What about you, Momma?"

"Bean, I feels fine" her mother replied. "Now I knows ya'll gonna eat some of Maw-Maw's good ol' cookin', and I don't want to hear no mess from you, Bean" she added sarcastically.

"No Momma!" Bean said sharply. "They done ate at church. I fixed them a big lunch before we left home." Even though the girls had eaten their lunches at church, they still wanted to sample some of Maw-Maw's excellent cooking. However, Bean rarely allowed them to eat at her mother's place because she was such a proud woman. So when Maw-Maw asked once more "Ya'll babies want to eat?" Bean gave the girls one of those "You better not take nothing" looks. They responded in unison, "No thank you, Ma'am."

"Ya'll git back outside-n-play", Bean said. "And stop gazing at that food on the table like you starved to death!"

"Bean, I don't know why you do them kids like that? I'm they grandma, and they can have anything I got in this house."

"Because, Momma. They done had enough to eat. They act like they ain't ate nothin before in they life. Ya'll get back outside-n-play, I said! Right now. I mean it! And Momma, I don't know why you fussin with me so much, because you use to be the same way, when we was some kids coming up. You know you wouldn't let us eat everywhere."

"I know that Bean, but I love my grandchildren so much and I want to do something nice for them when they come by my house."

"I know Momma, but they ain't hungry. They just want to eat because they see all that food on the table. That's all."

The girls went back outside, again. This time, they knew to stay clear of Paw-Paw's car. Playing on the front porch got a bit boring, though. Nita at a very early age had a fascination for nature, so she started looking as far as her eyes could see toward the roaring Gulf of Mexico. She observed closely the white caps on the waves as they rolled inward to shore. Captivated by the sight and sound of the Gulfs rushing, roaring waters, Nita began walking in the direction of the bellowing sea. The motion of the waves abducted her psyche momentarily, drawing her like a huge magnet. Mary and Lil noticed Nita's abrupt trance, and followed her under the same wizardry. As the three got closer and closer to the beach, the excitement of the rushing waves kept inviting them further. Foolishly, the innocent little ones kept walking toward the unfriendly Gulf, oblivious to the danger that lay ahead. Meanwhile, back inside the house, the adults continued to converse without an inkling of the girl's whereabouts, until Bryant, suddenly aware that their playful noise had faded, got up to check on them. He stepped out onto the porch to see where the girls might be. As he looked toward the beach, he spotted three little images headed straight for the mighty Gulf of Mexico. Bryant broke out into a speedy dash after them.

"Oh God, please don't let them go into the water" he prayed while racing onward. The girls never looked back as they kept walking toward the enchanting surf. After a strenuous effort, Bryant finally caught up to them. His sudden appearance stopped them dead in their tracks. With a heaving voice he said

"Na-na-na-na-now just where ya'll thank ya'lls going at?"

"Nowheres Daddy" answered Nita, as she bounced back to reality.

"Ya'll get on back to that house, and don't ever let me catch none of ya'll going to that ol' gulf again by yourself. You hear me?"

Sniffling they answered, "Yeah Sir, Daddy!" Fearfully, the little trio marched back toward Maw-Maw and Paw-Paw's place with their father lecturing them each step of the way. "Ya'll could fall in that ol' Gulf, and we'd never find none of ya'll again. Then what me and Momma supposed to do without ya'll? Go crazy? That ol' Gulfs mean. And it don't like no little girls messing around with it. Never, ever, go back to that beach again by yourself. You hear me Piggy-Pon-Tole? Toad? Bay-Bay?"

"Yeah Sir," they answered.

"Then, get on back to that house, right now and don't let me catch ya'll out yonder no more."

At the end of the day, when it was time for the Bartie bunch to leave, the Bishops reassured Bryant that if he and Bean needed anything to never hesitate to call on them. Paw-Paw's carpentry skills allowed him to make an excellent living, not bad for a colored man during those times. Bryant, however, had too much pride to take a cent from Bean's parents. He would rather live a life below the poverty level than depend on Maw-Maw and Paw-Paw for any financial support. That was just Bryant's nature. Nita, Mary, and Lillie influenced Lorina to walk early. Lorina had a strong desire to keep up with the bigger girls, so she refused to be left out just because she was the baby of the bunch. The girls looked out for each other, and they all looked to Nita for guidance as she was slowly becoming their second mother. At bedtime the four little girls climbed into bed next to each other. The space had gotten even tighter, but they never really noticed a difference because their love for each other outweighed any inconvenience. Sometimes, before they went to sleep, Nita entertained the group with a funny or scary story—until it got too noisy. Bryant would then go into the room to calm the girls down. Occasionally, he would let them carry on the ruckus, because he knew that they were just being little girls. "A little fun won't hurt that much."

Sometimes he even joined in on the good times. On one occasion, he got down on all fours, and crept quietly into their room. They could neither see nor hear him coming because their bed sat so high off the floor. Nita was in the middle of a scary story when Bryant reached the front of the bed. He pulled the girl's toes, and made beastly noises. They were all frightened to no end, until they realized it was him, and that's when they laughed themselves to sleep.

Many months zoomed by. Bryant on his way home from a tiring day in the field passed by Joe and Alice's place, and saw a small candle burning in their window. Curious about the flickering light, Bryant banged on the door. He banged again—still no response. After waiting patiently for a moment, Joe came to the door, very somber. He opened it up, just wide enough for Bryant to see the right profile of his face. Bryant wondered why Joe answered the door in such a concealed fashion.

"What's the matter, Joe? I see you got this candle burning in the window, so I just wanted to see if something's wrong with ya'll." Joe said not a word for a long moment, still only revealing the contour of his face. He couldn't speak, because his heart was too full to communicate to Bryant at that particular moment. "Joe, you sure ain't nothing wrong with you-n-your family?"

Joe tried, but he could no longer hold back his tears. Slowly, he opened the door completely. Bryant saw him standing there, with his rosary dangling over the fingers of both hands. That's when Bryant realized that something very serious had occurred.

"Come on in, Bryant" Joe said with a trembling voice and teary eyes. Once inside the house, the smell of death seeped through the dark, tidy, living room. Bryant saw Alice sitting in a straight back chair near the burning candle perched on top of the windowsill. Dressed all in black, she had a handkerchief draped across her mouth. She never uttered a word. She just sat there, staring into space, and shaking her head. The scene grew even more somber when Bryant saw in the flickering light a little wooden coffin sitting atop a makeshift bier in the middle of the floor. Joe glanced at the tiny box, and sniffled softly. The candle had almost burned down to the end, the flickering light fading away on the shadowy walls. The atmosphere grew gloomier and gloomier, as the candle gradually died.

Joe had made the wooden box himself, and lined it with white satin and lace. The mere thought of having to do such a thing for his own child caused Bryant much remorse.

"Ump, what a sad sight" thought Bryant, who walked over to the small coffin and there lay the most beautiful baby he had ever seen. He couldn't tell the sex of the child, just that it was very pretty, and dressed in a white satin gown. After viewing the baby's body, Bryant cringed. To suppress his own and the family's sadness, he offered a word of prayer. As he prayed, he realized how truly blessed he and his family were, mainly, because he and Bean had not thus far undergone such a traumatic experience.

"Father, bless this family during their hour of sorrow" he said with conviction. "In the name of Jesus, I pray that you touch they aching hearts. Amen."

Joe continued praying his rosary, and cried as he looked at his baby's flesh. Bryant stepped away from the little wooden box and shook his head drearily. Annie had been locked in her room all day, too young to understand death. The distraught child had been crying constantly over the loss of her sister, because she wanted so desperately to have a little sibling in her life.

"I'm so sorry Joe. I ain't knowed that Alice was in the family way" said Bryant.

"Thank you so much. The little baby was born dead" he replied. "Is there anything I can do for you or the family?" asked Bryant.

"No. Just tell Bean what happened."

"I will tell her, Joe. Now, if you needs something, don't be ashamed to call on us. And remember God loves ya'll, and so do we."

"Thank you, Bryant" Joe said sniffling.

As Bryant prepared to exit he said, "God bless you and he is going to see ya'll through this storm. The winds may be blowin real hard right now, Joe, but God's gonna send some sunshine after a while. You'll see."

"Thank you so much Bryant for everything" Alice said in a weak whisper. Joe showed Bryant to the door with the rosary clutched to his left hand "Thank you so much for praying for us."

Bryant told Bean the bad news soon after he arrived. The next day the Bishops held a private burial for the little baby out in a field in back of their house. A few days later, Nita and Mary picked some fresh wild flowers, and placed them atop the little grave. Meanwhile, the Bishops prepared for a rough road ahead to mend their agonizing hearts. The barn and pastures seemed to have a special effect on the girls' playful imaginations. They knew they were only supposed to play near the house where Bean could keep an eye on them. There was just something about sneaking off to the pasture, however, that made the endeavor more exciting.

"Lil and Lo were asleep in the house while Bean was in the kitchen preparing lunch for the family, and Bryant's noon meal. He was due back from the fields shortly to take a break from the hot sun. At about eleven o'clock Bryant always came in to eat and rest before going back out for a second round in late afternoon. Nita and Mary were playing together under the Chinaberry trees.

"Hey Mary, want to go to the vat to see the bugs?"

"No, Nita. Momma done told us not to go to them ol' pastures.. Remember?"

"Well, I'm getting tired of playing in the back yard all the time.

It just ain't no fun no more, Mary."

"Now Nita, you know we ain't supposed to leave without Momma knowing where we at."

"I know, but we can go see the bugs really quick, and then come right back. Come on Mary, let's go. Please? We won't stay long."

"Well okay, Nita. But we better hurry up, before Momma catch us going over there."

"Okay, let's go" whispered Nita.

The girls snuck off to the vat. Once they got there however the sun was too hot to stay for long.

"Mary, it's too hot out here, right now. Let's go play in the barn. It'll be cooler there."

"Okay Nita. I'm real hot, too."

Inside the barn, the girls set up an imaginary living room using bales of hay as furniture. Of course, Nita played her usual motherly role. She pretended to make a hearty lunch for both of them, while Mary sat on a wooden block pretending to drink a cup of coffee.

After they finished playing house, Nita had another bright idea.

"Mary, let me comb your hair like Momma do."

"Now, how you gonna do that, Nita?"

"I'll need a comb. So you wait right here til I get back. Okay?"

"Okay Nita."

"Now don't move Mary. You hear?"

"Okay, I won't."

Nita ran to the house as fast as she could to find a comb. When she arrived at the back door out of breath, Bean asked "What you n-Mary doing outside?"

"Nothing, Momma. We just playing house."

"Well, ya'll better be. Remember don't go too far away from here. I want to be able to see you-n-Mary when I look outside. Okay?"

"Yes Ma'am."

When Nita found a comb in their room, she left quietly, careful not to wake Lil and Lo, and raced back to the barn. Mary sat on the block without wriggling as Nita pulled the comb through her hair. Nita hadn't the slightest idea what she was supposed to be doing with Mary's hair, but she kept on trying to make it look pretty.

"Oh Mary, I forgot to bring the "Lucky Heart" hair grease with me. But that's okay, we'll use some of this right here."

"Some of what?"

"This right here, Mary." Nita and Mary had set up their living room furniture near a large container of axle grease.

"You sure Nita? Momma ain't never used that ol' stuff on my hair before."

"Yeah Mary. It'll be all right, you'll see. It feels just like the "Lucky Heart" grease, anyways!"

Nita grabbed a handful of the axle grease from out of the barrel and massaged it in, all over Mary's hair and scalp. Half the black smelly stuff was in Mary's hair, and the other half on their clothes. Mary just sat there without a fuss, letting Nita continue. After she finished, Mary's head looked like a slick black tar roof. Only a few ringlets of curls remained, motionless on top of her head.

"Mary, you look real pretty now. Come on, let's go show Momma and them, what I did to your hair."

"Okay" said Mary, without an inkling as to what she looked like.

Bryant had just come in from the fields for lunch, and was eating at the table when the two girls walked through the back door. Nita went in first followed by Mary, whose hair fumigated the kitchen.

When Bean and Bryant saw Mary's hair, Bean yelled "Oh Lord have mercy, Jesus!!! What ya'll done, done to Mary's head?"

"Come here, Toad" said Bryant. "Plague-take-it, that's that ol' axle grease, Bean. Ya'll been playin' out there in that ol' barn, uh?" he asked Nita.

"Yeah Sir" said Nita, dropping her gaze to the floor.

"I done told ya'll to stay out that ol' barn, already!" Bean hollered. "Ump!! Now, Bryant, how we gonna get this grease out of that kid's head?"

Bryant jumped up from the table, about to burst into laughter, tickled pink over the episode. He went outside, and pumped some water into a bucket, and then heated it in a big pot on the stove. Nita just sat there speechless, knowing that she had gotten herself into some hot water this afternoon. Mary didn't know what to do or say.

Once the water warmed, Bryant and Bean took Mary outside, and hung her head over one end of a wooden bench. They soaped and washed, and soaped and washed, and soaped and washed, until her hair was clean. Afterward, Bryant had to return to the fields, without finishing his meal. Nevertheless, he never scolded Nita for the mischief. The excursion turned out to be a laughing good time for him. All afternoon long, Bryant laughed and laughed and laughed as he recollected the image of Mary's hair dressed with axle grease. "Ole Piggy is always getting herself into something." Meanwhile, back at home, Bean reprimanded Nita for her role in the incident.

"Nita, the next time I catch you-n-Mary in that barn messing round with that ol' grease again, I'm going to skin both ya'll little legs. I mean it. I better not ever catch ya'll back out there again. This don't make no sense at all. Now I got to wash these clothes full of this ol' grease. Ya'll go in that house and you best not move till I say you can."

Nita and Mary went inside and stayed. Nita was so ashamed that she didn't have much to say for the rest of the afternoon. Besides, her feelings were a bit bruised because Bean had scolded her sincere efforts to make little "Toad" look very pretty. That's all Nita had hoped to do!

CHAPTER 5

This particular morning couldn't come soon enough for Nita. The six-year-old tossed and turned throughout the night, fantasizing over her first day of school. Bean woke up early to fix her and the other girls' breakfast. In the process, she draped a homemade blue dress over a straight-back chair in the living room to finish hemming it before Nita put it on. Bryant had saved up enough money to purchase a new pair of shoes for Nita, too, which would have to last her the entire school year. Nita passed her old pair on to Mary, who passed her pair on to Lil, who passed her pair on to Lo.

The stimulated pupil could barely eat breakfast on this special morning, taking only three bites of food and pushing the rest aside. After rushing through her meal, she jumped up from the table and dashed straight to the bedroom. A chain reaction occurred with her younger sisters following directly behind her. They acted as though it was their first day of school, too. Bean left a fresh bowl of water in the bedroom for Nita to wash her face and brush her teeth.

"Ya'll git back to that table and finish eating your breakfast. Nita hurry up and get ready for school," ordered Bean.

All three spirited little sisters trickled back into the kitchen, single file from the bedroom. They sat back down at the table to finish their bowl of cornbread and milk. Meanwhile, Nita brushed her teeth with baking soda. Afterward, she put some of the same under her arms for freshness—especially since she would be mixing and mingling with other children she had never seen before.

Extremely excited over her new dress, Nita almost tore it at the seam while rushing to put it on. Bean combed Nita's hair, as she sat on the edge of the bed, looking at herself in a hand mirror. Today, Nita desired every strand of hair to be combed neatly into place. When her mother finished, Nita gave her a big appreciative hug. The young girl really didn't look like much: a plain old hand-made dress, four plats in her hair, and a new pair of brown lace-up boots.

When she stared at her reflection in the mirror, however she saw far beyond her appearance. A much clearer picture projected her abundance of enthusiasm to discover the new world of literacy. With such a keen attitude in mind, learning would be no problem for the zealous young school girl.

The three-year-old Lorina was about to drive Bean to her last nerve. She walked around the house repeating over, and over again, in a childish tone: "Momma, where Nita goin, Momma?"

"She's going to school. And when you get old enough, so will you."

"But Momma, where you say Nita's goin?" asked Lo again.

"I done told you once already, she's going to school."

"Can I go with her?"

"No. You ain't old enough to go. You'll get your chance one day."

"But I want to go with her today, Momma."

"You can't go because you ain't old enough. Now that's enough."

When Nita walked out of the bedroom into the living room where Mary, Lil and Lo were sitting, she felt like Cinderella on her way to the big ball. Even though she didn't look the part, the other girls marveled over their big sister's appearance as she gathered her things together to catch the school car.

"Momma, I want a dress just like Nita's wearin when I go to school next year" Mary said.

"Me too, Momma. And I want some new shoes like hers, too," said Lil.

"Momma, I just want to go to 'cool with Nita. That's all" said Lorina.

Bean handed Nita an old syrup bucket packed with a lunch consisting of a fig preserves, and a fried egg sandwich made with fresh homemade bread, and gave Nita a final check before she left the house.

"You look fine my girl," said Bean.

"Thank you, Momma."

"Now Nita, you act like you got some sense up there at school.

If you don't, you gonna catch it, when you get back home, girl. You going up there to learn, and not to be silly."

"Yes Ma'am, Momma" said Nita, politely.

As Nita left the house and headed for the Front Ridge Road, Bean stayed behind on the steps with the other three girls. They watched each step Nita took, until she got to the side of the road. It was a sentimental moment for Bean, who wiped away a small tear. To see her first daughter off to school meant a whole lot to the family, because Nita was setting an example for the rest of the girls. Bean realized that her daughter's appearance was drab. She only wished that she and Bryant could afford to do better for Nita and the others. They were doing the best they could, and that's all that mattered.

When Nita got to the road, she looked back, and was her mother and three nappy-headed little sisters cheering her on. A wonderful feeling overtook her. Bryant saw his daughter at a distance from the cow pasture, and rushed over.

"Now Piggy-Pon-Tole you be a good girl up there. No acking the fool at school. Study your book and work real hard. Okay?"

"Yes, Daddy."

"One day you won't have to be poor like me and Momma. A learning can take you places you never been to before. Study real hard. The only thing that I can say, is that you do your best, and God will do the rest. You gonna rise up above this poor life one day. You always been a real lady to me, my girl. Keep it up! Listen to what your teacher say. And listen to ol' Bryant, because I knows what I'm talking about. I might not have much learning myself, but I knows I'm right about this. You hear?"

"Yeah Sir, Daddy."

"Now here comes the car. You be a good girl, you hear?"

"Yeah Sir, I will. Bye Daddy!"

"Bye, Piggy-Pon-Tole."

Pandemonium broke out on the steps, when the other girls saw the car drive up for Nita. Annie Bishop and Carrie Payton were already inside. Mr. Mose Lute, the driver, was a real nice old colored man who adored driving the kids to school. Nita waved bye to everyone, and then climbed inside.

"How you doing Bryant?" said Mose.

"I's fine. Now Mose, if she gives you any trouble, you just let ol' Bryant know, and she won't do it no more. I guarantee that. Okay?"

"Oh Bryant, she don't look like no bad girl to me. She's gonna be okay."

"But if she ain't Mose, you just let me know. Bye Piggy-Pon-Tole, and be good!"

"Yeah Sir, Daddy" said Nita.

As Mose drove off, Nita's three sisters yelled and screamed to the top of their lungs in the background, until the car was completely out of sight.

"Bye Nita!" they yelled. Bye! Bye Nita! Bye! Bye!"

"Momma, I'm gonna be just like Nita, when I get big" said Lo.

"Me too, Momma" said Lil.

"And Momma, I can't wait till next year comes, because I want a dress and some new shoes too, so I can look like Nita when I goes to school" Mary added.

"Ya'll all gonna get your chance to go to school one day" Bean told each of her daughters.

In the car, Annie and Carrie took Nita under their wings, and gave her some pointers about the teacher's rules.

"Nita, when you get to school, the teacher's name is Miss West" said Annie. "She's a real nice lady. You'll like her a lot."

"Whenever Miss West rings the first bell" Carrie explained, "all the students must line up outside the school. Then she will tell us when it's okay to go inside. And that's when we go. But not until she says so. Okay? If you move out of line before she says it's okay, that will make Miss West real mad."

"You must stay in line, too. No cutting" said Annie.

"Please whatever you do, don't break the line Nita! Next, we will go down a long hallway to put our lunch bucket up on the shelf. And when it gets cold outside, you hang up your coat on the nails sticking out of the wall in the same place. After you finish that, then you can go inside the classroom, and take your seat. You know what I mean, Nita?" asked Carrie.

"Yeah, I guess so," Nita said.

"It's not yeah" Annie insisted, "It's yes. Remember that because Miss West hates it when you use incorrect English. And please don't talk in class. That makes her very angry too. Okay Nita?" Annie asked.

"Yeah!"

"There you go again, with that "yeah". Remember it's yes. Not yeah!"

"Oh! Oh, that's right. Yes," said Nita with a smile.

Mose Lute smiled, too, as the two older girls shared with Nita some of Miss West's pet peeves. By the time they reached the Bazile Moore School, Mr. Lute had collected a carload of students.

Henry Schlesinger and Bud Welch were two boys among the girls that made the trip from the east side of the school. Some of the children who lived near the school walked there each day. When Mr. Lute unloaded the eastern bunch, he went west for another load.

"You'll do good,Nita. Just pay attention to Miss West and don't talk too much. You'll be all right, my girl," said Mose.

"Yes Sir."

The Bazile Moore School was a one-room building about four miles west of Bryant's home. It was named after its donor, who donated the property on which it stood. Miss West maintained six grades in one room. While one class received oral instruction and tutoring, the other five worked diligently on their specified assignments until their rotation for an oral lesson came around.

Everything turned out to be exactly as Carrie and Annie had explained to Nita. Once they arrived, she got so excited seeing all the new faces at school, that adrenalin rushed through her body.

"Ding-a-ling-a-ling" went the bell as Miss West rang it to signal the start of the first school day. All the students gathered to form a single line. Nita found herself a place in front of Annie and Carrie, and waited for further instructions about entering the school.

That first day of school, a fun day, went by in a flash. Miss West's limited intervals for individual instruction required Nita to pay close attention, so that she could grasp her work quickly. As the school day came to a close, Nita gathered her books to take home and show them to her sisters. Even though she didn't have homework in each subject, she still packed those books, anyway.

It was a difficult task for her to carry everything to the car, but somehow, she managed.

Meanwhile, back at the Bartie home, Mary, Lil, and Lo played in the front yard all day long. They kept on running in and out of the house, asking Bean over and over again, "What time Nita coming home, Momma?" Finally, after a very long day of impatience, Mary spotted the school car.

When the car pulled up in front of the house Nita said bye to Annie and Carrie, and got out with both arms full of books, her tablet, and her lunch bucket. She was so excited to see her sisters, she tripped over her own feet. Books and papers flew everywhere. The three girls ran after the flying papers and brought them back to her. She meanwhile gathered the rest of her things before they flew away. Lo ran inside the house to let Bean know that Nita had made it home from school.

"Momma, Nita's home from 'cool," she said, out of breath.

Bean rushed out of the house to meet her and the rest of the gang near the road. Afterward, they found themselves a spot under the mulberry tree in the front yard, and that's where Nita told them all about her first day of school.

"First, we had to line up before anyone could go into the classroom. We went down a long hallway to put up our lunch buckets. Inside the classroom, I shared a desk with Annie. The first grade class got their work first, then the teacher gave the other kids theirs. There were a whole lot of kids there I ain't never seen before. Today we did writing and spelling. Oh! And I have some homework to do tonight. Tomorrow we'll do arithmetic and reading."

"What do you mean rithmitic?" asked Lil.

"That's when you learn how to count, add, and take-away. You know, that kind-a-stuff," said Nita.

"That sounds real hard to me" Mary said.

"What's your teacher's name is?" asked Lo.

"Her name is Miss West. I like her because she is so nice."

Bean sat with the girls as they talked for hours about Nita's first day. While they were talking, Bryant wandered in from the field. He was happy to see his family in such a jovial mood, even though everything that could go wrong for him that day, had gone wrong. First, an old mule broke away from his plow and ran off. It took hours to retrieve it. Then, a White Chester sow broke loose from the pig pen. Bryant later captured her, and had to repair the hole. To make matters even worse, an old stray dog chased down some of his chickens and killed one. The girls, happy to see him, showed him Nita's books and told him all about her experiences at school. Rather than ruin his daughter's excitement because of his own stressful day, he resorted to acting like a vicious dog. When the girls approached him, he barked, snarled and snapped his teeth each time they tried to get close. At one point, Lo actually grabbed him by the arm, and he bit her, like an old mad dog would do. It startled her, and the other girls' play ceased momentarily. When Lil made another attempt, he bit her as well, but not very hard. Mary and Nita knew better than to try.

"Ya'll better leave him alone, before he eats ya'll up," said Bean.

When the fun and game suspended for a brief moment, Bryant made a quick exit, and went inside the house to take a hot bath. His cleverness enabled him to break away randomly, without the girls noticing his departure or feeling neglected. The girls and Bean continued to laugh at the silly incident, until it was time for them to go inside.

"Nita, go to the well and get some cool milk for supper," Bean said. "We'll take your books inside for you."

"Yes Momma."

On her way out to the well, Nita became very intrigued with spelling, as she'd learned how to spell some new words earlier that day. She tried to spell out the words for every object she saw on her way to the pasture or the easy ones, at least.

"Okay now, let me see. Cow. C-o-w. Cow. Okay, Cat. C-a-t. Dog. D-o-g, Dog. Vat. V-a-t. Vat."

Nita continued to spell as many words as she could. She pulled a gallon jug of milk up by a rope from the vat's well where the girls had explored the water-bugs. Not paying attention to what she was doing she pulled clumsily on the rope, causing the jug to bang against the side of the well and break. When she looked down, Nita saw milk spilling everywhere.

"Oh no! Ohhhh weee! Momma's gonna be real mad at me. Look at what I done now."

Too afraid to go back to the house, she prepared herself for a scolding as she walked home. Bean had already wondered what was taking the girl so long with the milk, and was headed out toward the pasture.

Nita heard Bean's call, and ran toward it. "Momma, Momma, I'm sorry, but I broke the jug of milk."

"Oh Lord! Now, how did you do that Nita? Well, that's okay don't worry about it. Mistakes will happen. But the most important thing right now, is for you to get a good learning. I just want so bad for you to do good in school. Let's go home. You'll have another chance to get milk out of the well, but you only gonna have one chance for a learning. Momma ain't gonna fuss at you this time. I just want you to do your best in school, so the other kids can be just like you. It's okay for us to be short for supper, tonight. We ain't got nothin but beans, rice and bread, anyways. Water'll taste better with that. Someday we'll have better food to eat, than what we got tonight. We are just going through a storm right now, but I know the Lord's gonna bring us through it all. That's why you got to study your books real hard, so you won't have to be poor like me and daddy. Always remember that. Okay?"

"Yes Ma'am."

They went home and after supper Nita and Mary helped Bean clean up the kitchen. Later on that night Nita sat at the table and did her homework by a kerosene lamp. She thought about what her mother told her earlier.

"I've gotta study hard, so I can make my family real proud of me some day."

One Saturday afternoon a few days before Christmas, 1941, Bryant rushed home by horseback from the B. Nunez General Store. When he arrived with a folded newspaper clutched under of his right arm, he ran through the house yelling at the top of his lungs for Bean. She was outback with her daughter's plucking feathers from the wild ducks he had acquired on an early morning hunt. Yelling loudly once again, Bryant finally got his wife's attention. She stopped in the middle of her work and came inside to see just what was agonizing him. The girls trickled in behind her because they, too, figured that something serious was troubling their father. When Bean got there, she found him in a stationary state of shock, still trying to figure out what was taking her so long to respond to his call.

"Bryant, what's the matter?"

"Everybody come inside and sit down" he said, quivering. "I, I, I, I got some bad news to tell you."

Everyone gathered together in the living room, hurriedly. Bean had no idea what Bryant was about to unfold.

"Oh Lord, what done happened Bryant?" asked Bean, trembling. "Is something wrong with Momma or Poppa?"

"No Bean, ain't nothing wrong with none of our folks. But when I was at the general store, Mister Newness gave me this paper that showed Poor Mister Eloi Conner's boys both got killed in the war."

"Oh no, Bryant!" screamed Bean.

Bryant heaved out a deep breath. "Ain't that something? Euclide and Andrew both died in the war. Look-a-here at the picture. Lord! Lord! Lord! They even got another picture showing that big ol' ship one of um was on when it sunk in the water way over sea. Look right there. Lord, that puts me in the mind when I was in the war."

"Not Euclide and Andrew, Bryant?"

"Yeap! Ump! Ump! Ump! They both dead, Bean."

Bean grabbed the paper from Bryant and read the headlines in disbelief. The girls remained quiet as mice, stunned over the bad news about the Conner brothers. Of course they didn't know the two white boys well, but they did know their parents.

"I wonder what poor ol' Miss Eloi gonna do now?" Bean said.

"I know she's about to loose her mind. That's why I hate them ol' wars in the first place. I don't know why they gotta fight'm anyways. They just killin all our good boys. Ump! Now what she's suppose to do now? Lord, I just don't know!"

"Ain't that something, Bean? Both of them's gone. You know what Bean? It ought to be a law for the army not to let two brothers serve in the war, at the same time."

"Yeah, you's right Bryant. But, you think the government cares about something like that?" NO! They don't care nothing about poor ol' Miss Eloi and the pain she gon suffer. It really don't make no sense, a-tall."

"Daddy, can I see the paper?" asked Nita.

"Here Piggy. You remember them boys?"

"Just a lil bit."

"I didn't think you would. You was just a lil ol' thing when they left here."

While Nita and her sisters looked at the newspaper article and at the pictures, a morbid feeling overtook each of them. Nita couldn't imagine what life would be like to lose her own sisters.

The paper showed a picture of the sinking "Utah," and a headshot of Fireman First Class Joseph Euclide Conner. The article read:

"Euclide Conner was killed in action, when the enemy struck Pearl Harbor, a territory of Hawaii, on December 7, 1941. He was born June 30, 1915, attended the Creole High School, and later became a farmer prior to enlisting in the United States Navy in Beaumont, Texas, on November 7, 1939." The article also showed a picture of his brother Fireman First Class William Andrew Conner, who was reported to be "missing in action in the Battle of the Java Sea engagement. He was aboard the "Arizona" when it sank. No word has yet been received from him since, and it is assumed that he lost his life in action against the enemy. Andrew was born September 20, 1921. He also attended the Creole High School, was a farmer, and had enlisted in the United States Navy on the same date as Euclide. Both men were the sons of Mr. and Mrs. Eloi Conner of Creole, Louisiana."

"Bryant, you need to go and see Mister and Miss Eloi. Tell'm I'm sorry to hear the bad news about Andrew and Euclide. Oh my Lord! They was some good ol' white boys, too."

"Bean, why don't you come with me?" It'll make'm both feel good to see me and you together."

"No Bryant, I can't go. My nerves too bad for something like that. Just tell'm I'm sorry to get the sad news."

"Okay Bean, I'll go by myself."

Once Bryant left the house headed toward the Conner's, Bean got out her rosary, and started praying for the brothers. Nita continued to look at the pictures in the newspaper. She said to her mother, while staring at the article, "It's gonna be real sad at their house for Christmas, Momma." Bean responded "It sure will, Nita. That's why we need to be thankful to the Lord that we all alive ourselves. You know Nita? When the storms of life blow real hard like this, a person's only choice is to turn to the Lord. That's the only way anybody can make it through a rough time like this."

Nita did well in school and she started taking on more responsibilities around the house, especially, after Bean finally gave birth to a son, Bryant Lee Bartie, Jr., born October 17, 1942. Bryant Jr., wasn't a very big baby, weighing just a little over five pounds at birth. He didn't cry much, just kicked his legs a lot. Bean tried to breast feed him, but he didn't particularly care for that. So she had to put him on the bottle, and boy could he suck. His little mouth worked vigorously whenever he sensed a nipple near. Bryant, elated over the birth of his son and also being his usual perpetual self immediately nicknamed the baby "Nip" because of his fascination for a rubber nipple. The girls loved the new baby, especially since he was a gender different from themselves. Each one of them fought over an opportunity to care for the tiny little boy. Lo kept inquiring "Why he always kickin' his legs so much, Momma?"

"He's just a little baby, Lo. That's why."

Bean's pregnancy turned out to be a very difficult undertaking. After Nip's birth, she grew emaciated and could only partake of minimal responsibilities around the house, so Bryant's mother came across the marshland from her home on the back ridge to live with the family to help out. "Big Momma Bartie," a strict disciplinarian, tolerated very little foolishness from the kids. To put it quite simply "Big Momma didn't take no mess." She had the girls walking the chalk line just like mice in the presence of a cat. Each one had responsibilities to contribute to the family's daily regimen, and everything had to be gotten done because there was no other choice in the matter. All Big Momma did each day herself was sit in her rocking chair with a salt cedar switch at her side, just waiting for any of the girls to step out of line. The appearance of the switch caused them to think twice before they misbehaved. If they tried her patience, she would sting their little legs without hesitation and show them just who was boss. Despite her disciplinary tactics, Big Momma proved a tremendous help to the family. Both Bean and Bryant appreciated her contribution during their time of need.

As time went on, Lil had grown to love animals. The family had a dog, several cats, and a tamed White Chester pig, which roamed the yard, freely. Bryant raised several other White Chester pigs in a hog pen on the east side of the barn. This particular area unfolded a pungent odor of sour food. The White Chesters, who were gluttonous for the slop, ate every meal as though it were their last. The smell had no bearing on their individual greed. The mere fact that they ate daily kept them quite content and fat. Each day a battle brewed between the pigs and field rats over a position at the trough. Neither competitor, however was afraid of the other, for they developed an immunity for one another, and stood their ground firmly in order to take in a fair share of food.

Lil loved the animals, endlessly. Like Nita, she developed a fascination for the fields and pastures. The adventure of being out in nature captivated her fullest attention. One day after playing with the tame White Chester pig, she went inside the house and confronted Bean. "Why is that ol' pig always diggin' holes in our yard, Momma?"

Big Momma intervened before Bean even had a chance to reply "That ol' pig likes to dig holes, so he can stay cool. That's why!"

"Stay cool," replied Lil.

"Yeah, stay cool. Because it's so hot outside" said Big Momma.

"Well, I'm sick of him diggin all these holes in the yard. You can't walk for'm," Lil said.

"I know. But that's how the Lord made'm" Big Momma spurted out. "So we just gonna have to live with God's plan."

"I guess so," Lil said, "but I still can't see why he wanna dig so many holes in the yard."

"Lil, leave them ol' pigs alone, girl, cause they might bite you or something" said Bean.

Later that afternoon, when Nita was still at school, Mary and Lo were in the kitchen washing dishes. Still perplexed about the pig, Lil decided to go outside and play with the White Chester some more. The two of them carried on an interesting conversation.

"Big Momma say you like to dig these holes, so you can stay cool, you ol' crazy pig."

"Grunt, Grunt" went the White Chester.

"Momma said you might bite me on my leg. But you best not try, you ol' crazy thing. Cause if you do, I'm gonna hit you back."

"Grunt, Grunt" said the pig.

"Is that all you know how to say is Grunt Grunt?"

"Grunt, Grunt" the pig said.

Just as soon as Nita came home from school, she immediately went inside to look in on her mother.

"How was school today?" her mother said.

"Good, Momma."

Big Momma asked "You got some homework to do?"

"Yes Ma'am" replied Nita.

"Well, don'tcha think you needs to get to doin it?"

"Yes Ma'am."

"Well it ain't gonna get done with you standing right here, looking me in the face, now is it?"

"No Ma'am."

"Okay then, get to that table, and don'tcha move til you through with all your work."

"Yes, Ma'am."

"And Mary, you go to the well and get some cool milk for supper. Lo, you go feed the pigs these left over table scraps right there" instructed Big Momma. "And where is Lil at?" she asked.

Nita, Mary and Lo all hunched their shoulders simultaneously.

"Lo, when you finish feeding them pigs, go look for Lil and tell her she gonna catch it, if she don't get in here right now and help the rest of ya'll with this kitchen."

Lo left the house with a bucket of slop, headed for the pig pen. The only problem was, she had never fed the pigs before. That was Nita and Mary's job. Lo was too afraid to tell Big Momma of her insufficient skills, so she ventured on without a clue as to how to pour the slop into the trough for the pigs to feed. The bucket got a bit heavy for her small, skinny body, so she resorted to using both hands to carry the heavy pail. The walk from the house to the pen was quite a distance, but Lo's bona fide struggle didn't impede her progress. In the meantime, she looked all around for Lil as she walked. "Ohh, Ohh, Big Momma gonna be real mad at Lil. I don't even see her nowhere. She's gonna be inna-lot-of-trouble when she get home, too." Lo stopped for a brief rest. Soon after she caught her breath, she journeyed onward with the bucket of slop dangling just above the ground.

Finally, after her super-human effort, Lo made it to the pig pen. The only problem was she saw three big field rats standing in the trough eating right alongside the pigs. She was too afraid to get to close to the pen, fearing the rodents might attack her. Lo knew that the pigs had to be fed or Big Momma would have a fit if she came back home with the same bucket full of slop. In the meantime, she saw an old stick lying on the ground near the pen. The little girl picked up the stick and threw it over the top plank of the pen, trusting that it would fall near the rats and scare them away. "Grunt, Grunt" went a White Chester pig, when the stick hit it on the head.

Lo's efforts did nothing, however, to frighten the huge field rats. They paid no attention to the stick once it landed on the floor of the pen. Instead, they kept right on eating, as though nothing ever happened.

"What I'm gonna do now? Them ol' rats still there, and they ain't even moved. I know what I'll do" she thought.

Lo picked up the bucket of slop, and ran towards the pen. Then, she stepped up onto the little platform that Bryant had made for Nita and Mary to make the feedings easier. Once her feet were planted solidly, she raised the bucket of slop over her head.

Immediately, an old White Chester sow sensed the little girl's presence by the smell of the sour food. The huge pig's head collided with the bucket and turned it over, spilling slop all over Lo's head and body. She ran home crying, and smelling just like a stinky ol' pig's pen. When she got there Bryant had just come in from the fields. First, he heard that no one had seen Lil for the past two hours. Then, Lo came home drenched in slop, and screaming at the top of her lungs. What could possibly go wrong next?

"Plague-take-it!" said Bryant. "Lo, what done happened to you, girl?"

Lo responded in a teary voice. "Daddy, them ol' pigs wouldn't move out the way, for me to feed'm. After I tried to make them move, one-of-um turned the bucket of slop over on my head."

Big Momma looked at Lo oddly. "Next time you better make sure them ol' pigs is out the way before you try to pour slop in they trough!"

Bean grew frantic, worrying over the whereabouts of Lil, and now Lo's incident with the pigs created even more anxiety. Bryant went out back and pumped some fresh water into a pail. Nita and Mary pitched in to help Lo get out of her smelly clothes. Soon after, they bathed their little sister and washed her hair thoroughly.

Then Nita and Mary washed Lo's soiled clothes, and hung them out to dry. Bryant struck out toward the fields to look for Lil, who still hadn't come home.

Meanwhile, Lil and the tame White Chester pig had already made their way to the field near Joe and Alice's place. Both were having quite a ball with each other. That old pig followed Lil's every command, except for one special request.

"You ol' crazy pig, you can dig all the holes you want to out here in the field" said Lil.

"Grunt, Grunt," went the White Chester.

"Go ahead. Dig I said," she demanded.

"Grunt, Grunt, said the pig, again.

"Big Momma say you like to stay cool. Well if you do, go ahead and dig yourself a hole out here. And stop diggin'm in our yard!"

"Grunt, Grunt!"

Lil popped the pig on it's back with her hand and said "And you best not bite me, either. Dig, I said!"

"Grunt, Grunt."

Irritated after a concerted effort to get the White Chester pig to dig a hole in the field had failed, Lil headed for her Uncle Joe's place. She was very disappointed over the pig's lazy attitude. Her main objective was to stop it from digging so many holes in the yard at home.

Nightfall found Lil and the pig heading home from the east alongside the Front Ridge Road. When Bryant saw her and the White Chester, he rushed over to them.

"Lil, where you been girl? We been looking for you all over the place."

"Daddy, I got tired of this ol' pig diggin' so many holes in our yard, so I took him out here in the fields."

"Now you know better than to just leave home without nobody knowing were you at!" scolded Bryant.

"Yeah Sir," said Lil in a scared voice.

"The next time you better let somebody know where you going, or it's gonna be too bad for you, girl! Now get on back to the house."

"Yeah Sir" responded the teary-eyed little girl.

Lil got a spanking later that evening for being away from home too long without her parent's permission. Afterward, Bryant gathered all the girls together and gave them a lecture. "Make sure when you leaves this house, that one of us grownups know where you going at. Okay?"

"Yeah Sir" responded each of the girls.

The day was very tiring, so everyone retired to bed early that evening. The girls were all sound asleep. So was Nip in the big rocker in Bryant and Bean's room. Later in the night, however, the pitch-black darkness brought with it the smell of smoke throughout the house.

No one in the house sensed anything as the thickening smoke expanded. Finally, after a bad nightmare, Nita awoke and found the house engulfed in a thick haze. She jumped up out of bed and ran to her father's room, screaming and coughing.

"Daddy, Daddy wake up!" she shouted. "Wake up Daddy!! Wakeup!!"

Bryant awakened instantly. He grabbed Nip, and helped Bean get safely out of the smoke-filled room.

"Nita get the other girls! Hurry up!!"

Nita rushed back into the bedroom, and woke up Mary, Lil and Lo, and they all rushed out of the house safely. Big Momma had already made it outside. As she slept in the living room, she was able to get out as soon as she heard the commotion.

"Everybody okay?" asked Bryant.

"Yeah Sir" answered Nita for the others.

Once Bryant got a headcount of the family, he went back inside the house to determine where the smoke was coming from. He found the source in an old armoire. A small fire had gotten started in the wardrobe, catching onto some clothing and other items inside.

Bryant ran outside and got a bucket of water. It took several more buckets to contain the fire. Soon after the fire was extinguished, the family returned to sleep in the smoky house. It was a nerve racking night.

The next morning, Bryant assessed the damages and found a gnawed box of matches. Presumably, a couple of mice had ignited the blaze in the armoire as they chewed on the match sticks. Bryant praised Nita for alerting him before the fire expanded further. No one was seriously injured during the mishap. Bryant and Bean did lose most of their sparse clothing however, the salvageable items were washed and hung out to dry before the morning prayer.

Afterward, Bryant thanked God immensely for sparing their lives.

"Thank you my Father for watching over us as we slept last night. In Jesus name I pray. Amen!"

CHAPTER 6

Over the years, a very close relationship developed between Nita and Mary, especially since they were in school together, where love had a chance to grow. Nita provided Mary assistance with her school work, as well as guidance on surviving as a poor, colored farm girl in the Deep South. Miss Helen Allen taught the girls at the Bazile Moore School, replacing Miss West, who decided not to return the following school year. Miss Allen boarded in Bryant's home during the six-month session. She was a strict, short, dark-complected instructor with a domineering personality. She let it be known to all her students that triviality had no place in the classroom. Nita and Mary had to be well behaved girls, because if they weren't, all Miss Allen needed to do was discuss their misconduct with Bryant. Both girls knew that getting him involved would definitely not be a pretty picture. Bean had taken on the job of preparing Miss Allen a hot meal for lunch each school day. It was Nita and Mary's responsibility to walk back home, pick up the lunch and bring it to Miss Allen at school. The walk was about three miles each way. The girls enjoyed the break, because it allowed them an opportunity to converse with each other outside the classroom.

"It's hot out here today, Nita."

"Sure is Mary."

"Nita, two times two is four. Right?"

"Yep! But the easiest way to remember your time tables is by memory."

"Okay. Let's see three times three is nine. Right?"

"Yep! Tonight, when we get home I'll help you memorize'm, so you can do real good the next time you have to say'm in front of the class. Okay?"

"Okay. Ohhhh! Nita look at that big ol' black snake."

"Where?"

"Over there coming out of the ditch. I'm scared he might bite us."

Mary grabbed Nita's arm as the snake crawled across the dusty, shell road.

"Nita, I'm so glad you with me, 'cause I don't know what I would do without you, girl."

"I'm always going to be here for you, Mary. No matter what happens."

Once the snake crossed their path, the two girls continued, their arms embracing each other's shoulders. They hopped, skipped, and jumped most of the way home.

During the excursion, they passed in front of the Hultons, a white family who lived on the Front Ridge Road about a mile west of the Barties. Each day, one of the Hulton boys waited for Nita and Mary' to go by. Sometimes he hid from them in tall bushes, or behind a huge oak tree. When they'd get near, he'd jump out and hooray the two, saying all kinds of hurtful things. He'd been carrying on like this ever since school had started that fall. Nita instructed Mary to ignore his remarks as they approached him.

"Hey ya'll lil nigger girls, now just where you think you two going?" said the tall, lanky, white boy.

"Mary, don't say a word to him. Don't even look at him. Just keep walking," Nita said in a loud whisper.

"Ya'll don't hear me talking to you? You silly lil pickaninny. I said, where ya'll think ya'll niggers going at?"

"Just keep on walking Mary... Pay him no mind."

"Okay" Mary said through her teeth.

The girls' hearts raced, even though Nita tried to maintain her composure. Mary, on the other hand showed her nervousness. The Hulton boy got real angry when they ignored his nasty remarks.

"Mary, we almost home. Just keep walking and don't say nothin."

"Ya'll some dumb lil nigger girls" he shouted at them louder. "I done asked you once, already. Just where you think you going at?" Nita whispered in Mary's ear. "On the count of three, let's take off running, and don't stop, till we get way down the road. Okay?"

"Okay" Mary whispered back.

"One, two, three. Go!"

They took off running as fast as they could.

"Hey, come back here ya'll lil niggers! Come back I said. Get back over here, right now!"

The girls ran for about a quarter of a mile, never once stopping or looking back. Finally, after their fatiguing sprint in the hot sun, they stopped for a brief moment to catch their breath.

"You ... okay ... Mary?" Nita asked, gasping for breath.

"Yeah!..." Mary huffed and puffed. "But that old white boy... really scared me ... Nita."

"Don't worry about him ... I ain't gonna let... nothing happen to you ... okay?"

"I know you ain't." Mary swallowed hard. "But I'm still scared. Crazy ol' white thang."

"He ain't gonna ... do us nothing, girl."

"You sure?"

" 'Cause if he try . . . we'll just tell Daddy. Okay?"

"I'm still . . . scared of him."

"Come on, Mary. We're almost home."

At the Bartie house, Bean looked them over. "Why ya'll sweating and breathing so hard?"

"Cause it's real hot out there, Momma" said Nita.

"Yea, Momma and this ol'—

"This ol' black snake we seen" Nita cut Mary off. "Almost scared us to death. Made us both run real fast. That's why we's sweating, and outta breath, Momma."

"What ol' black snake?" asked Bean.

"A big black snake we seen coming outta the ditch" Nita replied.

"Boy, he was a big ol' snake, too," added Mary.

"Ya'll better be careful with them ol' moccasins out there. Them things will bite you on the leg, if you don't watch out."

"Okay Momma" said Nita and Mary.

"Ya'll hurry up and eat your lunch, and then get on back to school."

"Yes Ma'm" they answered.

After the girls finished their meal, Bean handed each of them a syrup bucket, with their teacher's lunch packed inside.

"Ya'll be careful" Bean said, "and go straight to school. You hear me?"

"Yes Ma'm" said Nita.

"And leave them ol' snakes alone!"

"Okay Momma" said Mary, and she ran out the front door to catch up with Nita, so as not to be left too far behind. But the Hulton boy had found himself a comfortable spot under an oak tree about a mile down the road and was waiting impatiently for the girls to return. That ol' boy had been watching Nita and Mary for weeks, so he knew exactly how long it took for them to come back. Talk about a lazy, no-count-for-nothing boy. He'd dropped out of school some time before. The only thing he was good for was getting himself in and out of devilment.

He heard Nita and Mary talking on the way down the road long before they got close. The break had allowed him a chance to scheme a foolish prank. Before the two girls approached the Hulton house, they lowered their voices considerably.

"Hurry up Mary. Let's walk fast" Nita said in a low whisper.

"And please don't drop Miss Allen's lunch if that ol' boy starts picking at us."

"Okay Nita" Mary whispered back.

As they got closer to where he usually darted out from behind a tree, the girls picked up their pace almost to a trot. But once they were in front of the Hulton house, the boy jumped out from behind a bush with his pants pulled all the way down to the ankles. He stood there shaking his genitals at the girls.

"Ya'll lil niggers want some of this here big ol' thang?"

The girls screamed at the top of their lungs. Nita dragged Mary by the arm. "Come on, don't look at him. And don't you drop Miss Alien's lunch, either!"

The two sisters ran off, only stopping to gain their composure when they were much further down the road.

"You all right, Mary?"

"I guess so." But Mary had been crying, and was visibly shaken by the boy's unexpected nakedness. "I ain't never seen anything like that before in my life! You Nita?"

"NO, MARY!"

"I'm so scared, Nita."

"That's okay. Just promise me that you want tell nobody at school about this."

"I don't know, Nita. I'm real scared."

"I know you are. But the other kids gonna laugh and make fun of us if we tell them. We can't even tell Miss Allen nothing, okay?" Mary hunched her shoulders, "But that ol' white boy might try to hurt us again the next time we see him."

"I know. But if it makes you feel better, we can tell Daddy as soon as we get home after school. Okay Mary?"

"I don't know, Nita. I think we should tell Miss Allen."

"No Mary, you gotta promise me that you won't do that. Okay? I promise I'm gonna tell Daddy."

Nita tried her best to help Mary get hold of herself before they went into the classroom. Still shaken over the incident, Mary put the syrup can on Miss Allen's desk, then went straight to her seat and sat staring into space.

"Here's you lunch Miss Allen" said Nita.

"You lunch? Or your lunch, Wanita?"

"Excuse me. Your lunch, Miss Allen."

That is much better. Thank you. Now get your reading book out, and start looking through the next chapter. Mary, I want you to recite the number three and four time tables, in front of the class."

"Mary's mind wasn't on time tables. She kept visualizing the Hulton boy's naked body.

Nita whispered in her ear "It's gonna be okay, Mary. Just take your time and say them slowly."

"Mary, did you hear me?"

"Yes Ma'm" she responded.

"All right then. Start with the three's and continue through the four's."

Mary got out of her seat very slowly, and staggered to the front of the room. When she tried to open her mouth, however nothing came out. Mary stood there with a blank look. After a few moments, she started to cry.

"Why, what's wrong Mary?" Miss Allen asked, alarmed.

The classroom at this point was completely silent, all its attention focused on Mary. Nita prepared herself to rush out of the room if her sister lost her composure and spilled the beans about the Hulton boy's exhibition. Mary said nothing, however, and more tears streamed down her pretty, brown face.

"I don't understand Mary. Why are you crying?" asked Miss Allen.

Nita realized that she had to do something quickly, before her sister made a spectacle of herself in front of the whole class. "Miss Allen, she's crying because on our way back to school we see a big, black snake when we was bring you lunch back. It scared both of us. That's why she's crying!"

"Snake!" The entire class began to murmur in dismay. "A big black snake!"

"Where?"

"Okay class. Quiet please!" said Miss Allen. "Wanita it's saw, not see and your not you. As for you, Mary, you may take your seat, but tomorrow, no excuses will be tolerated." Miss Allen composed herself behind her desk, "I want you to be able to recite your three's and four's through twelve for each number, Mary. Do I make myself clear?"

"Yes Ma'm" the girl answered tearfully.

Nita let out a big sigh of relief. She knew that the Hulton boy's behavior had really affected Mary's sensibility and concentration. When her sister returned to her desk, Nita whispered, "Everything's gonna be okay, Mary. I'll tell Daddy as soon as we go home, so you won't be scared no more."

The rest of the school day raced by. On the way home in the school car, Carrie, Annie, Henry, and Bud all wondered about the big snake's whereabouts.

"Where did ya'll see that big ol' snake at, Nita?" asked Annie.

"I'll show you, when we get close to the place."

Mary said nothing as they drove onward, but when the car passed the Hulton boy's place, she cringed. Nita looked at her and whispered "It's gonna be okay Mary."

"What was that Nita?" Annie asked.

"I said right over there is where we seen that ol' snake," Nita responded.

"Over where?" Carrie asked.

"Right there, by the ditch" said Nita.

Everyone in the car laughed, including Mr. Lute. When he pulled up to the Bartie house, Nita and a somber Mary jumped out and rushed inside.

Once the girls settled in after school, Mary fed the pigs, and retrieved a cool jug of milk from the well. Nita swept the kitchen floor, and helped Bean fold some clothes and place them in their respective places. Lil and Lo were washing and drying some dishes. Soon after, Bryant came in from the fields, and began scraping scales off some fish that Mr. Rutherford had given the family for their supper.

But all evening long, Mary pictured clearly the Hulton boy's naked body. She just couldn't keep the thought out of her mind. In the meantime, Nita observed each step that Mary took. It wasn't hard to determine that the incident had shaken up her sister pretty bad. She figured she should tell her daddy right away. Poor Mary had almost broken the jug of milk when she pulled it out of the well.

"Daddy, what are you doing?"

"Scraping some scales off these here fish Mr. Rutherford give me."

"I got something I wanna tell you, about what happened to me and Mary on our way home to pick up Miss Allen's lunch, today."

"Okay daughter" said Bryant as he put the fish down. He listened attentively. Nita began telling him about the Hulton boy's foolish behavior.

"Say what, daughter?"

"Daddy, that ol' white boy was standing up there with his thing, pointing it at me and Mary!"

"What 'thing' you talking about Nita?"

"You know Daddy. A thing. That boys have. Different from girls." Bryant's eyes grew wide. "You sure that's what you seen, daughter?"

"Yeah Sir! And he really scared Mary real bad. She couldn't even say her time tables at school today when Miss Allen ask her too."

"Na, Na, Na, Na, Na, Na daughter you sure that's exactly what he done?"

"Yeah Sir. I'm sure, Daddy. And after that me and Mary ran fast as we could, cause we was so scared he might try to do us something."

"Did ya'll tell Miss Allen, what happened?"

"No Sir!"

Bryant thought this over for a moment. "Good! Okay now Nita, tell Mary don't worry bout nothin. I'll take care of that ol' white boy tomorrow."

"Okay, Daddy."

"Now tomorrow when you-n-Mary come home to pick up Miss Allen's lunch, I'm gonna be waiting for ya'll right here in the house. If he do the same thing just keep walking. Don't say nothing to him, okay? Then, when you get here let me know what he done. Ol' Bryant'll take care of him."

"Yes Daddy."

Bryant went back to cleaning the fish when Nita left, but he became so angry that he slipped and cut one of his fingers with the knife before he finished the job.

Nita and Mary sat at the kitchen table and did their homework once supper was over. Nita helped Mary memorize her timetables, and her sister grasped both the threes and fours quickly. Before Bryant went to bed he went into the kitchen and watched his daughters doing their work.

Miss Allen, Bean, Lil, Lo, and Nip all retired for the evening. Once the lights went out, Mary tossed and turned, waking up Nita in the process.

"What's wrong?" Nita whispered.

"I can't sleep."

"It's gonna be all right Mary. Daddy is going to get that ol' boy tomorrow."

Finally, in the early dawn, both girls fell asleep in each other's arms.

The next day sure enough, the Hulton boy was waiting for them to pass. He carried on his usual agitation as they walked by. Mary and Nita said not a word; just kept walking like their father had instructed.

When they got home, Bryant was there waiting for them. They ate their lunch, and gathered Miss Allen's food to carry back to school.

Bean was afraid. She didn't want anything to happen to her daughters. Nevertheless, she also feared Bryant would lose his temper, and get himself into some serious trouble.

"Be careful, Bryant with them ol' white people. They might try to hurt you."

"I ain't scared of none of them. And they ain't gonna be messing round with my girls. I don't care who they is. I mean that. Now, Nita, you-n-Mary go ahead. I'm gonna wait a ways behind ya'll on my horse. Don't never look back at me, once you start walking. Just look straight ahead the whole way. Okay?"

"Yeah Sir" they answered.

"Now, when you get close to him, don't scream or nothing like that if he got his pants pulled down. Just keep on walking. I wonna catch him right in the act."

In the afternoon, the boy had two pails of water ready to throw at the sisters once they reached his house. He had also plans to pull his pants down when they were close enough. As soon as Nita and Mary got in front of the Hultons, he didn't know that slowly and quietly, Bryant was riding his horse on the ridge to the right side of the road.

When Bryant saw the boy's partially nude body exposed, he kicked his horse into high gear. Just as the boy picked up a pail of water to throw on the girls, Bryant caught him right in the act. The bad ol' boy almost passed out when he saw Bryant headed toward him.

Nita! Mary!" yelled Bryant "keep on going to school, and don't look back."

Yeah Sir" they responded and picked up their pace.

Now just what you gonna do with that water boy? Throw it on me?"

"I, I, I, I, I, I, I, I, wa, wa, wa, wa, wa, wa."

"Pull up your britches!" Bryant demanded.

He pulled his pants up so fast, he ripped off most of his fly buttons.

"Look boy, the next time you mess with my girls I'm gonna break you neck. You hear me?"

"Yea, Yea, Yea, Yea, Yea, Sir!" he said. "Yea Sir."

"Don'tcha ever say nothing to them girls again. Do I make myself clear?"

"Yeah Sir!"

"Now git on home," Bryant shouted. "Don't ever let me catch you fussing with my girls no more." His horse kicked up a small dust storm, as Bryant chased the boy to the right side of the Hulton house. He ran the boy down to the ground, out of breath.

"I ain't gonna do it no more, Sir! Please don't hurt me" the boy said curled on the side yard in a fetal position.

"I better never catch you messing with them girls again. You hear me?"

"Yeah Sir, Yeah Sir, I, I, I, I, promise, I won't do it no more."

That was the last time Nita and Mary ever saw that boy on their way home for lunch.

* * *

All the children gathered around Bryant one Friday evening, and listened attentively, as he told a story about the disastrous storm that had swept through Creole in 1918. Story-telling was a delightful form of entertainment, since there really wasn't much else to do in a small country town. Nita, Mary, Lil and Lo were all dressed in their cotton night gowns as they sat on the living room floor in front of their father. Nip was asleep in Bean's arms, while Miss Allen sat in a straight back chair near Bryant. By a kerosene lamp he narrated his experience of being trapped for hours during the dreadful hurricane.

"I musta been about fourteen, when the storm hit August six, 1918. It was a real, bad, bad, storm. The wind blowed over a hundred miles a hour. I was helping Poppa and them out in the fields that day. He told me to hurry up, and go home 'cause the weather made up so fast. I didn't listen to him 'cause I wanted to finish up my work before the weather came through. But Poppa didn't stay a minute longer after he told me that. He got his tools together and commanded me and the rest of my brothers to quit, and head on home. He knewed something bad was about to happen."

"My brothers listened to Poppa. But as for me, I had to be a fool. I was too hard-headed to listen, so I kept on working and as soon as they left, sure enough the sky turned pitch black real fast.

So dark, till I could hardly see two foot in front of me. All at once, that ol' wind started blowing harder and harder. I didn't know what to do or where to run to. I said to myself, 'I should've listen to Poppa'. The wind blowed so hard, till it whipped my body like a cow whip, stinging me everywhere and blowing sand, dirt and leaves all in my face."

"I know the Lord was speaking cause he was angry at me for being disobedient to Poppa. I got scared. So scared, till I wet on myself and my clothes. That was the scariest feeling I ever had before in my life. Face to face with God. I just knowed I was gonna die. Ain't no way I could make it out of this storm alive. No way. Then, the wind picked up my whole body, about four foot off the ground, and slammed me against a big ol' tree. I fell down in a big ol' hole that was made by the uprooted tree when it fell over. All I could do was grab hold onto one of the roots to try and save my life. The wind kept blowing me up and down, and up and down. I wanted to just give up, but I couldn't. So I kept on praying to God to spare my life. At one point, I was holding on to the root of the tree with just one hand. I almost let go of it. But I didn't. I just kept on praying. I said, 'Lord please spare my life. I promise to do whatever my Poppa tell me to do, next time. Please help me Lord." "That's when the Lord gave me strength to grab hold to the root again, and hold on to it with both hands. Otherwise, the wind would've blowed me God knows where else. I'd probably be dead, and ya'll kids wouldn't even be here."

"The storm lasted for about three hours. I was wet, and dirty and found myself laying on top of a ants pile. Them ol' far ants got all over my body, and started biting me head to toe. They bit me so much till they poison me to sleep. Luckily, the wind stop blowing real hard. Otherwise I'd wouldn't been able to hold on no more 'cause I was too weak."

"Poppa and them just knowed I was dead when I didn't come home with the rest of my brothers. When the weather calmed down, him and my brothers Levion, Henry and Alcy came to look for me and they found me in the hole, stretched out. When Poppa first seen me, he just knowed the storm killed me 'cause I wasn't moving. I couldn't move cause them ol' ants had me pinned down. Poppa started crying. Levion and Henry runned over to me, to see if I was all right. Alcy stayed back to comfort Poppa. When they got to me, they pulled me outta the hole. Levion started shaking his head like there was no hope for me to be alive. That's when Henry wiped the dirt offn my face. After that, Poppa and Alcy came closer. And that's when they could see I was still living, cause they seen me breathing. Poppa fell to his knees and started praying to the Lord for sparing my life. My brothers prayed too. Talk about thankful for being alive!"

"After they got me home, they cleaned me up, and I stayed in bed for the rest of the day. I could hardly move. Poppa and them said that storm was one of the worst ones ever to hit this area. They said the "Ol' Rex" sunk in Big Lake with forty people on board.

Not all of them drowned, though. In all I thank the storm kilt twenty-nine people, and it tore up Lake Charles. A lot of buildings was blowed down to the ground, like the Ol' Lambert Chemical Co., the Long Leaf Lumber, Co., and J. A. Bel and Powell Mills. I also heard the Miller Brothers Garage's roof fell in and damaged over sixty cars in there. Pooh Ooooh! That was a bad storm. We ain't seen another one that bad since then. But ya'll know something? Through it all, God was on my side. Things could have been worst. That just goes to show, that if you put your trust in God, he will see you through any storm. Don't matter what kind it is either. I knows that for sure, cause I'm living proof. Bryant laughed out loud. "I'm still alive, ain't I?"

The girls, Bean and Miss Allen were mesmerized. Tears welled up in Nita and Mary's eyes. They were so grateful that their father's life had been spared. Bean had also survived the storm of 1918, but she had not realized until just then that her husband had gone through such a frightful experience. Hearing it for the first time sent cold chills up and down her spine.

"Mr. Bartie," Miss Allen said, "God must have been on your side."

"Daddy, you wasn't scared?" asked Mary.

"Yea I was scared, but I had to believe the Lord would see me through it."

"Ohhhh! Them ol' ants all over you makes me real scared," said Lil, cringing.

"Me to" said Lo, shaking her body as though the ants were crawling all over her at that moment.

"Daddy did many colored people die in the storm?" asked Nita.

"I don't know, daughter for sure just how many-colored folks died. But I do know that a whole family of them perished somewhere out there on the beach. Poppa told me."

"How old you say you was, Daddy?" asked Lo.

"Fourteen. I was a pretty big ol' boy, too. Yep! I was a lot older than ya'll is."

"I'm so glad you could hold on to the roots of that tree to save your life" Nita said.

"Me too, Daddy" said Mary.

"Ya'll remember one thing girls. In the midst of a storm, never give up, cause the time you almost let go, that's when the Lord will give you strength to pull yourself through it. Just trust the Almighty Master. He ain't gonna put no more on you, than you can bear. And always remember to hold on to his unchanging hands. There ain't nothing he want and can't do for you."

"And another thing" Bryant said. "No matter how hard the winds in this ol' life might blow, always keep the faith in the Lord because the quiet of the storm is sure to pass over."

CHAPTER 7

Mose Lute came early one mid-July morning in 1944 to chauffeur the Bartie family to church. Bryant paid him a dollar for his services each Sunday. Everyone was dressed in their best clothing. All the girls were school age, now. Nip was a toddler, and Bean was pregnant for the sixth time. The kids were delighted to ride in Mose's car because it sure beat the horse driven wagon they were accustomed to. Nita, Mary, Lil and Lo piled into the back seat, while Bean sat in between Mose and Bryant up front. There was always a feud over who would get to hold Nip on the way to Ebenezer Baptist Church.

"Okay girls, no acting the fool back there." Bryant said as Mose drove on. "Let him sit between ya'll, and not on your lap."

"Daddy, Lil won't let me hold Nip, first" said Lo.

"I done told ya'll to let him sit on the seat between you. And I ain't gonna say it no more."

The back seat got quiet. Before their father's abrupt outburst, Nita and Mary had been whispering in each other's ear regarding the good time they planned on having at Maw-Maw and Paw-Paw's house. Maw-Maw had asked Bean to let the two girls stay over after church for a couple of days to help her can some fig preserves, since a good crop of the fruit had been produced that season.

Maw-Maw desired to get her canning out of the way before the figs started to spoil. Lil and Lo were a bit agitated because they weren't granted the same opportunity as their two older sisters. When the family arrived at church, Bryant said "Remember, no talking in church."

"Yeah Sir" replied the entire back seat.

Bryant's warning, however, had no effect on Nip's demeanor. He started squirming around like a little worm on the church grounds, before the family even set foot into the sanctuary.

"That goes for you too, boy!" Bryant said.

But inside, Nip's wriggling didn't cease. He just couldn't keep still, and kept on talking loudly, twisting and turning himself so, until the commotion disrupted the pastor's sermon.

"Boy, you better be good cause Daddy gonna get you," said Nita.

"Nip, you better stop acting crazy" Mary whispered loudly to the hyper toddler.

"Daddy's lookin right at you, and you gonna get all of us in trouble" added Lil.

"Stop that boy" said Lo.

It was customary for the men to sat on one side of the house of worship, the women on the other. After a few minutes of Nip's disorderly conduct, Bryant rose from his seat across the church with a serious look on his face.

"Oh, oh," Lil whispered in Nip's ear. "There goes Daddy."

"And he got a real big frown on his face, too" Lo said softly.

"You gonna get it now."

Bean turned around in her seat, and gave Nip a look that said "You better quit while you ahead," but her warning came a bit too late. She and the girls knew what was going to follow. Nip ignored all this counsel until he looked up and saw his father staring him straight in the face. Bryant reached over Nita and Mary, who were sitting on the pew closest to the aisle, picked the little fellow up by the seat of his pants, then carried him out of church in that very same manner.

The congregation, Bean and the girls could hear Nip crying as Bryant spanked his little bottom.

Bean was about to have a fit, but she knew not to interfere with her husband's disciplinarian tactics. When Bryant and Nip returned to the sanctuary, the only thing that anyone could hear were sniffles coming from Nip's nose. Afterward, he lay down with his little head on Nita's lap, and fell fast asleep. Nita, Mary, Lil and Lo remained quiet as mice, and stayed that way for the duration of the service, too afraid even to breathe loudly.

Once the services concluded, the girls exited the corridor in a very orderly fashion knowing better than to aggravate their father further. Nip, meanwhile, had learned a valuable lesson, never talk or act the fool during church services.

After they had fellowship on the church's grounds for a while, Mose Lute picked up the family and took them to Maw-Maw and Paw-Paw Bishop's place. Bryant never once had to turn around to attend to any disorderly conduct in the back seat.

When the family arrived at the Bishops, Maw-Maw had fresh homemade rolls waiting for everyone. Nita and Mary jumped out of the car, and raced towards the big porch to see their grandparents.

"Hey, don't be runnin like a wild deer." Bryant shouted. "Slow down and act like you got some sense."

Nita and Mary stopped dead in their tracks, and began to walk like young ladies were supposed to.

"Hi ya'll babies doin?" Maw-Maw asked.

'Im all right!" said Nita.

"Maw-Maw, you got some good ol' hot rolls?" Mary asked.

"Plague-take-it!" said Bryant. "Did you take time to ask Maw-Maw how she feel first, before you start askin for something to eat?"

"I'm sorry Maw-Maw. How you and Paw-Paw feeling?"

"We been doing good, my baby" said Maw-Maw.

"Speak to the people first, before you go into they house" said Bryant. "You know I'm raising ya'll better than that."

Maw-Maw gave each of the girls a kiss on the cheek, and extended her arms toward Nip as soon as she saw him. "Come here my baby."

Nip reached for his grandmother. However, he wasn't his same usual self today for some strange reason, and Maw-Maw could sense the difference. "What's wrong with my baby?" she asked. Nip said not a word. "Momma," Bean answered for him, "he was so bad in church today, till Bryant had to take him outside, and skin them little legs. That's what's wrong with him."

"Oh no! Well come on my baby, and get some of Maw-Maw's hot rolls, that'll make you feel better."

Everyone followed Maw-Maw into the kitchen to sample her good ol' rolls. Nip ate his quietly, just as humble as a little lamb, while Maw-Maw held him in her arms, and served each family member. Bean and Bryant drank a cup of coffee along with theirs.

Maw-Maw put Nip down on the floor for a short moment. The little fellow eventually made his way over to Paw-Paw, who was sitting in his favorite chair at the table. Nip climbed up into Paw-Paw's arms with a sad look on his small face, and never said a thing throughout the entire visit. Bryant conversed with Paw-Paw and Bill, while Nita, Mary, Lil and Lo went upstairs to play. Bean stayed in the kitchen, and talked with her mother. Mose Lute sat in his car under an oak tree in the front yard, and dozed off briefly, until the family concluded their visit. After Bill finished talking with Bryant, he went to his room, and took a nap. He needed his rest, since he had become employed at Louisiana Menhaden, a lucrative menhaden fish industry located in Cameron whose fishing season began in April and ended in October of each year. Menhaden—commonly called Pogy fish traveled in large schools and were caught offshore by fish boats that trolled the Gulfs waters. Pogy fish averaged three quarters of a pound in weight, were six to eight inches long with big heads; had a slight hump on their backs and no teeth. They fed entirely on plankton, a minute floating life that dwelled in the sea. Pogy fish were too oily for human consumption, therefore they were not a sport fish that could be taken by a hook and line. Instead, several tons of the fish were captured in huge nets by Pogy boatmen, manning three boats. The larger menhaden mother boat carried two smaller purse seine boats that scanned the Gulf for a reddish brown area at the surface of the water in hopes of finding a school of fish feeding on plankton. Once a school of Pogy were spotted by the seine boatmen, they entrapped the catch in their nets while the mother boat closed in on the action. Each crew of men on the smaller boats worked together to spread their nets, called a purse seine, because the bottom of the net could be purced or drawn together in order to capture the fish. Once secured in the nets, the catch was later transferred aboard the larger boat and transported to the Louisiana Menhaden plant to be processed into oil, meal and solubles, and eventually marketed commercially. Pogy fish were cooked continuously with live steam that released an extremely pungent odor into the air. The oil from the fish driven out by the steam was used to manufacture paints, putties, lubricants, soaps, and for tanning leather. The solid protein portion of the fish known as press cake, once dried and ground, became an excellent nutrient for poultry, hogs and other livestock animal meals. Any remaining liquid after the oil and water had been driven out, called stickwater, was used mainly as a liquid fertilizer. No part of the fish was ever wasted. Because of menhaden fish oil, varnish dried faster and ink simply wrote better.

Bill had grown accustomed to the stinky Pogy fish smell shortly after employment, so did Maw-Maw and Paw-Paw.

Nevertheless, when Bill came home from work with menhaden oil embedded in his skin, he always took a hot sudsy bathe first to soak his body, so that he might alleviate the undesirable smell that seemed to hover in the Bishop's home.

When it was time to go, Lil and Lo wanted to stay with Nita and Mary badly, but they knew not to make a fuss today. They just climbed into the back seat of Mose's car, with Nip in the middle, and waved by to their sisters and Maw-Maw, who were standing on the porch waving back.

The evening rushed by. Nita and Mary had been playing outside all afternoon. Paw-Paw took himself a snooze, while Maw-Maw cleaned up the kitchen, and some canning jars for the fig preserves. Nita and Mary played in Paw-Paw's car for a long while. Then they chased some chickens and guineas around in the yard, and played house on the porch, until boredom interrupted their frisky spirits.

"I'm tired of playing on the porch, Mary."

"Yeah, me too, Nita. So what we gonna do next?"

"I don't know. Maybe we can go for a walk."

"Where to, Nita?"

"I don't know just follow me, Mary."

"But where? Do you think we should tell Maw-Maw?"

"No! We won't be gone long. Hurry up. Let's go, before she sees us and ask where we going."

"Okay. But where are we going to, Nita?"

"Well, maybe we can go looking for some seashells. I love to pick them up, because they are so pretty."

"Seashells? Where we gonna find some seashells around here?"

"Come on Mary, just follow me, and I'll show you where."

They struck out toward the beach looking for seashells.

"Look Mary, there's some way over there."

"Over where, Nita?"

"Look right there!"

"Now Nita, you know we ain't suppose to be going close to that ol' beach by ourselves."

"Come on Mary, stop complaining." Nita answered, sharply.

"Ain't nobody said we was gonna git in the water."

The girls strolled along the shore of the beach hand in hand, and gathered several pretty seashells as they went. As soon as they had a handful, they placed them in a little pile, then searched for more.

"These sure are pretty, Mary. Look there's some more over there."

"Over where?"

"Right there. Look!"

"Now, how we gonna git to them way over there, Nita? Shoot, we might git all wet trying to do that."

"Mary, let's take our shoes off. We can make it to them, if we try."

"But Nita! We gonna get all wet trying to do that."

"We ain't gonna get all wet, girl! Follow me."

The Gulf of Mexico rolled softly into shore bring with it a low tide which left loose sprigs of kelp and rockweed algae along the sands of the beach. The coastline near Maw-Maw and Paw-Paw's home yielded a pungent fishy stench, which the girls got use to over the years. A relinquishment of dead fish, and other sea dwelling organisms, whose corpses were eventually washed to shore, produced the freshly decayed flesh smell that hovered in the air. It wasn't like the emerging whiff was an intolerable annoyance to either girl's noses. Nita and Mary continued to collect sea shells joyfully, and paid no attention to the dubious smell or the Gulfs murky waters.

Sand pits resembling miniature islands protruded from the water where the Gulfs uneven surface had been revealed at low tide. Today, one particular sand pit close to shore attracted the girls' attention because they could see several beautiful shells, sparkling against the sunlight, positioned atop it. Nita and Mary decided to skip across the oncoming, ankle deep waves over to the small island to retrieve some of the irresistible, treasures that lay there. They made it to the pit in a playful manner after several leaps, as this sand pit was only a few feet away from the shoreline. The girls could still see their foot prints left behind in the sand along the edge of the beach, depicting their harmonious journey. Soon after, however, the trail of tracks began to wash away, as the motion of the dingy waves bounced backwards and forwards against the strand.

"This is fun, ain't it Mary?"

"Yeah! But we better not go too much farther out in the water because I'm getting scared. Remember, Daddy told us once not to mess around with this ol' Gulf because it don't like little girls."

They picked up several more seashells, and then raced back across the rushing surf to the strand. In just a short time, Nita and Mary had quite a few treasures. Afterwards, the sisters ran back to the pit, splashing the Gulfs waters all over each other. This time when they looked toward the shore, however, their footprints were washing away more expeditiously than before. An ascending tide was headed inland.

"Don't be scared, Mary. We ain't gonna go far. We made it to this sand pit, didn't we? Besides, how we gonna get to them seashells over there on that pit?"

"Way over there, Nita?"

"Yeah!"

"You must be crazy, girl."

"No I'm not crazy." She pointed to another pit a bit further away from the one they were standing on.

"All right I guess, but we still better not go too far out in the Gulf."

"Look at our footprints in the sand, Mary."

"Where Nita?"

"Oh, Oh! Too late the waves done washed them away." Nita laughed.

"Oh Nita, I never got a chance to see them." But she laughed, too.

"Come on Mary, let's go to the next sand pit."

The second sand pit was farther out into the Gulf. As Nita and Mary walked towards it, the waters came up to their knees.

"This is fun. Let's go to another one, Mary."

"NO Nita. You must be crazy."

"No I'm not. Come on, let's go."

Nita convinced Mary to venture on to an even farther sand pit. But once they got there and stood on it, the water was well above their ankles. In the meantime, the area around the pit started getting deeper and deeper. The two adventurous children played and danced from side to side for several moments. Nita glanced as far south as her eyes could see over the mighty Gulf of Mexico.

"Ain't this fun, Mary?"

"Yeah." But Mary was looking back at the shore now quite a distance away. "We better be getting back though. Remember what Daddy told us about this ol' Gulf. We done gone too far out, Nita because I can't even see our seashells in the sand on the beach, no more."

"Oh Mary. Don't worry. We'll be okay."

"No. We better go back now, Nita. I'm really scared!"

"All right scary cat, hold my hand."

Nita grabbed Mary's hand, and as soon as they stepped off the sand pit into the water, much to their surprise, the high tide was vastly upon them. When their feet reach the bottom of the Gulfs floor, the water was up to the little girl's chests. Mary squeezed Nita's hand securely. Nita sensed danger all around them in the rumbling surf, but she didn't want to let her anxiety be evident to Mary.

"Mary hold on to my hand real tight, and don't let go. No matter what happens. Okay?" Nita said, struggling to remain composed.

"Okay, Nita" Mary responded with a quivering voice as both she and Nita wadded slowly back towards the shore. The Gulfs charging waters were now up to their necks. The only visible thing in the roaring Gulf at this particular moment were two little nappy heads of hair, surrounded in a sea of doom. The two little colored girls fought boldly onward, trying to get back to the shoreline as quickly as possible. Mary's whole body shook, as did Nita's, while the agonizing journey to save their precious little lives carried forward. However, without the view of any protruded islands as a means to navigate a safe path back to the shoreline, their journey was variable at this point.

All at once, a huge, forceful wave came up from behind and rushed over the girl's bodies completely, knocking them underneath the water. Their heads were completely submerged for a quick second, but through it all Nita never let go of Mary's hand.

Each of them spat out a mouth full of salty water, and they struggled to catch their breaths, as soon as their heads surfaced. Both of them screamed loudly, but only God in heaven could hear their innocent, little cries for help, and he didn't verbalize an answer. The girls screamed louder and louder in the midst of the deep waters. Still no answer came from anyone who might rescue the two abandoned children at sea. What were they going to do? Who were they to turn to for help in this large, massive body of water?

"I'm so scared Nita" said Mary with jittery teeth.

"Just hold onto my hand, Mary and don't let it go."

Defiantly, the girls made it to another sand pit, just a little bit closer to the shore. Both children at this point were insanely petrified; both crying pitifully, afraid to continue on in the dangerous surf. Despite her tears, Nita tried to stay calm. "If we die today," she said to herself, "at least Momma, Daddy and them will find both of us together, hand in hand." She knew they'd have to battle the fierce waves and high waters in order to make it back to the shore safely. There just was no other choice in the matter.

"What we gonna do now?" Mary asked tearfully.

"Remember that time when Daddy told us about how he saved his life in that bad storm?"

"Yeah" answered Mary.

"Remember, Mary, he said in the midst of a storm, never give up on God. You remember that?" Nita said as the rushing waves splashed around them. Still tense, Mary answered "Yeah!"

"Then, we can't give up! We just can't! God, please help us make it back to the shore" was Nita's cry.

"I don't think we gonna make it, Nita" cried Mary.

"Oh yes we will, Mary. I know we will." Nita yelled over the bellowing sea.

Mary shook her head, hesitating as both girls took their next step together off the second sand pit. As soon as they'd done so, another monstrous wave rushed overhead, knocking Mary under the water completely. With the turbulent Gulf up to her own neck, Nita was uncertain for a horrible moment whether she still held her sister's hand. "Mary! Mary!" Once the wave passed, however, she pulled Mary up onto her feet, the little girl coughing and spitting out the salty waters that had been trapped in her nostrils and throat. They struggled forward, and never let go of each other.

"We gonna make it Mary. We got to trust God. Whatever you do, don't let go of my hand! We gonna make it!"

But right after Nita said those encouraging words another large wave rushed at them from behind, covering their entire bodies. Nita had never before felt death to be so near and so real. Their hands, however, remained undivided.

Finally, after their wearisome bout, the girls made it to the last sand pit nearest the shore. From that vantage, they could see the beach's sand, and some of the seashells that had been gathered earlier, still in the same pile where they left them. A sigh of relief brightened up their worn faces, as they both looked forward to reaching the shoreline. Nita and Mary knew that God had to have been on their side that day.

"Mary, we almost there. We just got a little ways left to go."

The girls took a moment to catch their breath on top of the sand pit before rushing through the final stretch of water. When they reached the beach, both of them fell down to their knees, embraced each other, and sniffled softly together.

"We made it Mary! Thank God we both made it and I will always be by your side."

"And I will always be by yours too, Nita." Mary responded in a tired voice.

Afterwards, they picked up their shoes with one hand, the seashells in another, and journeyed back towards Maw-Maw and Paw-Paw's house, both of them drenched from head to toe in the salty Gulfs water. Still visibly shaken from such a distressing encounter with the resounding Gulf of Mexico, the girls still had another storm to weather.

"Maw-Maw's, gonna git us, all wet like this, ain't she Nita?"

Mary said sniffling.

"I ain't worrying about that right now, I'm just glad the Lord spared our lives to even make it back to anybody's house."

"You right, Nita. We both could have drowned."

"God was just on our side today, Mary. You know something, Daddy was right again. You gotta just hold on, and never give up. The Lord will help you make it through any storm."

"Nita, I ain't never been this scared before, since that time that ol' Hulton boy pulled his pants down, and showed us his thing. Nita you have always been there for me, when I needed you the most."

"And I always will be, Mary until the day I die."

"You can count on me too, Nita."

Along the way, Nita and Mary saw Maw-Maw heading in their direction, half-way between the house and the beach. They could tell that she was really disturbed, once she caught sight of them with their shoes in one hand and clutching seashells in another. Nita said in a whisper "we can't tell her that we went real far out in the water, okay?" Mary nodded, agreeing."Remember not a word!" Nita murmured.

"Where ya'll been?" Maw-Maw yelled loudly before she caught up to them. "Ya'll got me and poor ol' Paw-Paw worried to death!"

"We been on the beach looking for seashells" spoke Nita.

"Well, whacha clothes doing all wet for?"

"We was playing in the water close to the shore Maw-Maw," said Mary.

"Playing in the water? Now ya'll knows, ya'll ain't supposed to be playing in that ol' Gulf water no way. Enough for ya'll both to drown out there. Lord, have mercy Jesus!! Ya'll two kids knows better than that."

"Yes Ma'm" responded Nita and Mary, simultaneously.

"Get on home right now! I don't know what I'm gonna do with you girls. Lord knows ya'll ain't suppose to go to that ol' beach by you self."

Paw-Paw, waiting on the porch had almost had a cardiac arrest. It wasn't until he saw Nita, Mary, and Maw-Maw coming at a distance, that he could let out a big sigh of relief. Maw-Maw continued to scold the girls, who were too tired and distressed to try and offer a creditable explanation.

"Don't ya'll ever go to that Gulf again by you self!" exclaimed Maw-Maw. "What you and Mary trying to do, kill poor ol' Maw Maw and Paw-Paw? Something happen to you kids, they just as well go ahead and dig two more graves to bury me and Paw-Paw right along with you. Ya'll can play all you won't to, around the house, but don't ever go back to that Gulf by you self again. Ya'll hear me?"

Nita and Mary didn't dispute the truth because they knew their grandmother was absolutely right. Later on that night, the two girls cleaned themselves up and went to bed early. In the middle of the night, however, Nita awakened with a frightful nightmare that reminded her of the traumatic experience she and Mary had undertaken earlier in the day. After settling down a bit, she thanked God immensely for sparing their lives, and made a promise never to go to the Gulf again—at least without adult supervision.

* * *

When the school car pulled up to the Bartie home, Nita and Mary got out first, then Lil, and then Lo. On that afternoon, Lil couldn't wait to get home so she raced ahead of the other girls. Their teacher, Miss Myron Hayward who boarded in the home of Mr. and Mrs. Bazile Moore had assigned Lil a poem for homework. She would have to recite it in class the next school day. She could hardly wait to practice on her mother and father. All the kids in the car including Nita, Mary, and Lo were so sick and tired of hearing her repeat that poem over and over. Right after Lil hit the front door of the house, she found Bryant who had just come in from a hard days work out in the fields. He was sitting in his favorite chair in the living room while Bean stood in the front doorway and watched Nita, Mary, and Lo, walk towards the house from the Front Ridge Road.

Soon after, the little chatter box Lil opened up!

"Little Charlie Chipmunk was a talker, mercy me.

He chattered after breakfast, and he chattered after tea.

He chattered to his father, and he chattered to his mother.

He chattered to his sister, and he chattered to his brother.

He chattered so much, he almost drove his family wild.

Little Charlie Chipmunk was a very tiresome child."

At first, Bean and Bryant were very impressed with Lil's narration of the poem. After hours and hours of hearing about the Little Charlie Chipmunk, however, the little girl drove the Bartie family wild! The other three sisters grew completely fed up, went outside to play, and so left their mother and father to weather the hilarious storm all by themselves. Bryant wanted to make Lil feel proud of herself, but at the same time, he also desired to silence the child because she was driving him and Bean into hysteria.

"What else did you learn in school today, Lil?" asked Bryant.

"He chattered after breakfast and he chattered after tea."

Continued Lil with a big smile on her face. "He chattered to his father, and he chattered to his----------"

The poem went on for so long, poor Bryant couldn't take it anymore. He left the house, and went to the barn seeking some peace and quiet there. When supper rolled around, guess who Bean sent out to the barn to tell him?

"Daddy, Momma said it's time for us to eat." And of course, on the way back to the house from the pasture, Lil started up again.

"Little Charlie Chipmunk was a talker mercy me."

All Bryant could do was just walk with his daughter, and pretend to listen attentively, to her chatter which he heard for the fortieth time by now. As they walked into the kitchen, he asked Bean.

"When do this kid have to say that poem, at school? All I hear is he chattered after breakfast, and he chattered after tea." Bryant moved his head in unison with each rhyming line.

"Oh Bryant, I'm sure her teacher will be real proud of her."

"She better be, Bean. Plague-take-it!' I done heard enough about that ol' Chipmunk for the rest of my life. Whoooooooof!!

Once the family gathered at the table, Bryant blessed the food.

Afterwards, the other girls looked at Lil, and said "please don't start." What did they even say that for? The chatter box opened up, again.

"Little Charlie Chipmunk was a talker mercy me!"

No one could get angry with Lil—she was so proud of herself—so the entire family just had to laugh together as they ate supper. Afterwards, the girls cleaned up the kitchen. Each of them did their homework by a kerosene lamp, and retired for bed, and so did the Little Chatter Box Lil, Mercy Me!

The next day at school, Lil stood before the class and recited the poem with such refinement that her efforts earned her an A. Miss Hayward was so impressed with the narration, that she sent a note home to Bean and Bryant emphasizing Lil's exceptional oral capabilities, and the positive influence they had made with her. At the conclusion of the poem, the entire class stood and applauded as Lil returned to her seat. Nita, Mary, and Lo were very proud of their sister's efforts. Of course Lil's hard work and consistent pestering eventually paid off. She had a big smile on her face for the duration of the school day. For once in her life Lil knew what it felt like to be a shining star.

Nita and the rest of her sisters grew to love and admire Miss Hayward. She was the epitome of femininity, and was the Bartie girls' most memorable mentor. An intelligent, well dressed, articulate, and beautiful lady, she was loved dearly by all her students as well. Miss Hayward was the kind of teacher that a student had no other choice but to admire and respect because of her extensive knowledge and magnetic personality. Miss Hayward touched the students lives in so many countless, wonderful ways, constantly emphasizing their need to become literate. She taught Nita, Mary, Lil and Lo to always "believe and be true to themselves, and to strive for excellence, never allowing anything or anyone to stand in the way of their dreams and aspirations."

Towards the close of the school day, Miss Hayward excused Nita and Rosie Andrews to go outside, each with an arm full of blackboard erasers, to beat the chalk dust out of each. Nita and Rosie had become the very best of friends. Even though Rosie dressed much better than Nita, that fact did nothing to tarnish their friendship. They cared a lot for each other and loved the opportunity to chat whenever Miss Hayward permitted it.

"Miss Hayward is the nicest teacher I ever had" said Rosie.

"She sure is Rosie. And she dresses so nice and wears the prettiest jewelry and shoes."

" I really like her Nita."

"I hope someday when I grow up that I can be just like her, and wear nice clothes too."

"Oh Nita, you look good every day."

"I know I don't, Rosie, because my Momma and Daddy's real poor. And I got so many sisters, a brother, and another baby on the way, till they can't afford to buy us too many nice things."

"Trust me Nita. Your clothes really don't matter to me. The most important thing is that you are my very best friend, and I like you just the way you are."

"Thanks Rosie. You are so kind. And you will always be my good friend forever."

Once they finished, Nita and Rosie went back into the classroom together and placed the clean erasers in their proper place near the blackboard. Nita took her seat feeling pretty good about herself. Even though her exterior fell short when it came down to pretty clothes, Rosie's kind words had lifted Nita's spirits and self esteem, and made her feel important, needed and loved.

She knew that Rosie was a true friend. Wasn't that what true friendships were all about, anyway? Regardless of the obstacles, adversities, or storms that life may yield, a true friend would never, ever turn their back and walk away. Instead, a real friend would always find a way to lift another's spirits at those not so pleasant moments when the weight of the world bears down a heavy load, or even simply when the storms of life may just be blowing a very mild breeze.

When the girls came home from school on the ninth day of February, in 1946, they found a pleasant surprise bundled up in their mother's arms. Earlier on during the morning Bean had given birth to a third son, Walter Charles. Nip, in the meantime stuck to his mother like glue. He wouldn't allow himself to lose sight of her, nor the new baby. Bryant didn't go out into the fields that day at all.

Once the birthing process had transpired, he stayed home to provide assistance to Bean. As soon as Nita, Mary, Lil and Lo came through the front door, they heaved out a joyful roar when they saw Walter, who didn't make much of a fuss over them though. He was a quiet little baby boy who sort of smiled as each sister took a turn to hold him. Of course Nip felt a bit rejected being as the attention suddenly diverted from him to Walter. Nip whimpered and cried as each girl awaited their turn to hold Walter for a short moment.

"It's my turn, Nita" shouted Lo.

"Okay, Lo. But don't be so rough with him," Nita explained, as she handed the baby over.

"Can I hold him next, Momma?" asked Lil.

"Yeah, but after you hold him, give him back to Momma, okay?"

"Yes Ma'm. It's my turn now, Lo!"

"All right, Lil."

A scuffle started when Lo refused to let go of Walter at Lil's request. Finally, Bryant intervened.

"Okay daughter, let Lil hold 'Ol' Dad' a little bit."

"Ol' Dad?" responded Mary, who was holding onto Nip in a loving manner.

"Yep! 'Ol' Dad'." Bryant exclaimed with laughter.

"Bryant you always coming up with some ol' silly name" Bean responded.

That's right Bean. Now let's see. We've got Ol' Piggy Pon Tole, Toad, Bay Bay, Pole, Nip and Ol' Dad" He laughed as he counted each on his fingers. "Plague-take-it Bean! Na Na Na Na Na Na we got a whole school house full of nothin but Bartie kids." Bryant laughed louder and harder.

The birth of Walter added one more mouth to feed for this poor, struggling colored family. It meant Bryant would have to work a little bit harder to put extra food on the table, but he didn't mind that the least bit. Bryant knew that God would provide a way for the family to survive. The Bartie's loved each other immensely, which was the true reason for their survival as a family. There may not have been much food to eat, but the love they shared for each other made up the difference. Many times when there was only cornbread and milk to soothe their hunger pains, the family was still grateful for God's blessings.

Approximately two weeks after Walter's birth, the little baby became extremely dehydrated. Bryant had to seek the attention of a local midwife to attend to the illness. It had become a difficult task for Ol' Dad to sleep at night because of a constant stream of diarrhea. Once the midwife examined the infant, she gave him a teaspoon of castor oil to negate the bug lurking in his stomach, and also recommended that Bean strain some oatmeal water with a teaspoon of sugar to enhance his nutrient intake. Bean was afraid the family would lose the new baby, however in a few days they saw a drastic improvement in Walter's health. Of course, Bryant took the matter to the almighty Master, who was the real reason that the young infant had been brought through his bitter illness.

"Bean, I know we was scared we might lose Ol' Dad. But you know something? All you got to do is look up, and extend your hands to God, and tell him that you gonna leave your worries with him. I know He'll see you through any storm."

"You so right Bryant. Sometimes we just seem to forget, about how good God really is. Just look at Walter. He's living proof, ain't he?"

"Plague-take-it, Bean you so right!"

CHAPTER 8

In May of 1946, the school term ended on a good note, with each girl advancing to her next respective grade level. Nita proved to be an exceptional role model for her younger sisters, taking on many responsibilities in the Bartie home such as cooking, cleaning, washing clothes, and picking cotton just to name a few. It was Nita who awakened before sun up to help her father milk the cows, and who made sure the other girls were up, bright and early, to get a fresh start out in the cotton fields. Once Nita finished her first set of chores, she lead the family in prayer, then helped with the preparation of breakfast. Soon after the school year concluded, all the Bartie children were required to contribute their fair share around the farm. Nip and Ol' Dad were too young to work out in the cotton fields, but they did help Bean in any way they could at home.

"Hurry up Mary, Lil, Lo, it's time to get moving!" Yelled Nita as she finished washing the last dish. She was using a dish pan full of water that sat on the table in the kitchen. The other girls hovered while putting on their clothes, dreading the hot summer's glistening heat that awaited them out in the cotton patches. The fields were about a half a mile walk from the shack. Sometimes the trek tired the girls out before they even got started. Nita, however, walked next to Bryant ahead of the others. Even though she, too, detested the summer's heat, she always tried to simulate a positive attitude for the sake of her sisters. As the girls walked towards the sea of pretty white cotton, mosquitoes and horse flies—which made picking the soft fiber a real annoyance— were already swarming around waiting to deflate the sister's already low spirits. The cotton crop grew on shrubs two to four feet tall. The immature flower bud eventually blossomed into an oval boll which split open at maturity producing a mass of long white seed hairs called lint that covered several black seeds. That season Bryant had done a good job decimating the infestation of the cotton boll weevil with a home-made pesticide. Usually, the insect laid its eggs in the boll of the cotton plant, and as the larvae fed inside, the crop was eventually destroyed. Bryant picked about 80-100 pounds of cotton per sack, however the girls were not quite as fast as their father. Sometimes at the end of the day collectively they would have accumulated over 400 hundred pounds of white fiber. The hardest part of the task however was to get the cotton from the fields back to the crib where it was stored in a bin. Each sack of cotton had to be compactly tromped over, sewed at the filled end with twine and then neatly stacked. Of course, Bryant was responsible for that technique. As soon as he had enough sacks of cotton accumulated, he loaded them onto his wagon and transported it to the 'Jiggy' Miller Cotton Gin. The gin separated the lint from the seeds, while compressing many sacks of the fiber into a bale weighing over 500 pounds. Afterwards, several bales of cotton were shipped out from the gin to different industries for making yarns, cloths and cordage; the left-over cotton seeds were used for cattle feed, oil and fertilizer.

What a picture! Four little nappy-headed girls with straw hats decked out atop their heads, all trudging slowly on the dusty pathway leading into the fields to partake in a full day's work with their father. They were all shabbily dressed, however; who needed to look good in the cotton patch? Bryant was all smiles. All four of his girls were by his side; a decent crop of cotton had matured in the fields; all the family members were healthy, and, of course he had the Lord on his side. What more could he ask for?

Once they arrived at the patch Bryant gave the girls specific instructions where to start picking the white stuff.

"Okay Piggy-Pon-Tole and Toad, here's a sack for you." He pointed into the field. "Ya'll start over there. Bay Bay and Pole, right here. Now Ol' Bryant's gonna be way over yonder. If ya'll need anything just holler" he said, then walked away over to the far end of the field. The crop was planted in furrows requiring Bryant and the girls to walk down the middle of each row, pulling a sack draped over their left shoulder as they bent over to pick the soft fiber. The posture in which they maintained yielded a throbbing pain in their lower backs, while their hands were scuffed and scratched as they pulled the lint from the shrubs.

"I don't see why we gotta pick this ol' mess anyways," Mary commented, making sure that Bryant was far enough down a row of cotton not to hear her grumble.

"Me either" added Lo. "I'm already hot and my back hurts. I wish I was back home with Momma. And these ol' mosquitoes about to kill me too."

"I'm about to faint" added Lil.

"Ohhhhh!" Lo pointed and screamed. "Look ya'll at that big ol thing right over there."

"Now whacha talkin about Lo?" Nita asked.

"Look he runnin real fast on that row right over there."

"Ah girl, that's just an ol' field rat." Nita replied. "He ain't gonna mess with you."

"How you know he ain't, Nita?"

"Because I done picked enough cotton in my day to know better. That's how! And if you look hard enough you can see the same ol' rat in our room at home. Ya'll know, he gotta big hole in the wall. And that's were he stay most of the time. Now git back to pickin cotton, Lo" commanded Nita.

"I can't Nita. I'm too scared of that ol' rat."

"I'm scared too, said Lil."

"Them ol' rats ain't gonna mess with ya'll" Mary added.

"Plague-take-it! You and Lo just wanna get out of working. But ya'll ain't foolin nobody today. You both gonna pick some cotton because you ain't going back home with Momma. So just forget it!"

"Mary's right. Lil and Lo, get back to work before Daddy come over here, and then we'll all be in trouble."

"I'm too scared, Nita," insisted Lo.

"Me too. And I hate them ol' mosquitoes" said Lil.

"I don't like them either," Nita replied, "but we still have plenty of work to do."

Lil and Lo sat down on their sacks pretending to be afraid of the field rat while Nita and Mary continued to pick. As the time passed slowly, Lil and Lo forgot all about the rat scenario, and decided to do some work before Bryant came over. Soon, it was getting close to ten o'clock. The sun hung high up, in the sky, beaming down on their tender, feminine, small-framed bodies.

Each girl had pulled several stalks of cotton lint from the plant and placed it in their respective sacks. Talk about hard work. It seemed like forever had come and gone before they would even get close to filling up a sack with the small white cotton balls.

"I'm so hot, I think I'm gonna pass out" Lo said.

"Me too" added Lil.

"I'm kinda getting tired myself said Mary.

"I don't see why we have to pick this ol' cotton in the first place" Lil complained.

"Why? Because we's a po family," Nita explained in a huff.

"And this is the only way Daddy can feed us."

"But still," Lo interjected. "We's just some little girls. And we's too young to be working so hard out here in this ol' heat, Nita."

"And all day long, too. You must be crazy!" Lil remarked.

"Okay! Okay! Let's take a short break. But afterwards we gotta get back to work." Nita took a deep gasp of breath as she wiped the perspiration off her face.

"Lord! Lord! Lord! It's hot out here, now" complained Mary.

The girls gathered in a small circle between a row of cotton and sat down on their sacks for a well-deserved break. The heat had really started to beam down upon them by then. They pulled their straw hats off and began to fan their warm bodies as the sun's rays blemished their complexions. Nita pulled out an ol' jug filled with drinking water, to prevent dehydration unfortunately, it did very little to cool them off.

"I can't wait until eleven o'clock comes, because I'm so tired," said Mary.

"Here! Each of you take a drink of this," Nita instructed.

"Ahhh! It's warm, but it's good," said Lil.

"Give me some," said Lo, then she drank several mouths full.

"Okay Lo, don't drink all the water up, save some for me and Mary."

Even though the tepid water was all they had to quench their thirst, the girls gulped it down like it was a real cool treat. A breeze blew over them, momentarily as they sat in the hot climate, but that merely delivered temporary relief. Bryant looked at his daughters from a distance and he thought to himself, "I wish they didn't have to work so hard out here in this hot sun. Maybe one day, God, you'll make a way for me to do better for my girls, and they won't have to."

Back in the circle of annoyance, the girls continued to complain about the heat, the bugs, the rat, or whatever other trivial thoughts came to mind. Their constant faultfinding had begun to aggravate Nita's spirits, causing her to stand up abruptly. Spontaneously, she started to reprimand the group for their pessimistic temperaments. "Y'alls complaining ain't gonna help none of us, so you can just stop it right now. Besides, we've got to help poor Daddy out. He's doing the best he can for all of us. He's gotta feed the family some kind-a-way. So the least we can do is to stop complaining, and be thankful. Things could be a lot worse, you know! Ya'll all better remember one thing each of us had better git our learning, so we can rise above these here ol' cotton fields one day. At least that's what Miss Hayward said. Otherwise if we don't, we'll all be stuck out here pickin cotton for the rest of our lives. A good education can take us far in life, so never give up on learning and bettering yourselves. Now let's get back to work before Daddy sees us playing around. It's almost eleven o'clock!"

The other girls listened attentively to Nita's wisdom, though her exhortation did very little to divert their attention from the heat. Their anguish was easily detected by Nita, so she started singing "Jesus Loves Me," a song they had all learned in a Sunday school class. As Nita began to sing, the other three girls joined in delivering a beautiful melody:

"Jesus loves me this I know.

For the Bible tells me so.

Little ones to him belong.

They are weak, but he is strong.

Yes Jesus loves me.

Yes Jesus loves me.

Yes Jesus loves me.

For the Bible tells me so."

As Bryant made his way over to the harmonizing group, he found them singing to the Lord, joyfully. He was so proud of them. A small tear formed in the corner of his left eye as he watched and listened to his inspirational daughters. The girls were finishing the last verse when they saw him coming. Immediately, Lil and Lo got excited, because they knew a well deserved break was close at hand. Bryant applauded the sisters' harmonious efforts at the completion of their song.

"That was real good! Now Piggy, I always knowed you could sang, but I ain't knowed ol' Toad, Bay Bay, and Pole could carry a tune like that. That was some good singin. Plague-take-it! Ya'll needs to sang that at church one Sunday."

"Is it time to go home yet, Daddy?" asked Lo.

"Yeah. It's about that time. Lord! It's so hot out here till I'm about to faint myself. Let's go see what ol' Momma's got-a-cookin in the kitchen," said Bryant.

The girls were so happy that eleven o'clock had finally come. Everyone walked home, wearily. Bean prepared beans and rice for lunch. One thing was for sure, meal times were especially important in the Bartie home. Everyone had to gather around the table, including the two little boys, and thank God for his blessing before a single fork was raise to a mouth. Once they finished eating, Bryant and the girls took a short, worthy nap, but at the conclusion of their sleep, it was back out into the fields again at three o'clock. They worked until dusk. It was a rigorous schedule, but that was life in "the forties," for the Bryant Bartie household. At the end of the day, the four little exhausted girls returned home. Each of them soaked in a hot tub of water, ate their supper, and retired to bed, all of them resting together after a debilitating day. While staring at the ceiling, Nita repeated over and over again to herself, "I can. And I will rise above these cotton fields of Creole!"

Only God listened to her serene whispers, that night. Her sisters were too haggard to even hear her. Nita smiled, shut her eyes tight, and made a wish. Afterwards, she dozed off, as though God had provided her with reassurance that someday she wouldn't ever have to labor in such an exhausting way any more. A happy smile remained on her face for the duration of the night. Everything was quiet in the house, except for a field rat fumbling around the girl's room below their very high, antiquated, iron post bed. Ironically, the old rat knew not to make much of a fuss that night. It moved about carefully and modestly, as if it realized that the girls had already had enough confusion earlier in the day from one of its kindred out in the cotton field. Apparently, the rat sensed the girl's sluggishness and knew that they didn't need any further turmoil to disrupt their peaceful rest. So the ol' field rat just retired tranquilly to it's familiar nest between the walls of the dilapidated, hot, humid shack, and shortly thereafter it fell asleep, too. Every living thing in the Bartie household was even-tempered on that night, as a higher being guarded their slumber!

Bryant's dwindling cotton crop worsened the following year due to the infestation of the boll weevil. He had to take on a lot of odd jobs to try' and make ends meet for his family. One day he heard through Mr. B. Nunez that additional help was needed for a large cattle drive taking place not far from his home. Out of desperation, Bryant sought temporary employment from Frank Rutherford, a white farmer who lived about a half mile east of Jim Rutherford's place. Bryant had never worked cattle in such a way before, but he learned the trade quickly, knowing that his family needed the extra funds to survive. Mr. Frank was impressed with Bryants capabilities and his eagerness to work, and continued employing him from time to time for occasional tasks as they became available.

A close relationship developed between the two men. Bryant became obsessed with the manner in which Mr. Frank provided a means for his daughters to obtain a college education. Bryant felt an added incentive to procure the same opportunity for Nita, Mary, Lil, Lo, Nip and Ol' Dad someday. "Education is the key to success thought Bryant. "I'm gonna make sure my kids get one, cause I ain't never had that opportunity before, myself. And I want them to do much better with they life than I done with mine."

Bryant's association with Mr. Frank's wife, Miss Delia, blossomed as well, which led to additional opportunities for the family. Miss Delia needed a domestic worker to assist her in the evenings around the huge ante-bellum style home. Bryant relayed the message to Bean and the girls. Nita volunteered wholeheartedly. She had a strong desire to work and earn extra money for the family. With Bryant and Bean's approval, she started working for Miss Delia in the afternoons. Nita worked three times a week after school, walking to and from the Frank Rutherford house from her home. She washed and folded clothes, did dishes, scrubbed the floors, polished furniture, and whatever else was requested of her services. Nita fell in love with the big house and Miss Delia, who was a very mannerly, good hearted, and attractive white lady. She taught Nita a lot about home etiquette, and developing self confidence. Nita was required to set the table with a linen tablecloth every evening, along with Miss Delia's fine bone china, silverware, cloth napkins, stemware and dinnerware.

"Okay Wanita, it's time to set the table for this evenings meal, My Dear."

"Yes, Ma'am."

"It's 'Yes Miss Delia,' Wanita. I don't like it when you say 'Yes Ma'am.' That sounds too subservient. And I'm also going to refer to you by your proper name: 'Wanita.' I don't like that shorter version.

It just sounds plain ol' country." Wanita wondered what she meant by that word 'subservient.'

"Once you finish in the dinning room, you may iron those shirts for Frank, and fold all the clothes in the middle bedroom, upstairs. Then you may fix yourself something to eat, My dear."

"Yes Miss Delia" responded Nita.

"Now, that sounds much more proper, My Dear," Miss Delia said, nodding her head approvingly.

"Oh, and Wanita, don't slouch when you walk, Dear. You're much too pretty of a girl to practice incorrect posture. Try to keep your back straight, your nose and chin pointed, with your head slightly tilted upward. Sort of with your nose stuck up in the air. That's it!" Miss Delia giggled. "And just glide gracefully across the floor like a lady should."

"I ain't never walked like this, Miss Delia," Wanita said balancing awkwardly.

"Look at my lips, Wanita. You haven't ever walked like that. Not ain't never. Now keep working at that walk. You will master it, with time. Just pay close attention to my two girls, and try to imitate them. They project good examples of what I'm talking about." Nita wondered what Miss Delia meant by that word, "imitate". And "project?" She pondered.

"Well anyways, she said I was pretty. Ain't nobody ever told me that before. I can't wait to tell Mary, Lil and Lo that Miss Delia said I was a pretty girl."

"Wanita," Miss Delia said, "let's go into the dining room now. I want to teach you correctly, the proper way to fold the dinner napkins, and to set the table correctly." Miss Delia showed Wanita how to fold a dinner napkin. "Okay, this is how you do it. First, fold this end of the napkin over like this and the other end like that. Then place the knife and fork on top of it and align the entire set to the right side of the plate. The stem ware goes on the left, My Dear. The smaller glass is for water, and the larger one for tea. Any questions?"

"No Miss Delia, I understand."

"You've grasped that very well. Not only are you pretty, but you're a smart young lady, too. Pretty and smart, what a combination! Carry on, My dear."

Once Miss Delia exited the dining room, Wanita thought out loud to herself" I wonder what she mean by 'grasped'? And I guess these here glasses is the stemware, and the knife and fork is the silverware. They must be rich, because we ain't got but one kinda glass to drink out of at my house, and they's some Mason jars. I ain't never gonna get tired of this job. I mean...I will never."

She was quite pleased with her new way of talking. "Now, that's better, Wanita," she said under her breath in a refined tone.

Mr. Frank, Miss Delia and their daughters always sat together as a family for meal times, which was also common in Wanita's home. After the Rutherfords recited their blessing, the food was passed around the table in a clockwise sequence, until everyone present acquired a sample of each dish. No one ate until each person was completely served. Afterwards, the neatly folded napkins were taken from the place setting and placed in their laps.

The family ate with one hand only, while the other stayed at their sides, away from the table. All of them gently patted their mouths in a proper fashion after several bites of food were consumed. Wanita fantasized as she watched the family exercise good eating habits from the kitchen. She yearned to teach the same etiquette to her sisters and parents. Of course Nita wasn't allowed to eat with the Rutherford's in the huge dining room. She wasn't even allowed to enter their home through the front door, only through the back entrance. Those were the house rules for the young colored girl, who suddenly became exposed to things she never experienced before.

At the conclusion of the meal, Wanita washed the dishes carefully, and placed them back in the beautiful cherry wood china cabinet sitting against a long wall in the dining room. Once Wanita's day concluded, she couldn't wait to get home to tell her family all about the exciting things that she had learned. Miss Delia allowed her to take the leftover food home to her family.

On the way home, Wanita tucked the bag of food under her left arm. With her nose and chin pointed, and head tilted slightly upward, she glided home along the dusty Front Ridge Road just as Miss Delia had instructed her to do.

The following day at school she asked Miss Hayward the definitions for 'subservient,' 'imitate,' 'project' and 'grasp.' Once Miss Hayward explained each of them to her Nita comprehended very well what Miss Delia meant the day before.

The next night, before supper, Wanita attempted to set the table for her mother in the same manner Miss Delia taught her, but she ran into much difficulty. First of all, Bean had no place mats, no cloth napkins, no fine china, and no stemware. There really wasn't too much Nita could do with cornbread and milk, either. The family usually just got themselves a piece of the cornbread out of an old black skillet sitting on the wood burning stove. Then, they chopped it up into a bowl of milk, and added a little sugar if desired. Wanita did the best she could with what she had to work with. Determined to use proper etiquette, she set the bare table with a bowl and a spoon at each place. Then she placed the cornbread in a plate, and put it on the table also. When supper time came, everyone gathered into the kitchen for the blessing. Even though things weren't quite as pretty as Miss Delia's beautiful made up dinning room table, Bryant did recognize Nita's efforts, and noticed the positive influence Miss Delia was having on his daughter. Her eagerness was what really counted, anyway. It was another reason for him to support the idea of his children obtaining an advanced education.

"Good job, Nita. That's what a good education can do for you."

"Thank you very much, Daddy. But it's Wanita not Nita."

"Plague-take-it! You really trying to get fancy on me, now ain't you? I knows it's Wanita because I'm the one that named you." He laughed.

"Still Daddy, Nita sounds too sub-ser-vi-ent, which means inferior. So we should practice the proper pro-nun-ci-a-tion of my birth name. Nick names or shorter versions are very country, at least that's what Miss Delia tells me."

Bryant, not knowing quite how to take this, returned to his milk and cornbread. Being in the company of Miss Delia increased Wanita's vocabulary after a few weeks and aided her with diction and enunciation as well. Whenever, she used incorrect English, Miss Delia corrected her on the spot. The atmosphere at the Rutherfords started molding Wanita into a very refined, young lady, herself. In turn, she tried to expose the same social graces, to her own family, particularly her sisters.

Bean was becoming a bit skeptical of the new emerging Wanita. Ever since she started working for Miss Delia it appeared as though her oldest daughter had gone through some type of metamorphosis, trying to duplicate the Rutherford's mannerisms, and speech. Bean just didn't want Wanita to have a rude awakening one day. The exposure was good; however it was Bean's intent to keep Wanita in check. The fact that she was a small town, colored, country girl living in the Deep South was not going to go away overnight. "No matter how fancy she thank she is" thought Bean, "she still gonna be a poor colored girl in the eyes of them rich white folks."

"Momma, the next time we have cornbread and milk," Nita said one day "we need to cut the cornbread into pieces and place them in a large tray, and then put the tray on the table, along with a container of milk. Once everyone has been seated, that's when we will pass each item around the table. Like this. See? Look at my hands." Wanita motioned in a clockwise manner. "Once everyone has a share of each item on the table, that's when we all may begin eating our food together. Of course we must say the blessing first."

"I see a lot of Miss Delia's ways done rubbed off on you" Bean said.

Momma, it's has rubbed off. Not done rubbed off.

"Understand?"

Bean nodded her head with a delayed cynical hesitation. Once supper was over, Nita and Mary washed the dishes, while Lil and Lo dried them. After that, they all did their homework. Then the girls wanted to know more about Miss Delia, and her beautiful home.

"She has the prettiest home I never seen before. Oops! I mean I have ever seen before. I ain't never, ever been in such a pretty house like that. And look you all, this is the way Miss Delia says a lady is supposed to walk. First, you should always keep your back straight. Then, point your nose and chin upward with your head tilted. Like this. Then, you just glide across the floor like a lady. You've got it?"

Lil and Lo tried first. They were a natural. No problem what so ever. Poor Mary, however experienced the most difficulty with her attempt to grasp the new found walk.

"That's okay Mary, it was even hard for me at first. Just imitate Lil and Lo and you'll get it, My Dear."

"Whacha mean by 'im-i-tate', Nita?" asked Mary.

"Mary, remember what I told you earlier. I'm Wanita now. And 'imitate' means to act or walk like Lil and Lo. Okay? Understand?"

"I guess so" said Mary as she tried to mimic her sisters.

"Oh, one more thing. Miss Delia says, you don't ever sit with your legs opened wide. Remember, we are ladies. This is the way a lady should sit. Like this. Not like that. Okay?" She demonstrated again. "Either cross your legs like this, or turn them to the side, and slightly cross them at the ankles, like that. Or you may sit with your legs very close together, like this. Never, ever with them wide opened. No one should ever be able to see under your dress, at anytime."

The girls caught on to the sitting technique, effortlessly.

"Very good Lillie, Lorina, and Mary. You've all done it correctly" nodded Wanita approvingly. "Guess what else Miss Delia told me?" she said with a bit of an attitude. Miss Delia told me that I was a very pretty and smart colored girl. Now what do you think about that?"

"Really? She told you that?" gasped Lil.

"Yes." Wanita pointed her nose high in the air.

"I really want to meet Miss Delia one day" said Lo.

"Yeah! Me too" said Mary.

"I'll have to ask her if it will be okay, first. But if she does allow you to, Lil, please remember to tell her that your name is Lillie, and Lo, that yours is Lorina. Mary you're fine. You have nothing to worry about because we call you by your proper birth name most of the time. She doesn't like it when you use the shorter version of your birth name. That is considered "COUNTRY!! Hee, hee! replied the three other girls, simultaneously.

"I can't wait to see her" replied Mary.

"Me either!" said Lil excitedly.

"Maybe we all can go with you the next time, you go Nita" Lo added.

"Maybe. But remember Lorina, I'm Wanita. And if I do bring all of you with me, you must promise me that you will act like ladies, talk like ladies, walk like ladies and sit like ladies. Okay?"

"YES!" responded the ecstatic group of polished, remade, young colored girls. It was all thanks to Wanita's tenacious persuasion.

Easter Sunday at the Bartie home that year was going to be a real joy. Wanita saved up enough money to buy Mary, Lillie and Lorina stylish, new-fashioned dresses to wear to church. The girls were so excited. For once their outfits weren't the same ol' homemade stuff they had grown accustomed to.

Bean ordered the dresses from the Sears and Roebuck catalog. Fortunately, the order showed up about two weeks before the holiday. Had the outfits not made it to the Bartie home on time, there would have been some disgruntled little girls once Easter morning arrived. Wanita purchased a navy fishtail dress for herself.

Mary's dress was similar to Wanita's, except hers was a chocolate brown color. Lillie and Lorina were to wear pretty pink dresses, with sashes that tied in the back. Wanita even managed to save up enough money to buy new ribbons for each girl's hair. What a marvelous day for the Bartie girls. They couldn't wait to wear their dresses to church.

In the meantime, there was a bit of pandemonium developing, particularly in the mind of Lorina. She had been fantasizing for the longest over wearing her new outfit. Every day she got out the Sears catalog and stared at the dress Bean had chosen for her and Lillie to wear. Lorina became obsessed with the picture of the little white girl, her hair cut into a short bob, who was modeling the outfit in the catalog. Lorina wanted to look exactly like the white child model. On the Saturday night before Easter Sunday, Lo went into the bedroom, picked up a hand mirror and began imagining herself looking precisely like the girl in the picture. But she figured out that something just wasn't right with the way she looked compared to the little girl in the book.

I can't understand why I don't look like that little girl" she pondered. "I just don't know why!"

Lorina contemplated it until a crazy thought overtook her mind. Out of desperation she jumped up from where she was sitting and rushed into her mother's room. The young girl searched and searched around until she found Bean's sewing basket. Inside she found a pair of scissors. Lorina headed back to her bedroom with a purposeful objective in mind. She looked at herself in the mirror again and said "Now, I know why I don't look like her."

That's when the desperate little child prepared herself to perform the inevitable.

"I'm gonna look just like that little girl in the catalog on Easter Sunday" she thought. Lorina grabbed the biggest lock of hair from the back side of her head and placed it between the very sharp blades of the scissors. She snipped off about four inches of her beautiful thick, long, course hair and the strands scattered everywhere over the floor. Afterwards, she picked up the mirror with much anticipation to ascertain the results of her efforts. Wanita walked into the room right then, to find her sister crying.

"Oh my God! Lorina what have you done to your hair, girl?"

"I cut it, because I wanted to look like that little girl in the Sears catalog" she sobbed.

"Oh no, Lorina!" said Wanita, with her hand gripping her mouth. "You look fine just the way you are. You didn't have to cut your hair to look like that little girl. Oh my God, come here."

Wanita embraced her little sister. "We can't tell Momma a thing about this, because if she finds out, she'll be real mad at you. Please promise me that you won't tell Mary or Lil, and that you will only let me comb your hair from now on."

"I promise," cried Lorina.

Wanita reached for a comb and brush and began combing Lorina's hair. She struggled to camouflage the huge missing gap in the back of her head.

"If Momma sees your hair like this, she's gonna know something's wrong with it. And remember, Lorina, you're a beautiful little girl. You don't have to look like any body else to be pretty. Okay?"

"Yeah!" Lo responded with a pouting face.

After much frustration, Wanita managed to make two big plats on each side of her sister's head. Then she placed a pink ribbon in both. When Lorina looked at herself in the mirror, she realized that she still didn't look like the girl in the catalog, however Wanita had done a wonderful job to make her feel good about herself. No one would be able to tell that her hair was unevenly cut.

That Sunday morning, when it was time for the girls to comb their hair. Wanita made sure that she did Lorina's so she could blend the longer portions in with the shorter part. Wanita assured her little sister again that she was much prettier than the little white girl in the Sears and Roebuck catalog.

The four Bartie girls had never looked as good as they did on that Easter Sunday. Bryant and Bean were so proud of them, especially Wanita, because she had willingly shared her hard earned money with the other three girls. By far, all four of them were the best dressed little girl's at church.

A few weeks later as Wanita was combing Lorina's hair, Bryant in passing noticed the two different lengths.

"Daughter, Na Na Na Na Na Na what happened to Lo's hair?" he inquired.

"She accidentally cut a big gap out one day with Momma's scissors, Daddy."

"Now Lo, the next time you needs your hair cut, just ask somebody. You know you can't do that all by yourself. Plague-take-it!" Bryant said. "Nita go get me Momma's scissors."

"Here Daddy," said Nita when she returned.

"Thank you. Now Lo, hold your head straight for me. Like this."

Bryant cut Lo's hair even to one length. He later told Bean of the mishap. She didn't scold Lo. She just said "Bryant, it's hard to keep an eye on all of them at one time. Them kids change every day just like the wind!"

CHAPTER 9

The 1948 school year found Nita attending the Hebert School, located next door to the Ebenezer Baptist Church, several miles away from her home. Bryant's brother, Henry, needed someone to stay with their mother, "Big Momma" while he worked the night shift at the Swindell Pogy Plant in Cameron. Henry detested the idea of leaving Big Momma home alone when he was away laboring. He expressed his concern to Bryant, who relayed the message to the most probable candidate, that of course being Nita. She was excited over the proposal, and willingly accepted her uncle's offer without hesitation. Since the Pogy industry was seasonal, Nita's stay at her grandmother's place would only last through the month of October.

Upon arrival at Big Momma's, Nita longed for Mary, Lil, Lo, Nip, and Ol' Dad. However, after a few weeks of adapting to an all-adult environment, she became eager to meet new friends at school, and also enjoyed all the attention her grandmother and uncle focused towards her. The experience of being away from her parents and siblings proved that she was maturing into a responsible young lady. Before school each morning, Nita first milked the cows, then fed the chickens, ducks, and geese. After those chores were completed, she hurried to get cleaned up so that she made it to the school car stop on time. From Big Momma's house to the back ridge road the walk was approximately two miles each way. Mr. Amedie Bargeman, a nice old colored man, who adored Nita, dearly, drove her and the rest of the students to the Hebert School in a Ford.

The First day at the new school, Nita quickly developed a close friendship with her Aunt Lucinda—Bryant's sister and her Uncle John 'Cass' Mouton's children Mary and Roland. Lucinda and Cass lived on the back ridge near Big Momma's home. Lucinda like her mother Big Momma was devoutly religious. She was as sweet as sugar, soft spoken, kind, had long silky hair, and loved to bake and cook. Cass was a short, stout man who talked very loud. The Mouton family attended Ebenezer Baptist, owned a large six room house, raised their own food in a nicely kept garden, as well as chickens and geese. Cass and Lucinda always made Nita feel welcomed in their home whenever Big Momma allowed her to visit them so that she wouldn't loose contact with children her own age.

Besides Mary and Roland, the Moutons had seven other children: Susie, Catherine, Kenneth, Viola, Joseph, Emma Lois and Geneva. Bryant and Lucinda shared very close ties. On many occasions, Lucinda allowed Emma Lois to spend extended periods of time at Bryant's place to help the family out when Bean was under the weather.

Mary and Roland assisted Nita in easing into the environment of the new school. Miss Sonobe Mack, a very pretty, light complexioned lady, who always kept her face made up charmingly with fresh lipstick and rouge, was the children's teacher. She took Nita under her wings and tried to introduce lessons that would reinforce a more positive future. Nita appreciated those conversations with her teacher, who encouraged her to think about becoming an educator one day. Even though Nita was a bit reluctant over the suggestion, Miss Mack continued to extend sincere and logical advice, in spite of her student's pessimistic attitude. Miss Mack's influence increased the young girl's self-esteem, and confidence.

"Being a school teacher isn't a bad idea, after all" said Nita.

"The only thing is, you have to know a little something about everything, and I don't think I'm smart enough for that."

"Wanita", Miss Mack replied, "if I could become a teacher, I know that you are very capable of doing the same thing. Never let anything or anyone impede your progress from reaching your goals in life. You are a very bright young lady, and would make an excellent teacher one day. I see a lot of potential in you, and I know that you can do what ever you want to, if you just put your mind to it."

Nita smiled after hearing Miss Mack's words of inspiration, and slowly started to consider her sound advice.

In the evenings after school, Nita gathered the eggs from the chicken coop. Nevertheless, Big Momma always made sure she did her schoolwork every night, after the other household chores were done. Nita adored her grandmother, even though Big Momma ran a strict household. On the weekends, the young girl's responsibilities were a bit more stringent, and included washing and ironing clothes, sweeping, and mopping the floors. One thing's for sure, Nita truly cherished the idea of having her own room. It made life so much more comfortable and easier, not having to share a bed with three other sisters.

Big Momma's neat and tidy home had a narrow front porch at the entrance, bordering a very large living room. Henry's bedroom was located in the center, directly behind the living area. The kitchen was partitioned off from the remainder of the house near the west side, with a short hallway that led to it. Three other bedrooms were aligned horizontally on the east side of the house, with a stairway tucked between Henry's room, and the furthermost bedroom, which was Nita's. The squeaky wooden stairs led to a fairly large loft on the second floor used mainly to store all types of preserves such as figs, pears, and peaches. Canned vegetables like corn, peas, pickles, tomatoes, and hot peppers were also stored in there as well. Big Momma occupied the middle room, while the front room was mainly used for overnight guests.

Big Momma was an excellent cook, who could fry some mouthwatering chicken, and she fixed the best jambalaya this side of the Calcasieu River, too. Henry—known by the family as Pat—labored, vigorously at the Pogy plant, so Big Momma made sure he was well fed after a long, exhausting day. Nita yearned constantly for her grandmother's cooking. Since there weren't as many mouths to feed at Big Momma's place, she always had a plenty of good food to eat.

Saturday morning brought Pat home early from work. As soon as he walked into the house, the entire place became folded in an odor of decayed fish. The smell was embedded into his skin and clothes. That pogy fish smell was the most repulsive scent that Nita's nose had ever inhaled. Pat soaked his funky attire in a tub of water saturated with Purex and detergent, hoping to dissipate some of the fusty stench. Afterwards, he relaxed in a hot bath to relieve himself of the strong whiff that had Nita a bit queasy. Pat worked as a helper at the Swindell Plant, so he was exposed to the smell his entire shift. Each time he returned home from work, soiled in the Pogy fish's juices, his presence was easily detectable. It took Nita a long time to get adjusted to the vile odor. However, Big Momma had already grown accustomed to the smell, so it wasn't anything unusual for her.

One morning, after Nita finished milking the cows out in the barn, she brought a fresh container of milk home for breakfast. Big Momma needed to get some things from the store, so she had Nita write each item down on a piece of paper, along with the exact corresponding prices. As Nita wrote out the list, Big Momma prepared a huge meal consisting of hot buttermilk biscuits, eggs, hominy, and fig preserves. Nita's eyes gleamed as she watched her grandmother place the food onto the table. "We ain't never had this much food on our table at one time before. Not for breakfast, we ain't" she thought, and continued to make out the grocery list.

"Nita, when you finish with my list, go get Pat and tell him, it's time to eat" said Big Momma. "When I'm finished cookin my food, I don't like for it to get cold. I likes for everybody to sit down, and eat it while it's hot. Then after we eat, me and you's gonna go to the store. Okay?"

"Yes Ma'am" answered Nita.

Pat was out back hanging his clothes out to dry, when he heard his niece's call.

"Uncle Pat, Uncle Pat, it's time for us to eat" yelled Nita approaching the Pogy fish odor hovering in the outdoor breeze, with one hand covering her nose.

"Okay my girl" he responded with a smirk. Pat looked at her peculiarly as she struggled to keep the reeking whiff from seeping up her nostrils.

When Nita and Pat arrived to the kitchen, they all sat down together, bowed their heads and said grace. The biscuits were piping hot. So was the hominy, and fried eggs. Nita opened her eyes, momentarily, to look at the stem elevating from the food. She had the hardest time keeping her head bowed and eyes closed until Pat finished saying the grace, especially with all that good food staring her in the face.

"Thank God for this food, we about to receive, Aman" he concluded.

"Aman" said Big Momma. "Pat how was work today?"

"Wasn't too bad, Momma. We had a lotta boats come in, so we was real busy."

"Well thank the Lord for that, cause that's more money you gonna put in your pocket."

"That's right Momma. And, Nita, how was school, yesterday?"

"It was real good, Uncle Pat. We studied geography."

"Hum! What you mean by that?" he asked.

"Our teacher taught us about the different continents found here on earth" Nita answered with a mouth full of food.

"Don't talk with your mouth full" snapped Big Momma. "Let your food go down first, then you can speak."

"Yes Ma'm" answered Nita. She gulped several swallows of milk to wash down the food in her stuffed mouth.

"Ump! I ain't never learnt nothing like that before, when I was a boy in school" answered Pat, quaintly. We just learnt reading, writing, and 'rithmitic. Boy, things sure have changed since then. That's why ya'lls chilluns so smart these days. Git yourself a good learning, my girl. You can't beat it with a stick. Maybe one day you might be a school teacher like Miss Mack."

"Uncle Pat, that's the same thing she keep on telling me."

"Oh yeah?" He raised an eyebrow.

"Yeah Sir. But I don't know if I want to be no teacher. I mean, that sounds like it'll be too hard for me to do."

"You can be anything you want to be, if you just put your mind to it," responded Big Momma, authoritatively. "Just trust in the Lord."

"Ge-og-lo-phy you say?" Pat questioned Nita.

"No, Uncle Pat, it's Ge-og-ra-phy. And Miss Mack said we must learn more about other parts of the world. Just because we live in Creole, don't mean there ain't no other people or places somewhere else."

"Miss Mack's right about that," Big Momma said. "Now, did you finish all your school work, yet?"

"Yes Ma'm, I did."

"Good. 'Cause you know Big Momma ain't gonna put up with no mess like that. You gonna get your school work first, fo you do anything else. Now after you clean up the kitchen, me and you gonna walk to the store. Pat I knows you tired and you have to work tomorrow, so we'll just walk instead."

"No Momma. I'm off. And ya'll don't have to walk to the store. I can go for you."

"That's okay Pat. Walkin ain't never hurt nobody. Besides, I got some things I want to talk to her about. So you go on, and get yourself some rest. I knows you tired. We'll be all right. She done wrote down everything what I need, so all we got to do is go, and get it. And tomorrow I'm gonna fix us a big meal, before we go to church."

"Okay Momma" replied Pat.

"Now Nita, don't sit there and play witcha food, girl. You can take all you want, but in this house we eats all we take" Big Momma said abrasively.

"Yes Ma'm" responded Nita very politely. However, on that morning, Nita eyes had been too big for her stomach, as she struggled to finish eating the rest of the food on her plate. Big Momma went into her bedroom and closed the door. Upon returning to the kitchen she mysteriously had the exact change in her hands. Nita wondered where the money came from. Afterwards, she put the change in a handkerchief, tied it up and then placed it in her bosom.

"Nita!" Big Momma said. "You ret-ta-go?"

"Yes Ma'm."

The walk to and from the store was about three miles each way, so it would take her and Nita a good hour and a half to make the trip, particularly, since Big Momma was a heavy set lady who walked very slowly.

"I'm only gonna bring the exact change with me. Just in case somebody tries to knock us both in the head, they ain't gonna git all my money if they do."

Big Momma didn't have much to say along the first stretch of the walk. She merely answered Nita when a question was asked of her. However, after walking for several miles through the marsh, she and Nita approached a house adjacent to the Back Ridge Road. A bunch of white children were playing outside in the yard. Once they got near at hand, the children stopped playing, and just stared at them, impolitely. All of a sudden each of them laughed loudly, in a teasing fashion. The kids never said anything derogative to Big Momma or Nita, they just continued laughing, simultaneously, accompanied by a rude piercing gaze, as though they had never seen any colored people before in their lives.

"Big Momma, why them ol' white kids over there lookin at us colored folk like we's crazy or something?"

"First, let me git one thing straight with you Nita. I ain't colored like the rest of ya'll. I's whacha call a mu-lat-to. Now you know what that means?"

"No Ma'm, I don't."

"Well you see my daddy was a white man, and my po Momma was colored. Being a mulatto is a lot different from being full colored. That's how come my skin's more lighter than most colored people." Big Momma chuckled proudly. "You see them kids back over there, they momma and daddy ain't teachin them no sense a-tall. 'Cause if they was, they wouldn't be lookin at me and you like we's the crazy one.

They's the one with the problem. I guess that's 'cause they ain't never seent many half-white people before.

We all got the same blood runnin through our veins. I don't know why they ackin the fool like that. Later on in life them same lil ol' white boys be tryin to git up under your dress, if you don't watch-um. I knows 'cause that's what happen to my po momma. In her day, a colored woman couldn't walk the street by they self, especially after the sun went down. Them ol' white mens would take-um, and do just what ever they please. And nothin was ever done about it either. Ump! And they make out they don't like no colored womens. Huh! That's just to fool they own kind. 'Cause when the sun goes down, your color don't make no difference to um no ways. You'll just be like another regular ol' white woman. They know good-n-well, they don't care nothin about no body's color, once they gotcha pinned down on the ground. They just be puttin on in the front of them other ol' white folks. That's all! Makin out they don't like colored womens. That's just to make they self look good in the day time. Them dirty dogs! But Baby don't ever let um catch you by yourself at night. You'll see zactly what Big Momma's talkin about. That's why us colored folks is so many different colors now, because of they ol' foolishness. And if you don't watch your self, they'll be runnin after you like some ol' stray dogs in heat. Baby, Big Momma knows what she's talkin about, 'cause I done be around for a very long time, and seent it happen to too many colored womens a many times before."

"Whacha mean by all that, Big Momma?" asked a curious Nita.

" You's a bit too young for me to explain most of what I'm talkin about right now. But there are some other things that I needs to bring out, because you gittin to be a big girl. Big Momma can tell by your bosom, 'cause they's really a-growin."

"My bosom is growing? What is that suppose to mean" asked Nita.

"Look right there" she pointed at Nita's developing breasts.

"You gittin real big, my girl. And you know what that means, don't you?"

"No Ma'm," Nita said shyly. "I really don't know."

"Bean ain't never splain that to you before?"

"No Ma'm."

"Ump! Ain't no need to be shame now, to talk about it. Well, Big Momma just gonna come on out with it, and tell it to you straight. You gonna soon be a young lady. And what that means is, things gonna start happening to you that you might not know nothin about. Or ain't never seent before."

"Like what Big Momma?" blared out Nita. Her curiosity was really challenged after hearing those words.

"First, one day real soon, you gonna think you bleedin to deaf."

"Bleeding to death? Oh my God!"

"Yes Ma'm, Nita. Big Momma wouldn't tell you no lie. It might hit you at school. At home in the bed. Maybe even at church or while you playin outside with your sisters. It might be anywheres. And it's gonna be coming from your private."

"From my private? What's my private, Big Momma?"

"You know. You private!"

"No Ma'm, I don't know nothing about no private. Uh Uh!"

"Doncha ever look at yourself sometimes child, when you take a bath, or use the outdoor toilette?"

"Yes Ma'm!"

"Well, I can't see how you can miss it, 'cause it's staring you right dead in your face. Well, anyways, that's your private. And you suppose to keep it private, too. Ain't nobody posta touch or play with it. You understand me? Nobody!"

"Um!"

"I mean that Nita. Nobody! God put you in charge over your body, and you ain't posta let nothin happen to it, until he ready. You understand?"

"No Ma'm, not really" responded Nita.

"You will in time. Now look, when you starts bleedin from your private, you gonna need to tell Bean as soon as possible. She will know what to tell you to do next. Ain't nothin to be scared of. It just mean that the good Lord cleanin you out, 'cause he ain't ready for you to start having no babies, yet. That's all."

"That's all? Having no babies? What's that got to do with me bleeding from my private?"

"Girl, how you think babies get here in the first place? I hope you don't think they just fall out the sky. No Ma'm. They's come from your private. You growin' up now, Baby. And you gonna start having these feelings for them lil ol' boys. But the thing you got to remember is, even though they might say they like you, they probably don't. They just trying to git up under your dress, so they can git you to do what they want to, and that's something you ain't posta be doing noways."

"Doing what Big Momma?"

"You know. Like having relations with them! That's what. You see, theys private is different from yours. Lil boys don't go through the same thing as lil girls do, 'cause they got a different kinda private. They ain't gonna bleed from theirs like no lil girls do. But Nita you watch um. 'Cause they gonna try they best to make your heart bleed. Now that's if you let um. You see, yous a real pretty girl. Kinda put me in the mind of my self when I was a child coming up. Them ol' boys gonna try to make you do some things with your private that you ain't posta be doin."

"I just don't understand Big Momma. Like what?"

"You just keep on livin, you'll see what I mean. Don't you let um fool you into doing nothin until the good Lord is ready. Girl, they'll ruin you for life. Even if you fall deep in love with um, don't be too quick to give your self up to um. A respectable lady always waits until theys married before they starts to have any kinda relations with a man."

"I'm lost Big Momma!"

"I knows you is Baby, but somebody got to tell you these things. You see, I was a married woman before a man could touch me. I made it real hard for um, girl. See, if you be to easy they just gonna treat you like some ol' cheap trash standing on side of the road. And, Honey, you got more class than that, 'cause you's just a chip offen the old block like me!" Big Momma laughed.

"Relations with a man? Before I'm married? Cheap trash? I don't understand none of that, Big Momma."

"Relations with a man, means goin to bed with him before you married. And you ain't posta to be doing none of that. The Lord speaks against all that ol' mess in the Bible. I can show you, when we get back home. That's why you see a lot of these same lil ol' colored girls round here in Creole, coming up with all these babys before time. That's cause they let them ol' silly boys fool um into doing something they ain't got no business doing in the first place."

"I'm kinda scared Big Momma" said Nita. Then her mind wandered back to the time when the Hulton boy confronted she and Mary.

"That's okay, my girl. You posta be scared. I was scared when I was your age too. You see, I ain't never had nobody to talk to me like I'm talking to you about these things. I can remember when my private first started bleedin, I almost lost my mind. I didn't know what to do and who to turn to. I thought I had done come down with some ol' silly disease that was gonna kill me dead. Then I finally realized I wasn't gonna die'cause it started happening every month around the same time."

"Really? Every month you say?"

"Yes Ma'm. That's right, every month!"

"Good Lord, that's really strange!"

"Sure is strange. But it happens that way. Ump! I can even remember the time when me and your grandpa first got married. Ain't nobody told me what I was posta be doin with no man. Shoots! The first time he tried to have relations with me, I nearly jumped outta the bed 'cause I didn't know that's what a man and woman was posta be doin. Nita, I know I ain't telling everything to you the right way, but at lease you will have some idea when these things start to happen and it won't be no shock to you. As you get older it's gonna make more sense. Right now I'm just trying to get you ready for that day. Understand?"

"I guess so... I mean... I don't know."

"While I'm talkin to you about this stuff, there is one more thing I want to tell you. Always remember to treat yourself and your private like it's gold, and you'll be okay."

"Now what's that suppose to mean Big Momma?"

"Baby, you knows gold is worth an awful lot of money, uh?"

"Yes Ma'm."

"Well then. If you treat your self... I mean you and your private like gold, you gonna be okay. What I really mean is don't just give in to some ol' boy 'cause your heart might be feelin one way and your head is tellin you to do something else.' You'll know when the time is right for you to start having relations. But as for now, you got to finish your school first, to make Momma and Daddy real proud of you. I knows you gonna be a teacher one day. I feel it in my heart. That's if you don't mess up first. You see a teacher is posta set a good example for herself and everybody else. That's how come she's a teacher. But you can't teach nobody else nothin if you don't teach yourself first. Now what that means is you got to hold yourself up high 'cause ever' body lookin at Nita to pattern they life after you. And a lotta people wanna drag you down to the ground. You understand what I mean?"

"I guess so" Nita replied. "But Big Momma, I ain't thinking about no ol' boys right now!"

"Yeah! That's what you say now, but give it a little time . . . your mind will change. Just remember every thing I told you today and treat your self like gold, you want have no worry, my girl.

"Cause we Bartie ladys don't take nobody's foolishness, noway." Big Momma chuckled. "Okay my girl?"

"Yes Ma'am."

"And remember girl, when you start bleedin from your private, tell Bean about it. She gonna know what to tell you to do. You might cramp a little bit in your belly, but that's natural. You gonna be okay in a couple of days. Then the same thing gonna happen to you all over again, every month till you get on up in age. So don't worry about it 'cause it ain't much you can do noways. That's just the way the good Lord planned it to be. Okay?"

"Yes Big Momma."

"Oh! And there's one more thing. I almost forgot! Always keep your private clean, and smelling fresh. Lord have mercy, ain't nothin worse than a grown woman walkin round with her private stankin someum terrible like an ol' polecat. Pooh Oooh! You talk about someum that smells bad. You see Nita, I's a big ol' woman. Sometimes I bathe myself two and three times a day, so I can stay fresh and smell clean all the time. And you know what?"

"No, what Big Momma?"

"People'll talk about you behind your back, just as soon as you walk away from um. They'll say some dirty, ugly, ol' stuff if you don't keep yourself clean, girl. You understand?"

"Yes Ma'm."

"Well good! Now, let's talk about something else," whispered Big Momma "cause we almost at the store. It's not nice to talk about this kinda stuff out in the public."

Nita only vaguely comprehended the true message that her grandmother was trying to express. However, it was good exposure. At least when growing up started to take place, Nita could reflect back to the conversation with Big Momma, and things might not be as complicated because of her familiarity with the subject matter.

While at the store Nita and Big Momma purchased everything that was written down on the list. Sure enough, the groceries totaled exactly to two dollars and ten cents. Big Momma pulled the money out of her bosom and paid the clerk. Then she and Nita picked up the bags and headed on back home. Nita wanted to continue the previous conversation.

"Big Momma, I don't quite understand what you meant by relations."

"Don't worry about it girl." Big Momma evaded the issue, fearing that she may have said a little too much already. "In time you'll see what I mean. Boy, it's show hot out here today!"

"Yes it is. Now Big Momma------------"

"I done told you already let's talk about something else. Hush that up now!"

"But I,-------------- "

"You know something? Your daddy is very special to me, just like you's special to Big Momma too. Yeap! Ol' Dutch was a real special child."

"Who's Dutch?"

"Oh, that's the nick-name I gave to your daddy when he was born. And you know something else, he was my only child born with a veil on top of his face."

"A veil on his face? What's that suppose to mean?"

"Well, the old people use to say long time ago, when a person was born with a veil over they face, they posta be able to see things other's can't see. Least that's what they use to tell me when I was a girl, your age."

"You say my Daddy was born with a veil over his face? What in the world is a veil?"

"You know. A veil. And that thing covered his whole face, when I birthed him. You know what? I got that veil saved to this day."

"Saved it! What do you mean you saved it?"

"Child, I still got that thing in a big ol' trunk at home in my room. I got all kinda ol' mess in that trunk. And I don't let too many folks mess around in there either, 'cause I don't ever want to part with all my stuff. And that veil is one of um. Huh! I show do. I got it wrapped up in a silk scarf, too."

"Wrapped in a silk scarf? Really?"

"Um huh! I'll have to show it to you one of these days."

"I can't wait to see it, Big Momma."

"That'll be fine when we have a little more time to look at it."

Finally, after a long tiring walk home, Big Momma and Nita were too tired to even think about looking through the things in the trunk. Later on during the night before she and Nita fell asleep, Big Momma was a bit worried over the things she discussed with Nita earlier. On the other hand, Nita longed for Mary even more now, because she had so many questions that needed some answers.

"Mary, I miss you so much. I wish you were here with me right now. I hope you're doing okay. There's so much I have to talk to you about. I can't wait to see you again" Nita said softly after saying her prayers. Big Momma prayed down on her knees, before she laid her head to sleep.

"Lord, I hope I didn't scare my grand baby too much, today. But she needs to know them things. Lord, you know how to fix it. I pray that you help her to grow up and make something big out of herself one day. Lord, I just don't want her foolin around with them silly lil ol' boys 'cause they might ruin her for life. I love her very much and I'm puttin everything in your hands 'cause I know you know what to do. Help her to be a good girl and please look after her all the time. In Jesus name, I pray. Aman."

As Nita laid in bed, she thought "I have got to see what's inside of that trunk, soon. Maybe tomorrow will be a good time." All was silent that night, as Big Momma, Pat and Nita slumbered through a quiet storm, till the morning hour evolved.

About a month later. Big Momma was outside in the back of the house talking with Pat while Nita finished washing and drying all the dishes in the kitchen. Once that chore had been completed, the girl's inquisitive mind kept tempting her to go and explore the contents of Big Momma's trunk. Nita knew that she wasn't supposed to mess around in there without her grandmother's consent. However, the thrill of not getting caught when engaging in mischief made the endeavor much more exciting. Ever since Big Momma told Nita about the trunk, she was having the most difficult time trying to patiently wait to see her father's veil. On each occasion, when she requested to examine the thing, something always interrupted the opportunity. That day, just so happened to be one of those days that Nita refused to be disappointed all over again. She prowled into the bedroom very quietly, determined to take a look inside the trunk.

In the bedroom, Big Momma's large iron post bed was neatly dressed in a beautiful, multicolored quilt that a relative had given to her handmade from scrap fabric. A large cedar chest sat along one wall, while the mysterious trunk flanked the foot of the bed. Nita struggled momentarily, to pull the heavy box far enough out onto the floor so that she could open it with ease. "Pop" went both latches on each side. No problem. The middle latch was locked, however, which meant she had to find the right key to open it. Nita searched everywhere. She looked in the cedar chest, at the base of the window, and all around the room. The key was nowhere to be found. Finally, she crawled under the bed. The only thing visible was a small wooden box tucked near the head, on the left side. "I know that key is inside of this here box" she thought. Anxiously, Nita pulled herself and the box from under the bed. Much to her surprise she found several stacks of currency inside along with coins neatly arranged in stacks as well. The eager young girl had never, ever seen so much money, before in her life.

"Oh my God! Look at all this money. Goodness! Big Momma is a very rich lady," she thought.

Once the clumsy child started fumbling around inside the box looking for the key, however several rows of the coins fell over. Nita's heart throbbed deliriously, fearing Big Momma's catching her rambling through the box.

"Oh my God, I hope Big Momma don't catch me. I gotta hurry up, and put these coins back in place, 'cause if I don't she gonna know that I've been messing around with her money."

Nita tried to stack the coins back in the same manner that Big Momma had them arranged, but one of her nervous fingers knocked over another stack of money, creating a nerve-racking situation for her to contend with.

"Oh no! She might send me back home for this! Lord, I don't won't her to think that I was trying to steal anything from her. I was just looking for that ol' key. Please help me Lord to put this money back like she had it."

"Finally, after struggling earnestly, Nita stacked every coin in separate rows, precisely the way Big Momma had them arranged previously. In the meantime, she heard her grandmother and Pat's voices near the corner of the house. The poor girl almost died on the spot, as she listened to them converse. In an instant, the two of them had made their way to the front steps of the house. Still holding onto the box, and kneeling down on the floor Nita whispered "Oh please help me Lord, to put this box back in place before she comes in here and catch me." But the tension caused Nita's nervous hand to knock over a few more rows of the coins.

"Oh Lord, have mercy Jesus, look at what I done now!" she gasped. "I'm gonna get caught, and that'll be the end of me. Hurry up, girl!"

Nita said softly while desperately trying to get the coins stacked into neat rows so that Big Momma wouldn't notice a difference. "Hurry up you crazy fool!"

Balls of sweat rolled off Nita's forehead, while she worked diligently. In a matter of seconds, all of the coins were put back, just the way they were originally, when the box was first opened. Nita closed the top, and placed the box back under the bed careful this time, not to create another reckless predicament.

"What I'm gonna do now? Big Momma and Uncle Pat done made it into the house. Oh Lord, help me Jesus" she begged. "That big woman gonna kill me, if she finds me in her room by myself."

It just wasn't turning out to be Nita's day because Pat had given his mother some money for her to put up for him. Once Big Momma made it to the living room, she immediately proceeded to her bedroom with the money in one hand, her handkerchief in another. Nita thought quickly, and picked her small framed body up off the floor. She ran over to the trunk and fell across it, pretending to be asleep. When Big Momma walked into the room, she saw her granddaughter's body stretched over the trunk. At first Big Momma wondered "what in the world is this child doin in my room?" Then she realized that Nita was probably trying to get inside the trunk to take a look, but wasn't able to open it, and eventually, fell asleep.

"Nita" called out Big Momma as she walked over and shook her by the arm. "Nita" she said again. "You all right?" No answer followed because Nita was still pretending to be asleep.

"Nita! Nita! You betta wake up from there, right now!"

Nita jumped up, abruptly. "Yes Ma'm" she answered very nervously.

"What you doin in Big Momma's room?"

"I, I, I, I wanted to see my daddy's veil in your trunk," she answered in a squeaky, innocent, humble voice. "But I couldn't get it open."

"Couldn't get it open? I know you couldn't. I'm the only one who knows were that key is. Anyways, the next time you want to go into that trunk you betta ask somebody first before you go messin round in my room. You understand me?"

"Yes Ma'am."

"Now you go in the living room, and wait there with your Uncle Pat, till I put something away. Then when I'm finished, you can come back in and Big Momma'll show you what's inside the trunk. But girl, don't be foolin round in my room no more, unless I tell you to. Specially, when I'm not in here with you."

"Yes Ma'm" responded Nita, with a soft sigh of relief as she exited the room.

Big Momma didn't scold Nita much, because she was well aware that on every occasion they were supposed to look at the veil, something always precluded them from doing so. However, she waited until Nita was completely out of sight before pulling the wooden box out, carefully, from under the head of the bed.

Meanwhile, Nita waited in the living room on pins and needles. In the interim, Big Momma made no fuss of anything being out of the ordinary, so Nita assumed concurrently, that she wasn't in any serious trouble. Big Momma opened the box cautiously and observed the currency, checking each stack of coins to see if it had been tampered with. "Um huh" she said to herself as her eyes reviewed the contents of the box. Afterwards, she put Pat's money in with the rest, and closed the top, then pushed it back under the bed. Nita made a wise decision when she stacked the coins back in place, exactly the way they were supposed to be. Had she not, Big Momma could have easily detected that someone had been messing around with her money.

"Okay Nita! I'm finished. You can come back in here now," yelled Big Momma from her bedroom.

Nita came fearfully back into the room, only to find that Big Momma had already opened up the trunk.

"Come on over here a lil bit closer, so you can see betta."

Nita's whole face was filled with excitement, as she and Big Momma reviewed the items inside of the trunk, together. The intrusive young girl learned a valuable lesson that day. The best thing to do when an anxious mind causes one to meddle, was to simply ask for permission, rather than try to take matters up in your own hand! Particularly, when dealing with Big Momma's stuff!

Everything was neatly placed in order inside the trunk. Nita saw long plats of hair wrapped in silk scarves which Big Momma said belonged to some of her dead relatives and her own children. Also included were several nice lingerie pieces that she had never worn before, beautiful embroidered aprons, and many colorful vanity scarves.

"Who's hair was this?" asked Nita.

"That's po momma's hair right there."

"Really? That hair was from my great-grandmother?"

"Um, Uh." Big Momma answered with closed lips.

"And who's that hair from over there?"

"That's for my daughter Mary. This one's for my daughter Sarah, and that's Lucinda's."

"You mean that's Roland and Mary's momma's hair?" Nita laughed.

"Um, Uh" Big Momma said, with little expression.

Nita continued looking at the plats of hair and other items in the trunk, as Big Momma searched around under some quilts for Bryant's veil.

"Yeap, here it is right here."

Nita's eyes got as big as marbles when her grandmother pulled out the white silk scarf, in which the "velum",—the proper term for the veil—was wrapped.

"Oh my God, is that it?" exclaimed Nita, excitedly.

"Yeap! This is it" responded Big Momma. She had a strange look as she unfolded the scarf which held the mysterious membrane.

The veil resembled the urinary bladder of a pig, something that Nita was very familiar with. During a butchery, Bryant had once extracted a pig's bladder and dried it out. Once it was completely dry, he had inflated it with air, and the children played with it as a substitute ball. But as Nita stared at the veil, Big Momma shook her head hesitantly. She knew something just wasn't quite right with it.

"Oh no!" shouted Big Momma, finally.

"What's wrong?"

"Looka here. This veil posta to be dry. But it's all wet and sticky, today. Something must be wrong with Dutch."

"You mean Daddy?"

"Yeah! It's gotta be something wrong with him. You see when everything's all right with him the veil is usually dry, and not all wet like this. I knows 'cause I been watchin this thing for years. And Lord knows, I know what I'm talkin to be the truth. Something's wrong with Dutch, you can believe that my girl."

Nita refused to believe her ears. How could Big Momma know that something was wrong with her father just by looking at his veil? But Big Momma's whole face displayed anguish. She hurriedly grabbed the veil and scarf from Nita, and examined it closely one more time. Then she wrapped it up swiftly, tucked it away back under the quilts, and shut the trunk closed. Once she pushed the box back in its proper place at the foot of the bed, she yelled out "Pat! Pat! Come on Nita, we needs to find Pat." She yelled out again for her son who came running into the living room to see what was wrong. Pat found Nita standing still, afraid to say a word because she feared the worst for her father. Big Momma's whole body shook all over.

"You needs to go," Big Momma insisted "and see about Dutch, 'cause something done happened to him. I know Pat, 'cause I can feel it."

"How you know that, Momma?" Pat inquired.

"I just knows Pat. Don't fuss with me, boy. Just go and see about your brother," she demanded. "Right now I say!"

Pat dashed out of the house and headed for his horse. Nita and Big Momma stood in the back doorway, and watched him saddle up the stallion. Once he finished, he rode away swiftly, headed to Bryant's place without a clue as to what he would find once he got there. Pat knew better than to argue with Big Momma though, so he did exactly what she told him.

After an hour's ride, Pat arrived at Bryant's front door. He rushed up the steps, and knocked loudly. Bean rushed to the door. "Pat you musta got the news about Bryant." She liked to knocked Pat down to his knees with that response.

"What news Bean?"

"Oh Lord! Ya'll didn't hear? Come on inside, Pat. Bryant's been in a terrible accident."

"Whatcha say? Is he all right?"

"When he was riding his ol' black mare on The Front Ridge Road, a car came alone and put a big hole in that ol' mare's side, and she died not long after that."

"Say what Bean? Kilt who?" asked Pat incredulously.

"The horse, Pat, not Bryant." Bean trembled. "Oh Lord have mercy, I'm so nervous, I don't know what I'm sayin half the time."

"You say a car hit um?"

"Yeah! Like to killed him too."

"Where is Bryant, Bean?"

"He laying down in the room back there. Go on in the house and see him."

When Pat walked into the room, he found Bryant lying painfully in bed.

"How you feel, Bryant?"

"Oh, I feel pretty good Pat. I'm just a little sore. How you knowed something happen to me?"

"Momma had a notion, Bryant. She told me to come and see about you. And boy was she right, too. I still don't know how she knowed it, but she say she felt something was wrong with you."

"I'll be alright in a few days. I just need some rest right now. I kinda hurt my leg real bad, other than that I'm okay."

"Anything I can do for you, Bryant?"

"No. Just tell Momma not to worry herself. How's Nita doin?"

"She fine. Talk about a real smart girl. She's been helping us out a whole lot."

"Well that's good. Don't let her be no lazy girl. Make sure she do her part, now."

"You know something Bryant? I believe she's gonna teach school one day, 'cause she's so smart."

"Oh yeah, Pat? Well that will be good if she makes something out of herself like that."

Pat stayed with Bryant for about an hour, then he had to leave because he worked the night shift at the plant.

"Well Bryant, you better take care of yourself, and quit riding them ol' horses late at night. You know that's dangerous these days especially with all them Fords out there on the road."

"Yeah, you right Pat. You better get on back home yourself before it gets too dark. I don't want the same thing to happen to you."

"You right, Bryant. I better be goin."

"Tell Momma and Nita I said hello."

As soon as Pat walked out of the room, Bryant fell back asleep. Mary, Lil and Lo couldn't wait to ask their Uncle Pat about Nita. After filling the girls in on Nita, Pat left for home. The girls were so excited to get the news about their sister.

"Okay Bean, I'm gonna go now." Pat said. "Now if ya'll needs anything, just let us know."

"Thanks Pat. We will."

"Uncle Pat tell Nita hello for us" said Mary.

"Yeah, Uncle Pat, tell her that we miss her, too" said Lo.

"And tell her we can't wait to see her real soon" Lil added.

"Bye, Uncle Pat" said Nip. Walter had been asleep during the whole visit.

On the ride back home, Pat couldn't get over how his mother knew that something was wrong with Bryant.

"How in the world did she know that?" he wondered.

About two Sundays later at church, Big Momma, Nita and Pat saw Bryant. He appeared to have recuperated fairly well from the accident, with the exception of a small limp in his right leg.

Everyone was glad to see him out and about. As soon as Nita got home, she asked Big Momma for permission to take another look at the veil.

"Okay Nita, we can look at it again" she replied.

True enough, when Big Momma pulled the veil out of the trunk this time, it was dry and rigid as it lay inside of the silk scarf. Nita couldn't believe her eyes. She glared down at the inanimate membrane.

"Big Momma, may I keep it?"

"No Ma'm! I can never part with that veil. 'Cause that's the only way I'm gonna ever know how "Ol' Dutch" is doin."

"That's okay, Big Momma. I understand."

Big Momma put the veil away, and locked the trunk. She looked at Nita with a smile, and said "see, I told you that I know what I'm talkin about, and I ain't got much learnin either!" And then she liked to killed herself laughing as the wind blew through her bedroom window.

Things were a bit slow at the Barlie house while Nita was away at Big Momma's. Mary inherited the over-protective big sisterly role, as the younger Bartie children started to look up to her during Nita's absence.

One summer day Bean and Mary were washing clothes out back, Ol' Dad was asleep in the bedroom, and Bryant was out seeking odd jobs as work on the Rutherford's premises had slowed down almost to a halt. Lil, Lo and Nip were chasing a vagrant cat around in the yard. The kids had fallen in love with the brown and white feline soon after it had spent a few days with the family.

Eventually, it became an important feature in their lives. An ol' mangy, stray dog had been lurking about the house as well, however vying for the same attention his major opponent was receiving. When the deserted hound showed up on the Bartie's door steps one morning, it was a mere skin and bones, topped with a very shabby coat of fallen black and white hair. The animal appeared to have been on it's last leg before landing it's temporary home. The dog's popularity was much less appealing to everyone except the very superstitious Bryant. He feared bad luck would overtake the household if the diseased dog was run off. God knows the Barties didn't need any more misfortune to come their way, so the canine was allowed to hang around too. Bryant fed the malnourished dog table scraps each day, in hopes of giving it a healthier appearance. The family didn't have a name for either the dog or cat. They merely referred to each, respectively by their species.

On this particular hot day, a wacky scenario initiated when Mary left the front door of the house opened as she went inside to get some more clothes to wash. Lil and Lo continued to chase the cat joyfully in the yard, while Nip tried to patronize the stray dog with some condescending attention. During the process, the ol' dog became enchanted with the cat's agility as it ran and played with the two girls. After watching the cat anxiously for a while the dog's canine instinct commanded him to interrupt their play and show him the respect he felt he was due. Abruptly, sparks began to fly. The children paused, and watched the excitement erupt. The dog started running the cat around, and around in a circle. Finally, the cat got tired of being chased by the dog so viciously, and ran directly into the house, the dog following directly in it's tracks.

Behind the dog sprinted Lil, Lo, and Nip. Mary heard the loud barking and snarling and rushed inside to see just what was happening. She soon joined in the chase with the rest of the gang. The pursuit wound up in the girls' bedroom. That ol' dog stood eagerly at attention in the doorway and barked loudly because he knew he had the cat cornered. There really was no other means of escape for the cat. It would have to come through him.

"Get away from that cat, you ol' crazy dog" Mary hollered.

"Leave that cat alone!" shouted Lo.

"Where's that ol' cat at?" asked Lil.

The dog responded only by continuing its loud barking. The kids could hear the cat's panicky cry in the room, but they couldn't tell from whence it came.

"Look ya'll that ol' cat back there" Nip pointed behind the dresser.

"Back where?" said Mary.

"Look right there" said Nip.

The kids put forth a concerted effort to pull the dresser away from the wall. Much to their surprise, the cat wasn't there.

"I don't see nothin back there" replied Mary.

"That's cause she ain't back there" Lil responded.

"Well, where she at then? I still hear her cryin but I don't see her" replied Mary.

"Ya'll move out the way," said Lo, and "let me see if I can find her."

One of the girls had left the top drawer open, and Lo pushed it back into place with a resounding "bam!" The children heard a loud screech.

"Wait Lo, you're hurting her" said Lil.

Lo pulled the drawer out once again, and slammed it back into place even harder the second time. "Bam" went the drawer and the cat made an even louder "screech", followed by a hurtful cry which frightened the children.

"Ya'll, I still don't see her" remarked Mary. "And I know she ain't behind the dresser, 'cause we done looked back there."

"She ain't back there, I done told ya'll that." Nip pointed to the front of the dresser. "She up underneath this right here."

"Underneath where?" asked Mary.

"Look she right there, see her tail" he showed them where the cat's tail hung from the closed drawer.

Sure enough once the kids figured out the cat's whereabouts, they found her lying on top of some clothes in the second drawer, her bloody tail nearly severed. Apparently, the cat had leaped into the convenient hiding place which the open drawer had offered, then fallen behind and dropped down on the pile of clothes in the level below. Lo's harsh pushing and pulling had not only crushed the cat's tail between the drawers, but its head, too.

"Move out the way" Mary told Nip as she reached inside the drawer and pulled out the animals' warm, bleeding body.

"Oh, Oh" said Lil. "I'm gonna tell Momma, ya'll done killed that ol' cat, Mary."

"I ain't killed nothing" snapped Mary. "Lo the one, who did it. Not me!"

"I ain't knowed it was stuck back there in the first place!" cried Lo.

"Roof, roof, roof, roof, roof, roof!" The ol' dog continued to bellow.

"Shut up your mouth, you ol' crazy dog" commanded Mary.

"Yeah, shut up!" Lil remarked. "Cause you the main reason why that ol' cat's dead anyways."

Mary led the befuddled group out the bedroom in a straight line towards the front door with the dead cat in her arms. Bean just so happened to walk in on the impromptu funeral processional.

"What that ol' dog doing in this house? And where ya'll going with that ol' cat?" asked Bean.

"He chased the cat in our room, Momma." Lo pointed at the dog.

"For what?" inquired Bean.

"Momma, that ol' dog chased the cat into our room," Mary explained "and she got caught between two dresser drawers."

"Why is that ol' thing bleeding all over the floor?" questioned Bean.

"Cause, Lo mashed it's head against the top dresser drawer while it was stuck on the bottom one" Lil replied. "That's what killed it!"

"Mashed its head with the dresser drawer? Now, how you done that Lo?"

Lo, in tears couldn't say a word. She just shrugged her shoulders.

"Ya'll bring that ol' dead thing outside, right now. And don't be bring no more ol' animals in this house again. I mean it!"

Once outside, the kids found a place under a china berry tree, and lay the cat down on the ground. Lil and Lo picked some fresh wild flowers and placed them all around its warm body. The dog was still barking continuously during the cat's final rites. "Shut up that noise, you ol' crazy dog!" Mary demanded.

Bryant wondered in from the fields and came immediately, upon this mock funeral where all the kids gathered around the cat under the tree.

"What done happen here?" he asked.

"Daddy, Lo killed that ol' cat. That's what!" responded Lil.

"I ain't done nothin" said Lo.

"Yes you did!" said Lil.

"No I didn't!" said Lo.

"All right. All right, that's enough of that" Bryant intervened.

"Move out of the way, and let me have that ol' cat."

Bryant proceeded towards the field with the cat's body in one hand and a shovel in the other. Everyone followed him to a place near the barn. He dug a shallow hole, and afterwards laid the cat to rest inside. The ol' dog quiet now that Bryant had arrived looked at the grave very somberly.

Mary turned to him. "It's all your fault. I don't know why you looking so sad. If you wouldn't been chasing the cat, she might still be alive now, you crazy ol' dog."

The dog just kept his head down, and sniffled through his nose, approvingly.

"Well, we gonna have to get rid of this ol' dog," remarked Bryant. "Cause he making too much trouble around here."

The next morning, bright and early, Bryant got up and carried the dog down to the coastal beach. As he prepared to walk away, the ol' black and white hound looked at him very pitifully. "You be a good dog, now and take it easy," Bryant said.

The ol' dog never responded. He just rested his head sorrowfully in the sand, and watched the white caps on the waves roll into shore while the wind blew over his meager coat of hair. He knew that this was his and Bryant's final good-bye.

CHAPTER 10

It was common practice for residents in the area to catch a ride with the postman as long as they desired to travel his same scheduled route and promised not to interrupt the mail service. Mr. and Mrs. Jim Bonsall—personal friends of President Franklin D. Roosevelt were the federal postmasters, who delivered not only mail between the small towns of Grand Chenier, Creole, and Cameron, but just about anything else that could fit snugly into the postal truck's cargo area. Bryant asked permission of the Bonsall's for Nita to obtain a ride each Saturday morning to and from the Roger's Grocery Store located in the heart of Cameron. Nita delivered fresh eggs to the merchant for sale in the market place. The revenue earned from the egg sales enhanced the family's monetary affairs immensely over a period of time. Bean and Nita cleaned the eggs, by wiping them with moist rags. Afterwards, they were placed in a zinc bucket with a bail for easy handling. Sheets of brown paper bags were carefully layered inside the bucket to protect the fragile commodity from possible breakage or damage during transport. To avoid altering the Bonsall's rigid schedule, Nita stood near the road with the securely packed pail and waited patiently for the mail truck's arrival. Once there, Mr. Bonsall placed the merchandise cautiously into the rear of the truck, while Nita rode in the back on a little wooden bench. They ventured onward from there, making several stops en route to the Roger's Grocery Store. Most of Nita's day was consumed by the long ride. Mr. Bonsall dropped her off with the eggs before his final mail stop culminated at the Cameron Post Office, then after completing his task there, gave her a lift back home en route to Grand Chenier.

Nita was held accountable for the beginning and ending inventories, offset by any profits justified during the day. As soon as she returned home, all moneys were reported to Bryant, who determined the legitimacy of the earnings. The practical experience she attained was invaluable. Not only did Nita's managerial skills increase tremendously, but she was allowed an opportunity to mingle with many residents along the postal route, and at the store. Bryant was very proud of Nita's eagerness, and the way she handled responsibility. The young girl's efforts left him in a firm contemplation of her prospects for the future.

Not a whole lot had changed around the Bartie home over the years. Nita, a mere fourteen years old now, did exceptionally well in school. She continued to display her motherly instincts amidst her younger sisters and brothers. "Thanks God for a good day at the store," she said softly to herself. "Cause Lord knows my family really needs this money."

Bean was waiting in the living room for her arrival, to determine if a profit had been attained this afternoon. "How much money we made today, Nita?"

"One dollar and twenty cents, Momma."

"Thank the Lord, because things is getting real tight around this ol' place. I just don't see how we gonna make ends meet."

"We'll make it Momma. I still have my job at Miss Delia's, and I'm willing to help out any other way that I can."

"Yeah, but things don't look too good for your daddy. Cotton ain't done nothing this year. Ump! I wish it was something else he could do besides working for that Ol' Mister Jim Rutherford. I can't blame your daddy. He's doing the best that he can, but things still lookin real bad for him. And Ol' Mister Jim keep on giving Bryant such a real hard time, because he be looking for work elsewhere. What Mister Jim think Bryant is supposed to do? Just let his family starve to death, because that ol' cotton crop didn't make a good one? Some of them ol' white people make me so sick to my stomach. They act like just because we's colored, we ain't supposed to have a good living. Shoots! Be left up to some of them, we'd still be in slavery."

"Try not to worry, Momma. As long as we got each other, we'll be okay. They can knock us down to the ground, and step on us too, but there is one thing for sure, they can't do, and that's tear us apart. We may be poor, Momma, but we got a lot of love in this family. And that's what's gonna get us through this depression."

"Yeah Nita, I guess you're right. I'm gonna start lookin for me a job real soon. Poor Bryant can't make it like this all by himself, not with all these mouths to feed."

"Momma, speaking of mouths to feed, where's Mary and the rest at?"

"Lil and Lo's outside, and Nip's back there in the room with Walter. Nita, you know something, I just don't know what's wrong with that boy. I can't get him to eat nothin."

"Who you talking about Momma?"

"Nip! That's who. I done tried and tried to get him to eat a lil something, but he won't. Shoots! I'm scared he gonna blow away in the wind, he's so poor. And Nita, I don't know what's wrong with Mary, either. She just stay locked up in that ol' room all the time, and won't come out for nothing. Lord have mercy, ya'll kids about to run me crazy. And Lord knows my nerves is real bad. I can't take too much more of this foolishness."

"Momma, I've noticed the same thing about Mary, too."

"Ump! I don't know, Nita. She act like she's sick, but she say ain't nothing bothering her. So I don't know what's the matter."

"That's strange Momma."

"Sure is girl. Nita, see if you can get Nip to eat something. I'll be back in a few minutes. I'm going down to Joe's. Him and Alice got some okra for us. Lord knows we can use anything somebody's got to give."

"Okay Momma. And try not to worry so much. Okay?"

"Child you just don't know the half of it. I'll be glad when this ol' storm that we's going through is over."

"I know Momma, it will be over soon. We gonna make it. Daddy's a real strong man, and he ain't never let us fall before."

"Yeah. But it gets real hard sometimes, child. Sometimes you just want to give up."

"Don't give up Momma. We'll make it. I know we will."

"I sure hope so, Nita. Lord, I hope so. Let me go. I'll see you after while."

"Bye Momma."

"And Nita, please see if you can do something with Nip. Poor lil thing. I feel so sorry for him."

"I will, Momma."

As Bean walked to her brother's house, she couldn't help but break down and cry. Times were very hard for the family. She was a young struggling mother, trying to make ends meet as best as she knew how. Big balls of tears started trickling down Bean's pale face as she sobbed loudly and cried out to the Lord. Meanwhile, a car drove by on the dusty road, and blew some grime into her already teary eyes, causing the white membranes to turn pink.

"I don't know what we gonna do Lord" she said out loud, as the car sped away. "I just don't know what we gonna do if things don't get better. How we suppose to make it? Just tell me how. Please help us, Lord, if you can. If it ain't askin for too much, please, I beg you Jesus, to help us. Lord Jesus get us through this storm. Please?"

After Bean's cry, she tried to regain her composure quickly before reaching Joe's doorstep.

"Okay Bean, get yourself together," she said softly. "I don't want them to see that I've been cryin" she mumbled and wiped away some of the smeared tears from her face. Bean brushed off her shabby clothes to look refreshed. The cry did her all the good in the world.

Back at home, Nita fixed Nip a small plate of food. He sat at the table and tried frantically to swallow it. Each time he put some into his mouth, however it just wouldn't go down his throat. He took the food out, and gave it back to Nita, who tried mashing it up.

"Come on Nip. you've got to eat something."

Nip spoke not a word as Nita tried putting some more food back into his mouth. Again, he took the food out with his fingers and gave it back to her.

"I wonder what's wrong with this little fellow?" Nita thought. She tried once again. "Come on Nip, you've got to eat. I mean it!" At that point, Nita realized that something was seriously wrong with her younger brother. Nita put forth one last effort. "Please eat something Nip."

The poor little boy tried, but he just couldn't swallow the food. Nita removed the plate from his reach. "I've got to figure out what's wrong with this boy" she thought. Nip sat there and stared at Nita pitifully. He knew that something was wrong, too, but didn't know what. His somber appearance touched Nita's heart. It appeared as though he was trying to say "Help me please," but just didn't know how. Nita refused to let another moment pass with him in this condition. She reached over the table, and placed her hand at Nip's forehead to check his temperature, finding that it had escalated tremendously.

"How do you feel, Nip?"

"This hurt right here, Nita" he said, and pointed at his throat.

"Oh, okay" Nita said. "Right there?"

"Yeah" he answered in a babyish voice.

"Okay, open your mouth up real wide for me."

When Nita looked inside, she couldn't believe her eyes.

"Oh my God!" Nita continued looking in the little fellow's throat, though he was getting very frustrated keeping his mouth open so widely for so long.

"Okay Nip, you can close your mouth now. Come with me, I want you to lie down in our bed, and stay there, until I come back. I've got to go find Momma."

Nip did exactly as Nita told him. Once he was in bed, she pulled the covers up to his weakened, frail chest, and he didn't move. Nita dashed out of the house as fast as she could to find her mother. On the way to Joe's place, she saw Bean at a distance walking towards home with two bags full of okra. Once Nita caught sight of her mother, she sprinted in that direction.

"Momma. Momma, come quick" Nita blared out breathlessly.

"Child, what's the matter with you?"

"It's Nip, Momma!"

"What's wrong with Nip, girl?"

Nita struggled to catch her breath, and tried to speak at the same time. "Momma, Nip's throat is all red inside. I think that's why he can't eat nothing." She breathed hard from her running.

"And it looks really bad too."

"Here girl, take one of these bags" Bean instructed. She and Nita walked swiftly home. When Bean arrived at the house, she found Nip in the girls' bed with the covers draped across his body, in the same position in which Nita left him.

"Open your mouth wide, son."

Sure enough when Bean looked inside, she could see exactly what Nita was talking about.

"Oh Lord" Bean cringed. "Don't let him move, Nita. Stay here with him, until I get back. I'm going out to the fields to find Bryant."

Bean dashed out of the house and headed for the fields, while Nita stayed behind to comfort her little brother. On the way there, more tears welled up in Bean's eyes as she rushed to find Bryant.

"What's next Lord?" she asked. Bean really didn't want to question God's will, but sometimes one has to, in order to find some comfort to life's variations.

"Why Lord? Why? Ain't we tried to live right?"

No answer came from the man upstairs, even though she knew that she wouldn't get a verbal response, anyway. She walked faster and faster. The faster Bean walked, the more grief stricken she became. "God I can't take much more of this mess. Now, you gonna have to help me, Lord."

Once she reached the edge of the field. Bean yelled out to Bryant, who stopped in the middle of his work as soon as he heard her shout. Approaching Bean hastily, he sensed something had his wife very disturbed.

Bean broke down, and cried in her husband's arms. "Bryant everything is going wrong. We almost living outdoors. The cotton crop ain't done nothin this year, and because of it Ol' Mister Jim Rutherford won't to run you off his property. Just who do he think he is anyways? Treatin us like we's some dirt. Bryant, we ain't gotta pot to piss in, and hardly no money to make ends meet. What we suppose to do? And now we about to loose Nip" she cried. "I don't know why the Lord is putting us through so much. Why Lord? Why? Please just tell me why?" she shouted.

"Na Na Na Na Na Bean" Bryant said as his stutter kicked in.

"The Lord ain't put nothin on us, that we can't bear. Everything's gonna be all right." He said, while caressing and comforting his wife.

"Bryant, I just can't take this no more. I mean, I don't know why the Lord is making it so hard on us."

"Plague-take-it! You better watch out how you talk to the Lord, Bean."

"Bryant, you need to git home quick. Something's wrong with Nip. His throat's all red inside, and he's burning up with a fever," she sobbed. "I'm afraid we gonna loose him, if we don't get him to Dr. Carter."

Bryant let go of Bean, abruptly. "I'm going. But remember Bean, God don't put nothin on you, that you can't bear. He's just testing our faith right now. Bean, don't let that ol' devil fool you, because he'll knock you down to the ground, and leave you there. I ain't worried about nothin because God have always been on our side. Ain't nobody ever said this life was gonna be easy, anyway. Git yourself together, woman, and quit doubting the Lord."

Bryant left Bean standing alone in the fields and rushed home to see about his son. She, meanwhile, looked up to the heavens. "I still don't know how come that man's got so much faith in you. I mean, look at him, he about to loose everything he's got! He just might loose one of his children!! But he never gives up on you, Lord!"

Once Bean finished releasing her frustrations, she thought about what Bryant said earlier, and started realizing that she too needed to turn all her troubles over to God.

As soon as Bryant made it home, he found Nip under the covers with the other children gathered around him in bed. "Open wide son." Bryant looked inside his son's mouth, and saw definite signs of an infectious inflammation everywhere. Quickly, he ran out of the house into the barn, saddled up his horse, and brought it to the front yard. By then, Bean had made it back home, too. Bryant picked up his son's weak body, and placed the boy on the saddle in front of him. He held onto the reigns firmly with one hand, and the other gripped Nip around his waist. "Giddy up horse" he yelled out, and off they trotted to Dr. Carter's home. The rest of the family watched as the horse kicked up a small dust storm on the dirt road while racing onward.

The trip to Dr. Carter's didn't take very long. Once they arrived, Bryant held Nip in his arms as he banged on Dr. Carter's front door.

Dr. Carter came quickly, and directed Bryant and Nip to his office. "Lay him down here on the bed, Bryant. Open wide son."

"Ahh," said Nip.

"Um huh. Um huh" said Dr. Carter as he looked around in there, and swabbed the little boy's throat. "Okay son you may close your mouth now."

"What's wrong with him Dr. Carter?"

"Bryant, your son has a serious case of diphtheria."

"Diptheory, you say Dr. Carter?"

"Yes Bryant. Diph-the-ria. It's a contagious disease harbored in his throat."

"Ump! I ain't never heared of that before. Diptheory, you say. Is he gonna be all right?"

"Yes Bryant, he should be" Dr. Carter said hesitantly. "But make sure you give him two teaspoons of this red liquid medicine, three times a day. Open wide again, son. Now Bryant, you see how I'm swabbing his throat?"

Nip gagged as Dr. Carter coated his throat with the antibiotic.

"I want you to swab his throat twice a day with this bottle of medicine just like I'm doing. Okay?"

"Yeah Sir, Dr. Carter. I can do that."

"Give him a few days, and he should start eating solid foods again. Whatever you do, make sure he takes all of his medicine now. I guarantee you'll see a big improvement in him soon. If not, don't waste any time in bring him back to see me. Okay?"

"Yeah Sir! But Dr. Carter, there's one other thing. I ain't got no money to pay you sir, but I can do a little days work for you for helping my boy out. Things is lookin real bad at Mister Rutherford's and for my family."

"Bryant, don't worry about that right now. You just get on home with this sick boy, before it gets too late. You can pay me whenever you can. I know you're a man of your word, and I understand your situation. The most important thing is for this kid to get well."

"Thank you so much Dr. Carter. God bless you Sir, and I'm gonna pay you as soon as I can. Sir."

"You're quite welcome, Bryant. Hurry home and put this boy to bed. Don't worry about a payment to me right now. Just get moving!"

"Yeah Sir!"

A few days later, Nita watched Bean swab Nip's throat.

"Momma, may I try?" she asked.

"Here. You can try, Nita" responded Bean.

The medication proved to be satisfactory. Soon afterwards, Nip was able to eat solid foods, again. When Nita went to school the following day, she discussed her brother's condition with Miss Hayward. She told Nita that diphtheria was a contagious bacterium, which meant the other children in the family could catch the disease from the boy if his eating utensils were not sterilized. Nita explained to Bean exactly what Miss Hayward had shared with her.

They made sure that Nip's plate, fork, and glass was isolated from the rest of the family's. After each use, his utensils were scalded with hot water from the kettle to insure that proper sterilization had been done. It wasn't long thereafter, that he began to gain weight, and his playful energy was restored. The family was happy to see Nip at his old self again. Of course, Bryant thanked God immensely for getting his son through the storm.

One Sunday morning, everyone was up early getting dressed for church. Everyone except Mary, however, who just couldn't get it together. The other children didn't linger because they knew how important it was to be dressed and ready on time for departure to the morning service. Nita had notice a change in Mary's behavior over the past month. She neglected to discuss the dilemma which had her sister so perplexed, though Nita's dedicated involvement with household chores, and tending to Nip's illness had made her inadvertently fail to set aside some quality time for simply conversing with her sister. It wasn't deliberate, it was just that Nita had so many other things going on at the same time. On that day, however, she vowed not to let another second transpire before getting to the bottom of Mary's somber nature. Once Lil and Lo finished dressing, Nita instructed them to wait in the living room. The two younger sisters regarded her request without opposition. When they exited the room, Nita sat down on the bed near Mary, and looked directly into her big beautiful brown eyes. "Mary what's wrong with you?" she asked.

A hesitant Mary didn't respond right away because she didn't know how to tell her older sister just what was troubling her.

"Mary what's wrong?" Nita asked politely once again. "You know you can talk to me about anything."

Mary said not a word. She simply looked at Nita dismally.

"Now Mary, I know that something is wrong with you because I've noticed a change over the past few weeks. Did someone try to hurt you?"

"No," she answered in a whisper.

"Is your throat hurting you like Nip's?"

"No." She shook her head while dangling her fingers.

"Then what's wrong Mary? Because I know something just ain't right."

Mary, remained silent, but Nita didn't stop with her persistent questions. "Okay, Mary, if nothing hurts you, then maybe you're going through something you don't know much about."

Nita had touched a sensitive nerve. Finally, after a moment of complete silence, Mary responded with an approving node of the head.

"So someone did do something to you, right?"

"No!" she shook her head.

"Then you've got to be sick? That's the only thing that I can think of."

Another agreeable nod came abruptly as Mary looked at Nita with a small tear forming in the corner of her right eye.

"Do you want to share with me what the matter is?"

Mary began to cry, softly. Nita's sympathetic instincts commanded her to move closer to Mary, and place an arm around the girl's shoulder in a comforting manner. "It's okay to cry Mary."

Only sniffles could be heard.

"I'm here for you. You know you can tell me anything, and I promise not to tell anyone."

Mary turned and rested her head on Nita's shoulder. Nita held on to her for a short moment, without saying a word. Then she spoke softly.

"Mary, you don't have to tell me right now. But you gotta hurry, and get dressed for church. We don't want to get daddy mad at us. After church, you and me can take a long walk, just like we use to, and then you can tell me everything. Okay?"

Mary agreed, and finished dressing quickly. "Whatever's bothering you, you know that I'm here for you, and you don't have to worry. Me and you have been through a lot together. So don't be scared to talk to me," said Nita.

Soon after, Nita and Mary joined the rest of the gang waiting in the living room for Mose Lute to take them to church. Everyone followed

Bryant out to the car, when Mose arrived, then the entire family, including Bean, loaded up and drove to Ebenezer.

Church was an all day affair that Sunday. It started at about nine o'clock and lasted until two-thirty in the afternoon. Of course after the service was over, it was a ritual for the family to make their usual stop at Maw-Maw and Paw-Paw's place, which took about another hour. Mary was very uneasy throughout the service and the visit at her grandparents. She couldn't wait to get back home to converse in private with Nita.

Finally, after a full's day agenda, the family returned home. Mary jumped quickly out of her clothes, but Nita took her time, getting undressed, which really irritated her restless sister.

"Hurry up Nita, I don't want the others to follow us."

"Okay Mary, I'm going as fast as I can."

"Well I just don't want Lil and Lo to come walking with me and you."

"All right then, I'm almost done."

As soon as Nita finished Mary said softly, "Let's slip out through the back door, so they won't see us leave."

The two girls crept out the back door without anyone noticing their disappearance.

"Let's walk towards Annie's house, Nita."

"Okay Mary. Now, tell me what's wrong with you girl?"

As they strolled along the dusty road, Mary kept her shy head focused at the ground. She didn't know where to begin. Nita sensed her shyness, so she reached out and held her sister's hand for support.

"Come on Mary. You can tell me now."

Nita looked directly into Mary's eyes, which had become a pool of glassy tears. She tried to speak, but nothing came out.

"Take your time Mary, and tell me what's on your mind."

"Okay Nita," she said in a trembling voice. "I mean, I don't know' why I've been bleeding so much. I think I'm gonna die, Nita, because this is the second time it has happened to me. Each time there was blood everywhere. I know I probably got some ol' crazy disease like Nip. That's why I'm too scared to tell Momma and Daddy, because they ain't got no money for me to go to Dr. Carter."

"Oh Mary!"

"I know I'm gonna die, and I ain't never gonna see you, Lil, Lo, Nip, Walter, Momma and Daddy no more."

"You say you've been bleeding?"

"Yeah Nita. I ain't never seen this much blood before in my life to come out of me at one time. I'm so scared, until I don't know what to do. And sometimes my stomach feels like it's gonna burst wide open. Oooh it hurts so bad," she sniffled. "I know I'm just gonna die real soon, Nita."

"Oh Mary, my dear," Nita said calmly. "Where you been bleeding from?"

"Down there, Nita." Mary pointed below her waist.

"Mary, is that why you've been so sad, lately?"

"Yeah. I mean, I guess so," she quivered.

"Well let me tell you something, my dear sister. You don't have to be scared no more. It's a natural thing for this to happen to you, at your age."

"How do you know that Nita?"

"Mary, the first time I ever heard of such a thing was from Big Momma, and no, it ain't happen to me yet, even though I'm fourteen years old."

"It ain't never happened?"

"No, not yet. But you know something, Mary, what's real funny?"

"No, what Nita?"

"The first time I ever heard of such a thing as bleeding from down there was when me and Big Momma took a long walk to the store. I remember her telling me that I was gonna start bleeding from my private. I didn't even know what she was talking about."

"Your private?"

"Yeah Mary, let me explain. What Big Momma meant when she referred to down there," pointed Nita, "as my private is what you really call a vagina."

"Va-gi-na, Nita?"

"Yes. A vagina."

"What is that suppose to mean?"

"It is a female sex organ. Each month young girls like you and me go through a men-strul-al cycle. And what that means is you discharge blood and dead cells through your vagina, because you didn't conceive a child during the month."

"Girl, what do you mean conceive a child?"

"You know. Have a baby, Mary. Big Momma told me that the Lord be cleaning out your system because he ain't ready for you to have no baby just yet. And you can't have no baby unless you have relations with a boy."

"How you know about all this stuff, Nita?"

"Remember when I went to stay with Big Momma?"

"Yeah!"

"Well, one day she and I took a long walk to the store, and she tried to explain all this stuff to me as best she could. Some of it I understood, and some of it I didn't."

"Really Nita?"

"Yeap. But one day during lunch Miss Hayward explained everything to me. It made more sense after she took the time to do it. But I still must give Big Momma the credit because she did her best to help me to understand the changes that I was about to start seeing. It's a natural thing for this to happen to you Mary at your age."

"Really Nita?"

"Yeah girl!"

Nita proceeded to explain to her sister all the knowledge that had been thoughtfully passed on to her by Big Momma and Miss Hayward. The two young girls continued down the dusty road, hand in hand.

"Well Mary, you have to have sex with a boy before you can get pregnant."

Nita's low voice was occasionally interrupted by Mary's alarming cry: "Sex?—Get pregnant?—Girl you must be crazy now!"

"Okay, Okay, wait a minute and let me explain. You see, a boy's got a different sex organ from a girl. Remember that time me and you saw that ol' Hulton boy with his pants pulled down to his ankles and what he was shaking at us?"

"Oh yeah! I will never forget that Nita."

"Well that's what a boy's got. Now when a boy and a girl get together to have relations—Ooops! I mean sex—that's how you get pregnant and have a baby. So, if you don't have sex, you can't get pregnant. If you ain't pregnant, your body releases the eggs that weren't fertile. Now I can't tell you much about having sex, because I ain't never done that with no boy before, and I don't think you have to worry about that either. I, I, mean I hope not."

"Girl, you know better than that. I ain't thinking about no ol' boys."

"Good then. Now, the most important thing for you to know is that each month the same bleeding that you are having right now is gonna happen until the good Lord says it's time to stop. Which is a mighty long time."

"Plague-take-it!" Mary said.

"So remember now, it don't mean that you're gonna die each time this happens every month. It's just the way the Lord made us, and that's how he wanted to get rid of any unused eggs still inside your body." Nita laughed as if this was some kind of joke.

"Tell me something Nita, when did you and Miss Hayward have enough time to talk about all this stuff?"

"One day when all the students were outside of the classroom she asked me to stay in with her, and then she explained everything to me. Just like Big Momma, she told me that I needed to know these things because I was becoming a young lady, and she didn't want me to be surprised when it started to happen. I love both Miss Hayward and Big Momma. I look up to and trust them both."

"You say you ain't never had your period yet?"

"No not yet, Mary. Miss Hayward told me not to worry, though. She just said that I was late, and that it will happen sooner or later."

"And Nita you say you got to have sex with boys to have a baby?"

"Yeah, Mary. The only thing I can tell you about that is—Big Momma told me some boys will try to make you do things you ain't suppose to do with your vagina. She said a good girl will wait until they're married before they start having sex. And that's what I plan on doing. And you should do the same thing too. No matter what those boys tell you, either. Don't let them fool you."

"All this stuff sounds real crazy to me, Nita."

"I know it do because this is your first time ever hearing about it. But it ain't crazy. It's for real, Mary."

"So I guess I ain't gonna die? Right Nita?"

"No Mary, you want. You're just growing up, my sister."

"Whoooof Nita! I feel so much better now."

"There is one other thing, Mary."

"What's that Nita?"

"You need to tell Momma about all this. Miss Hayward says that you should wear sanitary rags during your period, and keep yourself real clean, before, during and after. Momma will know what to do. Okay?"

"Yeah. Boy, I feel so much better after talking to you. I knew you would know what was wrong with me. You are so smart."

"I ain't that smart, girl. I'm just glad Big Momma and Miss Hayward was there for me. If I'm not around, and Lil and Lo starts to feeling the same way as you, it is your duty to explain to them everything I told you here today. Okay?"

"Okay Nita, I promise, I will."

"Good! Now is there anything else you want to ask me?"

"No. I'm just glad I ain't gonna die now. Nita, I don't know what I would do without you girl. I love you very much."

"Good Mary. You know that I love you too. Well, let's go see what Annie's doing."

Annie was sitting under an oak tree in the back yard when Nita and Mary arrived.

"Hey Annie, what are you doing?" asked Nita.

"Nothing. What you and Mary doing all the way down here?"

"We just wanted to take a long walk. That's all."

"Did ya'll go to church today?"

"Yep!" responded Mary with a big smile on her face. She felt like living again.

"Guess what ya'll?"

"What?" responded Nita and Mary.

"Miss Hayward told me at school on Friday" Annie said with her know it all attitude, "that next year we gonna be going to school with colored kids from Grand Chenier, Creole, and Cameron."

"REALLY!" said Mary.

"Oh Mary, I didn't tell you that?" asked Nita.

"NO. I DIDN'T KNOW THAT, GIRL!!" replied Mary, excitedly.

"That's right. We will be going to school with kids from The Rose School in Cameron, The Bazile Moore School, The Hebert School by Ebenezer Baptist Church, and the colored kids from Grand Chenier. I don't know the name of their school. Miss Hayward just said they hold school in some church house over there."

"I can't wait," Annie added. "It's gonna be a big school too. Much bigger than the one we go to now."

"Yeah, it should be a lot of fun" said Nita.

"Plague-take-it! I can't wait for school to start next year, either" replied Mary. "What's the name of the school gonna be?"

"Well, Miss Hayward said it's gonna be called The Cameron Consolidated School" Nita remarked very obnoxiously.

"Ah Nita, you think you know everything," laughed Annie with a chip on her shoulder.

"No I don't" responded Nita, defensively.

"All the kids know that you are Miss Hayward's pet anyways." Annie laughed.

"I ain't nobody's pet. Miss Hayward is just real nice to me. That's all."

"Nita's the teacher's pet!" Nita's the teacher's pet! Nita's the teacher's pet!" Annie and Mary teased Nita mercilessly, and that made her a bit frustrated, however she realized that she did have a special relationship with Miss Hayward, unlike the rest of the school children; who all naturally sort of envied her. Nita didn't let Annie and Mary get the best of her, though. "At least somebody thinks I'm special" she thought, and joined in the fun with the other two. The girls played and teased Nita for the duration of the afternoon.

The current school year came to a close on a good accord. Each of the Bartie girls, Nip and Annie went on to their next respective grade levels. The summer flew by. All the colored kids in the area were happy because they couldn't wait for the fall school term to commence to meet new friends and attend the new school.

Consolidating the schools meant a better education for the Negro children in the lower Cameron Parish area.

CHAPTER 11

What a close call for the six innocent Bartie children, who were left home alone. Bean and Bryant were away seeking an employment opportunity for her. Things had gotten so bad for the family financially, until Bean had no other alternative, but to try and find work. Nita had diligently tried to bake a cake to ease the pain of hunger amongst her complaining siblings. The children attempted to keep themselves warm from mother nature's frigid weather as they stood in the kitchen, lined up for a piece of their big sister's meager breakfast. Unfortunately, as the cake was being passed around, Nita dispersed too much kerosene over the wood in the stove. All the children except Walter were standing near when the fire started. A black cloud of smoke, and the smell of charred wood quickly engulfed the entire house. Fierce flames and crackling sparks raced to the top of the chimney through the metal stove pipe like a dramatic fireworks display.

The young innocent children choked and coughed and quickly lost their sense of direction in the haze. The poor kids could barely see two feet in front of their faces. It was urgent that they get out of the kitchen quickly, or all of them could eventually perish due to smoke inhalation. Nita acted responsibly once she recognized the danger that confronted them. Time was of the essence, and not much of it could be wasted.

"Mary, where are you girl?"

"Right here!" Mary yelled to Nita gasping her breath.

Nita felt her way through the smoke, and found her sister.

"Hold on to my hand and don't let go." As Nita and Mary staggered through the fume filled room, they came across Lo.

"Hold onto Mary's hand," Nita instructed.

Lo immediately caught hold to Mary's hand, who was still holding onto Nita's. The three sisters heard the cries of Lil and Nip who were lost near the living room, wandering around in a daze.

Nita, Mary, and Lo located them by the sounds of their distressed voices. The children kept close to one another, hand in hand, as Nita led everyone out of the house.

Once outside, they coughed, cried and trembled from the chilly temperatures that awaited them.

"Where's Walter at?" rang out Mary.

"Oh my God, he's still in the...," Nita cried. "Don't anybody move. Mary, make sure all ya'll stay right here, until I get back. I gotta go see about Walter."

Mary was too frightened to even respond when Nita dashed back into the fuming house to rescue her little brother. She didn't bother to go into the kitchen where the fire originated because she knew that he wasn't there. Her intuition led her straight to Bean and Bryant's room, and that's where she found the young boy asleep in his parent's bed. Nita shoved his body several times, trying to awaken him, but no response followed. "Oh my God" she thought

"I've got to do something fast."

It took all of her strength to maneuver the boy's body out of bed. Once Nita got him down on the floor, she grabbed both of his arms, and struggled to pull him into the living room. She coughed and fought for breath, dearly. Nita knew she and Walter had very little time. Out of breath, Nita could only pull the boy by one arm. She almost gave up, agonized by fatigue and stress. Walter became coherent then, and that's when he and Nita were able to safely feel their way out of the house. The two of them joined a heartening Mary, Lil, Lo, and Nip who were standing in the yard barefooted, and inadequately dressed for the cold weather. They were so happy to see that their older sister and baby brother had made it out of the house alive. Each child huddled together to try and keep warm.

They watched the flames blare swiftly out of the chimney. Nita stood guard, and wouldn't allow anyone access back into the smoky quarters.

When Bryant and Bean returned home, they found the children standing helplessly in the front yard with a cloud of smoke hanging over their heads. Once they saw their parents arrive by horseback, a sigh of relief covered each of their traumatized faces, because they knew that Bryant would comfort their fears. He jumped off of his horse hurriedly, and helped Bean down afterwards.

"Daughter, what done happened here?"

"Daddy we was cold" Nita said. "So cold until I lit a fire in the"

Nita tried to explain but couldn't continue. She just broke down and gently cried.

"That's okay, daughter. I know you was trying to keep the other's warm. It's all right cause' I'm home now. You don't have to cry. The rest of ya'll all right?"

The group of children stood with jittering teeth, and shivered without responding.

Bean had already rushed over and tried to put her arms around as many of them as she possibly could. "Lord have mercy Jesus, ya'll all could've burnt up in the fire!" she cried.

Once Bryant saw that everyone was all right, he made his way inside the house with a pail of water to contain the blaze in the kitchen. Afterwards, he opened every window to allow the smoke to escape. He brought some old blankets outside for the family to keep warm with until the air cleared inside. Everyone sat close to one another under the quilted covers. As soon as things settled down considerably, Bryant motioned to the family that it was okay to enter the smelly house. Fortunately, no one suffered any serious injuries, and very little damage was assessed to the property. God knows the family could do without any tragedies or additional financial burdens to conquer. The only nuisance lingering was the smell of kerosene and charred wood which everyone adjusted to in due time.

Later in the afternoon, the burnt smell still hovered over the house. Bean prepared some beans and rice for the family to eat, while Nita assisted in her usual manner. Nip sat at the table, and all of a sudden he said "Momma can I have a piece of cake?"

Nita could have fallen off the face of the earth at that moment. She immediately gave Nip one of those "you better shut up your mouth" looks.

Nip ignored his sister's facial gesture.

"We ain't got no cake boy," Bean said.

"Momma, I wanna piece of cake! Please?"

Lord knows, Nita had already been through enough stress for the day, and for Nip to bring up the cake almost gave her a heart attack.

"I done told you once already boy, we ain't got no cake."

Nita gave Nip another alarming look, however it did no good because the boy wouldn't shut up his mouth about the infamous cake.

"Momma, look it's right here" he pointed, and pulled back the cloth blind that surrounded the bottom portion of the safe. When Bean saw a quarter of the cake remaining in a tin pan on the shelf, Nita trembled.

"Where ya'll got this of cake from, Nita?" inquired Bean.

"I made it this morning, Momma," she answered guiltily.

"Uh huh. I guess that's how that fire got started in here, uh?"

Nita was speechless, too afraid to say another word. Bean gave Nip a piece of cake, then kept on about her work. Nip ate without the realization of the mess he'd gotten his sister into.

But Bean wouldn't allow herself to scold Nita, realizing that there really was no sense in rekindling any fires. Instead, Bean took a deep breath. A feeling of guilt had suddenly overtaken her. The painful thought of losing her children played tricks with her mind.

"Lord, I'm so glad you spared them kid's life," Bean prayed silently. "Ain't no need for me to fuss at Nita. They was hungry, and she did the best she could to feed them. Ump! Thank you Jesus for being there with them, while me and Bryant was gone. You the main reason why they still alive right now!"

Five months swiftly passed into the school year. The students adjusted fairly well at the new Cameron Consolidated School, although each time a student from Cameron or Creole met up with one from Grand Chenier, a fight was sure to erupt. It was clearly understood. Mary tolerated very little mess from anybody at school. She protected herself from the hostile students by using her long fingernails as a means of defense. The very first day of school she and a girl named Mae West from Grand Chenier got into the biggest skirmish on campus. When the fight was over, both girls had clawed each other to the point of dribbling blood. Mary not only fought the girls, but she also wasn't afraid to lock horns with the boys, either. It was a good thing that Nita, Lil, and Lo were around to try and talk some sense into the girl's head because if Bryant found out about her fighting at school, she was going to be in some serious trouble.

The Cameron Consolidated School was housed in a large single story facility located on the Front Ridge Road, about two miles west of the Bartie home. To the right of the front entrance of the building was Mr. R. S. Guice's office, the first colored principal in the lower Cameron Parish area hired by Mr. "Red" Hackett, Superintendent of the school board. Other faculty and staff members included Miss Manilla Allen, Miss Geneva Mouton, Miss Baker, Mr. Isaiah Pierce, Mr. John A. Parker, and Miss Myron Hayward. Across from the principal's office were two adjacent classrooms, which led to a much longer hall running east to west on the back side of the corridor. There, several partitioned classrooms were aligned in a row, equipped with large folding doors that could be doubled back for easy conversion into a fairly large auditorium.

The facility also had a stage to carry on school programs and assemblies. Miss Hayward, entertained the colored residents in the area with a "Womanless, Manless Wedding" at the school; having the men dress up as women and the women as men. One of the largest crowds ever turned out for the drama. Miss Hayward possessed a knack for putting on such amusing productions that promoted social graces for the students and their parents. Being that church was the only other form of entertainment during this era, these types of festive events were a welcome change by all who attended.

Nita, as a high school sophomore, had matured into an attractive young lady, though she possessed a "countrified" look about herself. Because the Bartie girls were very pretty in their own special way, they were extremely popular. Nita and Mary played on the basketball team, and both were cheerleaders.

One afternoon, after the 3:30 P.M. The school bell rang as it always did—exactly on time, all the students of Cameron Consolidated rushed into the hallways en route to their respective buses. The Bartie kids sat near the front, since they were amongst the first to unload. Nita and Mary had just settled in the very first seat, when the bus rolled away from the campus. About a mile east down the dusty gravel road, the bus driver, Cleveland Washington, noticed that an accident ahead occurred. Cleveland was a student himself, filling in as bus driver for his grandmother, Ida Washington, who had become ill recently. He parked the bus at the school during the day while attending his classes. Cleveland demanded that the students calm down quickly once he recognized one of the cars involved in the mishap. Upon approaching the scene he pulled the bus over to the far side of the road and stopped. He stuck his head out of the window to find out if everything was okay.

"What happened here Lee Boy?" he inquired.

Seeing the two wrecked cars, all the children on the bus went into hysterics. Even Nita and Mary rose from their seat to get a closer look.

"Everybody sit down and be quiet!" Cleveland demanded.

Silence ruled the bus, instantaneously, as Cleveland awaited an answer from an attractive young light-reddish, colored gentleman, who was the driver of a maroon convertible Chevrolet.

"What happened Lee Boy?" asked Cleveland again.

"Oh, I lost control of my car in the loose gravel. And this man right here, sideswiped me when we passed each other by. The highway patrol is on the way. I'll be okay, Cleveland."

At the moment Lee began talking, Nita got up from her seat, and poked her head out of the window. She and Lee caught each other's eyes and stared for a long moment.

"Boy, what a good-lookin fellow," thought Nita. "And would you look at them pretty green eyes? They're making my heart skip a beat."

Lee on the other hand thought "My, my, my, my, my, what a pretty girl."

Cleveland broke the two's concentration when he cranked up the bus engine. As the bus drove away, Nita kept her head protruded out of the window until she could no longer see Lee in sight.

"Please sit down, Nita" requested Cleveland as he drove the bus onward.

Nita, still in a deep trance, sat back down next to Mary, speechless. An inexplicable strangeness captivated the teenager's entire soul. She just couldn't quite shake the erratic, but so sweet sensation that had just come over her.

"Nita? What's wrong with you girl?" inquired Mary. "It's time for us to get off the bus."

A tug-of-war match developed between the two sisters. Mary had to literally yank Nita up from her seat. Eventually, they both exited the bus with Lil, Lo, and Nip. Nita lagged behind the others, however, still in a mellow mystification as they all walked home.

During the family gathering at the evening meal, Bryant recited the blessing with a pious anointment, thanking God immensely for his generosity and grace. Nita heard not a word of her father's obliged praise. Her mind was far, far away in another world. After dinner, Mary—who couldn't quite figure out what exactly had come over her sister—got extremely irritated in the kitchen.

"Girl, you better wash these dishes right the first time, cause' I ain't gonna be washing them all over again, for you. Especially, since I'm the one who got to dry um, too" Mary snarled.

"All right Mary", Nita snapped. "I'm doing the best that I can."

"No you ain't! Look at this glass, girl. And at that plate! And this fork. And that knife. They still got food all over them."

The fussing got so out of hand between the two sisters, until Bryant had to go into the kitchen, to settle the disturbance.

"Ya'll both betta straighten up in here, or it's gonna be too bad for you. You hear me Nita?"

"Yeah Sir!" she answered, breaking out of her bewilderment.

"Mary, you understand me?"

"Yeah Sir!" she responded with her bottom lip poked out in an act of retaliation towards Nita.

"All right Mary, you can just pull in that bottom lip. And ya'll betta hurry up with them dishes, so you can start doin your lessons. And I bet not have to come back in here no more, cause' if I do, ya'll both gonna git it!"

The girls calmed down after Bryant's reprimand. Soon after, the kitchen became spotless, they started in on their homework. In the midst of the laughter and chatter of the other children Nita's mind drifted back to the quaint young fellow whom she only knew as Lee Boy.

There was no rest for her embroiled mind all night long. The next morning she awakened bright and early, made up the bed, swept the floor, prepared breakfast for the rest of the family, washed the dishes, and then got dressed for school. Before the bus arrived this morning, her mind was still boggled with thoughts of Lee. "Why am I thinking so much about some guy I don't even know nothing about? I barely know his name. I mean, I don't even know where he's from or nothing like that." The bus pulled up in front of the house as she continued to ponder the mystery.

"Mornin Nita!" Cleveland said. "Boy, you show up early this mornin. Do this every day, and me and you gonna git alone just fine."

"I will Cleveland" Nita answered, sharply.

When the bus pulled into the school's driveway, there was an extreme volume of talking and laughter going on amongst the students inside; all except for Nita. She didn't concern herself with such trivialities today. Instead her beautiful big brown eyes focused straight ahead with a vacant stare across the school yard.

Once the highway patrolman had determined who caused the accident, the wreckage was cleared. Lee rushed home to Grand Chenier, almost involving himself in another mishap trying to get to a friend's house as fast as he could. "I gotta see Punkin, today. He will know exactly who that pretty girl was that I saw on the school bus, earlier."

Lee flew down the eastbound gravel road at a high rate of speed. Once he reached Grand Chenier, he had no plans on stopping by his parents house to inform them of the wreck. Instead, he went straight to James January's house, a boy everybody called 'Punkin'.

Punkin and his family lived in a small shotgun style home owned by Mrs. Annie Miller. Punkin's father Clem had been employed by the wealthy Crain family for several years. Clem was an averaged built, dark complected man who wore his hair slicked back with grease, and he loved to play the guitar. The man never took a lesson in his life, but could make that guitar say just about anything he wanted it to and was the musician for the local colored church. Clem also loved cars, particularly sports cars. Punkin's mother, Annie Mae—known by everyone in the area as "Coonie" was a heavy set woman as sweet as honey just like her mother Willie 'Will' Dozier. Will and her husband Letchet lived nearby with their three other children: D. Y., Carrie and Jimmy.

Coonie was the first to come to the door in response to Lee's eager banging.

"Hey Coonie, is Punkin home from school yet?"

"Yeah Lee Boy, he's home. He back there in the back with Clem helping him clean some fish and crabs. How's Lillie and Simon doin?"

"They all right I guess. I just had a wreck way down there by the school house. I ain't told Momma and them nothing about it yet. I know when she finds out, she's gonna have a fit."

"Ah no, Lee Boy. You say you had a wreck? You messed up your car pretty bad?"

"Yeah! It's all bent in on the left side, Coonie."

"Ah no. Now how you done that Lee Boy?"

"I lost control of it in the loose gravel."

"You all right?"

"Yeap! Go over there and see it for yourself. It's all messed up."

As Coonie left to take a closer look at the car, Lee walked to the back of the house in search of Punkin. He and his father had already scaled a half bucket full of fish.

"Well Sir, Punkin" said Clem. "Look at Ol' Lee Boy."

"How ya'll doin?" responded Lee.

"Yea Sir Boy, how's that pretty little varoon car of your's?"

"Not good, Clem. Some white guy sideswiped my whole left side, not far from the school house on the Front Ridge Road."

"Ah you gone, Lee Boy! Well Sir! Now just how did that happen?"

"I lost control of it in the loose gravel. When he seent me coming, he couldn't help but hit me and tore up the whole left side of my car."

"Not that pretty lil ol' varoon car, Lee Boy?"

"Yep!"

"Ah you gone!"

"Go see for yourself, Clem." Lee was hoping Clem would leave so he and Punkin could talk in private. Sure enough the father couldn't stand to hear much more about a wrecked sports car without investigating it. He stood up and made his way around to the front of the house.

Punkin wanted to see, too. "Is it all messed up bad, Lee Boy?"

Lee placed a restraining hand on his friend's shoulder. "It's pretty darn bad, Punkin, but that ain't why I came up here."

"Oh no? What's wrong?"

"Well Punkin, I saw the prettiest girl I ever seent before in my life today. She had her head sticking out of the school bus window, right after I had the wreck."

"Oh yeah? Do you know her name?"

"No I sure don't. I don't even know who she is. Much less what her name is. All I know is that she was a very pretty girl, and I gotta find out just who she is."

"Well tell me Lee Boy, what did she look like? And who's bus was she on?"

"Punkin, she was riding on Cleveland Washington's bus headed this way. That's all I know."

"Um. Did they have a bunch of other girls on that bus with her?"

"I guess so. I really don't remember."

"Did four of those girls look a lot alike?"

"I guess, Punkin, from what I could tell. Why you asking me all these questions?"

"Where was she sitting at on the bus?"

"In the very front seat on the right side."

"Was there another girl sitting next to her who was a little bit darker than she was with long pretty hair?"

"You know something, Punkin, there was another girl sitting next to her a little darker with long hair. That's right—sure was. I take it you know these girls."

"Lee Boy, they sound like them Bartie girls. Now the one sitting next to the dark one you say is the one you like, right?"

"Yeah! That's the one."

"Is she a real bright skinned girl, with a lot of thick hair and got a real pretty face?"

"I'm sure that's the one. What's her name?"

"It's Wanita, but everybody at school calls her Nita. Her sister's name is Mary, and everybody calls her Toad. And boy can she fight. You better not mess with ol' Toad. Man, that girl will scratch up your face if you try."

"So, you say the one I like is Wanita. Right?"

"Yea. Her name's just like my sister."

"Who? Cee Cee?"

"Yeah! My sister Juanita. Now Lee Boy, I hope you know that she's much younger than you are. She can't be no more than fourteen years old."

"That ain't nothing, boy. I don't care. I really like what I saw today, and that's that."

"Another thing Lee Boy, they daddy's real strict on um. You ain't gonna be able to get close to them girls. They say Mr. Bryant don't take nobody's mess. And since you much older than she is, I know he ain't gonna go for that."

"Well Punkin, I don't care. I gotta try. If I don't, I'll never know what could've happened. Will I?"

"I guess so. But you better not get your hopes up too high cause' them some good girls, and they daddy ain't gonna let them go nowheres with nobody. Not even you."

"So, what do you think I should do?"

"I don't know Lee Boy."

"Punkin, maybe you can tell her that I really like her."

"Tell her what?"

"That I really, really, really like her a whole lot."

"Noop! I can't do that. But I tell you what, maybe you should write her a letter and tell her yourself. I'll give it to her tomorrow. That way she'll know that it came from you and she won't think that I'm just making all of this up."

"Punkin, that's a good idea. I'll write her tonight, so that you can give her the letter tomorrow."

"Okay Lee Boy, I can do that."

"Now Punkin, you say her name is Wanita, right?"

"Yea, Wanita Bartie."

"Punkin, I knew you would know who she was. I owe you one."

"You don't owe me nothin. But remember now, what I told you about they daddy. He's real hard on them."

"I know that already," responded Lee very sarcastically. "If I don't try, I'll never know will I?"

"No you sure want. But remember what I told you. Mr. Bryant don't take no mess from nobody. And it don't matter who you are, either."

"I won't forget Punkin!"

Clem and Coonie returned from the front of the house just as Lee and Punkin finished their conversation. Punkin walked Lee Boy to his car and took a closer look at the damages. Later that night, Lee drafted the most convincing letter of his life.

Dear Wanita,

Ever since I saw you on yesterday, I can't get you off of my mind. Each time I open my eyes you are there staring me straight in the face. I really want to get to know who you are. Hopefully, you will feel the same as me. Until I see you again, I will always remember your beautiful smile and face.

From the heart,

Lee J. Harrison

The next school day, as soon as Punkin saw Nita he rushed over to her, very excited to deliver the message from Lee.

"Hey Nita, somebody from Grand Chenier really likes you."

"FOR REAL!" exclaimed Nita with a cheesy smile.

"Um Huh!"

"Well, what's his name, then?"

"Here, everything is in this letter" said Punkin as he handed the note to her.

"Oh my God" Nita replied. "I can't believe he wrote to me."

Nita took the note, and ran straight to her classroom. Once she got there, she opened it reading silently and slowly to herself. She almost had a fit right there on the spot. She thought about Lee for the rest of the day, completely forgetting about her studies. Nita carefully wrote Lee Harrison back, only using correct English and diction to express her thoughts precisely:

My Dearest One, While time permits and thinking only of you, I decided to express my feelings, after seeing you for the first time on yesterday.

I am interested in dating you, however my parents will not permit such a thing, presently. I know that you will perhaps not tolerate someone that you cannot go out with on a date, but I would still like to know your feelings, anyway. Even if you choose not to see me. Please write me at your earliest convenience with your response.

With all my Love,

Wanita Cecil Bartie

During the afternoon recess, Nita gave the letter to Punkin.

"Hi James would you please be so kind to pass this letter on to Lee for me?"

"Sure Nita, I'll give it to him. I know he's gonna be glad to get it to."

"You think so James?"

"I know so, Nita. I'm sure he will."

"Thanks so much" replied the love-bitten girl.

When Nita arrived home later that afternoon, she could hardly do her household chores. Bean observed the big change that had come over her daughter in recent days, and began her interrogations.

"Nita, girl what done come over you? You been acting real silly for the past few days. I ain't crazy. You been half doing your work, and walking around here like you high as a kite. Now what's wrong girl?"

"Ah Momma, ain't nothing wrong with me. I don't know why you would think something like that."

"Yea there's something wrong all right, cause' Mary done told me. She say ever since you seen some ol' boy from Grand Chenier, you been acting like you ain't got no sense a-tall."

"Momma, Mary don't know nothing," answered Nita, abrasively. She thank she do, but she don't know a thing."

"And what's that ol' boy's name?"

"What boy you talkin about Momma?"

"You know who I'm talkin about. Don't play no games with me, girl!"

"Okay, Momma. His name is Lee J. Harrison, and he is from Grand Chenier."

"Lee Harrison, you say? Is that Lillie and Simon Harrison's boy?"

"I guess so, Momma. I really don't know his people. I barely even know who he is."

"Girl, that boy don't want you. Besides, he's too old for you in the first place. And you know Bryant ain't gonna go for no ol' mess like that. I can tell you that right now."

"I already know that, Momma, but I still like him."

"Now just tell me how you gon like somebody you ain't never even talked to before? Let along only seen once in your life. That don't even make crazy sense."

"I don't know Momma. All I know is that I ain't never felt like this before."

"The best thing for you to do is to keep your mind on your lessens and off them ol' boys."

"Yes Ma'am" answered Nita, disappointedly.

After supper, Nita couldn't concentrate on her studies. Later that night she went to bed hoping to dream about Lee. She twisted and turned herself on the mattress like a maggot, which really annoyed Mary. At 4 A.M. she was awakened abruptly by the first crow of the rooster.

"Girl, stop pulling the covers off me, and go back to sleep" demanded Mary.

Nita couldn't go back to sleep, however, so she just lay there with a few tears welling up in her eyes. "Nobody understands me" she thought. "I thought Mary would, but she don't even care."

After a sleepless night, Nita was happy when morning came. Anxiously, she got up and did her usual household chores before dressing for school. She stood alongside the road, and waited for the school bus to approach. Once the bus pulled up, she spoke to Cleveland, politely.

"Good mornin', Cleveland."

"Mornin Nita" he replied startled. "Boy I sure don't know what's gotten into you lately. Now don't get me wrong, I'm not complaining about it, but whatever it is, I sure hope it keeps you catching the bus on time" he laughed.

Nita didn't answer, just rolled her eyes, and took the front seat. Cleveland blew his horn loudly again to alert Nip and the rest of the sisters of his presence because they were nowhere in sight.

"How come you out here so early every day? Mary asked snidely as she climbed up into the bus. "I guess you still got that ol' boy on your mind."

"Stop, Mary. Cause' I'm not in the mood today. Okay?"

Cleveland snickered.

Nita could not wait to get to school, hoping that James would have a response from Lee concerning the letter she'd sent to him the day before. As soon as the bus pulled into the driveway, Nita was the first one off. She spotted James from a distance. His facial expression conveyed good news. Eventually, when they caught up with each other, he handed over another note from Lee, and she grabbed it excitedly. "Thanks James" she said and detoured into the restroom.

Hello Nita,

I received your letter yesterday, and I desire very much to see you. You must make some sort of arrangements with your parents, so that we can visit each other. You are the girl that I have been waiting for.

I'm for Real,

Lee J. Harrison

Nita read the letter several times, but wondered immediately how she could make such an arrangement with her parents "There is just no way Daddy is gonna let this boy visit me," she thought.

"I'm too young for him, so I just better get it off my mind right now. Oh! But I just can't. I wish I could, but I can't. I know he ain't gonna won't me. Just like Momma said, I'm too young. He's probably already got somebody else."

Nita remained hysterical for the remainder of the day. Once the final bell rang, she was the first to get on the bus, and decided to discuss her new love interest with Cleveland.

"I knew it was something different about you Nita. You've just been acting too strange lately. Well! Let me see. I've been knowing Lee for a very long time. He's a good guy, just a bit possessive. You'll find out once you get to know him better."

As soon as Nita saw Mary, Lil and Lo headed towards the bus, she abruptly ended the conversation. Later on at home, she did her usual chores. Nita didn't tell Bean a thing about the letters she had been receiving from Lee, however, in fear of her disapproval. That night Nita contemplated the circumstances:

"Lee works offshore on a boat out in the Gulf, seven days on, and seven off. Tomorrow he will be gone out for a whole week. At least that will give me enough time to think about how I'm going to ask Momma and Daddy to at least let him come over to our house for a short visit. I have to ask them, if I expect to keep him."

Lee (Lee Boy) Johnson Harrison was born in Grand Chenier, Louisiana on August 15, 1928 to Simon and Sue Ordella Olivia Harrison. Simon and Sue were married September 1, 1927 in the home of Ed Stein. Previous to their marriage, Sue gave birth to a daughter named Betty Lovenia (B-Bean), born December 28, 1926.

Everyone in the area knew Sue as "Lillie", a nickname given to her by a half-sister, Irene "Pinee". Lillie, born August 19, 1908 was a short, dark complected, well figured domestic worker who was an excellent cook and flawless housekeeper. Lillie's daughter B-Bean was raised by another half-sister, Willie (Will) Dozier. Adam Nunez's wife, Leonna, had given birth to a son, Bobby, so Mr. Adam—as Lillie referred to him—had some business going on in Texas City at the time. He asked Lillie to assist the family as an attendant until everything was completed there. Lillie agreed and left her infant daughter Lovenia in Will's care. When Lillie returned home from Texas City, Will had fallen in love with and became very attached to B-Bean, and wouldn't hear of parting with the little girl. Lillie, however, disapproved and so lived with Will for some time thereafter. Unfortunately, times got hard for Lillie's parents, so she had to seek additional work to contribute her fair share to the family's well-being. After much stressful contemplation and pondering over the child's plight, Lillie came to the conclusion that it was in the best interests of everyone for Lovenia to remain in the custody of Will Dozier, who eventually raised the child through adulthood.

Lillie's mother, Frances January (born October 20, 1888, in Cameron, Louisiana), was part Negro, part Cherokee Indian, and the granddaughter of George and Winnie Wilder, originally from Mississippi. George and Winnie gave birth to a daughter named Sarah, who met Nathaniel Ben West, from Mermentau, Louisiana. Ben had a wife named Angeline when he met Sarah; who had several children out of wedlock with him. Ben and Angeline West's children were Rachel, Sarah, Mittie, Harriet, George, Ester ("Ethel Mae"), Hattie, Dewy (Duval), Sherman, Florence, Gladdie ("Gertie"), Edith West and a stepdaughter Lurman Jones. Ben West and Sarah Wilder's children were Frances, John ("Boy"), Andrew, Tom, Eddy, and Willie West.

Frances West-January was a tall, slim, dark-complected and attractive lady with distinct high cheek bones. She had a long, pointed nose, and fiery gray, piercing eyes that looked directly through a person. She was an extremely intelligent, well-read colored lady, who knew the Bible very well and didn't believe in much trivial talk. Upon completion of the sixth grade, Frances could have become a school teacher had she completed another year. Instead, she chose a profession as a licensed midwife, however, and delivered countless numbers of colored and white babies throughout the Grand Chenier area. On January 6, 1908, Frances married Charles January, the son of a former slave John January. John had been bought and sold on several occasions during his period of slavery. Originally from Lafayette, Louisiana, after he became a free man he adopted the name January from the last white family he had served. In 1847 John January and his wife Belle Rose moved to "Cheniere Perdue," an area on the opposite side of Grand Chenier along the Mermentau River. They settled on the "Jean Vileor Theriot" estate as tenants helping with the farming and cattle raising. The marriage between John and Belle Rose produced eight children: Jane, Koetess, Zelia, Charles, John "Jean", Joe "Feast", Jewel, and Jice. Belle Rose also gave birth to a very light complected son named Anthony Miller, fathered by a white man. Very' little information was really ever known about Anthony because he left the family at a very early age.

Charles January was a short, dark, proud, fairly handsome man who had lost one of his fingers in a cotton gin, several years back. His first marriage to Ellen Frank ended after she died of an apparent heart attack. The union between Charles and Ellen Frank gave them ten children: Joe, Sue, John, Ida ("Chink"), Willie ("Will"), Anthony, Frank, Antney, Jim ("Jim Black") and Irene ("Pinee"). His second marriage to Frances West bore that couple seven more children: Sue Ordella ("Lillie"), Emmaline Clara, Ethel Mae, Ben Davis, Phillip Ray, and Pinky Lovenia, who died of pneumonia, as an infant. Charles died on March 2, 1945 and was buried in the St. Martin DePorres Cemetery in Grand Chenier.

Lee's father, Simon Renus Harrison—known as ("Red")—was a charming, reddish complected gentleman, who stood about 6'5" and enjoyed fishing, shrimping, traveling, and gambling. He was bom May 6, 1905, to Joseph (Joe) Harrison (a very tall, handsome, sporty fellow, born in 1878) and Mary' Frank. Simon was the only child that Joe Harrison and Mary Frank had together as a couple out of wedlock.

Joe Harrison later married Sue Williams. Her father was John Williams, who married Charles January's sister Zelia. The union between Joe Harrison and Sue produced seven children: Georgia ("Sister"), Dorothy ("Pat"), Ann, Betty Cornelia, Ernest ("Jack"), Billie and Joseph, Jr. However, Sue Williams had three other children, previous to her marriage to Joe. They were Manuel Nash (whose father Willie Nash was one of the first colored school teachers at the Shady Grove Baptist Church located across the road from St. Martin DePores Cemetery. The school was established in approximately 1896); a daughter Frankie Reed (fathered by Frank Reed, who was Joe Harrison's half brother), and Douglas ("Booger") Schlesinger (whose father was Albert Schlesinger, a Caucasian man). As a young boy Simon grew to love dearly his maternal grandmother Clarinda Dozier, and his paternal grandmother Seen Mayne better known as "Maw" (born December 25, 1860). After the abolition of slavery, Maw was raised with the Doxey family in Grand Chenier. Maw's father was an Irish immigrant, and her mother Jeanette Dozier-a former slave was murdered by a white man. When asked whose child she was carrying at the time, Maw's mother revealed the name of the unborn baby's father. The White man had a wife and family of his own, so when he later heard that he had fathered a mulatto child, he took a shotgun and blew Maw's mother's brains right out of her head on her own front door steps. Unfortunately, the man was never tried or convicted for her murder. Quite a woman to reckon with, "Maw" was an attractive, feisty, light brown skin lady, with beautiful coal black, wavy hair and a very well-defined figure. She smoked a pipe, loved to talk, and didn't mind speaking her mind. During the course of her employment as a domestic servant for Mrs. Alcide Miller. "Maw" mothered eight children, all born out of wedlock. Six of the eight were fathered by men other than Negroes which included: Steve, Agnes ("Coot"), and Rosa Sturlese. Their father was an Italian immigrant named Manuel Sturlese, a peddler who came to Cameron and later opened a general store. Another child Charlie Davis was given the surname Davis at birth nevertheless, Charlie's father was Manuel Sturlese as well. Maw changed Charlie's surname because she was afraid Manuel Sturlese would take her son; given Manuel had only fathered two daughters with his wife Leontine Archer during this time period. Annie Miller whose father was Raphael Miller, the son of Mr. and Mrs. Alcide Miller. Another son Frank Reed was fathered by one of the first white physicians in the Grand Chenier area. Lillian Stewart's father was Henry Stewart, and Joseph Harrison's father was an educator from the north. Lillian and Joseph were the only two children fathered by Negro men. Sean "Maw" Mayne's first and only marriage was to Ozimae Savoie, a Negro man; no children were conceived to this union which lasted for a very short period of time.

One thing's for sure Lee Boy and Nita did have one thing in common, their family lineages both consisted of flavor and cultural parallelism. However, their upbring had occurred on two opposite ends of the spectrum. Unlike the hovel Nita was reared in, Lee Boy's principal dwelling place was a striking two story early American villa which belonged to his father Simon's mother Mary Frank and grandmother Clarinda Dozier. Located on the banks of the Mermentau River near the "Pull Rope Ferry" in Grand Chenier, the property was prime real estate. Back when Lee Boy was a mere two years old, in order for citizens to cross the Mermentau to an area called "The District on the other side, they had to board a man powered ferry, propelled by pulling a rope which stretched from one side of the river to the other. Lillie and Simon moved into the villa with Mary and Clarinda about three years after they were married, occupying the second floor. At the time Simon was employed as a boat captain on the "True Friend", vessel owned by Mr. Lee R. Nunez. Lillie did days work for several white families in the area. Lee Boy was a mere two years old.

In addition to their own son, Lillie and Simon raised her half brother "Jim Black" January's son John Albert (Son) January, a few years older than Lee Boy. At a very early age, Lee Boy had little inkling that he was colored. Two of Lee Boy's best friends were white boys, Dean and Cleveland Miller. The only time he really hung around other colored children was at "The Grand Chenier Colored School" held at the St. James Church of God in Christ, located in "The District." One of Lee's teachers , Miss Flowers, boarded in their household. Other teachers who taught him were Miss Bernice Washington and Miss Manilla Allen. It wasn't until later on in his life that Lee Boy realized there was a true difference between Negroes and Whites.

After Grandma Clarinda and Mary Frank passed away, Simon inherited the home and all of it's authentic furnishings. Five years later, however the home was confiscated from Simon, due to an outstanding debt owed claimed by a local white merchant. Though Simon couldn't read or write, he was smart enough to know that the storekeeper beat him out of his inherited property because of an unresolved misunderstanding. After that misfortune, the Harrisons and Son January wound up homeless for a short period of time.

Lillie had been doing some washing and ironing for an aristocratic white family known as the L. O. Miller's. Lillie's mother Frances had held the job first. Frances passed the job on to Willie Dozier, who passed it on to Lillie. Dr. Laurent O. Miller and his wife, the former Annie Tabachick, had been searching for a full time maid. Since Lillie did such an excellent job doing their laundry, Dr. Miller offered her the employment opportunity after hearing about her stroke of bad luck. Dr. Miller even built a small two room house on premises of his large estate for Lillie and her family to occupy. The house had a combined living room and bedroom, along with a kitchen-dinning area. The Miller's paid Lillie $2.50--a day which began at 7:00 A.M. and ended at 1:30 P.M. She cooked, cleaned, washed, ironed and prepared three meals each day with all the trimmings. She also had the responsibility for serving at special events: whenever the family entertained local guests, the clergy, politicians, duck hunters or relatives. In addition to her daily chores, Lillie also assisted with light gardening duties.

The Millers truly loved Lille and her family, and the Harrisons loved the Millers in return. They treated each other with respect, and skin color never had any true relevance in the eyes of either household. Dr. Miller was a short, honest, truthful, stem, intelligent gentleman who loved to play "bridge", "beau jeau", "rook" and dominoes. He also enjoyed reading the New Orleans Time Picayune, and was a big advocate of education. He often lent money to local high school graduates who desired to attend college.

"Doc" as most people in the Grand Chenier area referred to him had received his medical degree in 1908 from Tulane University's Medical School located in New Orleans, Louisiana. So had his brother Dr. Martin O. Miller, who chose to remain in the New Orleans area after graduation. "Doc" had encountered Annie Tabachick at his parent's home (Mr. & Mrs. Eugene Miller), while he was still attending medical school. She had come to Cameron Parish because Eugene Miller was searching for a school teacher to educate his children and others who lived in their neighborhood.

"Miss Annie" arrived in America from Czechoslovakia at a very early age. Her family settled in Georgia before she and her mother relocated to Grand Chenier. She was an avid reader, a good manager, not very tall, but definitely a striking lady of class and style. Miss Annie sometimes liked having physical aliments, too. She also enjoyed reading the Saturday Evening Post. During the depression, when money was tight, all the family's periodicals were canceled except for The Post and The New Orleans Time Picayune.

Miss Annie wore very simple, but expensive clothing. "Doc" had most of his suits tailor made. During World War II, he desired to buy two pair of pants to go with a single jacket, but wasn't able to do so. Mixing and matching clothes were something simply unheard of during this era, which led him to eventually have his clothes tailored. He mostly wore seersucker suits in the hot summer months, and these he bought off the rack.

In the year of 1935, "Doc" consulted an architect to sketch out plans for a sturdy "storm proof' home not to exceed $ 10,000 in cost. After construction got underway, however, the huge estate far exceeded his initial price. The structure was built on 2 ½ foot brick blocks. After the floor and beams were installed, the house sat about 4 ½ feet off the ground, a total of 8 feet above sea level.

There was a large kitchen and pantry where Lillie spent most of her time. The home was also furnished with a study and formal living and dinning rooms. The mosquito trap front entrance invited guest to enter and a small screened-in porch, located in the back of the house, displayed an array of beautiful hanging plants. A cozy breakfast room sat near the spacious kitchen. The bathroom, and three large luxurious bedrooms including the one occupied by "Doc" and Miss Annie, was downstairs. Constructed with sumptuous glass French doors, their bedroom adjourned an enchanting spacious screened-in front porch. This made it convenient for them to contemplate the full moon lodged against a charming starlit sky on warm, romantic, summer nights. Beautiful oak wood floors graced most of the house throughout, and these were always waxed to perfection. Each piece of miniature tile on the bathroom and kitchen floors was individually laid, these coverings made from the finest of ceramics available. Miss Annie decorated the place with nothing but the very best early American antique furniture, and exclusive pieces imported from her native country. Other unique features of the house included a fabulous indoor balcony with double doors that opened from an upstairs bedroom overlooking the formal living area. Here a comely black baby grand piano resided. The living area was also adorned with a fire-place which communed with the study. Two massive, varnished beams traversed the living area at the ceiling level. A distinguished grandfather clock stood near the beautiful, discriminate, tasteful, winding staircase, near a built-in bookcase that enclosed the finest of lavish crystal, figurines and porcelain. Only original, magnificently aesthetic artwork hung on the walls throughout each room. The second level of the house contained another bathroom, and two more huge bedrooms, one of which had a vaulted ceiling. The other room contained the entrance to the balcony. Both rooms were equipped with abundant walk-in closet space. The screened windows surrounding the home were used to invite the cool Gulf coast breezes in on those hot, humid, days and nights typical of Louisiana. The family feasted off the finest of china, drank from the best stemware, and manipulated their meals with the most eloquent silverware that money could purchase.

The grounds were just as impeccable as the edifice. Flourishing fig, pear, peach and persimmon trees decorated the north west side.

Several huge, shaded live oak trees were aligned along the road in the front yard. Broad decorative oleander shrubs bearing fragrant rose, white and purple colored flowers were strategically placed throughout the yard, producing a collage of colors when they bloomed in early spring. Miss Annie attentively groomed the flower beds, which held ornamental azaleas, crepe myrtles, tulips, roses, Easter Lillies, gladiolas, and gardenias to name a few of many flowers, shrubs and other seasonal plants which embellished the estate. Gardening just so happened to be one of her favorite past-times, which she definitely possessed a green thumb. Any visitor to the estate could easily detect that floriculture was Miss Annie's niche as they strolled about the massive, picturesque courtyard. "Doc" himself cultivated an impressive vegetable garden located near the fruit trees, where he raised most of his food. A large cistern outside the kitchen window stored rain water, mainly used in his practice and to quench the thirst of the flowers, plants and shrubs as needed on hot dry days. A deep fresh water well, with a rope and bucket had been installed near the cistern and this was chiefly used for drinking purposes. The Miller Estate was simply aristocracy at its finest.

"Doc's" office was located in the front of the house near the road, allowing his patients easy access. He had no established office hours, basically making himself available whenever the ill needed to see him. Whether colored or white, day or night, "Doc" was accessible to provide whatever medical attention necessary. In earlier days, his mode of transportation had been by horseback. Then he moved up to a horse and buggy, and later to a Buick. "Doc" and Miss Annie had three lovely daughters: Emily Josephine (Shutzie), the oldest; Annie Laurie (Punk); and Marilyn Cornelia (Te-Cum), who was the youngest. She was a mere seven years old, when Lillie first went to work for the family.

One funny fact to note about this elaborate estate and all of its luxurious amenities was that while the Millers didn't own a television set for the longest time, Lillie and Simon did. Often times, one could find "Doc", Miss Annie and their girls over at Lillie's place watching TV in her living room. "Doc" particularly loved baseball games. One memorable occasion occurred when Miss Annie and her next-door neighbor, Emma Nunez spent the entire day watching the coronation of Queen Elizabeth II, of England.

In Grand Chenier, Lillie Harrison was the "Queen of the Colored Society" simply because her home was the gathering place for most of the colored residents, friends, relatives and just whoever wanted to stop by for a visit. Lillie's doors were always open being that she was such a popular lady amongst both colored and white folks. The lady was an excellent cook, and it may well have been her delicious food that lured so many visitors to her place. She prepared Irish Potato Hash regularly for "Doc", this being his favorite dish 365 days of the year. "Doc" also loved rice and gravy, and fresh steamed vegetables from his garden. Lillie and her family always had something good to eat in their home, whether it was fresh beef, pork, poultry, seafood or nutritional fruits and vegetables. Whatever the Miller's ate, so did the Harrison's. Generally, on Sundays "Doc" would say to Lillie "I think I have a craving for baked chicken, today. Fix one for us and one for your family." The result would be the best mouthwatering birds either family could sink their teeth into.

Lillie also held the title as the best-dressed colored lady in the community, always looking exclusively fashionable each time she stepped out, which was mainly to church. She probably was the only Negro lady in the whole state of Louisiana who owned a pair of alligator shoes and matching handbag. The envy of onlookers was evident as Lillie strutted her stuff through the doors of the St. James Church of God in Christ—a sanctified church, looking like a cosmopolitan northern city lady. Many of her outfits were tailored by a white seamstress, and were rarely duplicated by others. She also wore stylish clothes from Muller's Department Store of Lake Charles.

On one occasion, while cleaning the study in the Miller estate, Lillie found a snake coiled up in a chair. The poor lady ran out of the house screaming so loudly, she alarmed the entire neighborhood. Frog legs were a no-no in Lillie's kitchen as well. She couldn't stand to see them jump in a skillet of hot grease while they were frying. To sum it all up, Lillie was just an all around, sweet as sugar, colored, trustworthy lady. "Doc" was very trusting of her, too. He would send Lillie to Lake

Charles with weeks of cash earned in his practice for depositing at the Gulf National Bank, and never on a single occasion did he ever come up short or ask her for his deposit ticket.

Simon Harrison, on the other hand, was quite a character himself. He loved to spend his money having a good time, especially on his many excursions to Lake Arthur, Louisiana. Simon often borrowed money from his boss, Lee R. Nunez, because he was too afraid to ask Lillie for cash when he was broke.

In Lillie's eyes, Simon was just what the doctor ordered. Quite an athlete, he played first-base on Frank Reed's colored baseball team, a minor league squad that entertained residents in the area. Nine of Frank Reed's own sons played ball on the same team as Simon.

That rascal could hit a baseball! In almost every game, Simon batted at least one home run to save the day. In addition, to being a boat captain, no one in the area, could out-swim him, or dive like him either. He could swim from shore to shore of the Mermentau River in a flash holding his breathe under water for many seconds without coming up for air. Once on a trip back from Lake Arthur, Simon purchased a quart of boot-leg liquor while he was there. Mr. Nunez wouldn't allow the stuff on the True Friend, so Simon had to sneak the bottle aboard. Before the boat reached the dock, Simon threw the liquor over the side at a point where he could remember to find it later. Once the boat docked, he went back to the very same location, dove in, and found the bottle at the bottom of the river. Simon, unlike Lillie, was Catholic, but rarely attended church. He just simply liked to let the good times roll!

In 1935 Lee Boy's environment allowed him to experience a lifestyle much different from other colored children in the area. Growing up in the heart of the business district of Grand Chenier, amongst the well-to-do white-folks, was an experience within itself. Dr. Compton (a white dentist) and his family lived next door to the Miller Estate to the north. To the west were Mr. and Mrs. Lee R. Nunez. Along the river bank was Joe Jone's home, the first postmaster in the area, who also owned a store. Alcede Miller, Raphael Miller and Paul Nunez all had stores along the shores of the Mermentau. The Immaculate Heart Conception Catholic Church was within walking distance from the Millers. Henry

McCall owned a dock on the riverbank, where the Margie ported. Nuness Miller owned another dock where the Wynnona ported and Paul Nunez's dock serviced the Delta owned by Adam Nunez. Those three boats were the only means in and out of the "island" of Grand Chenier, as most people referred to it before the road from Creole to Lake Charles was constructed. Anything bought or sold in the Grand Chenier area had to have been transported by one of those three boats. The Wynnona was a double decker that mainly transported people to and from Lake Charles. The Margie mostly carried people and cargo, while the Delta made three trips a week to Lake Arthur, taking about four hours each way. The cost was fifty cents for a one way fare, and the patrons had to spend the night because the boats made no return trips until the next day.

Another boat, The Summer Girl, also serviced the Grand Chenier residents. The baseball field where the colored teams played their games was located directly in front of Doc's office on the McCall property. Of course they played only during the daytime because there were no lights available for night activity. Most of the teams they played came from Lake Arthur, down the Mermentau River. Lee's great-great grandmother Seen Mayne lived close by in the same area, where she was employed as a maid by Miss Edna Nunez. Lillie's mother Frances January lived on premises at the "Ol' Captain Miller" place a few blocks away from her job. Frances worked for Randolph Fawvor before gaining full time employment with Mr. and Mrs. Lee R. Nunez, who lived in a moderate four bedroom home. Frances had the responsibility of fixing breakfast and lunch, washing and ironing clothes and doing household chores. She was an excellent cook, and loved to bake. Probably this was where Lillie acquired her incomparable culinary skills. Frances made the most delectable Pecan Crispie Cookies and mouth watering Pineapple Cake, and these became regular Sunday afternoon treats. Frances was like a mother to the Nunez Family.

"Miss Emma," as Frances referred to Mrs. Nunez, was a U. S. Postmaster who took over the job after Joe Jones passed away. The post office had originally been located on the Nunez's front porch. Over a period of time, the mail traffic increased tremendously.

Though this consisted mainly of letters, a very few packages were being sent, nevertheless, the large volume of mail eventually created the need for a larger Post Office. The Nunez's constructed the building in their yard and leased it out to the government. Miss Emma worked along with Jim Bonsall and Bobby Doxey, who mainly delivered the mail in the rural areas. Originally from Jennings, Louisiana, Emma Tabor had come to Grand Chenier aboard the Delta to visit her sister who boarded at Miss Bessie Nunez's place. There she met Lee R. Nunez and afterwards "it was love at first sight." From this union they had three sons: Lee Jr., Garner, and Tommy, all of whom Frances helped raise. Mr. Lee, as Frances referred to him was a hard worker, a good citizen, and a very particular gentleman who wanted everything done right the first time. Mr. Lee drove no other car but a Ford. The Nunez's were Methodist, and boarded area school teachers in their home for the local school system. Both the Miller's and Nunez's were very neighborly and each family loved Frances as well. Lee Boy enjoyed visiting his Grandma Frances. It was a short walk through the yard of the Miller Estate for him to get to the Nunez place. Frances loved her grandson, Lee Boy. Whenever he stopped by for a visit she always had something sweet for him to eat.

As a kid growing up, Lee Boy was one of the first children in the area to get a bicycle. Lillie and Simon purchased him one, which had to be shipped from Lake Arthur. He couldn't wait for it to come in, worrying his parents to death daily until its arrival.

Once he got the bicycle, a white friend named Jennings B. Jones used to chase after him for a ride. One of Lee Boy's most memorable cultural experiences was helping "Doc" mix different types of medicines in his office. Lee Boy was also fascinated with Doc's hand crank telephone located in the estate. In order to ring Doc's phone, one had to turn the crank one full turn and then two short ones. As Lee Boy got older he chaffered the doctor around in his Buick to various Louisiana and Texas cities. Lee Boy even talked different from the other colored kids in the area, simply because his environment dictated a more refined speech. He was a very well dressed kid. Of course Lillie Harrison would have it no other way. She wore the best, so did her son. Exposure to college life occurred when "Doc" had him to drive Te-Cum and a friend, Mage "Shoe Fly" Meaux to Louisiana State University at the start of each semester. The trips allowed Lee Boy an opportunity to experience college atmosphere first hand, as well as to sample amenities offered there. By the time T-Cum started LSU, her sisters Emily and Annie Laurie had already finished college, each with degrees in commerce.

Lee Boy's first real job was with Crain Brothers, a company that manufactured "Marsh Buggies", owned and operated by John Paul Crain. Lee worked as a helper, building and repairing the vehicles whenever they required maintenance. After working with the Crains for a period of time, Lee Boy purchased his first car, a black Plymouth for $600 from Mr. Lee Nunez's brother Ed. Lee Boy was also one of the first colored boys in the area to have his own bank account.

At the age of 19, Lee Boy got another job with his father as Co-captain on the True Friend. He and Simon alternated seven day shifts. The True Friend was a standby boat for the very first platform oil well drilled in the Gulf of Mexico, about a mile and a quarter off the shore of Cameron in block 2. Three oil companies, Pure Oil, Sun Oil, and Superior Oil, were involved in the joint venture. Nine wells were drilled, which included one straight and eight directional holes. The group of wells later produced about 3,000 barrels of oil per day. Soon after working on the "True Friend", Lee purchased, a maroon convertible Chevrolet.

As time went on, he matured into a very handsome, young fellow, who had no other choice but to be a spiffy guy. Lee Boy and his sister Lovenia were not that close growing up as children, simply because she lived in a totally different world than his. They saw each other on occasion; however, when she left Grand Chenier to finish high school at the Sacred Heart Catholic School in Lake Charles, their relationship stagnated. Once Lovenia graduated she moved on to San Francisco, California, to live with Simon's half baby sister Annie and her husband D. Y. Dozier, Will's son.

Even though Wanita and Lee lived on opposite sides of the tracks, it was evident that the two were attracted to each other.

Nevertheless, Lee Johnson Harrison was made of the stuff, that all the colored girls in the lower Cameron Parish area longed for. It would be a question whether or not Wanita Cecil Bartie had a big enough hook to reel him in.

About 5 A.M. on the morning after Nita had gotten her second letter from Lee Boy, Bean was up bright and early. She had to be to work at the Crab Factory in Cameron, promptly at seven o'clock.

Bryant had saved up enough money to purchase the family an old second hand, blue Chevrolet. Nita usually got up early every morning to open the crude barn doors so that her mother could back the car out safely. As she was holding the door, Lee Boy and his mother Lillie passed by on the road headed to Cameron. When Lee Boy saw Nita standing near the barn doors, he started tooting his horn like crazy. Of course Bean questioned his actions.

"Who's that Nita? And why is he blowing his horn out from under the hood of that car?"

"I don't know, Momma."

Bean narrowed her eyes. "He act like he know you from somewhere, the way he blowing that horn."

"It's getting late, Momma. You better hurry up so you can make it to work on time."

"I still wanna know why that boy was makin so much racket when he passed by here."

"We'll talk about it later, when you get home."

"You bet we gonna talk, because you know your daddy don't go for you seeing no boys. You ain't nothin but fourteen years old. So you can just get that ol' mess out of your head right now."

That's exactly what Nita didn't want to hear; not this morning at least. She watched Bean drive away on the dusty shell road.

Suddenly, a thought challenged her mind "I've got to convince Momma to talk to Daddy for me so that Lee can come to visit me soon. Somehow I got to find a way."

Nita rushed into the house, made up the beds, and dressed for school. She put on a white blouse with cotton lace trim and a skirt starched and ironed so stuff it could almost stand up by itself. In a matter of minutes, along came the old yellow school bus.

Cleveland with his usual frown in his forehead, and a slight grin on his face, opened the door. Nita got on the bus first, and he gave her a teasing smile.

"Don't start with me Cleveland because I'm not in the mood for your mess today. Okay?"

Cleveland remained speechless, and waited for Mary, Lil, Lo and Nip to board. Once all of them were on the bus, they journeyed onward to school. As soon as Punkin spotted Nita on campus, he ran over, and handed her a note from Lee Boy which read.

"Keep sweet for me, until I return home next week." Signed Lee J. Harrison

After reading the note, Nita reached down to her ankles and retrieved up her exhilarated heart. Once it was back in place, she clutched her books with both hands across her breast and stared into the blue, picturesque sky above. "At least I have something good that will carry me through the week, until he returns home from the Gulf she thought.

CHAPTER 12

The 1950's cotton season saw it's worst crop ever, due to the infestation of the boll weevil, and a dreadful drought which lasted several months. Though money was very scarce, Bryant wanted to reward his children for their unresentful assistance while laboring so industriously out in the hot cotton fields. In order to accommodate his desire he sought suggestions from the Sears, Roebuck catalog. During the course of scanning many pages, finally a green "army style suit" caught his eye...good for Nita, Mary, Lil and Lo he thought. Investigating further, he found pictures of a white cotton twill shirt and some denim trousers.

"Now let's see, I'll get this for Nip and Ol' Dad." Bean respected his kindhearted intentions, however she insisted that the army green infantry attire was not quite feminine enough for the young ladies. With Bean's persistent influence, Bryant changed his mind, and agreeably decided on a more stylish, feminine garment which Bean felt was sure to bring a smile to each girl's face. Even though Bryant really couldn't afford the purchase, somehow he found a way to come up with the money. The Bartie children appreciated their father's sincere sacrifice, and couldn't wait to wear their new outfits at the start of the school year in the fall.

One of those fall mornings started off with disaccord for Bean, bringing with it some dull, gloomy weather lurking over the sky. "Why should this be a good day anyways, when everything else is wrong?" she thought. With that notion in mind the surroundings quickly became suddenly more dismal, and cloudy. It got so dark, Bean had to put her sewing aside as she couldn't even see how to thread the eye of a needle. She had been working at the Crab Factory in Cameron, about two days a week for some time now. Her boss had promised to increase her work days if the crabs continued to be plentiful like they had been in the past few weeks. All the kids were in school except Walter so her days off were peaceful. Walter had been spending some time with Maw Maw, too, which allowed Bean a well deserved break.

Usually, when the weather got this bad, Bean covered the mirrors in the house immediately with a cotton sheet on the first occurrence of thunder or lightning. This was a family ritual which had been passed down through generations. Afterwards, she would lodge herself in a corner and just sit still, until the storm passed. It was a house rule "never to sit near an open window, for fear of being an easy target from a strike by lightning." Occasionally, she said her rosary aloud, or read the 23rd Psalm to ease the tension before the weather erupted. Nevertheless, for some strange reason today, she felt less fearful than she had been in the past. Instead, she just sat in a corner, and looked about her house as though it was her last time doing so.

A strange indescribable sense overtook her, yielding, concurrently, an unprecedented, empty, repulsive feeling of disappointment, pity and rage.

All of a sudden, a long streak of fierce lighting flashed through the house, at that very moment causing the dark living room to brighten tremendously, breaking her intense concentration.

Frightened by the suddenness, she jerked her head in response to the flash's expeditious presence and departure. Bean jumped up from her seat and lit a holy candle that her mother had recently given to her. She placed it in a living room window sill and watched the light flicker back and forth in conformity with the rhythm of the wind and rain as the gusts blew against the pane. Many thoughts raced through her mind as she reminisced the good and bad times that the family had shared in the old run-down house.

The pouring, wind-driven rain continued to pound on the roof-top, delivering a multitude of noises which sounded like hail on one occasion, and pop corn on another. The throbbing sound changed sporadically, like a pendulum, from vigorous to mild, as the winds blew overhead.

Bean rose from her seat with teary eyes, and disgustingly glanced around the house. Times were even harder than they had been previously for the Bartie family. Looking down at her rough, scarred, worn hands, Bean wondered just how they were going to survive if things didn't improve soon. Bryant was away looking for work because he just wasn't "cutting the mustard" for Mr. Jim Rutherford. Mr. Jim was outraged over the desolate cotton crop harvested this season. Lately, he had been taking his frustrations out on Bryant, who was after all experiencing the same financial instability. Bean was worried sick about her husband. "He's trying so hard, Lord," she thought. "I hope he's okay, out there in this rain on that ol' horse, lookin for work. Ohhh! The thought just sends cold chills all over me just to think about how Missa Jim talk to Bryant like he's some ol' dog. I hope and pray to the Lord, that he'll reap what he sows. It's ashamed for him to treat a grown colored man like my Bryant so dirty."

Once the storm settled down into a light rain, Bean walked over to the window and watched the precipitation fall for several moments. "I guess the storm is just about over now. I wonder were Bryant is? Lord I hope things went good for him today."

Afterwards, Bean turned away from the window, and walked somberly through the house. "I can't believe we been living in this ol' piece-a-junk for so long. We just as well be livin outdoors somewhere." Bean mumbled to herself. "Look-a-there, you can see clean through this ol' floor onto the ground. Ump! And this ol' roof leaks like a basket when it rains." Bean picked up a pale of water, and threw it out the front door. "We been here for so long, till we done got use to it now. Missa Jim know he can patch up this ol' floor for us. But he don't care nothin about no colored folks. That's a shame!!! Things is just gittin worser and worser, around here instead of better. And this ol' place ain't fit for a dog to live in."

Bean continued criticizing the house by finding fault with her own efforts to beautify it. "Look at this ol' Sears, Roebuck catalog paper, falling all off the wall. Ump! The rats and roaches done ate most of what's left of it, anyways. I don't even know why I put it up there in the first place. I guess I wanted to cover up these big ol' cracks right here. Shoot, they hit you right dead in the face, soon as you walk through the door. I don't know myself sometimes, why I even try to fix up this ol' place. It don't do no good, no ways, cause' it still look like the inside of a barn."

She walked into the kitchen where she likewise couldn't find much to praise. "This ol' stove is the ugliest thing I ever seen before in my life. Just to think, it almost burnt up my kids last year. I never really did like using it, but that's all we have, and I gotta make do with it. And look at this ol' piece-a-table and chairs. We ate a lot of meals off there. It's about to fall down, now. Lord knows me and Bryant can do better than this."

Without pausing she found herself in the girls bedroom. "Them girls don't need to be sleepin all on top of one another" she thought, while fluffing the pillows. "They need much more space than this. And that ol' mattress smell like wet duck's feathers every time it rains. I hate that ol' mildewed, damp smell. Pooh! It makes me sick to my stomach. It ain't them girls fault they got to sleep on this ol' mess, but that's all we got."

Finally, in her bedroom she stopped at the door. "Now, this is real pitiful. And just think, them two boys gotta sleep up in here with me and Bryant, cause' we ain't got enough room for them nowhere else. They ought to have they own room too, and not be stuck up in here with they momma and daddy. Just what do ol' Missa Jim think, anyways? Treating Bryant like some ol' stray dog.

He ain't gotta take that mess no more. I don't know what we going to do, but we gotta find a way to do better than this."

Once Bean had mentally torn apart the interior of the farm house, she fantasized over what it would be like to live in a place that was more pleasing to her own tastes. "One of these days, I'm gonna have me a beautiful home" she smiled. "With lots of pretty furniture, and enough rooms for my girls and boys to have they own. Oh yeah, and a big ol' nice kitchen like Momma's got with a great big ol' stove. I can't wait till we get out of this shack. You hear me Lord? I can't wait. I'm tired of this ol' white man's foolishness. I'm tired of it!" Bean found herself standing again in the kitchen with both arms extended to the ceiling. "I'm tired, Lord!! Lord, I'm tired of this! Please Lord, help Bryant find him a good job, so we can all get out of this hole we livin in." Bean pulled her arms down, slowly. She covered her face, and fell to her knees crying out, "Please help us Lord. I beg you. Please," she said in a whisper, "Help us real soon."

Afterwards Bean got up with a sigh of relief, feeling somehow that she'd at least released some of her frustration. Within a moment, however an angry knock almost broke the door in from the other side. A few seconds of silence raced by. Then a second set of knocks blared out much harder, and louder than the first. Bean rushed to the front door to see just what the problem was. She sensed that a very disgruntled person was out there, so she called through the door before opening it.

"Who is it?" she demanded.

"Open up this damn door, Bean, it's Jim Rutherford."

Bean pulled the door open, immediately.

"Yeah Sir, can I help you?"

"Where the hell is Bryant, at?" shouted Mr. Jim.

"He ain't home, right now" she answered adamantly.

"Where the hell is he then?"

"I already said he ain't home, and I don't know where he at."

"Oh no?"

"No Sir. I done told you once."

"I know you know where he's at, Gal. Now who you think you foolin? When I needs him, I need him right now. Not tomorrow, not yesterday, or the day before, but now, and when I say now, I mean now. Do I make myself clear?"

Bean steaming, said not a word. She glared back at Mr. Jim with repulsive eyes, and stood her ground.

"I'm gonna ask you one more time, Gal, where the hell is Bryant?"

Bean put her hands on her hip. "I done told you once, I don't know where he at," she shook her head with each word. "And I'm not gonna say it again."

"Oh yeah, so you don't know, huh? Well, I want you to tell him one thing for me when he gets home. You tell him that Mr. Jim said he wants all ya'll niggers off this property pretty damn quick. Okay? You tell that nigger that for me when he comes back. You hear me?" Mr. Jim pointed his finger in Bean's face.

Bean was furious. This time when she spoke, she didn't bite her tongue. She looked him straight in the eyes without blinking, and said "That's fine, Missa Jim, cause it's your house. But you know something? You can have this ol' raggedy shack, cause' it ain't fit for a dog to live in noways."

Mr. Jim was speechless. His complexion turned red as a crawfish. He walked off with Bean shouting to the back of his head.

"And another thing Missa Jim. You must think we's a buncha cows out in the pasture somewhere. You treat some of your own cattle better than you do us."

Mr. Jim kept on walking, pretending not to hear her remarks. He knew Bryant was out looking for work elsewhere, which caused his resentful attitude. Bean, clearly temporarily insane at this point, kept yelling at the top of her lungs.

"We might be colored, but we's worth much more than this ol' trash you got us livin in! You can have it! We don't need nothin from you no more!"

Mr. Rutherford slunk away, and Bean felt relieved, but figured that the comments had only made matters worse. During those times, such verbiage from Negroes was literally not tolerated by too many white people. Still, she'd held onto her dignity and pride, and had waited a long time to speak those words. And at least for once in her life she'd stood up for her husband, herself and her family.

The poor, fed-up woman realized, however, that the family had no other choice but to move. Bean paced the floors back and forth until Bryant came home. When he arrived after dark, she told him about the unpleasant conversation with Mr. Jim. Bryant didn't waste much time talking about the situation. He immediately walked over to Jim Rutherford's home without an inkling as to what he would say or how to approach the situation. One thing was for sure, he didn't appreciate the manner in which Mr. Jim spoke to his wife. "What ever your will is Lord, let it be done," Bryant said. "I'm puttin every thing in your hands." He walked along the shell road, up to Mr. Jim's place and knocked on the back door.

"Who the hell's out there?" Mr. Jim lashed out.

"It's me, Bryant, Sir!"

Mr. Jim opened the door at once. "Oh I see you bouta day late," he said sarcastically.

"Missa Jim, I knows you mad cause' Bean done told me. But I got six kids, and a wife to feed and I---------"

"You shut up your mouth nigger. I don't care nothin about your problems. I got problems of my own. Ain't you supposed to be workin for me, and not everybody else in Creole?"

"But Sir, I can't--------- "

"I don't want to hear your complaining, Bryant. Haven't I been good to ya'll niggers?"

"Yeah Sir, and we's thankful Sir. But that ain't gonna put no more food on my table."

"I don't give a damn about what it ain't gonna do. I just want ya'll niggers off my property, and pretty damn quick. You hear me, boy?"

"Na-Na-Na-Na wha-wha-wha we supposed to do. Sir? You know we ain't got nowhere else to go."

"That sounds like a personal problem to me. You should've thought about that, when you was running all around town trying to work for everybody else but me."

"But Missa Jim, can you please give me just a little time to find us another place?"

"Hell no, boy! Who do you think I am? You ain't gonna pull that stuff with me!"

"Missa Jim, I been with you for a long time and I done worked my fingers to the bone for you and your family. I can't believe you gonna treat us like this."

"Well Bryant, finally you're smart enough to figure something out on your own. That'll teach you the next time from running all over the place looking for another job. You should've been satisfied. But no! My place wasn't good enough for you. That's what's wrong with ya'll colored boys. A white man'll give you niggers a inch, and ya'll will try to take a mile every time. Hell, no!

I'm giving you to the end of this week, and Boy I want you off my property. And if you ain't gone by then, I'll see that the Law removes you, them nigger kids and smart mouth wife of yours, and all ya'lls belongings. You hear me Nigger?"

"Okay Missa Jim. But you know something you don't have to call me and my family no niggers. You see I's a proud, honest colored man. I might not have much learning, but I works hard to take care of my family. And you know something, Sir, sometimes a man gotta do what he supposed to do, whether he colored or white. If you want us to leave, we'll go. We ain't got much choice.

But you see Missa Jim, I knows a man, who sits high and he looks low." Bryant became a bit emotional at this point. His hands and voice trembled slightly as he spoke. "You see Sir, God ain't gonna let me and my family fall. He ain't never done it yet. Suddenly, Bryant's emotions switched from sentimental to irate. "Now let me git one thing straight with you, Sir. As long as you live, don't you ever, never call me, my wife or my children a nigger, again. And I mean that Sir! Just cause' I'm colored, don't mean I ain't a man!!"

Bryant turned and walked away. Mr. Jim just stood in his doorway, overwhelmed by Bryant's actions. He watched him walk into the dark night.

As he went inside his house, Mr. Jim thought out loud. "I don't know what's come over these niggers, now days. They used to not talk back to white folks like that, but darn near all of um is down right smart mouthed. I just don't know what this world is coming to, especially when a nigger talks that way to a white man. That's okay by me, Bryant Bartie, cause' you the one's gonna fall flat on your face. And when you do, you better not turn to me for no help, Boy! Ump! We'll see if your God can save your black behind then!!!"

* * *

As soon as Bryant returned home, he informed Bean and the children that they would have to move real soon. Bean had already knew the consequences at hand, however the children really didn't comprehend the bad news at first. Nita and Mary were disappointed because they didn't understand the whole content of the situation.

They only realized that they were going to miss seeing Annie, though they'd still have an opportunity to see her at school. Many fond and spirited memories had been shared at the Rutherfords place nevertheless, those times were about to end. It was time for the Bartie's to move on with their lives. It was unfortunate that life in that old house had to end in such an abrupt, harsh manner, but that was life in 1950 for a poor colored family in southwest Louisiana. "Sometimes a man's gotta do what he's supposed to" Bryant repeated to his family. "Even when the storms of life might be blowing real hard and hope ain't nowhere in sight."

After an extended search for another residence Bryant found the family an old, dilapidated, unpainted rent house west of the swing gate off the Front Ridge Road, not far from Maw-Maw and Paw-Paw's place. Although the interior reminded them a lot of the Rutherford's farm shack, they dared not allow such an agonizing recollection an opportunity to impair their perspective on their new living environment. At least this place would provide the Bartie's with a fresh beginning, something they really needed at this point in their lives.

Bryant moved what little makeshift furniture they owned to the new place by horse and wagon. Everything else was transported in the Chevrolet. One positive thing that came out of the move was the fact that this house was much larger than the previous one. Nita and Mary shared a bedroom together, Lil and Lo occupied another, and Nip and

Walter slept on cots in Bean and Bryant's room. The house even came equipped with a larger kitchen, which made Bean tickled pink. The living room was good sized as well, and a porch ran all across the entire front of the grayish homely domicile. An old, dull looking barn could be found out back and of course the children loved to play in there. Lil, Lo and Mary named the house "The Grey Derby" because of the fact it hadn't seen a good coat of paint in quite a few years. In just a few months everyone adjusted well to their new quarters especially the kids. The children enjoyed watching the white caps on the Gulf of Mexico roll into shore.

They'd always had an inexplicable fascination with the Gulf, and now that they lived closer to it, their fondness increased even more.

When they first moved in, "The Grey Derby" didn't have any electricity, but that wasn't the case for long. Bean and Bryant had adjusted well to Nita's boyfriend, Lee J. Harrison, and he'd learned the electrical trade while working offshore on an oil rig. Lee-Boy wired the entire house so the family could hook up to the local utility company, and Bryant got a kick out of touching a switch and having a light appear right before his face. Lee's electrical capabilities definitely increased his brownie points with Bryant, and the Barties began to allow him to visit Nita more and more often.

Bean got more days work at the Crab Factory in Cameron, Bryant landed a seasonal full time job at the Swindell Pogy Plant and things began to look up for the entire family. On one occasion after work, when Bean was headed home, she stopped by the Roger's Grocery Store in Cameron to pick up some items for the evening meal. A nice white lady from Pearl River, Louisiana by the name of Miss Bessie Terry approached Bean in need of a cook for her cafe. After a few minutes of conversing, Bean's and Miss Terry's spirits connected and instantly, right there on the spot, Miss Terry offered Bean the job. She accepted at once and became the first colored cook to ever work in the all white establishment.

Bean felt like a new person with a new lease on life. Finally, she could see her family making gradual headway in a positive direction. The determined woman began to save her pennies monthly, and started fixing up "The Grey Derby" with new furniture, draperies and bedding.

Her concerted efforts produced a complete makeover for the interior. Thanks to Bean's authentic taste, and decorative ability the old house may have resembled a shack from the road, but inside it was fit for a king. This had been something she'd always dreamed of accomplishing.

Once the family moved to "The Grey Derby", Nita maintained her job at Miss Delia's. She worked one evening per week, spending the night with Mr. and Mrs. Ennis Andrews who lived near by. Bryant got their permission for Nita to do so because his and Bean's work schedules were too irregular for them to provide her transportation to and from work. Mrs. Andrews was an overly-protective, proper-speaking, strict old lady who Nita addressed as "Miss Rosa".

Nita and Lee's relationship had continued to blossom as the months rolled by, and Lee soon knew Nita's schedule like his own. On one occasion he decided to stop by at the Andrews house once Nita got off work. Unfortunately, he decided to do so unannounced.

Miss Rosa met him at the door, which she blocked with authority. Nita, who'd just come in from Miss Delia's, could only wait in the next room, listening with her ear to the wall as Lee Boy discovered his blunder.

"May I help you son? Miss Rosa asked, as though to say now just what are you doing on my doorstep, anyways?

"How are you doing Miss Rosa?"

"I'm fine" she responded, without cracking a smile.

"I, I'm here to see Nita" Lee said, a bit shyly.

"I beg your pardon?"

"I'm sorry, Ma'am. May I please come in, and visit Nita for a short moment? Please?"

Miss Rosa stood with one arm crossed over the other, looking Lee directly in his eyes. "Certainly not. I cannot allow this young lady to have no company while she is under my care. The best thing you can do young man is to go on home."

Lee's face turned beet red.

"Now, you can visit her when she's at her Momma and Daddy's house, but you're not gonna visit her when she's here with me. NO SIR!"

Lee turned and walked quickly away, without a word. Miss Rosa, her nose pointed up in the air, bowed politely and said "And you do have a good evening, young man." She watched Lee walk all the way to his car and then closed the door once he drove away.

Nita stayed in her room pretending she knew nothing of the visit. Miss Rosa later told her husband Ennis about the incident.

"Yeah, he thought he was gonna come on in here, and see Wanita, but I got him straight right at the front door, and sent him on home. The idea of such a thing." The couple both laughed throughout the night, each time the thought of Lee Boy's visit surfaced in their thoughts.

More so than ever, Nita continued to carry on her motherly instincts towards the younger Bartie children. Especially since Bean and Bryant were away most of the time working. As she was the oldest, a lot of times the other children were left in her care. Nita's youngest brother, Walter, now four years old, had developed an affinity for dogs. He had an ol' dog that followed him everywhere he went. If the family didn't know were Walter was, all they had to do was look for the dog and the two of them were sure to be in each other's company. Walter was a good child, outside of the fact that he wet the bed frequently. This really disturbed Nita, as she had to clean up his mess. Otherwise, he really never gave the family much trouble.

The last time he'd had an accident, Nita had threatened him with a spanking if he did it again. But, sure enough this particular morning Walter awakened and found himself in a puddle of urine.

He got so scared, he ran out the house and hide in the barn, knowing Nita was going to be very upset once she found out.

While in the barn, Walter fell asleep on a sack of feathers that Bryant had been saving to make pillows. When Nita discovered the mess he made in the bed, she became furious, but she couldn't find him anywhere. If she'd known where to find him, she probably would have let him have it right there on the spot, but Nita looked all throughout the house, including under the bed, and Walter was no where in sight.

Nita went outside and yelled for him, but still there was no sign of the boy anywhere.

"I wonder where that rascal is ?" she thought. "He's gonna really get it, when I find him because I done told him already about wetting in the bed. Shoots, I'm tired of cleaning the mattress, washing his sheets and then hanging them out to dry. Walter! Walter!" she yelled again.

But Nita soon panicked after she'd been searching for awhile. She didn't know what to think. "Oh, I hope the little fellow didn't go to the Gulf, alone," she said out loud. The mere thought of a four year old being out by the rough waters created more anxiety than Nita could stand. She looked every where. She even asked the other children if they'd seen Walter, but no one knew exactly where he was.

She kept on searching, until finally she saw his dog lying down in front of the barn. When she got closer, the dog got up, and went inside. "Walter? Walter!" yelled out Nita. She followed the ol' dog into the barn, and there Walter was, asleep on a sack of feathers.

"There you are. Oh thank God" she said with a sigh of relief. But the boy didn't move. When Nita tried to get close to him, the dog suddenly attacked, and bit her several times on the arm. Nita, startled ran out the barn with blood gushing out all over her clothes and herself.

When she reached the house, she told Bean about her attack. Her mother paused long enough to clean Nita's wounds with peroxide and put some medication and bandages on them. Though worried stiff about her youngest child's safety, Bean went to the barn and tried to retrieve him, herself.

The ol' dog gritted his teeth at her, as soon as she got close. Bean just witnessed what happened to Nita, and didn't want to be victim number two. Instead, she snuck around the barn and entered from the back, very carefully, so the dog couldn't see her.

She grabbed an old stick lying near some hay and poked the boy on his shoulder to try and wake him from his sleep. It took several attempts, but finally he awakened. On the way home, Bean walked ahead of Walter and the dog because the animal wouldn't allow her to get close to him.

Nita showed Walter what his dog had done, but from that point, on she never threatened to spank him for wetting the bed again; at least not as long as the dog was nearby. Everyone concluded that dog was Walter's guardian angel.

The weeks of the school year flew by, and all the children did exceptionally well in their respective grades along the way. Times at "The Grey Derby" had gotten a whole lot better, too, particularly, since the installation of the electrical lights. Studying became a much more enjoyable task, compared to yester years of reading and doing homework by a kerosene lamp. Lee Boy was drafted into the armed forces, however and Nita became a very lonely teenager. His absence made it difficult for her to concentrate on school work, do household chores, or even make important decisions about her future. Lee's mother, Lillie, almost had a fit when she first heard of the news of his being drafted. It was a good thing Lillie's heart was strong as it had been, she probably would have been stricken with an attack right there on the spot.

The United States was involved in the "Korean Conflict" at the time of Lee's military conscription, and he was stationed at Camp Chaffee, Arkansas. Nita feared for his life daily. Lillie lost a lot of weight, and wasn't quite as sociable as she had been in the past, mainly due to the fact that her only son was being trained to fight in a war that could possibly take him overseas to a foreign land. She often stayed down on bended knees, praying to the Lord for his safekeeping while he was away at boot camp.

Lee Boy wrote to Nita almost every day. She made it a point to be first in line to collect the letters from the box on the scheduled days that the mail ran. The box was located at The Front Ridge Road, approximately a quarter of a mile east of the "The Grey Derby". She enjoyed the walk to and from there as it allowed an opportunity to read Lee's letters privately, being that this year was one of high anxiety for the perplexed teenager. At the mere age of fifteen, a lot of changes were taking place in Nita's life. The young man she fell so deeply in love with was many, many miles away. She also had to deal with the fact that, if other arrangements were not made for the 1951 fall semester the end of the school year could very' well be her last opportunity to attend public school.

Unfortunately, Cameron Consolidated School was not certified to promote any students further than the tenth grade. It had always been Nita's dream to finish high school and continue on to college, thanks to Miss Hayward and Miss Mack, those ladies who'd been so inspirational in keeping the young lady focused in the right direction. If Nita was to achieve her goal of attaining a high school diploma, her only choice would be to move away from Creole.

The problem was her parents really couldn't afford to send her away. What was she to do? And who would she turn to for guidance? During the course of Lee's absence, instead of releasing the overwhelming stress, she kept a lot of emotions bottled up inside. Nevertheless, Nita realized that she was too talented, and too smart to let her qualities fall by the wayside. In order to deal with the crisis, she resorted to prayer for direction, and left everything in God's hands. "Lord, I need you more than ever in my life now. I can't handle this all by myself was her nightly prayer. Nita had no other choice but to remain spiritual. This was the only antidote to get her through this ambiguous storm, whirling through her mind.

CHAPTER 13

Things have a way of working out for those who love the Lord, particularly if one believes and remains positive. Wanita Cecil Bartie did not let an overbearing altercation restrain her ambitions of moving ahead in life.

Nita's consistent perseverance allowed her to enroll at the Booker T. Washington Senior High School in Houston, Texas, during the summer of 1951. Enthused and motivated about completing her education, she studied diligently and earned enough credits to complete the eleventh grade at the end of the term. The fall of the very same year found her as a senior at the distinguished, culturally oriented, predominately Negro, Phillis Wheatley Senior High School, located in the heart of Houston's fifth ward. All this was thanks to Lee J. Harrison. His stay in the armed forces turned out to be a very short one due to an honorable discharge, mainly because of his affiliation with the oil industry. Wanita had been corresponding with him regularly, so he was well informed of her determination to obtain a diploma. When he returned home from Camp Chaffee, Arkansas, the first thing he did was to communicate her dilemma to a relative living in Houston. It was through his efforts that she was able to get past a major obstacle tarnishing her dream of becoming the first Bartie in her immediate family to graduate from high school.

After receiving Bryant's approval and blessings, Lee made arrangements with his mother's sister, Ethel Mae, and her husband, Adolph Dozier. They agreed wholeheartedly for Wanita to board in their home so she'd have a chance to complete her final year in high school.

Slowly all her dreams were becoming a reality. Before Wanita's move to Houston, Lee gave her a ring. He'd confronted Bryant after a church service one Sunday to seek his permission for her to wear it. Bryant's blunt response was "I don't mind her wearing it. But plague-take-it she's gonna finish high school before she can get married, Son!"

Being that she was a poor sharecropper's daughter from southwest Louisiana, who knew only life on a farm and in the cotton fields of a segregated southern town, Wanita's matriculation proved to be a difficult one. Moving to Houston was quite a cultural shock, as she had to adapt to and keep stride with a new lifestyle in a thriving metropolis. The city was very fast paced to say the least. It had several tall buildings in it's vibrant downtown area, concrete everywhere, streetcars, and even traffic lights: all of which Wanita was completely unaccustomed to. The biggest challenge that stood before her, however was being able to compete with a variety of students from different cultural backgrounds and economic standards. She was exposed to students whose parents were doctors, lawyers, pharmacists, educators and clergymen. The language of Houston was much more upscale than the country jargon she spoke. Wanita had to be very conscious of her articulation and diction. It was a personal aspiration not to let her accent be viewed as a crutch, simply because it caused her to stand out like a sore thumb. Instead, she worked hard to refine her speech, so she could fit in with the rest of her more polished peers. On many occasions she reminisced about her Creole yesteryears, recalling how she, her sisters and brothers used to ride on their father's open buggy, back before Bryant was even able to think about purchasing the family's first car. It amazed her the way that life brought about changes. Now, she lived in a society were automobiles were a commonality, and street cars available for those a little less fortunate. Wanita didn't let the fast pace or refinement of the city threaten her will to succeed. She took advantage of every opportunity placed before her, never once forgetting nor being ashamed of her heritage or background. She strove forward, smoothing out many jagged edges that stood before her, while adapting to life's adversities.

"I guess we never really had a decent place to live in, much less a nice family car" she thought. "But those things are just materialistic. The most important thing is for me to set an example for my younger sisters and brothers, so that maybe someday they can complete their education like me. Daddy always said an education is something no one can take from you. I've got to get mine. I have no other choice."

Ethel and Adolph Dozier lived in a one-bedroom apartment in "The Courts" on Pannell Street, several blocks from Market Street were Phillis Wheatley High School was. The place had a small kitchen and a combined living and dining room where Wanita slept.

One house rule everyone had to abide by was to be up early each morning in order to make it to their destination on time. Adolph (generally known as "Tug") worked as a stevedore for the Missouri Pacific Railroad Company in downtown Houston. Ethel, known by everyone as "Mae," was employed as a private home domestic worker for Mr. and Mrs. Eugene Shepherd, who lived on Binz Street in the section of town called "Sugar Hill". Mr. Shepherd was the president of the Falstaff Beer, Co., and Mrs. Shepherd a housewife. Mae's duties included washing clothes, ironing, and household cleaning—all for three dollars a day. She'd been a mere fourteen years old when she left Grand Chenier, after marrying Adolph on October 26, 1932. The Shepherd's were one of the first families she worked for. Mae heard of the opportunity through a neighbor who lived in "The Courts." Mrs. Shepherd exhibited a great deal of patience after hiring Mae, as the girl from Grand Chenier really knew nothing about house cleaning. Mrs. Shepherd taught Mae to improve her domestic skills. The previous maid had been fired because she was not reliable or dependable, creating the opportunity for Mae. One thing was for certain: Mae was very prompt and rarely missed a day's work all of which kept her employer very happy. Leaving home at such a young age hadn't helped her situation much, however she'd learned a lot of things through trial and error. Somehow, thanks to her husband's assistance, Mae managed to keep pace with the big city life. Tug took Mae under his wings and helped her to mature into a well dressed, well groomed "lady", to say the least. Both he and Mae wore the finest clothes they could afford. The Doziers always looked like they were worth millions each time they stepped out. Mae was a well-shaped, stunning, brown skinned woman, who turned a lot of heads with her captivating walk. One evening, on an excursion to "The Harlin Grill" in the Fourth Ward, a colored police officer directing traffic saw her approaching West Dallas Street. He immediately blew his whistle to halt the traffic, then motioned for Mae to cross the street. He just wanted to get one more long, good stare at her coke bottle shape and that exaggerated walk, as she glided across the street with grace and style. Tug was a neatly groomed, proud brown skin fellow, who's pet peeve was to wear nothing cheap. "If you gotta buy just one dress a year, don't let it be nothing cheap," he always told Mae. Their jaunty demeanors transferred over to their home as well. The Doziers didn't own much, but what little they did have, they took very good care of keeping their place very neat and orderly.

The first day of school for Wanita at Wheatley was quite a day to reckon with to say the least. She awakened bright and early, barely sleeping the night before due to the excitement and anticipation of going to a new school. Tug was first to leave as he had to be at work by six o'clock. Mae wasn't too far behind, leaving in plenty enough time to catch the seven o'clock streetcar. Before she left the apartment, she peeped in on Nita, who was in the bathroom washing her face.

"Now you sure, you know how to get to Wheatley, Nita?"

"Yes Ma'am" she responded.

"Do you need anything before I go? Need some money?"

"No Ma'am."

"All right. You have a good day and study hard. I'll see you when I get back home from work. Be careful and don't talk to no strangers on your way to school. Oh! And don't get into nobody's car either. Houston's a bad place. It ain't like it is back home. You got to be real careful out here, cause' it's dangerous."

"Okay, Aunt Mae. I won't."

Mae rushed out of the house in a fast walk. Nita was still primping in front of the bathroom mirror. She wanted to look extra special today, since she'd be the new kid on the block at Wheatley. The innocent little country girl chose a lavender dress and a pair of strapped sandals, and did everything possible to make her hair fall into a "page boy" style. Nevertheless, it appeared to be a bad hair day, because the only thing it did was frizz up. Nita was considered to be a pretty young lady in the country environment from whence she came, but she'd soon find the girls in the city were several steps ahead of her when it came to appearance.

As soon as she was dressed, she sat down at the table and ate grits, eggs and bacon for breakfast all of which Mae had left in the oven, covered with foil paper. So excited about the first day of school, Nita only picked over her food, hardly eating any of it.

When she finished, she threw most of it away and rinsed the plate in the sink. She washed and dried her hands, brushed her teeth, grabbed her notebooks and pencils and strolled out the door not knowing what the day would bring. On the way, she saw several students who appeared to be high school aged walking in the same direction. "I guess they're on their way to Wheatley" she thought. She extended them a smile, but they ignored her cordiality and kept on walking as though she didn't exist. "Well that's okay. They don't know me anyway. Maybe they'll be friendlier, once I get to school." As Nita continued down the sidewalk, she noticed a distinct difference between the students in Houston and those back home in Creole. Most of them were very well dressed and the girls looked like they'd just come from the beauty shop that morning. Once Nita got to the steps of Wheatley, she stood for a moment in awe. It was a huge new school, and almost triple the size of Cameron Consolidated. Inside the student council was on duty in the hallways, making sure the flow of students in different directions stayed consistent and precise. Nita asked one of the councilmen for directions to the principal's office. "Keep straight down the hall, look to your left, and you'll see it after you past the water fountain" he pointed. Once there, the counselor was very cooperative in helping Nita select the required core courses she needed to graduate in the spring. Once she finished getting her records validated, it was off to Mr. Bank's first period math class, already in progress. "Come on in and have a seat" said Mr. Banks, so Nita found herself a seat all the way in the back of the class.

"What is your name?"

"Wanita Cecil Bartie, Sir!"

"Wanita?"

"Yes Sir."

"My that's a pretty name. Um! You don't look familiar. Have you always attended Wheatley?"

"No Sir. I'm originally from Creole, Louisiana and I last attended Cameron Consolidated School before completing my junior year this summer at Booker T. Washington High here in Houston."

"Booooooo" said the class. "Hee, hee!"

"I see. Welcome, my dear. I hope your senior year here at Wheatley will be a pleasurable one. Class let's welcome Wanita Cecil Bartie."

No one responded to Mr. Banks' kind gesture, though. Everyone just looked at Wanita peculiarly. Afterwards the comments began to flutter. "Girl, look at her. Uh! She got to be from the country" said one snobby young lady. "And look at them ol' pitiful lookin shoes" said another. "And will you look at that barnyard dress" responded someone else. "Lord that hair don't look like it's seen a straightening comb in years" said another egotistical female as she shook her own. A few of the boys turned and looked at Wanita, laughing while they stared. She fought to hold back the tears. The poor little country girl thought she'd looked admirable when she left home that morning. Her new classmates confirmed however, that she clearly did not measure up to their metropolitan standards.

Mr. Banks sensed Wanita's feelings were affected, ceased the continuous flow of snide remarks. "Now class is that the way we treat a new student here at Phillis Wheatley Senior High?" Most of the students rang out again, collectively, with laughter. Mr. Banks was furious. "All right class that is enough of that triviality.

"Quiet, please," he shouted. Then, sternly, without cracking a smile he added "Where ignorance is bliss, Tis folly to be wise." At this point, if a pin dropped all the students were sure to hear it. "This is no place for your foolishness and I will not tolerate it. Some of you ought to be ashamed of yourselves for such stupidity. Wanita, you may take a seat here in the front."

"That's okay, Mr. Banks, I'm fine right here" she said, with her head buried behind a math book.

"Are you sure you don't want to sit near the front?"

"No Sir. I'm fine right here" she responded timidly.

"Okay class just for that nonsense, I'm assigning homework on the first day of school. I want you to complete all of the problems at the end of chapter one."

"But Mr. Banks—" said one girl.

"That ol' thang sittin over there caused this mess!" said another.

"Don't you Mr. Banks me. You all better have your homework done tomorrow" he ordered. "And correctly!"

No other comments surfaced after his statement. Everyone began thumbing through the first chapter. Wanita sat in her seat and mentally tore herself apart. "I don't know why I wanted to come to this ol' school anyway. I wish I was back home with Mary and the others. At least at Cameron Consolidated no one made fun of the way I dressed or looked." Suddenly though, a positive voice interceded from out of nowhere. "Okay Nita, get a hold of yourself girl. Don't let negative comments stand in the way of you reaching your goals. No one ever said it was going to be easy. Now you get it together, young lady, and don't worry about what they say. You know you're smart, and you'll make it through this storm."

Once the school bell rang concluding the first period, Wanita waited in her seat until the room cleared out completely before getting up to proceed on to her second period class. Mr. Banks observed her delayed reaction, and met her on her way out.

"Wanita, I must say that I really admire you for striving to get your high school diploma. The counselor has informed me of your circumstances. Most of the people who laughed at you in here today really don't understand the sacrifice you're going through to complete high school."

Wanita smiled bashfully and said "thank you Sir" in a whisper.

"It says a lot about your character and determination. Always remember one thing; don't ever be ashamed of who you are or where you've come from. Just keep the faith and you will succeed at anything you attempt in life. Keep your mind focused. Outer beauty is only skin deep. It's the inner qualities that really count."

Nita exited the classroom with a small tear in the corner of her right eye. Mr. Banks walked back to the front of the room and erased the blackboard.

Wanita searched for her next class with a bowed head, too ashamed to look anywhere but down as she passed through the hall. But one young lady had noticed how the other classmates ostracized her earlier. When this girl saw Wanita, she rushed over, immediately.

"Hello, my name is Verda Mae Deavers" she said with an extended hand.

Wanita was a bit apprehensive but did remember how Verda Mae had been the only person in the class who'd extended some warmth towards her.

"Hi" responded Wanita, in a soft timid tone.

"I understand you're from Louisiana?" said Verda Mae.

"Yes I am."

"Well, how long have you been living in Houston?"

"About four months."

"How do you like Wheatley, so far?"

"I don't know. I mean—I guess it's all right."

"Listen, there's no need for an explanation. I do understand. I mean, I know some of the others in class was kinda harsh, but honestly, I do want to be your friend. You appear to be a very genuine person. Why don't you join me for lunch? That way we can get to know each other better."

"Are you sure you want to be seen with me, Verda Mae? I mean, I don't want to cause you any trouble."

"Trouble?" Verda Mae cracked a smile. "Are you crazy girl?"

"No. But—"

"Then what's the matter?"

"Okay. Okay, Verda Mae. That'll be fine."

"Good. I'll see you at twelve noon. Meet me in the cafeteria. Okay?"

"Okay—I will. Thanks so much."

At least Wanita felt a whole lot better after meeting Verda Mae. She needed a shoulder to cry on, especially after her demeaning experience in the math class. Nita's next classes weren't as traumatic as the first period. As a matter of fact, the day softened as it went along. Nita made it to the cafeteria and, while waiting in line to be served, spotted Verda Mae. The girl had already, found the two of them a seat. Another young lady saw Nita and approached her from behind.

"Hi. You must be Nita" she said joyfully.

"Yes," responded Wanita, a bit puzzled.

"You don't remember me?" the girl asked, nodding her head as though Wanita should know who she was.

"Kinda. Sort of. But I've forgotten your name."

"Girl, I'm Gloria. Gloria Dozier."

"Gloria Dozier? Let me see. The name sounds familiar, but—"

"You don't remember me? We met this summer at Uncle Tug's house. I'm his niece. Him and my daddy are brothers. Remember?"

"What's your daddy's name?"

"Bishop. Bishop Dozier!"

"Oh! Now I remember you. I forgot you told me that you attended Wheatley. I guess it just slipped my mind."

"Yeah girl, nothin but the big Wheatley. Where you sittin for lunch?"

"Right over there with my friend Verda Mae. Do you know her?"

"Sure do!"

"Would you like to join us for lunch?"

"Love to girl."

"Good. I'm so glad to see you, Gloria."

"Me too. So, how's everything going so far on your first day?"

"I'm too afraid to say. I mean. After my math class this morning, I thought about going back home to Louisiana."

"What you mean by that?"

"Well, there were some girls in my class that made fun of my clothes, my shoes and my hair."

"Who were they, Nita?" Gloria asked, gritting her teeth.

"Girl, I don't know them. All I know is they were very pretty and every strand of their hair fell into place, especially compared to this moss sitting on top of my head."

"Oh, girl, don't say nothin crazy like that. You're a very pretty girl. Now you know they had to find something wrong with the new girl on the block. These Texas girls are something else. They see you have a lot of potential—and you do—they gonna try to cut you down to the ground just to make themselves look good. Nita don't worry about them. We gonna fix um. I'm gonna take you to my hairdresser, myself. She'll fix you up real pretty. Then let's see what they have to say."

"Will you really, Gloria?"

"Yeah girl, she'll have you lookin like you belong on the cover of Ebony Magazine."

"Well I don't know, Gloria. I mean, I don't have that much money. So—"

"So what? It don't cost much, girl. We can go after school tomorrow. She's closed on Mondays."

"Gee! Thanks Gloria. I'll tell Aunt Mae when I get home after school. Thanks so much!"

"Girl, you my kin people. I'm supposed to look out for you. I bet when she gets finished with your head you ain't gonna recognize your own self. Now who you say them ol' girls was?"

"I don't know them."

"Well don't you worry about them no more. I'm gonna get you all fixed up girl."

Wanita and Gloria joined Verda Mae at the lunch table, and after conversing with the two young ladies, Wanita regained her self-confidence. Gloria was a very popular girl: a majorette in the marching band, association with her could only increase Wanita's popularity as well.

Wanita's last class for the day was Speech with Mr. Olivier. Again, she sat as far back as she could in the classroom. When Mr. Olivier saw her, he walked over. "Now tell me something, why is a pretty young lady like you sitting all the way in the back of my class?"

Wanita responded with shrugged shoulders.

"I tell you what, you appear to have a lot of potential. I want you to do the first oration before the class this afternoon."

"Who me?" responded a doubtful Wanita. Her heart pulsated instantaneously.

"Yes you, Wanita. Come along to the front of the class. Okay class, Wanita Bartie is going to do an interpretive reading of

"Judgment Day" by James Weldon Johnson. I would like your undivided attention focused on her at this time. All right Wanita you may begin."

Before Wanita read, she said "Mr. Olivier, may I recite it? I've committed "Judgment Day" to memory."

"Splendid! I prefer you to" responded an excited Mr. Olivier.

"You may begin!"

Wanita stood before the class, perfectly posed, and began her rendition of "Judgment Day". She spoke with such clarity, articulation, enunciation and eloquence—thanks to Miss Myron Haywood, who tolerated nothing less than the best when reciting—that the entire class was overwhelmed. At the conclusion, Mr. Olivier was so impressed that he stood up and applauded.

"Bravo! Bravo! Magnificent!" The rest of the class followed his lead. "You must try out for the debate team, young lady" he commanded. "You must!"

Wanita felt absolutely grand after receiving so many wonderful compliments for her efforts. What a way to redeem herself, after everything that had happened. If only "the math class snobs" could have been present to hear her interpretation.

She could hardly wait to get home and share both the good and bad news with Mae. After she finished recapping the day's events, Mae got an idea and immediately rushed to her closet to pull out some of her own things.

"Nita, from now on, Aunt Mae wants to see whatever you have on every day, before you go up there to Wheatley. And here's a dollar for you to get your hair washed and pressed tomorrow evening, when you go to the beauty shop."

"Thanks so much Aunt Mae. I really appreciate everything."

"You're welcome, Sweetie."

That night after supper, Nita completed her math problems and wrote a letter to Lee and another to Mary. She took a hot bath and retired to bed, but before dozing off to sleep, she thanked God for the good and bad that had occurred to her on that stressful day.

"Thank you Father for making me the way you did. It hurts sometimes when people say ugly things about me. Teach me how to ignore negativity, and help me to appreciate and accept who I actually am. Please continue to allow me to do well in school. I pray for Momma, Daddy, Mary, Lil, Lo, Nip, Walter, Bill, Big Momma, Maw-Maw, Paw-Paw, Aunt Mae and Uncle Tug, and last but not least Lee and his family. These blessings are asked in your son Jesus' name. Amen."

Out went the light!

It's amazing how the latest hairstyles and clothes can change a person's whole perspective. To say the least Wanita's fresh new look definitely turned a lot of heads at school. Of course some heads refused to gyrate regardless of her efforts. "The snobby math class" bunch simply ignored Wanita's indisputable improvement in appearance. Even though she'd blossomed into a swan over a short period. The "Alleged Elite" still found means for persecution. On one occasion while class was in session, she could hear several blatant commentaries being disbursed from the opposition.

"It's about time she done something with that nappy stuff sittin on top of her head," said one member. Another snoot focused on Nita's dress code. "Ohhh and girl, I see she's been shopping downtown at Foley's a real store for a change. Well thank the Lord, she done found something more in style to wear, instead of that red checkered, country barnyard mess, she's been killin me with since school started."

"Ooops! There's just one other thang ya'll," said another.

"What's that girl?" asked all of the snobs in unison.

"She still ain't done nothin about them ol' scuffed up brown, pitiful lookin sorry sandals."

"Now girl, you know you wrong for that."

"Well that's too sad for the poor lil ol' country girl from LOUIS-ANA," laughed the "head snob" in a cynical, badgering tone. Her nose was stuck straight up in the air, and all of them continued to pour fuel on the fire.

"I don't care what they say about me," thought Wanita. "They're just jealous because my stuffs finally lookin good. Oh! Ya'll wanna talk about my sandals, uh? Well they might be scuffed, but what does my sandals have to do with the rest of me, anyway? It ain't the shoes, baby. It's what's in them. And ya'll just jealous because what's in them is lookin better than each of you."

Afterwards, Wanita sat prissily in her desk, displaying a "how do you like me now?" temperament towards "the snobs." Her obvious self-assurance spontaneously brought their "fault finding" session to a halt after a while. Quite frankly, Wanita wasn't going to let anyone, particularly arrogant classmates, dampen her vivacity with trivial remarks ever again.

Wanita became more enthused and excited day by day as her stay at Phillis Wheatly increased. Her persistent temperament, magnetic personality and strong voice brought her membership in the school's "Glee Club", as well as a significant role on the renowned "Debate Team" alongside the incomparable Barbara Jordan. A mentor whom Wanita admired tremendously and wanted to mimic in every way possible, Barbara was one of those students who commanded respect from the faculty and her peers at Wheatley. Definitely, Barbara was a young lady of authentic character, one most likely to succeed in the days ahead. Wanita felt not only honored, but privileged to be in her company. "When Barbara Jordan speaks everyone listens," the students all agreed. She possessed a charismatic aura that attracted many followers. As a part of the debate team, Wanita began to interact with several of the more intelligent students. Her participation also allowed her an opportunity to visit other schools, making new friends along the way. Much of which was thanks to Mr. Olivier, who saw many hidden talents embedded in this shy, polite, intelligent country girl from Creole, Louisiana. He took Wanita under his wings and cultivated her into a polished debater, encouraging the young lady to develop an eminent vocabulary. Being a member of the "Debate Team" and the "Glee Club" were absolutely her most cherished moments at Phillis Wheatley. Thanksgiving Day was always an immense celebration for both Third and the Fifth Ward. The gridiron rivalry between Phillis Wheatley and Jack Yates High School drew well over thirty thousand colored folks to Jefferson Stadium down on Scott Street every year. Everywhere, the scene showed nothing but well-dressed people Turning out in droves to witness "Bloody Fifth" as it took on "The Trey" in a football game guaranteed not only to be exciting, but entertaining as well. Folks couldn't wait to wear their new outfits, some purchased months in advance specifically for the classic. This annual occasion was inscribed as one of the largest fashion galas and gatherings among Houston's Negro society during this time period.

Lee arrived in town for the festive event. Wanita and Mae got up early that morning perfecting every detail about their appearances. It definitely would have been a horrendous day had she nor Mae not previously had their hair done. An unhurried Lee was badgered by the group for his spiritless demeanor because he took his dear ol' time to get dressed. Everyone else in the house was all set to go, but they had to wait patiently, for him to finish. It was evident that he had no perception of the importance of the day's event. His nonchalant mood worked on Mae's last nerve. By the way she rushed around in circles desiring to look her finest, you could swear she was an alumna or even a student of one of the schools. Mae had on a tight fitted, red, wool dress, which accentuated her figure and big beautiful legs. She accessorized her outfit with fine costume jewelry, including a pair of high heeled black, suede pumps all purchased from Foley's Department Store. Combined with Mae's walk, only God knew what the scene would render, once she made her entrance at the stadium. Both she and Tug were hoping for cold weather. Mae wanted to sport her fur stole, and he had purchased a new, all wool, charcoal grey top coat to show off at the game. The weather didn't cooperate with their wishes however, it turned out a bit brisk, but definitely not cold enough for a stole or top coat.

Wanita looked very classy in a navy blue, quilted wide skirt, along with a matching white cardigan sweater set. Lee had even brought her a new pair of shoes to compliment her ensemble.

Wanita's main objective was to walk into the stadium with her arm in Lee's, directly past "the snobby math class" crew all for some added retaliation and fun. She trusted they'd get an eye full of her new shoes and good-looking boyfriend. Lee J. Harrison had truly outdone himself that day. He looked like he'd just stepped off the cover of Ebony magazine in his baggy, navy blue, three-button, wool suit. His white banded collar shirt and the black Stacy Adams Knobs—spit shined to a tee—only added to the picture. Lee's hair tapered perfectly to both sides, brushed back in a crest of curly waves that set off his well-manicured mustache. The boy was cleaner than the "Board of Health." There was no way anyone at the game would mistake him for a Louisiana country boy.

Wanita was tickled pink over her main man's appearance. Of course Tug looked very sporty, too, in his black and white combo. He wore a nice white, banded collar, double pocket shirt with a small strip of a black handkerchief showing just above the right pocket. The neatly starched shirt was gently tucked into a pair of black, baggy, pleated wool slacks held up by a pair of black suspenders. The black and white "Specs" on his feet fully complemented the entire outfit.

All of them would definitely be the talk of the town, when they strolled into the stadium.

Things went as planned. The parade turned out to be a success, with Wanita and Mae very proud of Wheatley's showing. Once the quartet arrived at the stadium, Mae's adrenalin rushed over her body even as she set her foot out of the car and onto the parking lot.

All eyes in the general area were upon them. It was evident that they were being admired from afar. Wanita saw several girls looking in Lee's direction, so she quickly grabbed his arm in an unmistakable "he's already taken" manner. Mae had her nose straight up in the air and twisted graciously next to her husband, who was proud he was the winner of the prize. After purchasing their tickets, they preceded through the entrance gates while the many onlookers gazed: Mae thinking "I know I'm MISS IT, today!"

She engaged more fiercely in her patented walk, and confirmed its effect when several mature gentlemen stopped dead in their tracks as she passed. Dazzling each of them in turn, she finally strolled by and headed for the stands.

Once there, Wanita suggested they find a place near the band, where the student body usually sat. She spotted "the snobs" instantly, way before they saw her. Wanita's heart raced with excitement. She checked behind to make sure that Mae and Tug were near. Then Wanita got herself together and strutted her stuff, not quite as fiercely as Mae, but with perhaps more social grace, and proceeded to pass directly before her rivals with Lee at her side. The "head snob" along with their dates saw her coming and motioned to the others, and they all stopped and got a long good stare. Those boys couldn't touch Lee J. Harrison, with a ten foot pole.

"There they are" thought Wanita. "Okay girl, do your thing."

One could tell by the looks on their faces that the opposition was in awe. Not a word was spoken. They continued to stare at Wanita and Lee, who found a place about three rows in front of them. The snobs were forced to look at them the entire game. Wanita knew she had the best seat in the house. Throughout the game she stood and cheered on several occasions, looking slightly over her right shoulder to make sure that the snobs were getting the full treatment. Mae observed Wanita's play by play reactions throughout the whole game and mimicked her playfully—besides she knew very little about football to begin with. When Wanita stood and cheered, Mae did the same thing. "What better way to be seen!" thought she. They both had a lot of fun, as Lee and Tug calmly held to their seats. Those two Negroes didn't want to tarnish their cool, macho image. Jack Yates turned out to be the victor of the match-up and on the way back to "The Quarters," Lee continuously teased Wanita over Wheatley's loss. "Now you know Yates had the best band at halftime, too. And Lord knows they had the best football team," he commented.

Wanita ignored his blab and just looked out the car window as they rode. "We may have lost the game," she thought "but I won the battle. It was my day to shine!" She took a deep gratifying breath, shut her eyes and laid her back on the seat. "Mission accomplished," she said with a big bright, smile. Meanwhile, Mae's feet were a bit sore; probably, from too much twisting in those high heels.

Lee visited Wanita in Houston on several occasions, once accompanied by Bean, his mother Lillie, Cleveland "Sang" Reed, and Mary, too. Sang and Mary courting, somewhat, at the time. Wanita was so glad to see her mother, Mary and Lillie. Saturday morning was always a big shopping day, so the whole crew took a streetcar to downtown Houston. Lillie, Bean and Mary were amazed at the tall buildings, the stores, the ride on the streetcar, and all the diverse people shopping. On the way, Mae kept everyone In stitches with the story about her first visit to downtown.

"The first time I went was with Tug's sister "Sister". I wasn't nothin but fourteen years old, when I married Tug, so, ya'll know I was as green as grass. I ain't never been out of Grand Chenier before, much less shopping in a big city like this. That day, me and Sister was walking down the street by Foley's, and I ain't never seen so many people before in my life, walking on the sidewalk. Me and Sister was walking together and looking in the showcases and I was speakin to all of the people inside of there, as we past them by. I found it real funny, though, because they never spoke back to me! Now each of them had a big ol' smile on they face, and I must admit, I smiled right back. They kept on smiling at me, but never once did they speak! So, I said to myself, something ain't right with these Texas folks. They ain't friendly like the people back home. I spoke to them again, and they still didn't say nothin. They just kept on smiling at me, with they silly self. So finally, I got tired of that ol' mess and I said to myself, 'I'm gonna quit speakin to ya'll, if ya'll don't say nothin back.' Well guess what? They act like they heard me and still didn't say nothin! Boy I was mad then. So, I asked Sister. I said. Sister what's wrong with these ol' crazy folks out here in Houston? They act like they can't speak to nobody. They just look at you real stupid, with that ol' silly grin on they face all the time."

Sister looked at me real funny and said "what people you talking about Mae?" Then I pointed and said "them ol' silly folks standing up there."

"In where Mae?"

"Them fools right there!" Then Sister said "Lord have mercy Jesus. Them ain't no real people up in the showcase, Mae. They's what you call a statue. A statue looks like a real person, but they ain't really real. The people from the store put them in the showcase to show you what women's and men's clothes, Foley's got on sale on the inside."

Then I said "no wonder why they don't speak to nobody, they ain't real people." So then, I told Sister, "that's the first time I ever seen something like that before in my life." Me and Sister both cried laughing after that happened. Boy! I sure can get things so mixed up, backwards, loud, and wrong, every time, till it's pitiful."

Everyone was in tears after Mae shared her experience of seeing the first life sized fully dressed mannequin in a showcase window at Foley's Department Store.

"Okay, now don't ya'll make fun of me too much. I wanted to tell you that story so ya'll don't make the same mistake as me, when we get downtown. Cause' ya'll know, we's all from the country, anyway" replied Mae.

"Oh, we want do that, Ain't Mae," said Wanita, full of laughter. After the bunch had gained their composure, the street car made a stop were they needed to depart, and everyone got off, following the signal of Mae's head gesture. She directed them to Grayson's Department Store. Lillie, Bean, Wanita, Mary and Mae went inside to browse. Lee and Sang decided to walk further down the street to take a look inside a nice men's haberdashery. Sang hadn't eaten anything the whole morning long, trying to be cute in front of Mary. He was getting really hungry, though, as the day progressed, but never made mention of finding something to cure his hunger pains. After about thirty' minutes of looking through the merchandise, Lee suggested they head back to

Grayson's to see what everyone else was doing. As they were walking back Lee looked up and saw the Rice Hotel.

"Hey Sang, look there's the Rice Hotel. Look right there! That's one of the tallest buildings in Houston."

Sang looked up at the high-rise hotel, then passed out cold onto the street. Lee laughed at first when the boy fell to his knees, but afterwards realized that Sang wasn't worshiping the building or playing around. Lee immediately, tried to revive him, but Sang just lay there stiff as a board. A large crowd of people gathered around to get a closer glimpse of the commotion.

Back at Grayson's, a white lady who'd seen what happened and informed the sales clerk who was assisting Mae, Lillie and Bean. After hearing the news they all stopped in the middle of trying on dresses and went to investigate themselves. When Mae and the others approached the herd of people, Mary shouted "Oh my God! It's Sang lying down in the middle of the sidewalk." A policeman was yelling "Back up. Back up please, so he can get some air. Backup. Back up will you?"

Sang came through it all after a few minutes of darkness. As he gained his consciousness, the only thing he saw was a sea of legs standing over him. Wanita and Mary rushed towards Sang and Lee.

"My God," asked Wanita. "What happened, Lee?"

"I just pointed at the Rice Hotel, Sang looked up at it, and then fell out cold."

"Fell out?" inquired Mary.

"I told him to eat something before he came downtown, but he wouldn't listen."

"Oh Lord have mercy, what done happened to Sangy Boy?"

Mae asked gasping for breath. The attention shifted suddenly from Sang to her. The crowd was sure she would fall out next.

"Mae! Quit actin the fool!" Lillie shouted. "Can't you see Sang must be all right? He standing up on his own two feet. Ain't he? My goodness!"

"Oh Lord! Oh Lord!" Mae shouted over and over. Finally, after realizing that Sang was all right, she calmed down.

"You know ya'll January's like to put on anyways" Lillie said.

"Oh hush up."

Everyone laughed. However Sang's encounter broke up the shopping spree. Of course the sales clerk at Grayson's was very upset because she had a big job of putting back all the outfits Mae and the others left behind, in addition to losing a pretty hefty' commission. Mae hailed a cab. En route home, Mae's last words were "See, laughing catches. Sang, you laughed at me first when I told ya'll about the statues at Foley's, now look at what done happened to you! Goodie, goodie, goodie!"

Later on that evening, Mae and Tug took Lillie and Bean to a nightclub called "The Gayporee." Lillie was dressed to kill in a nice wool navy blue pencil strip suit, white blouse, black alligator purse and matching shoes, with her black hat tilted to one side. Lillie looked very affluent and felt she'd turn many heads when she stepped out. Bean was striking, herself in a black coat dress with gold buttons, a multicolored scarf around her neck and a pair of shoes that accentuated her purse. She let her long, beautiful, wavy black hair flow down her back. Without a doubt, Mae and Tug were in their usual spiffy attire. They all had a blast that night.

Bean couldn't get over how the people in Houston danced so differently from those back home in Creole.

The very next morning found everyone up early attending the seven o'clock service at Lyons Unity Baptist Church. Wanita sang in the choir. She was so proud to have Bean, Mary, Lillie, Lee and Sang stand when the visitors were acknowledged. After church, Lillie and Bean prepared a large meal for lunch. Mae sort of sat around and watched because she hadn't quite mastered the art of cooking like her sister and Bean. The food was so good everyone stuffed themselves to the fullest.

That afternoon, slowly came to a close. It was time for Lee and the others to return to Louisiana. Wanita became sentimental as they loaded up the car preparing for the long ride home. She watched Lee and the others drive away from "The Courts," till she could no longer see the car in sight. It had been wonderful seeing her mother, Mary and Lee, but the time had come once again to get focused back on her school work. Wanita didn't have long left before her final year at Wheatley would come to a close.

"There will be some more good times to come," she thought, while completing her math problems for Mr. Bank's first period class.

"Oh what a joyous day this was."

All 226 seniors positioned themselves in two lines in the lobby of the auditorium, preparing to make their final stroll down the aisle before a standing room only audience. Wanita with an abundance of pride stood amongst her class dressed in her cap and gown, anxiously awaiting the start of the graduation ceremony.

Bean, Bryant, Mae, Tug and Lee were already seated inside. The class sponsors were all insisting everyone be "quiet please," though they said it softly. The band queued the start of the processional.

Bean kept turning around in her seat to see if she could locate Wanita, but she had no such luck. There were too many graduates to single her daughter out from the group. Bryant sat next to his wife with an inflated chest, overcome with joy. He was so proud of Wanita's accomplishment. Mae, Tug and Lee were esthetic as well.

Wanita Cecil Bartie, a poor sharecropper's daughter from Creole, Louisiana had beaten the odds of defeat by graduating in the top ten of the 1952 class of Phillis Wheatley High School, making her the first Bartie in her immediate family to obtain a high school diploma. The day had finally became a reality. What a feat! The music played triumphantly, as the graduates strolled down the aisle onto the large stage.

"Bryant, I don't see her, yet," said Bean.

"She'll be coming, soon," he responded.

Bean's entire face lit up like a light, when she spotted Wanita walking very dignified amongst the others.

"Look Bryant!! There she is," she yelled with a smile from cheek to cheek on her face, calling loud enough for Wanita to hear as she passed their way. Wanita looked absolutely splendid in her black cap and gown. This was definitely not your typical country girl anymore. Nita had become very sophisticated over the past year. Every strand of hair in her short "Bob" was perfectly cut, and her face was made up to a tee.

Once the graduates were seated on stage, the program continued as printed. After a scintillating speech provided by the valedictorian, the time arrived to recognize the top ten students of the class. As principal John Codwell called out the rankings, Bryant and Bean could scarcely stay in their seats, until they heard the name "Wanita Cecil Bartie" announced clearly over the microphone. When she stood for recognition, Bryant, Bean, Lee, Mae and Tug cheered immensely and Wanita heard the thunder roar onto the stage. The audience applauded responsively just because of her family's proud exertions. Bryant wiped away a well of tears from both eyes. He bowed his head. "Thank you, Jesus, for hearing my prayers. Thank you Lord!" He turned and looked at Bean. She too, had been crying right along with him. For once in their lives, they felt good all over.

Wanita owed a great deal of thanks to Lee, who'd made it possible for her dreams to become a reality. She was grateful to Mae and Tug, and especially her parents for their support and prayers. When Wanita walked across the stage to receive her diploma, she couldn't help but to burst into tears. "I did it" she said over and over. "I did it."

The crowd responded to her emotions. At the conclusion of the ceremony Bryant looked up one last time and said "Ol' Piggy-Pon-Tole, I knew you could do it."

Afterwards, Wanita said farewell to her friends and the faculty. She had only just begun a life that would yield countless challenges and adversities, leaving behind an invaluable experience that would forever be engraved in her memory. She'd proven herself an example of integrity. If one truly believe in themselves, all goals are achievable through constant perseverance.

CHAPTER 14

The clear, blue, picturesque sky sat over a horizon of bright, glistening sunlight, beaming down onto Lee's car as it made the final turn off the Front Ridge Road, headed west for "The Gray Derby". The trip from Houston to Creole took several hours to complete, but it had been a good day for driving. Not a whole lot had changed in the area, since Wanita left. Nevertheless, her siblings were in for a big surprise, as soon as they caught sight of her. Wanita had put forth a concerted effort to look distinctly fashionable, being that her sisters, brothers, and other folks in the area, hadn't seen her in quite some time. Mary, Lil, Lo, Nip and Walter could barely wait to greet and congratulate the young lady for her remarkable feat of attaining a high school diploma. Wanita's accomplishment was something Bryant preached about daily, as an example for all his children to pattern their lives after.

Lil spotted the car first and ran through the house yelling "Nita's home, ya'll! Nita's home." Each of them rushed out onto the front porch. When Wanita stepped out of Lee's car, all eyes marveled over the sophisticated, refined, citified looking teenager, who dazzled them with her resplendent, delightful, smile. Mary, Lil and Lo were so excited they had to pause for a long moment before approaching their own sister. They were all finding it difficult to conceive just how polished Wanita had become over the past year. Neatly dressed in a stylish yellow spring dress gathered at the waist with a white belt, she also wore a white straw hat, with matching gloves and shoes. Her hair was cut into a neat flip style. Wanita had learned quite a lesson at Wheatley after having a "bad hair day," and had vowed never to let such a dire experience demean her appearance again.

Once out of the car, she pranced towards the family, daintily, with her precisely made up face. This was a far cry from the plain, simple country girl they once knew, who'd left home determined to advance her intellect. Wanita had reason to be proud and to look absolutely her best. It was evident that her stay in Houston had completely transformed her into a young lady of class and style. Lil got caught up in the moment and let her mind wonder taking herself off to a fictitious school in another city, then returning home looking like a princess. Mary ran over to greet her first, with Lo not far behind.

"Look at you, Nita," said Mary. "Boy you sure look good girl!"

"And look at them clothes. I want me some just like that" responded Lil.

"Nita, I want to see your class ring," Lo begged.

"Here it is," Wanita responded with an extended hand.

"Ohhh, it's very pretty'. Look ya'll," said Lo, raising Wanita's hand once again, for everyone to observe. "It's even got Phillis Wheatley, Class of 52 on it."

"Let me see" Lil pleaded.

"Me too" added Mary'. "Boy, I can't wait to get mine next year.

"Nita, please tell us about school and how it was living in Houston" said Lo. "Oh, and one more thing. I want to see your diploma too!"

"Okay. I'll show everyone once we get inside the house. Well hello Nip and Walter. Now just don't stand over there lookin at me like I'm a stranger, come on over here and give your big sister a hug!"

The boys responded to Wanita's request while Lee was getting her things out the trunk of the car. Nip and Walter after they exchanged greetings gave him a hand. Mary, Lil, and Lo trailed behind Nita into the house like three admiring, lambs. Bean and Bryant were waiting inside to welcome her home.

With everyone gathered in the living room, Wanita handed out gifts to her parents and the others: small tokens of gratitude. "It's not a lot, but I just wanted everyone to know how much I appreciated all the support and encouragement, you've given me over the past year." Afterwards, she shared some of her experiences about school and living in the big city. Mary's mind was drifting from the conversation, imagining what it was going to be like for her once she got to Houston in the fall. Mary had completed the tenth grade that spring at Cameron Consolidated. Bryant, being a very assertive father, had already made arrangements for her to board with Tug's sister Hortense "Sister" Campbell. Mary planned to attend Jack Yates High School in the Third Ward.

"Here Nita, this came in the mail for you" said Bryant.

She reached for the letter anxiously, opened it and read silently, only for a moment before sharing the good news with her family.

"Oh my God!" she shouted. "It's a letter from Grambling College, accepting my application for the fall semester! Thank you Jesus" she yelled out, with both hands extended in the air.

"What's that you say daughter?" asked Bryant inquisitively.

"Daddy, I'm going to be a freshman at Grambling this fall. Can you believe it?"

"You say you gonna be going to Grambling College? Well plague take it that sounds real good to me. Ain't that something Bean? Nita's going to Grambling."

"I'm so happy for you, my girl. All I can say is just keep up the good work" said Bean.

"Yea, keep up the good work and always keep God first in your life, cause he's really been good to you daughter."

"You're right Daddy, he sure has been."

Bryant sat back in his chair with a feeling of humbleness and dignity, simultaneously. "Nita's going to Grambling and Mary's going to Houston this fall. Plague-take-it Bryant, I got two down and four more to go. That ain't bad for an ol' uneducated, country, boy like me," he laughed. Especially after the Barties had been through so many trials and tribulations in the past, it was definitely a good change in pace to get some positive news. Bryant knew how the Lord always had a way of turning things around, when least expected. All it took was a little faith and patience.

Everyone was elated over the good news. Suddenly, Wanita was emerging into a positive role model, not only for her family, but for many colored children in the area as well. Bryant and Bean welcomed the good news without opposition. They were very pleased for Wanita to further her education on the collegiate level.

Once the excitement dwindled, Lee and Nita were off to Grand Chenier to spread the good news to Lillie and Simon. En route Lee suggested the two of them stop by his Uncle Frank Reed's place of business for a Coca Cola to celebrate Wanita's continued success.

Frank Reed, Lee's uncle stood about 6 feet, 2 inches, with a shock of white hair, tipping the scales at 210 pounds and looking very much like a "Dago". Born in Grand Chenier in 1881, when the land was mainly used for farming and fishing, Frank Reed didn't believe in none of this latter day offshore, oil drilling, monkey business that was going on currently. At the age of 21 he married Jeanette Jones (Aunt Duke), when she was a mere 14 years old. Many times he would say "I got my own baseball team" making reference to his nine boys, all of whom played on his team, not to mention the three girls besides.

As a survivor of the disastrous 1918 storm, which had been a tremendous blow in his life, Frank Reed had regained his momentum by using good business sense and purchasing approximately 80 acres of fertile land the following year. This investment proved to be very advantageous for him, particularly as that type of acquisition was nearly unheard of for a colored man during that era. He grew cotton, raised cattle and later opened a little store not far from his large, roomy house, selling all types of dry goods including cigarettes, beer, and cold drinks. Once the business began to prosper, a juke box was installed for added entertainment. The store was located about a mile west of the Mermentau River, right before the town of Grand Chenier. It was a nice place where a lot of colored residents would congregate particularly before and after attending services at the St. James "Sanctified" Church of God in Christ. The church was located in "The District" near the "Pull Rope Ferry" which crossed the Mermentau River, into the Grand Chenier area from the northwest side of town.

Frank Reed was a smart, hard working colored man to put it quite candidly. His day first began at 5 A.M. sharp, when he fed the pigs and cows. Then he labored in his garden and the cotton fields when those were in season. Being a man of large stature, he always worked up a hearty appetite for Jeanette to deal with. She enjoyed preparing his most preferred dish: "Jemaline", a jambalaya blended with shrimp and crawfish. The ol' Grand Chenier native also spoke "Cajun French" of the bayou country more regularly than not. As a favorite past time, he played the harmonica. A great believer in sittin up straight in a chair or saddle, one could often hear him say "Look at cha, why you sittin dare all slumped over? You got to sit up straight, if you're really alive." His choice of religion was Roman Catholicism, though he rarely attended church and had very little interest in politics. Frank Reed didn't do traveling either very much. Cameron Parish was all the world he knew or needed to know. Over the years, Frank had discovered television and become an ardent baseball follower, watching the games every Saturday night. If there was an exciting game on the tube, there was no need for anyone to try and get him to serve them a thing out of the store, as long as his eyes were glued to the set. They might as well hang it up until the final ending expired.

To sum it all up, Frank Reed was just an all around, good ol' guy, whom the community adored. Lee and Nita were no exceptions. They loved to drop by "Uncle Frank's" place for a Coca Cola and to listen to the latest music blaring out from the juke box.

That day happened to be one of those they dared not pass his place by, especially since so much good had come Wanita's way over the past year.

"Hey Uncle Frank."

"How you doin Lee Boy? I see you got that pretty lil ol' gal with cha again. Now you listen to me, Lee Boy don't you let her get away from you, cause if you do , you the one gonna be a real sad puppy" he laughed.

"I won't Uncle Frank. At least I don't plan on it, no time soon. Guess what?"

"No, what Lee Boy?"

"I know Momma and Daddy done told you that she finished high school last week in Houston."

"Matta of factly, Simon told me that the other day. That's real good my girl. You a pretty, lil ol' smart thang, ain't you "chere"?

"Thank you so kindly" responded Wanita with a smile from ear to ear.

"You ain't gonna believe this, but she's going to Grambling College this fall" bragged Lee Boy.

"Say what?"

"Yeap! Grambling."

"Now Lee Boy, I know you better treat her right cause she's high up there. That's a real good girl, boy. You don't find too many like her walking around here these days."

"I'm gonna hold on to her if that's the last thing I do, Uncle Frank. I ain't letting her go."

"Now. For that good news ya'll don't owe me a penny for them dranks. Them cokes is on me, this time."

"Thank you Uncle Frank."

"Yes, thank you very much for your generosity" added Wanita. Wanita and Lee finished their cokes and departed. Frank Reed watched them admiringly as they got into the car and drove away. "That boy sure got himself something there," he thought and walked back inside the store.

When Lee and Nita arrived at the Miller Estate, Lillie was doing some ironing for Miss Annie with a carbide iron. Each time she used that iron it brought about an excruciating headache, possibly from the discharged carbon dioxide gases that were released during heating. Poor Lillie kept on ironing, though, despite the pain she suffered.

"Hey Momma" said Lee.

"Well Lee Boy, I see you got Nita with you today. How you doin my baby?"

"I'm fine. How are you?" asked Nita.

"Well my baby, I can hardly see. Everytime I use this ol' iron I gets real dizzy, with a real funny feelin' all across my fore head. Sometimes I feels so bad, til I got to go lay down. But after a while, that ol' feelin just passes off. That's a funny thing, ain't it?"

"Maybe you should stop using that iron, if it causes you that much pain" said Wanita.

"Oh Nita don't worry about me, Sugar. I'm gon be okay. I been using that ol' iron for years now, so I done got used to it."

"Guess what Momma, Nita's got some good news for you."

"What's that Lee Boy?"

"She's got her papers from Grambling College today and will start school up there in the fall. Ain't that something?"

"Ahh shuckin now, what you say Lee Boy?"

"Yep. Nita's going to Grambling."

"Boy, God sure is good, ain't he? I'm so proud of you my baby. Ain't that something. Grambling College. I know Bean and Bryant is tickled to death over that. Ya'll I made a good pineapple cake for Miss Annie, let me cut you and Lee Boy a slice for all that good news."

"That sounds good, Momma" said Lee.

"Lee Boy, I know Simon and Momma gonna be real proud of Nita when they get the news."

"Where is Grandma Frances at?"

"She's over at Miss Emma's. You and Nita ought to walk over there and say hello."

"Maybe later. This cake sure is good."

"Yes indeed" concurred Wanita. "It is simply delectable. I enjoyed every bite."

"Why thank you my dear. Eat all you want. I'm just so happy for you till I don't know what to do. You keep that up and you'll be something big one day."

"Thank you very much. I appreciate your encouragement."

"I think I'm gonna lay down for a few minutes cause my head is about to fall off. I just don't know what's wrong with me no more. Sometimes, I just git these ol' dizzy spells."

"Okay Momma, get you some rest. I promised to bring Nita back home early. We'll see you later."

"Ya'll be careful on them ol' dangerous roads. And don't pick up nobody in your car on the way, Lee. They got some real tricky people out there."

"We won't Momma. You just take it easy, now."

"I will. This ol' headache'll pass after I git up. Then I'm gonna finish my ironing."

"Bye Momma."

"Ya'll be careful!"

As the weeks passed, the hot humid summer weather brought with it a wealth of "Love Bugs," "Mutt and Jeffs," or "Jack and Jill's,"... or whatever other cognate name the inhabitants of Grand Chenier were willing to tack onto the black and red, flying, twin nuisances joined at the tail. The only thing the pesky insects were really worthy of was basically ruining a car's paint job with their acidic juices as soon as their delicate bodies collided into the finish.

Lee was very annoyed over the bug's presence all over the front end of his car. One day he decided to give the vehicle a well deserved wash to remove the splattered mess stuck onto the grill. For what reason? He knew not himself because as soon as he washed the oozy insects away and drove down any country road once more, the same coating would reoccur. Being that he was so meticulous about his car's appearance though, there was no way he could bear to have it looking dull and dingy. Besides, a filthy automobile took away from that distinctive style he dared not tarnish. He labored earnestly with the wet car and a polishing cloth, finally accomplishing an expert shine to his liking. The labor helped him to alleviate some legitimate tension which had been engulfing his psyche lately.

Lee's mind was so consumed with Wanita Bartie it caused him to lose sleep at night, struggling desperately in his thoughts to determine whether or not he had a true place reserved in her life. Although Lee was quite excited over her motivation to succeed and make something of herself, he was also experiencing an insecure feeling that was simply driving him loony. The more he thought about Wanita going off to college, the more precarious his temperament became. Lee realized he had to do something profound in order to secure a stable relationship with the young, strong-willed coed he so truly loved.

Once his car glittered in the sun light from the wax job, he jumped in it and took off for a long drive to finish clearing his vulnerable mind. "I'm afraid that Nita will forget all about me, once she gets to Grambling," he pondered, driving down another dusty, insect infested Grand Chenier road. "I love her...and I have got to find a way to hold on to this girl."

Lee kept driving and driving and driving. Finally, without a notion even knowing that he was headed in that direction, he wound up in front of the Cameron Parish Courthouse. Invariably, he went inside and purchased a marriage license. Even though he and Wanita had entertained the thought many times before in the past, she however had always been a bit apprehensive because her parents wanted her to at least finish high school and give college a try before tying the knot.

After the license was acquired, he brought it home and kept it hidden in a secret place. Neither Lillie, Simon, Bean or Bryant had any inkling of his plans. Lee and Wanita continued their passionate love for each other despite the fact that the decision of a life long commitment lingered near. Still afraid to take the plunge, Wanita was in doubt over her father's approval of such a sacred covenant, even though she knew deep in her heart that Lee was the man she truly loved. However, Lee's persistent spirit, combined with an emotional craving to make Wanita his bride, finally led to the naïve couple's secret, impromptu elopement. One contingency was asked of Lee before Wanita finally agreed. "You must allow me to further my education at Grambling College or the marriage is off."

Lee agreed wholeheartedly, without any opposition to this plan. June 24, 1952, in Lake Charles, Louisiana on a hot humid Tuesday found Wanita Cecil Bartie looking like royalty. She was dressed up in a nostalgic, baby blue, ankle length, sleeveless flared taffeta dress, belted at the waistline with a silk chiffon overlay. She wore a pair of high-heeled white pumps. A string of off-white twisted beads, along with a pair of matching earrings accentuated her neckline. A floral arrangement that matched the dress exactly adorned her head, draped to the right side. Her thick, beautiful black hair flowed from under the flowers in a neat "Bob" style.

Wanita's make up had been applied to complement all of her facial features. The pretty, comely seventeen year old bride looked like a princess from a make believe wonderland. She dazzled the eyes and heart of her twenty-four year old fiancee, Lee Johnson Harrison.

He, likewise looked undeniably handsome in his nicely tailored, one button, tan, loose-fitting jacket, along with a white linen shirt and a pair of full-pleated, brown, tailored, baggy slacks, which fell perfectly from his waistline down to the heel of his shoes. He'd chosen a multi-colored brown, white and maroon necktie with diamonds impressed all over it, to fully accessorize this combo. To top off the timeless outfit, he wore his black "Stacy Adams Knobs" with white stitching around the sole. Lee and Wanita looked absolutely exquisite on the day of this very special beginning of their lives. Finally they'd be together as one.

Unfortunately, no invitations were mailed out. The "Traditional Brides March" was never played on this day. There were no brides maids or groomsmen, family, friends or onlookers present to marvel at the sensational bride's breathtaking stroll down the aisles as she met her knight in shining armor. Instead, only she and Lee and Judge Murray Anderson were present at the very simple, expeditious nuptial, carried out according to the couple's own concealed plan.

"My don't you two make a stunning couple?" said Judge Anderson. Please repeat after me. I, Wanita Cecil Bartie, do take Lee Johnson Harrison to be my lawful husband, to have and to hold? In sickness and in good health? Til death do us part."

Lee repeated the same vows along with Judge Anderson.

"I now pronounce you man and wife. You may kiss your bride."

Lee gave Wanita an affectionate kiss that lasted a long second. They signed their licenses and departed as man and wife without a single grain of rice hailed over their heads.

"Good Luck to both of you" said Judge Anderson.

"Thank you very much" was their appreciative response. Afterwards, they went to a photographer to have their pictures made. Both of them produced a nice, cheerful, bright smile. The pictures turned out very elegantly, to say the least. Lee and Wanita resembled a celebrated couple from the cover of a brides magazine standing together for the first time as Mr. and Mrs. Lee Johnson Harrison. The Harrison's had lunch at a colored restaurant on Enterprise Boulevard, then headed back to Creole.

Lee and Wanita both agreed not to tell their parents just yet about their secret elopement. When they pulled up to "The Gray Derby" Wanita reached over and gave her new husband a peck on the cheek. He responded with much more intense passion. They both got out of the car and he walked her to the front porch.

"Good night, Honey," said Lee.

Wanita responded with a soft tone "Good night and do have a safe trip home."

"Remember not a word to your parents" whispered Lee into her ear.

"Okay, I promise" she whispered softly, back.

Later on that night, reality set into Wanita's mind. The young innocent teenager began to realize what a tremendous commitment she and Lee had made earlier in the day. She lay in her bed, tossing and frantically. Everyone else was asleep. Big balls of tears rolled down her face, these arriving with a simultaneous feeling of joy and pain. Nita was happy because she'd married the man of her dreams, but also worried over the fact that her parents knew nothing of their secret. Bryant was sure to have a fit once he found out. He wanted to give Wanita a nice, big, church wedding. As her thoughts raced, she continued to cry, wondering if she had made the right decision.

"I don't know how I'm gonna tell Daddy and Momma that I'm married," she sniffled. "I just don't know how.

Mary heard her sister's murmurs and awakened abruptly.

"Nita, what's the matter? Why are you crying?"

"Oh Mary, it's nothing. Just go back to sleep."

Wanita tried to regain her composure.

"There's got to be something wrong with you girl. What is it?"

"Oh, don't worry about me Mary. I guess I'm just afraid of where my life is taking me so fast. That's all."

"What do you mean?"

"Oh, I don't know." Wanita gasped for her breath. "I mean, things are happening so quick and I guess I'm just afraid."

"Well don't cry about it Nita. Be happy because things could be a lot worse. I wish I were in your shoes. I mean, you're very pretty, smart, intelligent...you speak very well, you're going to Grambling this fall and you have a nice boyfriend. The list goes on...you have so much to be proud of."

"I don't think so," thought Wanita. Then she blurted out "What did you say Mary?"

"I said...I wish I were in your shoes" whispered Mary.

"Mary there's something that I------------- "

"What's that, Nita?"

"Oh, never mind. Go back to sleep, I'll be all right."

"Nita, are you sure nothing happened between you and Lee on your date?"

"No Mary! Why would you say a silly thing like that?"

"Come on, Nita. You're my big sister and I know you very well. I just can't help but feel that something is wrong with you girl, and you ain't telling me the truth."

"Go back to sleep Mary, we'll talk in the morning."

"Nita?" Mary whispered after a few moments.

"What's that Mary?"

"Remember that time when I first started having my period? Girl, I got so scared I thought I was gonna die. And you explained everything to me so clearly. Remember that?"

"Yes, I do. Quite well, Mary."

"Well all I'm saying is you were there for me. So I want to be here for you. That's all. If you want to talk about it, I'll understand."

"I know Mary and I appreciate your concern. But I'll be all right. Have a good night, okay?"

"Well, at least I tried Nita. But there is one last thing I'm gonna say...you can't make me shut up until I say it either."

"What's that, Mary?"

"Remember the time you told me what Big Momma told you about having relations with a boy?"

"Yes, I do."

"Well, could that be why you are crying tonight?"

"Of course not Mary. Just go to sleep, girl."

"All right. I give up. Have a good night, Nita. But if you wake up later and want to talk, I'm all ears."

"Thanks Mary. I'll be fine."

All night long, the marriage haunted Wanita. What was supposed to be the most exciting day of a girl's life, instead had Wanita's mind swirling around like a storm. There was just no way she could tell Mary first, before informing her parents. Especially after making a promise to Lee.

The summer months raced by. Lee and Wanita remained secretly married, without speaking a word to anyone. Bean, however being a mindful mother, noticed how Wanita's behavior had changed with the passing months. Until recently, Wanita used to ask for permission to go out on dates with Lee, but lately the young lady had started going and coming more nonchalantly.

Wanita even had the nerve to break her curfew on several occasions! Her unjustifiable manner continued, despite Bean's frustrated awareness of it. Then one day, after Bean's patience could no longer embrace Wanita's unrestrained conduct, there arrived the inevitable confrontation.

Wanita dressed very nicely, was sitting in the living room waiting for Lee to pick her up. When Bean walked in and saw her all ready to go, she exploded.

"Nita, now just where you think you goin at girl?" You ain't ask me or Bryant nothin about leaving here with Lee. You think you can just walk in and out of this house as you please? You better think again, cause you got another thought comin."

Wanita paused for a long moment. She knew that her mother was on to something. "Oh, Oh" she thought. "I'm in some hot water now."

"I'm gonna put an end to this mess right now. You hear me? I mean that."

"Yes Ma'me" responded a meek Wanita without rebuttal.

"As long as you under this roof, you gonna live by the rules in this house. And I don't care if you are going to Grambling in the fall either. Until you get your own place, my dear, you gonna respect mine. So don't pull this mess with me no more. You hear me? Answer me then, when I'm talkin to you, girl."

"Yes Ma'am" responded Wanita in a very timid voice.

Just about the time Bean finished chewing out Wanita, Lee drove up and was knocking at the front door, very candidly. Bean being the type of woman she was, let loose on him too.

"Oh come on in Lee! Now I"m gon tell it to you straight! I don't mind you and Nita goin out together, but we's got rules in this house and Nita already done broke um. I don't know why she acting like she ain't got no sense a-tall. Here lately you and her been goin and comin as you please. I'm gon stop this mess today. Now, I'm tellin the both of you, I want Nita back home no later than twelve o'clock tonight. I mean that. And if you can't have her back here by then, she just as well stay home, now. And the next time ya'll plan on goin somewhere, Nita better start asking me and Bryant both, or she ain't goin no where. My nerves is too bad to be puttin up with this ol' silly mess."

Lee and Wanita were speechless. They stared at each other with a strong realization. Lee spoke first.

"Miss Bean," he trembled. "Where's Mr. Bryant?"

"Bryant? He's out there in the back washin his clothes."

"Would you please go and get him? Me and Nita have something we would like to talk to the both of you about."

Not liking the sound of this, Bean forgot her anger and rushed out of the house hurriedly to find her husband. When she and Bryant came back inside, they found Wanita in a pool of tears, sitting very close to Lee on the sofa. Bryant looked at his daughter, inquisitively.

"Why you cryin, Nita?" he asked.

That particular question brought with it even more tears. Bean found herself a seat opposite Wanita and feared the worst.

In a quivering manner, Lee said, "Mr. Bryant, Miss Bean", then stopped in the middle of his sentence. The anticipation almost killed the Barties. Lee took a deep breath after the pause and blared out in a hurry "Nita and I are married. We have been for two months now. We got married this past June twenty-fourth in Lake Charles. We've been keepin it a secret because we were too scared of what you both might say."

A long moment of silence covered the living room. It was probably the longest moment that Wanita and Lee ever witnessed before in their life. The atmosphere was more like a funeral than a joyous announcement to celebrate a marriage. Bryant's whole face flushed. His mouth fell open, slightly. Lee and Nita were able to detect that he was very disappointed. Not because of whom Wanita had chosen to marry. He and Bean were very fond of Lee Boy. It was because they chose not to get married in the church. Being an ardent Christian, Bryant felt their wedding was not blessed by God. He was also resentful over the fact that his permission was never sought. Those two factors really agitated him the most.

It took a while for Bryant to accept the fact that his oldest daughter was married, however, through much strife, he realized that Wanita had made a conscious choice on her own. Even though he experienced some difficulty in doing so, Bryant's resolution not to interfere with his daughter's decision helped him to concur with her wishes. Eventually, he accepted the truth and wished she and Lee well in their future together as husband and wife.

About a week before Wanita's departure to Grambling, she and Lee caught a train in Lake Charles and headed to New Orleans for their long awaited honeymoon. Wanita was fascinated over the train ride, however when they approached the metropolitan area, it got a bit scary as the train made its way over the murky waters of the Mississippi River, high above it on a very narrow bridge. Once they reached Canal Street, Lee hailed a cab which took the couple to their hotel room. New Orleans was a beautiful place with a lot of culture. Later on that evening, they had dinner with some of Lee's relatives, the Butch Reed family. The Reeds were a very polished group of people, who had the table sat to perfection. The finest of china and stemware graced each place setting. The visit was a pleasurable one. After a fun-filled three days, the couple returned home to Grand Chenier, making a formal announcement of their marriage to relatives and friends.

Things got a bit sentimental around "The Gray Derby" as Wanita packed her things to head to Grambling. Mary, Lil and Lo had so many questions concerning what it felt like to be a married woman. Wanita explained as best she could, however, there really wasn't much to tell because she had only spent a short time actually with her new husband during the two month period. While she was getting her things together, tears welled up in Mary's eyes, realizing Wanita probably wouldn't be coming back home to share the same bedroom with her anymore.

"Nita, this is it girl...Ain't it?"

"Why would you say such a crazy thing like that, Mary?"

"You know it is. Once you leave home this time, we only gonna see you, when you come back for a short visit. You have a husband now, and that's were your attention will be focused."

Wanita looked at Mary with a strong cognizance of the reality of her words.

"You know something Mary, you are so right. Everything has happened so fast. I never even thought about it that way before, until you just made me realize the truth. Oh my, Mary," gasped Wanita "We want be sharing this room anymore! Will we?"

Mary moved closer to her sister and started helping her fold some clothes, then placed them in Wanita's only suitcase. Her bedding was packed into boxes and they put her dresses in paper bags.

"I feel like I'm losing you Nita" cried Mary.

"Oh Mary. You will never loose me. It's just that the time has come for me to broaden my horizons, so that I can reach some of my goals. That's all."

"I know Nita. But you don't understand. It just won't be the same around here without you. You know, I think about all the good times me and you shared together as kids. And you know that we've always been close. Real close as a matter of fact. And now you're leavin me behind to start a new life of your own. That's so hard for me to accept."

"Oh Mary, don't say that. You have a lot to look forward to. Remember you're going to Houston in a few weeks. You'll love it there. It'll give you a chance to meet some new people. But the most important thing of all is for you to get your high school diploma. Next thing you know, you'll be off to college. Maybe even Grambling, and that would be absolutely wonderful." "Well, I guess you're right. We are growing up very fast.

Sometimes I wish things would slow down a bit. But I guess that's life.

"Me too, Mary. Life must go on and things do change. But I'll never change the love that I have for you in my heart."

"Oh Nita! I love you so much and I'm gonna miss you girl."

"I love you too, Mary, and you will always be a special part of me. Never forget that as long as you live."

The two girls embraced, as they sat next to each other on their bed for the last time as roommates. A stream of tears trickled down each face.

"Please write to me sometimes and let me know how things are going in college," cried Mary.

"I will, Mary. I will" responded a tearful Wanita.

Once they finished packing all of Wanita's things Lee had already driven up to the front yard. Wanita washed her tear-stained face and brushed off her clothes before greeting he and his mother Lillie. She'd come along for the ride and to keep him company on the way back home. Bean met Lillie at the front door. The two of them went into the kitchen to talk. Wanita did a final check to make sure she hadn't forgotten anything.

Bryant was out back doing some chores, with a well of tears in his eyes. He was very happy for his oldest daughter, despite the drama that had occurred a few weeks before. He couldn't help but to be emotional. Even though it was a trying time for him, Wanita was proving that she wasn't going to let adversity stand in the way of her will to succeed. He had to respect her for that.

Once Lee, Nip and Walter had everything packed inside of the car, the entire family gathered in front of the house to say good-bye to Wanita. All eyes at this point were leaking. Lil and Lo said their farewells, first. The boys were next, followed by Bean and Bryant.

"You be a good girl up there, Nita, and study hard," sniffled Bean. "You're goin to Grambling to make something of yourself. I got faith that you will succeed."

"Thank you for everything, Momma. I love you so much. I mean it from the bottom of my heart."

Bryant came over and gave her a big hug." Always keep God somewhere close in your life. He'll see you through any storm. Remember the time I told you about me as a boy when I got caught in that Ol' 1918 storm? God saw me through it all, daughter, and he'll do the same thing for you. This is just another storm that you have to weather in your life. It ain't gonna be easy. I know that to be true because if it was every body would be goin to college too.

But you's a real smart girl, and I knows you gon make it. I'll be prayin for you, my girl."

Wanita broke down, relinquishing a feeling of guilt after Bryant gave her his blessing.

"I'm going to make it all up to you some day Daddy. You'll see!" she sobbed.

"Just be true to your self and God. As for me, Ol' Bryant' I'll be all right, cause I already done consulted the Almighty Master."

"Mary, I'm gonna really miss you girl," she cried.

"I'll miss you too, Nita," confirmed Mary with glassy eyes.

Wanita and Mary held onto each other for a long moment, then Nita turned away and got into Lee's car. Everyone watched them drive off. Nita looked back one last time to wave. Meanwhile, Lillie, in the back seat was in a pool of tears. One thing's for sure, though, it was evident that the whole family truly loved Wanita dearly. Even more reason for her to succeed. She didn't want to let any of them down.

The ride to Grambling was a long one, taking at least six hours one-way. Wanita had never ventured to the northern part of Louisiana before, so the ride would definitely produce different scenery along the way. At first the trip went as planned. The trio made it to Alexandria in about three and a half hours.

Unfortunately, when they got there, Lee's car was smoking something terrible. He pulled over to a service station. The attendant discovered a problem with the transmission. The dilemma would cost $60 to rectify and require at least three hours of labor.

Lee informed the mechanic of Wanita's limited time schedule, so he worked diligently to get the vehicle operable. Once the job was completed they were back on the road.

The further north they traveled, the more the terrain changed. North Louisiana was a very hilly country. Finally, after a very exhausting trip, they made it to Grambling College, ("The college were everybody is somebody") by night fall. The campus was very well manicured with several large buildings scattered throughout.

Lee pulled over to the side entrance and asked a young gentleman were the freshman female dorm could be found. He pointed them into the right direction. Wanita checked in, without any hassles.

Most of the freshman girls had arrived earlier during the day, however there were still a stream of them coming in after sun down.

Wanita was a bit ashamed when she saw most of the other coeds had nice trunks and footlockers to transport their personal belongings.

She, Lee and Lillie, however carried her things into the dorm in paper bags and boxes. "That's okay" she thought. "I'm not here to look flashy, I'm here to get a college education." Once over the initial shock, she settled into the barrack style dorm where she would spend the rest of the semester along with several other young ladies.

Another tearful farewell came when Lee and Lillie departed for Grand Chenier. They all exchanged good-byes. She watched them drive away slowly and then went back inside to get acquainted with her new roommates. Time flew during the evening. Once all conversations ceased, the lights went out for the night.

Wanita awakened early the next day for registration. Once dressed, she went to breakfast in the dining hall. After returning to the dorm, one of her roommates asked "Did you lose this Wanita?"

Her eyes got as big as marbles. "Oh my God, I sure did. Thank you very, very, very much!" she responded in a huffy voice. It was her tuition money tied up in a white handkerchief. Talk about high anxiety. Once the paranoia settled, Wanita registered for Math, Biology, English, American History and Social Problems. Initially, nursing was her first career choice. Unfortunately, there were very few opportunities in Cameron Parish for colored nurses, so she chose Education as an alternative instead, with an emphasis in Biology and Chemistry. She reasoned that this would provide an easy transition into the medical field if future opportunities ever developed.

Later on during the day, the freshman girls were given a guided tour of the academic halls, the library, the administration building and the physical education department. Meanwhile, at the student union, they were introduced to a posh group of young ladies wearing pink and green who appeared to be the society girls on campus. Another group, whose noses weren't stuck quite as high in the air as the first wore red and white. These girls were a little more diplomatic. Then there was a smaller group of ladies wearing blue and white who were very down to earth young ladies. They were nothing fancy, but the most cordial of all of them. Wanita had never heard of a sorority before, much less had an interest in pledging one. However, she pretended as though she knew exactly what the other freshman girls were gaggling over as they intermingled with some of the sorority sisters from each group.

One very pretty, fair complected, hazel-eyed "Creole Girl" from New Orleans was talking with a friend. "My Great-Grandmother was a 'pretty prissy, fair skinned lady!' So was my Grandmother, and my mother, too. So what does that make me? It was true, she had long, sandy-blonde hair and looked Caucasian.

The coed's friend looked her over and said, "Pink and Green, of course. But, I know I'm too dark for those stuck-up girls," she said sarcastically in retaliation. "Anyways, I've always had a fascination for "Ducks" and the art of quacking. So what does that make me?"

"A Quack-Quack" answered the 'Creole girl' holding her nose with a disfigured smile. "Now just don't stand over there looking all crazy Wanita, what's your preference, girlfriend?" she inquired.

"Well, I don't think I'm pretty enough to be a society girl. Besides, those young ladies remind me too much of a snobby group that harassed me to death, when I was going to Phillis Wheatley High School in Houston, Texas. Now let's see. I grew up on a farm and heard enough ducks quacking in my day. So, I guess, I really don't have but one other choice. Right?"

"Oh no, Chick, you got to be joking! Look at you, girl. With your light skin, pretty hair and face," responded the Creole beauty.

"I know you gon wear some pink and green with me. Girl! It's written all over your face."

"Light skin? Pretty face? And Lord don't let this nappy hair fool you my dear. So what does all that trivial mess have to do with me pledging a sorority?" Wanita inquired, puzzled.

"In due time, my friend, you'll see what I mean. All the pretty, light-skinned, girls like me and you have no other choice but to keep that ol' tradition a going, cause you know what they say about the girls in the pink and green don't you?"

"No, I'm clueless."

"Look at them, Wanita. That's why they are smiling at the both of us, girl. We look just like them. I'm gonna get them greek letters if that's the last thing I do."

"Well, I don't know about me. I mean, I'm a married woman and I've got to stay focused on finishing college, not hob-snobbing on the social scene in a sorority here at Grambling."

"Listen girl, don't let any of those other sororities sell you none of their monkey business. If you pledge any thing, it better be the pink and green, my dear. Okay? Take my advice, if it ain't pink and green then just don't pledge nothin at all. Girl, my goal is to become Miss Grambling. In order for me to do that I have to be popular on campus. And the pink and green will surely help me to. The Creole girl strolled past Wanita with her hair swinging daintily, right before the faces of the sorority sisters. One of the members acknowledged her performance with a prissy head gesture of approval. The other two sorority sister groups looked at "Miss Thing" then at each other and nodded disapprovingly. Their noses and mouths up simultaneously. "She belongs with that bunch of snobs over there" pointed out an unidentified member of the red and white crew. However, the pink and green sisters did extend Wanita a warm inviting smile to chat with them about their sorority. Wanita just smiled back after that scenario and moved on with the rest of the freshman girls to their respective academic departments to meet their advisors.

Nita's freshman year at Grambling proved to be an academic success, and she was cultivated into a mature, well disciplined, confident, appealing sophomore, who turned a lot of heads on campus during her second year. Representatives from three different sororities approached her again to join their pledge lines, however she declined each offer, insisting that "getting an education was her main priority." College life provided an invaluable experience by advancing her cultural well-being. For the first time in her life, Nita heard a musical composition performed by a real orchestra; the St. Louis Symphony, and she also got an opportunity to see the nationally renowned drama "John Brown's Body" starring Ann Baxter and Tyrone Power. Of course she never lost touch with her spirituality. At Grambling, attending the church of one's choice was a mandatory dictum, but on one hand no one had to boost her hunger for the word because she was well aware of the many blessings God had brought her way. Being away from Lee for semesters at a time was taxing on their marriage, nevertheless they found a way to survive the adversity and the absence from each other. He visited her as regularly as possible on his seven days off from the Gulf, but the drive and distance got old very quick.

The second year at Grambling, Nita purchased a nice trunk to transport her personal belongings for the 1953 fall semester, desiring not to share the same embarrassment she weathered the year before. Things were rolling along as scheduled by the spring, with her progressing right on target according to the degree program. She excelled in Chemistry and Physics, and did exceptionally well in Speech and English. Living on campus continued to be a lot of fun, however at the close of her second semester she discovered that there would be an addition to the family. It was an alarming time for Nita because she had met so many new friends, and attained a wealth of knowledge and culture. But the road ahead was about to take a detour.

The last day of school found the sophomore in an assembly with President Ralph Waldo Emerson Jones speaking diligently to the student body. He told the students to be careful and mindful of themselves during the summer months until the fall semester was upon them once again. He also said "Kiss Momma, Kiss Poppa, and Kiss the Mule, when you go home. Never be ashamed of who you are or where you've come from."

Tears welled up in Wanita's eyes as the program progressed. She realized that she would be leaving Grambling for good, to take on a new challenge of motherhood.

"Well, that's okay, Wanita" she said to herself. "At least I've got two years down and two more to go." She placed her hands onto her stomach, looked down and spoke softly to the tiny life forming inside of her. "I'm gonna get my education, if it's the last thing I do. I've promised myself, Daddy, and now I'm promising you. I must set a positive example for you to follow some day. Education is the only way the colored race can survive and overcome racism. Yes, I will finish college one day" she reassured her unborn child.

"I'll get through this storm, you'll see, my dear!"

The little fetus responded back with a jolt of confidence to his mother's abdomen, as though to say, "Don't give up, Momma because I know you can and will succeed."

Wanita walked around campus for the last time and said farewell to the faculty and all of her friends. Even though she realized that her education would be intermittently interrupted for the interim, she never once allowed the idea of finishing college to fade. Nita's stay at Grambling enabled her to mature into quite a young lady.

"School is just on hold for now, but with God's will, I am gonna get my four year degree" she said confidently, with a full and an incontestable mind. She looked back at the administration building for the last time, turned and walked away in the direction of her dorm.

One things for sure, it was all going to be left up to Wanita to keep her dreams alive. This was just another one of life's storms that she had to weather. Anyone's dreams can persist, however, with a profound sense of strength, determination and the will that only comes from within only shall one survive.

CHAPTER 15

The year was 1957. Approximately, 4,600 inhabitants lived in the lower Cameron Parish area. It's economy was based on the extraction, transmission, and processing of crude oil, which was a large contributor to the economy. A huge pipeline was built to transport the crude, its path manually dug out by hand and shovel and extending for miles and miles to the Intracoastal Canal; a manmade canal which ran from east to west and provided a convenient outlet to the Gulf of Mexico via the Calcasieu River.

Several colored men worked on the pipeline project, which took many years to complete. The oil started out being transported by barge from Block Two in the Gulf, then was stored in large tanks at a location in Creole near the beach by St. Hubert's Catholic Church. At this point, the crude was transmitted into the pipeline. Once it reached the Intracoastal Canal, it was stored again in larger 5,000 barrel tanks, until loaded onto barges and transported to refineries throughout Louisiana and Texas.

The parish maintained excellent water routes facilitated by the Intracoastal Waterway. A deep ship channel existed in the Calcasieu River, primarily because of a large rock pile called "The Jetties". Built at the mouth of the river, "The Jetties" extended approximately 30 feet out into the Gulf. It's general purpose was to keep the water level into the river deep and constantly flowing.

Comparably, the Mermanetau River in Grand Chenier could not handle vessel traffic as large as the Calcasieu could. The point where the Mermentau connected to the Gulf was too shallow, and in order for large boats to pass to and from the Gulf, a high tide had to be present. One notable improvement in Grand Chenier during this time was that the "Pull Rope" ferry had been upgraded to a mechanical vessel, and later finally replaced by a wooden bridge.

The Grand Chenier Bridge, located near Miller's Cafe, owned by Mrs. Malize Miller, was built with a crank shaft at midpoint of the structure. A worker would manually operate the shaft to open and close the bridge each time oncoming marine traffic had to pass. With the construction of new roads throughout the parish, over a period of time the boating industry—namely The Wynonna, The Delta and The Margie — experienced dwindling business in the Grand Chenier area. Cargo and other items could now be transported by trucks, lessening the need for the marine vessels.

The Crain Brothers Company, however grew in leaps and bounds, and provided several employment opportunities to area residents. Two ferry boats in the town of Cameron were operable during this era. One transported vehicles from downtown Cameron over to Monkey Island, a small island where the U. S. Coast Guard maintained a base. Once on Monkey Island, if a traveler desired to cross the Calcasieu River, they drove approximately four more miles to another point on the island and caught another ferry. That ferry brought them to the Johnson Bayou Louisiana Highway 82. The dirt and clam shell road ran along the coastline for quite a distance through a community called Holly Beach, then on into the town of Johnson Bayou and culminated at the city of Port Arthur, Texas.

Other lucrative industries in the parish in the late 50's included trapping, fishing, agriculture and seafood. The trapping of furbearing animals, alligators, and the transporting of their hides and meats, were important economic operations. The seafood industry played a significant role in the areas' prosperity as well, being that the town of Cameron ranked amongst the nation's leading fishing ports. Many area residents found work at several seafood factories beheading shrimp, which paid thirty-five cent per three gallon bucket. Also, the Louisiana Menhaden, Swindell and Smith Menhaden fish plants made a tremendous impact on the regions local economy.

In the area of agriculture, rice was the principal cash crop, particularly in the northern part of the parish. Livestock provided the second most important source of income. No railroads existed in Cameron Parish, however there were many graded, dirt and shell state highways and parish roads located throughout. The St. Gabriel Hospital was located on the second ridge in Creole next to Dr. George Dix's home, not far from the Sacred Heart Catholic Church.

The landmark Cameron Parish Courthouse still stood in the town square. Our Lady Star of the Sea Catholic Church was another notable landmark located east of downtown. The Cameron Consolidated School for colored children increased its enrollment and had received accreditation to award twelfth grade students with high school diplomas. The Creole High School for white students was renamed South Cameron High.

A sense of ownership developed throughout the lower Cameron Parish colored community. Since the economy was so profitable, many colored people took advantage of the situation by purchasing their own property. In Cameron, nice two and three bedroom homes sprang up, mostly in an area known as the "The Yellow Jacket" section of town. This area, also called "The Front" was located approximately three miles east of downtown off the Swindell Road, near the coastal beach. In addition to residential property, one could also find small proprietary businesses such as grocery stores, service oriented companies, cafes, boarding houses, nightclubs and even houses of worship. Rapheal Bargeman owned a plumbing company; Oliver "Noosh" Moore owned "The Yellow Jacket" nightclub; Lillian Stewart owned the "Sweet Dreams" café and bar; and Sophie Savoy was a nightclub proprietor as well.

Many transient colored workers connected to the Menhaden industry boarded in this area on a seasonal basis. There were no concentration of Negroes in one single area of Creole or Grand Chenier like in the neighboring town of Cameron. Basically, most colored residents in both towns lived spread out along the main roads, back ridges, and along the coastal beaches. Despite the fact that the living in Cameron Parish had its advantages for both colored and white residents, things still remained segregated and the colored people dared not cross those established boundaries set forth by the white residents. "For White Only" signs were posted in most Caucasian establishments, and these meant exactly as they read.

Getting a college education appeared to be a forfeited dream for Wanita. Nevertheless, she never lost sight of the idea of fulfilling her goal. The conviction had to be put on hold, however, at least for the time being. She had two boys to rear.

Gregory Orlando was born September 17, 1954. Bearing the same complexion as his father, his features nevertheless borrowed a little something from both Lee Boy and Nita. The toddler had a thick head of black hair and kept a constant smile on his little face.

A very smart kid right from the start, Gregory became very protective of his baby brother, Marlon Van, born July 30, 1956. Marlon's skin tone was light as a little ghost like his mother. He looked mostly like Lee Boy, and had sandy blond hair, and hazel green-colored eyes; a definite Harrison trait. Nita chose to name the boy's after two Hollywood actors, Gregory Peck and Marlon Brando. Both little fellows were as cute as could be. Nita made sure they stayed clean and fresh, and looking simply adorable in the latest fashions. She probably spent more money on the boy's apparel than on her own.

The Harrisons made up a small, happy, middle class family. They lived in a cozy two bedroom, brown slate siding, home consisting of a kitchen-dining room, living room, bathroom, and a garage for Lee Boy to park his 52 Ford. Of course they had a telephone connected to a party line. Nita's grandpa Paw-Paw, and his brother Pierre Bishop, built the house from the ground up. Lee Boy still worked as a Co-captain on the True Friend, while Nita was a housewife. Before the home was purchased, she and Lee lived with his parents at the Miller Estate. Lee Boy and Nita's house was located about a quarter of a mile east of the Immaculate Heart Conception Catholic Church, and about a half mile west of Curley Vincent's General Store. They had been living there for about three years. Their small home faced the south, along the main road in Grand Chenier. The coastal beach was approximately four miles out. Marsh land and acres of surface water separated the coastline from the main road. Very few homes were built on the south side of the road because of the swampy soil conditions. John Albert (Son) January and his family lived next door to the west of Lee Boy and Nita, while Miss Manilla Allen owned the home to the east. She'd only live there during the week, while school was in session. On the weekends. Miss Allen commuted back and forth to her hometown of Jennings, Louisiana were she also spent the summers at the close of the school year. On the east side of her home was a lane that dead-end at the Mermentau River. Lee Boy's parents Lillie and Simon occupied the first white painted house north of Miss Allen down the lane and were the only colored family living there amongst other white residents. Lee Boy and Nita had very little furniture in their place outside of a few pieces in both bedrooms and a chair in the living room. Nevertheless, it was a good living. A far better one than Wanita knew while growing up as a sharecropper's daughter.

Son January purchased his family an older home from Mrs. Alcede Miller, and was the first resident to live at that location. The January's had been there for five years, before Lee Boy and Nita built their home. Son's house was a moderate, two bedroom structure, with a large porch running across the entire front. Like Lee, Son also owned a Ford, and he was married to Jeanette Mayne, daughter of Henry and Clara Mayne. They had five children: John Albert, Jr., Laura Mae, Jimmy Lee, Pamela Sue, and Lynn Dean (Donald), who was a mere toddler. Laura Mae however lived with Son's Aunt Willie Dozier in an arrangement similar to the one Lee's sister Lovenia undertook during her childhood.

Lee's parents Lillie and Simon were making steady progress. He could walk through his back yard to get to their two bedroom house. They had a kitchen, a living room, a bathroom and a large hurricane fence surrounding their property. Simon and Lillie had been there for twenty-two months. Lillie was so proud of her house.

She still worked for the Millers, although Doc had passed away some time before from a massive heart attack, presumably caused by stress and overexertion. At this time, Miss Shutzie and Miss Annie were the only two occupants of the Miller Estate. Miss Punk and Te-Cum were living away in Baton Rouge and New Orleans, respectively. Simon was still employed by Mr. Lee R. Nunez as a boat captain, and Lillie's mother, Frances, who now lived with them, continued to work for Mr. Lee Nunez's wife, Miss Emma.

Simon owned two cars, an old Pink and Blue Plymouth, that he called "Pinky" and a brand new blue 57 Chevrolet. Lillie and Simon's phone was connected to the same party line as Lee Boy and Nita's. Time brought about a lot of changes for Bean and Bryant.

Finally things had started to look up for the Barties. The Lord had allowed them to move away from "The Gray Derby" into their own new, pink colored house, with three bedrooms, a kitchen, a dining room, living room, and a bathroom. Bryant was still employed at the Swindell Pogy Plant and Bean continued to work at Miss Bessie Terry's Cafe in Cameron. Mary was attending Dillard University in New Orleans, majoring in nursing. Lil and Lo both earned scholarships to Grambling College, pursuing education degrees. Nip now a high school student, and Walter in mid-high were attending Cameron Consolidated. Bean and Bryant's home was within walking distance from the St. Hubert Catholic Church in Creole. Bean's son Jimmy (Bill) had married Susie Mouton, Bryant's sister Lucinda and John Cass Mouton's daughter. Bill and Susie bought themselves a new home about a mile from Bean and Bryant's place, midway between the front and back ridges on the LaSalle Road. The road was named after Bill's grandfather Joe LaSalle, who owned several acres of property there. Bill and Susie had six children; Jimmy Jr., Cheryl Eugenia, Kathy Sue, Harold Curtis, Marvin Kent, and Melvin Brent, who was a mere infant.

Maw-Maw and Paw-Paw Bishop still lived at the Ol' Bishop home place along the beach. Maw-Maw's mother Grandma Louisa and stepfather Grandpa Seedy Andrews, lived about a quarter of a mile west of the Cameron Consolidated School in a small shack. One of their daughter's Lucille, married Adam Moore and they lived next door. Lucille and Adam's daughter Charlene Moore Galloway lived in the area as well. Joe Bishop and his wife Alice were still tenants on the Rutherford's property. Their daughter Annie had married Dalton LeBlanc and a baby girl named Vickie was born to this union. Dalton and Annie lived on the back ridge headed west towards the town of

Cameron, off the main road. Big Momma and her son Pat still lived on the back ridge.

Another son, Alcy Bartie, and his wife, Stella lived about a quarter of a mile west of their home. Alcy's brother Levion Bartie was the same distance to the west of his place at the entrance of the back ridge road.

Despite the segregation in lower Cameron Parish, the living conditions had improved tremendously for its colored population. Frank Reed's place of business in Grand Chenier continued to thrive as a favorite gathering spot for Negroes. Frank Reed's half brother Steve Sturlese owned and operated a grocery store about a mile west of the Ebenezer Baptist Church. On many occasions after service, the members of Ebenezer would congregate at the store where they purchased "Ike & Mike" cookies and cold drinks for refreshments. One thing's for sure, the place of worship continued to draw a full house each Sunday being that was the only true social interaction outside of the night clubs.

Late one Sunday afternoon in January, 1957 Bean brought her grandmother and step-grandfather over some food and stayed for a short visit. Grandma Louisa and Grandpa Seedy Andrews owned very little. Their home was probably in worse shape than the one Bean and Bryant had lived in back on the Rutherford's property.

Not far from the colored school, the Andrew's home was simply a large, plain, single room shack that had two double beds located by the front door. A wood burning stove stood in one corner near the rear of the place. An old table and chair set was in between the stove and a cedar clothes press in the other corner. A few pieces of furniture sat aimlessly aside the beds on top of a very crude wooden floor. The interior of the domicile yielded a musty, charred-wood, pungent odor that engulfed one's nose immediately upon entering.

Grandma Louisa was a very dark, petite, short lady, who was as sweet as sugar. Much taller than his wife, Grandpa Seedy was sort of a handsome, extremely fair-complected fellow with dazzling gray eyes and a medium build. He and Grandma Louisa were a lovable, poor couple, adored by all who knew them. They had very few worries in the world, simply because their lifestyle was uncomplicated. The two were thankful just to be alive and grateful for the roof that stood above their heads, even though their surroundings left a lot to be desired.

Bean made it a point to visit the couple as often as she could. Grandma Louisa appreciated seeing her granddaughter, and what ever extra food Bean had she'd share with Louisa and her husband. During the course of Bean's visit, another grand-daughter Charlene Galloway; Grandma Louisa and Grandpa Seedy's daughter Lucille's girl stopped by with her two children, Delores and James. Grandma Louisa was obsessed with her great-grandchildren and always enjoyed having them over.

"Hey Grandma Louisa and Grandpa Seedy!" Charlene said in greeting. "How ya'll feelin?"

"I feels pretty good," Grandma Louisa replied. "But poor ol' Seedy ain't doin too good."

"Oh no? What's wrong Grandpa Seedy?"

"I don't know, my girl. I gotta ol' hurting in my back and it won't go away."

"A hurtin in your back? Now were you got something like that from, Grandpa?"

"Ump! I wish I could tell you myself. I thank it's from that ol' cold I got the other day, done settled back there. Shoots! I don't know."

"Well, you better take care of yourself. Oh Lord! Cun Bean, how you doing? I didn't even see you sittin over there!"

"Doin good, Charlene. Boy, them kids sure growed up, didn't they?"

"Yep! They got big overnight, Cun Bean. How's Nita doing with them two pretty lil ol' boys of hers?"

"They fine. Me and Bryant seen'm today, after church. Only thing is, that little one won't have nothing to do with me. No sir! He stay stuck up under Nita like glue. Now the oldest one'll let you touch him, and hold him all day long. But not that baby, Charlene! That rascal don't do nothing but cry all the time!"

"Oh, don't worry Cun Bean. He'll grow out of that, when he gets older. He's just a little baby right now. That's how James used to be with people. He wouldn't even let Grandma Louisa or Grandpa Seedy touch him, till he got to be a big ol' boy. Now they can't get rid of him."

"I'll sure be glad when Nita's baby hurry up and grow out of that ol' mess, cause that little sandy headed rascal just wanna cry all the time."

"Bean! You mean Nita got two boys now?" said Grandma Louisa. "Lord have mercy, I ain't knowed that!"

"Momma didn't tell you, Grandma Louisa?" asked Bean.

"No. Mary ain't told me nothin! Bean tell ol' Nita to please stop by for me and Seedy to see them lil boys. And I bet theys some pretty lil things, too."

"Yea Cun Bean," said Charlene. "Tell Nita to bring them by, so they can play with Delores and James."

"Bean, you tell ol' Nita Grandma Louisa gon git her, if she don't come by here and see us real soon. Now whatcha say they names is?"

"The oldest is Gregory and the baby is Marlon."

"Gregley and Marvin. Boy that sure is some pretty names."

Meanwhile, James let out a loud sneeze, alarming the entire house.

"Sounds like he's coming down with a cold, Charlene."

"He is, Cun Bean. I took both of them to that ol' carnival in Cameron yesterday, and he ain't had nothing on his head, when it started raining. That's what's wrong with him. I done told him to keep that cap on his head, but he won't listen."

"Give him some hot tidy tonight, before it gets too bad" suggested Bean.

"That's a good idea, Cun Bean. Grandma Louisa, you got some lemons?"

"No baby, I sure don't."

"That's okay I'll stop by the store on our way home. Cun Bean did Nita bring her two boys to the carnival?"

"Ah no. They too young for something like that, right now. It probably was too cold, for them."

"Yeah, you right. We should've stayed home too. But you know how these kids can get. And guess what ya'll? When we was at the carnival, yesterday, they had this ol' Gypsy woman down there tellin people's fortunes. She was a real light skin lady all dressed up in a long black dress, and she had a big ol' crystal ball. At first when I seen her, I passed on by. I said to myself, I don't believe in that ol' mess. But then I got to thinking to myself, I said...Hum!...It ain't gonna hurt nothin to try... just this one time."

"For real, Charlene?" responded Bean excitedly.

"Yes Cun Bean. So I went to talk to her. HONEY! That ol' Gypsy woman had her face all made up real funny lookin, with a whole lot of black stuff all over and under her eyes. She looked like she was half dead to me. It scared me to death, just to look at that ol' ugly face. Cun Bean, I ain't never seen nobody look that bad before in my life. So anyways, once I got over the face, crazy me got out my dollar and handed it to her. I told Delores and James to stand back...off to the side out of the other people's way for a minute. Then, Cun Bean, she told me to put my hands over that ol' crystal ball and then rub it...three times like this."

Charlene commanded everyone's full attention as she rubbed her hands together and continued to tell the story.

"Cun Bean...She said 'open your hands up real wide, so I can see.' Just about the time she started reading my fortune. Floyd Bargeman and his wife Mae West walked up from behind. I looked up and spoke to them both. Then that ol' Gypsy said 'Wait a minute ya'll!!' Real loud. 'Don't move!' She looked down at my hands hard, hard, hard, for a long time. And then she started rubbing that ol' crystal ball, sayin 'crystal ball, crystal ball, crystal ball. Tell me whacha see for them all!!!!!!'

"Oh Lord. What happened then, my girl?" asked Grandma Louisa releasing a loud clap, and a curious snicker.

"That ol' Gypsy rared back in her chair and she looked at me and shook her head. Then, she looked at Delores and James real funny. Then she frowned at Mae West and her husband Floyd in a crazy ol' way. After a long moment of silence she said 'It don't look good for none of ya'll standing around me here today.' She kept on lookin at that ol' ball, and then at each one of us. Then she said in a loud whisper 'something real bad is gonna happen to all of you this summer!' Floyd looked at his wife like he was crazy. As for me, I didn't say a word. So she said it again. 'Something real bad is gonna happen to all of you standing right here, before me.' Then Floyd got down right smart mouthed and asked 'Well tell us what's gonna happen to us, if you know so much.' That ol' Gypsy looked at us, and said 'ya'll and a whole bunch of other people gonna die this June, right down here in Cameron!' Cun Bean, Floyd Bargeman laughed real loud at her. 'Don't laugh at me, son!' she said. 'Cause you might be real sorry you did later on.' And then Floyd got so mad, he pulled Mae West away by the arm and said 'come on Mae let's go. We ain't got to listen to that ol' foolishness! As they were leaving he shouted back at her 'How a whole bunch of people gonna die in Cameron this June, anyway? That don't even make no sense!' Cun Bean, after that...Floyd and Mae West walked away...Falling out laughing."

Grandma Louisa's living room was speechless for the moment. So quiet, if a pin dropped each of them could have heard it hit the floor. Even the kids were still, as Charlene somberly continued the story.

"But ya'll know something, I didn't laugh at her. I just got up from my seat with a real funny feeling and said thank you, Ma'am. Then I grabbed Delores and James and told them to come on let's go home. That ol' woman had done scared me half to death. All day long, today, I been having that same funny feeling, I had yesterday. Delores and James was so mad at me because they wanted to stay and ride some more rides. But I couldn't stay out there no more. After hearing all of that ol' mess my head started killin me. So we just came on home."

"Lord have mercy, Charlene. You know they say it's something to that ol' mess."

"Really Cun Bean?"

"Yes Sir! Bryant told me just this afternoon that ol' woman you talkin about told his son Raymond and his wife Lula the same thing she told ya'll. They was down there at that carnival yesterday too."

"Who Cun Bean?"

"You know Bryant's son Raymond...married to Lula Andrews."

"No Cun Bean...I didn't know Cun Bryant had a son named Raymond."

"Yea Honey! Bryant fathered that boy with Miss Melete LaSalle way before me and him got married years ago. But he never stayed with us though."

"Ain't that something. So she told them the same thing too, uh? Well, I guess it is something to it...Ain't it?" Charlene appeared as though she had suddenly started believing in the misfortune.

"Honey, I heard they can tell you a lot of things."

"Well, Cun Bean what in the world was she tryin to tell all of us?"

"I don't know Charlene. No Sir! I sure don't."

"Well, I hope she is dead wrong. I know I ain't ready for me or my kids to die this summer in June. Ump!!! We ain't lived long enough yet."

"I know whacha mean, girl."

Bean, Grandma Louisa and Grandpa Seedy looked at Charlene, peculiarly. Charlene shook her head and said "Well I guess we better be goin on home, kids. Now you really got me scared Cun Bean. Ya'll take it easy. It was good seeing you."

Charlene appearing even more disturbed after sharing her experience with the Gypsy departed with her children.

"Ain't nothin to that ol' mess, Bean" Grandma Louisa said. "All them thangs won't is ya'lls money. But they ain't gon git mines. I already ain't got much as it is, and I ain't gon throw it away on foolishness like that. Now that ol' woman got my baby all shuck up.

Shoots! They ought to have a law, to stop them ol' suckers dead in they tracks before they let um in Cameron. Scaring up the folks like that. That don't make no sense a-tall!"

"I don't know, Grandma Louisa. I always heard you better pay attention to what them ol' Gypsies say. At least that's what Momma told us. I'm only going by what she said. Momma even told me that ol' Gypsy told my brother Joe, his wife Alice and Annie the same thing."

"Ump! Now where Mary git that ol' silly mess from Bean? I know she ain't got it from me. Cause I ain't never believed in that ol' stuff before. The next time you-n-Charlene want to throw ya'lls money away, just give it to me...before you waste it up on that foolishness!" Grandma Louisa laughed very resonantly.

"Sometimes you just never know!" remarked Grandpa Seedy.

"Especially, living in this ol' world. Anything can come true. Oh Lordy! This here ol' back sure gon kill me if I don't do something about it pretty quick."

"You better go to the doctor Grandpa Seedy and see about yourself."

"I reckon so, Bean. I reckon so."

Cameron's thriving economy brought with it a lot of partying and good times because people had money to burn. The Front was the place to be for colored folks in Cameron, especially on Friday and Saturday nights. Sometimes the back streets where the night clubs resided witnessed a traffic jam with mobs of people and bumper-to-bumper cars. Many colored folk drove from Creole, Grand Chenier and as faraway as Lake Charles, Lake Arthur and Port Arthur, Texas just to come and party in Cameron. The fact was things had gotten a bit out of hand on The Front. Gambling, plenty of fights, wine, women, prostitution, illicit love affairs, and fornication were prominent. People just weren't living the life they were singing and praying about. Many colored ladies desiring a man, hung out on The Front looking not only for the available, but the attached married men as well. To some it made no difference.

On June 23, 1957, Rev. R. B. House was preaching the 11:00 o'clock morning service before a packed congregation at the Ebenezer Baptist Church.

"The Lord's gonna blow through Cameron like a storm, and clean up all of this sinful mess going on 'round here. He's tired of all ya'll serving everybody, and everything but Him. The Lord is tired, Cameron. He's tired. And if people don't start praying and living right, he's gonna clean up this mess real soon! Don't get caught out in the storm, without the Lord on your side. It'll be ashamed, if you die and loose your soul to worldly sin. Church, it's time to let go of the evils of this ol' earth and turn your life over to Jesus."

Rev. House's tone of voice changed from a roaring lion to that of an humble lamb, as he closed his sermon. "The Lord can and will see you through the wind, rains and floods that's going on in each of your lives. All of you sitting here today. Just trust the Lord, people. Let him be your guide. Because without him you want see the Kingdom of Heaven. The doors of the church are opened.

COME TO JESUS. RIGHT NOW. HE'LL SEE YOU THROUGH THE STORM!

After Rev. House concluded his very powerful, moving message, the services were dismissed. The reverend left each member with a sense of self evaluation. Many people were touched by his inspiring words of true devotion that lifted the name of Jesus in such a zealous manner. Bryant, Lovenia, Nip and Walter gathered outside on the grounds to greet Lee Boy, Nita, Greg and Marlon. Mary, Lil and Lo were home from college. Mary walked out of church looking like a chocolate southern belle. Lil looked subtly sophisticated, and Lo resembled a Hollywood movie actress.

It was amazing how going off to college had a way of refining the appearances and attitudes of the Bartie females. Today, there was no way one could take either of the girls for a once-poor sharecropper's daughter. And Nita looked absolutely stunning.

Even though she had given birth to two sons, she somehow maintained the figure she'd had as a coed. Bryant walked around the church grounds with an inflated chest. He was so proud of his girls, who were doing extremely well in college. The girls had many relatives to say hello to. If they didn't take out time for greetings, some of their kin folks would probably think that getting an education had swollen their heads, or that the girls had suddenly become to stuck up in the midst of their success. As Nita looked at her sisters it brought back a lot of memories of the days when she attended Grambling. She was so proud of them because each had blossomed into a fine young lady in her own special way. Once the whole crew had said hello to practically all the members of the congregation, Big Momma, and her sons and their wives-which took-forever, the whole family departed for Bryant's place.

Later on that afternoon, Lil invited Lo to ride along with her over to the home of Betty Jane LeBlanc, who lived east of the Cameron Consolidated School. Lil and Betty Jane had been best friends in high school. Betty Jane was several month's pregnant, and since she was about to become a mother, Lil wanted to catch up, on all the happenings that had been going on in her life. Betty Jane was as attractive as both Lil and Lo. A classy looking young colored girl, she'd married a young man by the name of Charles LeBlanc. Of course Lil and Lo chose to wear fashionable cool outfits to weather the hot sun. Mary didn't go with them because she had some pressing issues to discuss with Nita over the phone.

When Lil and Lo arrived, Betty Jane was thrilled to death to see them. She looked absolutely wonderful, even pregnant. The girls talked for hours and hours and hours. The evening went by in a flash, and then before they knew it, it was time for Lil and Lo to head back home.

"Bye Lil and Lo. Thanks so much for coming by to see me."

"Take care of yourself, girl, and don't do too much until after the baby gets here. Okay?"

"I won't Lil. Bye Lo, and say hello to Mary and Nita for me."

"Bye Betty Jane. Take care now!"

"Lo," Lil said during the drive home. "Betty Jane looks absolutely beautiful."

"She sure does Lil, but she always has."

"I've got a wonderful idea, Lo. Why don't we give her a baby shower?"

"Good idea, Lil. I'll tell Nita and Mary about it too. Maybe we can have it at Nita's house in Grand Chenier."

"Good thinking, Lo. We can invite all the girls that went to high school with us and have a wonderful time together. You know...sort of like a reunion, but to celebrate Betty Jane's pregnancy. It will be good to see everybody again."

"Sure will! I'll get in touch with Nita as soon as we get home to ask for she and Lee's permission. We have to do some quick planning.

The baby looks like it's about to pop out in a matter of days. And I definitely want to do something special for my dear friend before the baby arrives."

"I totally agree, Lil."

Meanwhile, Mary and Nita were conversing over the phone. "Nita! Girl, I couldn't wait to get back home from New Orleans, so we could talk."

"Really! What's going on Mary?"

"I don't even know where to start. Things in my life have gotten a bit complicated to say the least."

"Mary, are you sure you want to discuss this matter over the phone? Remember other ears could be listening, and that may not be such a good notion."

"You're so right, girl. I never even thought about that. And I don't want my business up and down this Front Ridge Road. But I really need to talk to you, Nita."

"Mary...I don't think it's safe over the phone."

"Okay...Let's change the conversation. This can wait until next Sunday, when we're in the company of each other. Nita, on a different note how is Annie and her pretty little daughter Vickie doing?"

"I don't know Mary. I haven't seen Annie in quite some time. I guess they're doing fine. Remember all those good times we shared together as kids...She...Uncle Joe... Aunt Alice...Those were some good ol' days."

"Yes I remember them very well, Nita."

"You know Mary, with the boys and all, I don't get a chance to do much visiting or to see too many people, unless they're at church."

"That's true, Nita."

"The last time I heard from Annie was when Momma spoke to her about three or four months ago."

"Oh yea?"

"Um uh. Guess what girl?"

"What Nita?"

"Annie told Momma that she and Dalton were in Cameron this past January at the carnival, and some ol' Gypsy woman was telling everybody that they were going to die in June. Can you believe that?"

"Die in June, Nita? What kind of silly mess is that?"

"That's right, girl. That ol' Gypsy told both Annie and Dalton. Momma said Annie got so upset after hearing that, it liked to drove her crazy."

"Really girl?"

"And you know what Mary? Momma said that ol' Gypsy told Charlene the same thing, too."

"Our cousin...Aunt Lucille's Charlene?"

"Uh, huh, girl! Sure did."

"Nita, I don't believe in that ol' psychic stuff. I think it's make believe if you ask me. Besides, if it were factual, why hasn't anything happened to any of them yet? Shoots...the month of June is almost over, so that should tell you something right there."

"Excuse me!!! But ya'll betta believe in it," rang out an angry, feminine voice convincingly. "I was at the carnival myself and she told me the same thing!!"

"NITA WHO WAS THAT, GIRL?"

"I guess someone's listening in on our conversation, again."

"Yeah, I'm listening to ya'll crazy fools" responded the snooping person.

"Well excuse me, but what are you doing eavesdropping in on our business?" inquired Mary.

"I got ears, don't I? And I think that's why the Lord gave um to me, so I can use um' to hear. Right? OH!!! And by the way I do pay my phone bill every month...NOW!!! So that means I can listen in whenever I want too."

"Mary I think it's time for us to hang up the phone," said Nita, digustedly. "I can not tolerate much ignorance."

"OH! So now I'm gittin on your nerves, uh? Ya'll ol' Bartie girls think ya'll know every thing just cause you done went off to college.

Well let me tell you one thing, Baby...I'm just as smart and just as pretty as the both of ya'll ol' ugly thangs. And I ought to know what the woman told me. I don't think I'm deaf. And if ya'll don't believe it, maybe you should've went and seen her for yourselves...Witcha silly self...Thinkin people got to lie about something like that. I ain't got to lie. I swear on top of my momma's grave, she told me that...And anyways, what I got to lie for...to ya'll? Ya'll ain't nothin!"

"Wait just a minute. No one's questioning your integrity' Miss Nosy Rosy. But I do think that you extended your opinion to us, without our consent, my dear friend. And if I'm not mistaken, I also think it was you who so rudely interrupted this conversation, blasted Nita.

"First of all...I ain't your friend! Missy! Second of all...you and Mary don't have to believe it, cause I can care less about what ya'll thinks!"

"Mary, where ignorance is bliss, Tis folly to be wise."

"Nita, I know what you mean girl. It is time for us to hang up this phone."

"Good! I'm glad ya'll ol' crazy girls is gittin off the line. I ain't got time to listen to no more hum bug, anyways. I have better things to talk about to my friends... instead of talkin to you silly thangs!"

"See Mary that's the main reason why you shouldn't discuss your private business over the line."

"Look girl, ain't nobody thinkin...nothin...about none of ya'll ol' business. You ain't got no private business noways. Not as long as you talk on this party line, you don't. If ya'll was so smart...you art-to-know that by now!"

"I guess she does have a point. I'll talk to you later, Mary."

"Okay. Bye Nita."

As soon as Mary hung up the phone, Lo ran through the house screaming.

"Wait a minute, Mary let me talk to Nita before you hang up the phone."

"Oh, Oh, too late Lo. Some ol' rude girl wanted to use the line."

"Ah Mary, I wanted to ask Nita if we could have a shower for Betty Jane at her house."

"I'll mention it to her tomorrow. You know what Lo? That ol' girl on the party line just snapped us both up about an ol' Gypsy who was at the carnival in Cameron this past January telling people's fortunes. She supposedly told a lot of people that they were going to die this month. So I said I didn't believe in that ol' stuff. What did I say that for? That girl got so upset with me and Nita, she almost came through the phone."

"Really Mary? That's the craziest thing I ever heard before in my life. How would an ol' Gypsy know something like that?"

"The girl on the line said she told her she was going to die this June. So I don't know!"

"My what a nut. Who was she in the first place, Mary?"

"Girl, I'm not sure, but I think I have an idea after she swore over her dead mother's grave."

"Well she's crazy, whoever she is. How in the world is she and all these people in Cameron suppose to die in June?"

"Lo, girl! I don't know. Nita said Momma told her that Charlene and Annie both went to see the same ol' lady and she told them that too."

"Really Mary? Oh well! I sure hope she's wrong."

"Anyway, the month of June is almost over and nothing has happened yet...So what do we have to worry about? Now, on a good note Betty Jane looks wonderful, girl."

"Does she really Lo?"

"She sure does," interrupted Lil. "Now what's this mess, I overheard the two of you talking about an ol' Gypsy at some carnival in Cameron telling everybody that they were going to die...this year...in June?"

CHAPTER 16

On Tuesday afternoon at 2:30 P.M., June 25, 1957, Nita had just put Gregory and Marlon to bed for a nap. The family didn't own a television, so her only form of entertainment was reading magazines or listening to her small radio. The day was so hot and humid that the window fan caused more frustration by merely circulating warm instead of cool air. Lee Boy wasn't due back from his seven day shift until Wednesday.

Nita stepped out onto the front steps of her house to try and find a cool breeze somewhere in the air, but no such luck. Her eyes wondered across the marshlands; nothing interesting was in sight except for three tall white cranes standing on top of a log in the ditch on the other side of the road. Nita stood there for a moment and thought "Will I ever finish college, some day?"

After seeing Mary, Lil and Lo, she'd gotten a bit sentimental. The notion of college lingered, before being interrupted by a babyish cry coming from the boy's bedroom. Once she heard the baby's shout, her mind found its way back to reality. She rushed inside the house to see what the whining was about. Marlon's pacifier had fallen out of reach, so she placed it back into his mouth and gently rubbed him across his back. He fell asleep instantly.

Nita glanced over at Gregory who was in dream land. She knew everything was fine with him because of the peaceful smile on his little face. An ol' horsefly swarmed almost cheerfully around his infantile body, however Nita ran to the kitchen and picked up a fly swatter and returned with it. She chased the fly out of the boy's bedroom and into the hall. Finally, after cornering the nuisance, she swatted it off the wall. The boys paid no attention to her maternal exertion, as they continued in their deep sleep.

Afterwards, Nita went to the kitchen and got herself an ice cold glass of Coke to try and find some relief from the hot weather. Then, she went into her bedroom and fell across the bed to finish reading an Ebony magazine. "Think It Over" by B. B. King was blaring out of the radio. She got up to turn the volume down, hoping the noise hadn't already disrupted her two young son's sleep. She listened for a moment to hear if another cry would follow.

Before she was able to turn the knob, however a news bulletin interrupted the music on KJET:

"A storm has been spotted about 380 miles out in the western quadrant of the Gulf of Mexico, by a U. S. Navy Reconnaissance plane. No need for immediate panic. However, heavy rains and high winds are predicted for tomorrow through the weekend. Now back to some more music with 'Oh What a Nite' by The Dells."

"Good! Whooooooof! Maybe the rain will help cool things off a bit. It is just too hot!" Nita wiped away some sweat from her forehead and continued to read an article. Eventually, shortly thereafter she fell asleep.

All along the shell roads in Grand Chenier, Creole, and Cameron, the next day dawned on crawfish crawling out of the marsh. They were everywhere; so plentiful people merely walked the road and picked the critters up with their bare hands by the five gallon bucket full. Lillie, her mother—now known as Grandma Frances,—and Nita's neighbor Jeanette joined in the excitement with the rest of the folks. Jeanette's husband Son was away at work at the Swindell Pogy Plant in Cameron. Simon was awaiting Lee Boy's arrival from his seven day shift. Simon was due to start his shift later that afternoon by taking the True Friend to the Intracoastal Canal to complete a job there. Nita sat inside her house and listened to all the commotion going on out on the road.

Everyone was overwhelmed by the numerous crawfish crawling in every direction.

"Boy, this is a lot of crawfish, ain't it Momma?" said Lillie.

"Yea Lillie, it is," said Grandma Frances. "I'm gonna get some for Miss Emma. Her and Mr. Lee like'm boiled."

"My kids love'm that way too. I'm gonna get as many as I can" said Jeanette.

"Ya'll know something Lillie and Jeanette?" said Grandma Frances. "This ain't a good sign when you see all these crawfish crawling from out the marsh. We ain't never had nothing like this happen in Grand Chenier before. Not in all my years of living here."

"I know what you mean, Momma." Lillie replied. "Something is wrong. This is the most crawfish I ever seen before in my life, too. Just crawling along the road in Grand Chenier."

"I don't care what ya'll say," Jeanette remarked. "I'm gonna get as many of um as I can. Cause at least we ain't got to pay for um. These things is real high up in the store."

"Yea, you right Jeanette. They sure are high. So I guess we need to stop complaining and be thankful to the Lord they out on the road for us to pick up so easy. But I still say something is wrong."

"Momma, you're right. It's been so hot lately and the old people used to say pay close attention to the animals because they can tell you a lot of things about the weather. Lord knows they always knew what they was talking about, them old people." Then Lillie pointed at the road. "Look at that big crawfish right over there by your foot, Jeanette!"

"Oh! Now I see it. That is a big one! Boy it's really getting hotter and hotter, ain't it ya'll?"

"Whoooooooof! It is Jeanette," responded Lillie.

"Jeanette...Momma did I tell you that Simon's Uncle Frank Reed got a house full of his grandchildren down there?"

"No, I didn't know that."

"Me either, Lillie."

"Um hu! His little granddaughter whose name is Jeanette just like yours..and named after her grandma Aunt Duke...and they little grandson Frank came from Lake Charles to visit them last week.

Their other grandson Bobby Sims was already down here before them two came. Then Aunt Duke went to California last week and brought two more back with her."

"Really Lillie?" said Grandma Frances.

"Simon told me that Aunt Duke was supposed to get in early this morning with Rebecca and Geraldine."

"Now what's them kids last name?" asked Jeanette.

"Guidry."

"Lillie, Lee Boy ought to bring Gregory and Marlon down there to see their little cousins," said Grandma Frances.

"I'm gonna tell Lee Boy to do that. That's a good idea."

"Now Momma Lillie, talkin about California, how's your daughter B-Bean doing?" asked Jeanette. "And what about her husband Blick, and they kids Joyce, Cindy, and Juan?"

"They all right Jeanette. You know B-Bean and them kids are supposed to be coming down here sometimes this summer.

"No, I didn't know that. Now what's B-Bean's husbands real name?"

"William. William Avant. They just call him Blick for short.

"That's right. I couldn't think of his name the other day for nothing," said Jeanette. "I believe I've got enough crawfish for the whole year. I'm going home."

"I think we have enough too Momma."

Grandma Frances, Jeanette and Lillie gathered enough crawfish to last for quite awhile. Once they got home, they washed the crustaceans several times before boiling them.

Later on towards the evening, the beautiful blue skies became obscured with heavy, dark, gray clouds. Nita stood on the front steps of her home and sensed the change in the weather. "Boy this sky just doesn't look good. Something's wrong. I mean, all these crawfish crawling out of the marsh, and now these crazy, colored-looking skies just popped up. I wonder what's going on with Mother Nature?"

As soon as Lee Boy got home from work Nita discussed the weather with him and then she called Mary to see how she and the rest of the family was doing.

"How's my little fellas doing?" Mary asked.

"They're fine. I just finished bathing them, and put'm in the bed."

"Nita! I ain't never seen so many crawfish before in my life.

People were walking all along the Front Ridge Road...picking them things up, girl."

"They were doing the same thing here in Grand Chenier. Momma Lillie gave us a whole bunch of those things. I don't know what we're gonna do with all these crawfish. That's why I was calling you, to see if ya'll wanted some."

"I don't think so, Nita. We have plenty. But Momma did say that Grandma Louisa might."

"That's a good idea. I'll save her some and maybe me, Lee and the boys can bring them to her tomorrow or Friday. She's been dying to see Greg and Marlon anyway!"

"I'm sure she'll appreciate the crawfish because you can't keep those things in the box too long. Please bring the boys by to see her. She wants to see them so bad."

"I will Mary. How's the weather down there?"

"Nita, it looks real funny. And Momma said with all of these crawfish crawling out of the marsh something bad is bound to happen."

"I think she's right girl."

"How do ya'll know something bad is gonna happen?" blared out a voice over the party line. Ya'll ain't God are you?"

"Oh Lord, Mary. Here we go again. I guess some people don't have anything else better to do with their time, but to sit and monitor other people's phone calls. How annoying! GEE!!

"You're so right, Nita."

"Well, if ya'll don't want them ol' crawfish, I'll take some of them for myself," laughed the outlandish female.

"Why don't you tell us who you are?" responded Nita. "Maybe we will share some of them with you."

"Click" went the receiver.

"Mary, tell Momma and the others hello for me. I sure hope this weather clears up soon. I was hoping for rain, to kind of cool things off, but now, I don't think that was a good idea at all. I'll call you tomorrow. Take care Mary!"

"Bye Nita! Kiss the boys for me."

"Okay. I will. Have a good night and keep an eye out on the weather."

After Lee Boy and Nita ate supper, they decided to go to bed early, since the weather made up so terribly, outside. The east wind's velocity increased something fiercely as it hollered, while the rain slammed against the window panes throughout the house. Nita was too afraid to lay down in bed, so she sat up and talked to Lee.

"Something's just not right, Lee. I mean these howling winds are very frightening."

"They say that there is a storm out in the Gulf, so I guess that's why we're getting so much of this wind and rain."

"Yea! I heard the same thing on the radio, yesterday. I ain't never seen the weather act like this before. Have you?"

"No!! I haven't. But, come on Honey, lay down and try' to go to sleep."

"I just can't sleep right now, Lee. You know something?"

"No! What Honey?"

"I've got a funny feeling that this is going to be the last night we sleep together in this house, ever again."

"Oh Honey! Stop talking crazy! It's just a little storm. It'll past soon."

"No Lee. I really mean that!"

"Well I'm too tired to even think about something like that right now. Goodnight!"

"Goodnight, Lee."

Unable to sleep Nita kept going back and forth to check on the boys in the back bedroom. During the course of the night, she discovered rain water everywhere in the bathroom, so she got a towel and blotted up the puddle. However, this was to no avail as the rain kept beating against the pane and seeping through the eastwindow. She tried placing a towel at the window seal to stop the rain's steady flow, but that did very little. After trying so persistently, to keep the water out, Nita simply went to bed. She didn't attempt to awaken Lee Boy. Nita lay in bed and prayed to God, for she sensed something unusual in the making. Thursday morning at approximately 5:45 A.M. Son and Jeanette were lying in bed together. Son's head was at a point were he could see clearly out of the south window of their bedroom.

"Jeanette, when did they build that levee out there in the marsh?"

"It's always been out there. Son. Shut up and go back to sleep."

"Aw, Jeanette! I ain't been gone, but three days. And I know, ain't no dragline can build a levee in just three days."

"Son, I said shut up please! I done told you, I'm trying to sleep. That levee has always been out there."

"Well, I sure don't remember seeing it there the last time I was home."

"I wish you would go to sleep, Son. You making me real sick!"

Cooperating, Son tried to go back to sleep, but he just couldn't. He lay in bed for a short moment, then raised up again because he saw something white moving back and forth about the levee.

"Jeanette! Look!!! I believe I see a big ol' white crane moving on that levee way out there."

"Son, if you don't be quiet, I'm gonna knock you over the head. Ain't nothing out there, I done told you once!"

"Jeanette, what ever it is, it's moving back and forth a whole lots!"

Son kept on looking, as far as he eyes could see from the vantage of his bed. Then he jumped up! "BOOM!!" Both of his feet hit the floor. He ran to the front door, quickly, and opened it up. That's when he saw the white caps on the waves of the mighty Gulf of Mexico, rolling directly towards their house.

"JEANETTE! JEANETTE! JEANETTE! OH LORD HAVE MERCY JESUS!!! he shouted. "THAT'S THE GULF OF MEXICO COMING THIS WAY!!! "

Jeanette got out of bed to take a quick look for herself.

"HURRY UP! GET THEM KIDS UP! WE AIN'T GOT NO TIME TO WASTE!!!!!

Son threw on the first pair of pants and a shirt he found lying in a chair next to the bed, and out the door he raced on his bare feet. Next door at Lee Boy's home. It was about 5:50 A.M. Nita awakened before he. She was staring out the east window of the bathroom at the grayish-colored skies. About a quarter of an inch of water had accumulated on the floor overnight. She reached for a towel to wipe it up. "This sky just doesn't look right" she thought as she continued looking out the window. Weary over the sky's appearance, Nita went to the living room window to get a better look outside.

"OH MY GOD" she gasped. She saw the white caps on the waves rolling inward towards the road. Nita ran to the back room to awaken Greg and Marlon. A loud banging rang out simultaneously at their front door.

While Nita was in the kids room. Lee got up quickly, to see what the commotion was all about and opened the front door.

"LEE BOY!!! yelled Son. "YA'LL BETTER GET UP FROM THERE! LOOK! THE WATERS DONE COME UP! GET UP!

GETUP! IT'S THE GULF, LEE. HEADED STRAIGHT TOWARDS US!!!!!!!!!! Son, calling the last words over his shoulder, was already sprinting toward Lillie's house.

Nita's heart pounded in bewilderment. She grabbed the first thing she saw in sight; an old pair of pants and a shirt flew onto her body as she pushed her feet into a pair of rubber thongs. Lee put the first thing on that he could find. Meanwhile, once Son reached Lillie's yard, he was so ecstatic, he jumped completely over the hurricane fence that surrounded her home without being conscious of his actions. When

Lillie opened up the door, after his banging, Son found her already awake, doing some ironing for Miss Annie.

"COME ON!!" he shouted. "LET'S GO!"

"Go where Son? What's the matter with you. You crazy or something?"

"COME ON MOMMA LILLIE. THE WATERS DONE COME UP!!!"

"SON! Quit acting the fool. What water you talking about?"

"COME ON MOMMA LILLIE LET'S GO!"

"Whacha talkin........?

"THE GULF IS COMING OVER THE ROAD, RIGHT NOW!! WE AIN'T GOT NO TIME TO PLAY."

"What...why...well let me call B-Bean and tell her what's happening, first."

"YOU CRAZY? LOVENIA IS SAFE...SHE'S ALL THE WAY IN CALIFORNIA. WE'S THE ONE IN DANGER! COME ON LETS GO!!

Son left Lillie's place and ran back to his house as fast as his legs could pump.

Meanwhile, Lee Boy had rushed to the boy's room and grabbed Greg. Nita already having Marlon in her arms. She picked up his old diaper bag and tossed a few clean ones inside. Then she raced to the kitchen, grabbed a couple of bottles of juice and milk, and threw them in with the diapers. By the time she, Lee and the boys stepped down onto the bottom step in their front yard, the beige colored, murky Gulf waters were lapping at their ankles. They held the boys up high, away from the smell of decayed matter mixed in with the surf. Shingles on the rooftops of the houses nearby flew off like feathers and scattered about them. The winds howled something dreadful.

It was a good thing Son was in a state of panic. Had he not been so consumed with informing Lee Boy's family and Lillie, and only concerned about himself and the safekeeping of his own household, the Harrisons may not have been so lucky as to get an advanced warning. Even though Son's car was parked right outside next to his house, he was obsessed with the thought of getting a ride to higher ground with either Lee Boy or Lillie. The excitement caused him to simply forget all about owning a car! Once Son, John Jr., Jimmy Lee, Pamela Sue, and Jeanette with Donald in her arms reached Lee Boy's house, both families rushed over to Lillie's place.

"COME ON MOMMA LILLIE! LET'S GO!" cried Son.

"COME ON MOMMA. PUT THAT STUFF DOWN AND LET'S GO. WE AIN'T GOT NO TIME TO WASTE!" shouted Lee Boy.

"Ya'll please let me call MY DAUGHTER!" cried Lillie.

"NO MOMMA! WHERE'S THE KEYS TO THE CAR?" demanded Lee Boy.

"Look!!! They right there on the table."

"COME ON GRANDMA FRANCES. WE GOTTA GET OUT OF HERE!!! yelled Son.

Finally, after much chaos and the eventual willing cooperation of six adults, three children, two toddlers and one infant somehow all climbed into Simon's brand new '57 Chevrolet with Lee Boy at the wheel. They headed east up the Grand Chenier road, all of them inside feeling the waves from the Gulf swishing against the car as they pushed onward. Strong winds made it even more difficult for Lee Boy to maneuver the automobile in a steady path, as the car load of colored people struggled to reach higher ground. Each adult and small child looked terrified, while watching what once was the marsh in front of their home quickly swallowed by the Gulf of Mexico.

"Lee Boy, where we going at?" asked Son, very huffy.

"I'm, I'm, I'm going to try to make it up to Mr. John Paul Crains. His place is on the highest point in Grand Chenier."

"You crazy Lee Boy?" bellowed son as the waves rushed over the hood of the car and the winds made it even more difficult for them to hear themselves talk. "We ain't gonna make it that far. Look...the water is coming in the car now."

"Let me out right here, Lee Boy. I ain't going no further!" remarked Grandma Frances, very bold.

"No Momma," said Lillie. "Leave Lee Boy alone...Let him drive!"

"Put me down right here!" demanded Grandma Frances.

"Everybody be quiet!!" shouted Son. "Shut up!"

"That's okay Son," Lee Boy said nervously. "I'll put her down at Mr. Lionel Theriot's."

"Thank you!!!" yelled Frances. "Because ya'll's a bunch of crazy fools if you think you gon make up to Mr. John Paul's house."

Lee Boy drove the car off the road and onto the ridge. They put Grandma Frances down at Mr. Theriot's place, where she got out and rushed inside.

"Oh Lord, Ya'll" screamed Lillie. "We gon loose Momma...She ain't gon make it by herself."

"Let her go Momma," said Lee Boy. "Get back inside...we've got to let her go."

By the time the car made it back to the main road, the waves were splashing over the windows.

"STOP LEE BOY!!! Put us down right here" screamed Son.

"The car's gonna drown out. We can't go no further...Stop I say? Don't you see the waves hitting the windshield? Stop this car Lee Boy... If you don't stop it I'm gonna jump out now!!! "

Lee Boy didn't want to abandon Son and his family, so he pulled up to Mr. Alcy Theriot's place. There everyone jumped out in their bare feet deserting the car on the ridge, as they waded through the surf over to Mr. Curly Vincent's home seeking higher ground. Waves came splashing against their knees. During the struggle the wind blew shingles, debris, leaves, and branches stinging them across their faces. John Jr., held onto his brother Jimmy Lee as they braved the waters, while Son and Pamela Sue trotted through the surf hand in hand. Lee Boy clutched Greg tightly in his arms as he pushed forward, and Nita maintained a strong hold on her baby, Marlon. Jeanette held Donald close to her bosom, while Lillie rushed alone, sad and by herself among the colossal waves. Nearby oleander trees had already been uprooted and leveled by the surf, as the group of relatives struggled to get to Mr. Curly Vincent's front door in the midst of the bawling winds.

Lillie stopped for a quick moment and looked back to the west, one last time. She wiped away a small tear from her right eye and wondered if she would ever see her mother Frances and her husband Simon again!

Thursday morning June 27th, 1957 turned out to be a very lamentable experience for all residents living along the lower Cameron Parish coastline.

From Johnson Bayou all the way to Grand Chenier, people were only haphazardly warned of the malicious hurricane that emerged in the warm waters of the Gulf of Mexico. Like a thief in the night, the virulent calamitress proudly waltzed unexpected into the lives of her innocent victims. Resembling a black widow in attendance to a funeral, this "gaudy gal" was dressed in dark, dismal clouds of destructive winds that ranged to speeds of 125 m.p.h. Haughty, she rolled inland on a 10 foot high tidal wave gritting her teeth as manifested by ravaging, briny, white caps which chewed a path of havoc along the way. Escorted by intermittent rain, the unbiased antagonist screamed resoundingly, sounding more like a mammoth freight train than a natural phenomenon as she slowly rumbled through Cameron Parish. There was nothing feminine about this sinister cyclone, which conveyed a familiar, pungent odor constituted of marsh residue. The "Portrait of Death", her character had no respect for a person's race, creed, color or religion.

The feral female had already made plans in advance to selfishly annihilate anything and everyone that stood before her. Why had she come?

Only God in heaven truly knew the answer to that. A deadly trail of ruination would definitely be left behind as evidence of her malicious assemblage. To put it defiantly, this terrible day in June had relinquished to her a golden opportunity to command absolute respect from all. There was nowhere to run and nowhere to hide from her deadly winds and rambunctious waves.

Many affected by the extravagant lady's devastation thought the whole world was being destroyed by water a second time on this catastrophic morning. However, that was not God's true intentions for her being. It simply was the malevolent mistress's noble day to reign as "Queen of the Winds and Seas".

Her name was AUDREY!

As soon as the Harrisons and the Januarys reached Mr. Curly Vincent's front door, he threw it open to let them in. Another colored couple, Ermie and Cliff Bargeman showed up shortly, thereafter. Mr. Curly's daughters Melba Lou and Olga, hurriedly lit a candle and placed it near a Blessed Mother's statue in one *of* the bedrooms. The Vincent's were already rushing to desert their home, however, and desiring to seek protective shelter on the second level of their barn.

The barn was located to the east at a distance of several yards. Mr. Curly suggested that everyone evacuate the residence along with them, but Lee Boy and Son refused. He didn't waste any additional time trying to sway their thinking. Curly Vincent, his wife Helen, their two daughters, and two sons David (Dee Dee) and Lynn left the colored families behind. Together, the Vincent's braved the high waves en route to the barn.

As soon as they departed, AUDREY'S rough waters lifted Mr. Curly's general store completely up off its blocks and sent it smashing directly into the right side of the house. The store hit—BAM!!, then crumbled into splinters, apparently from an explosion, and the impact caused the front door to break open with great force. The house filled up with water rapidly and the children let out a loud scream as the waves came barreling through. Nita, Jeanette and Lillie worked tirelessly to keep the kids contained on top of a high bed in one of the bedrooms. Cliff and Ermie locked themselves in another room and never ventured out to extend any assistance. That left only Lee Boy and Son to try and halt AUDREY'S rumbling surf from egoistically making herself at home. Come on! We got to close that door, or we all gonna drown in here!" yelled Lee Boy. "Help me push this sofa in front of it!"

Nita, Lillie and Jeanette's hearts accelerated one hundred miles per hour as the waters quickly rose above their knees. The ladies sensed an immediate danger all around them, so they resorted to prayer, silently, amongst themselves. In the meantime, Lee Boy and Son labored diligently to stop the water from surging inside.

"Lee Boy! Push that chair over here…Bring that table too."

"Okay Son!"

"Hand me that hammer right there!"

"Here Son!"

God must have heard the lady's praying for the door was successfully nailed shut. The winds continued to wail, while erratic rains poured down turbulently, with the Gulfs murky waters oscillating back and forth, gushing against the front portion of the house. Time crawled by. Mr. Curly's son, Dee Dee, left his family in the barn and headed back to the house to see if everything was all right with the colored group. He treaded through the waters firmly gripping the fence each step of the way. Though things remained horrendous for the first half hour of the stay at the Vincent home, the candle in the bedroom never stopped burning soon after Dee Dee made it back to the house and crawled in through a window.

At 8:00 A.M. sharp, AUDREY'S forceful winds and turbulent surf worsened and the home began to shift more vigorously.

"Lee Boy! You feel that?"

"Oh Lord Son! I believe the whole house is gonna float off into the water."

The ladies and children let out another loud piercing cry as they felt the entire structure swaying back and forth, rhythmically conforming to the motions of the brawling waves.

"Lee Boy! We got to do something quick or we just gon float away like a log."

"Quick Son, open the doors and the front windows, so the water can run through the house."

"You must be crazy Lee Boy!! We all might drown up in here."

"Son!! That's the only way we can survive. We got to let the waters run through the house. If we don't its just gon float off its blocks like a boat…You already seen what happened to the store a few minutes ago… Open up the front windows and that door…I'll get the ones on the side. Come on and give me a hand Dee Dee."

The house rocked, twitched and lifted up and down like a see saw with each intrusion of the oscillating waves. The wobbling motion felt like a boat wavering on a rough, high sea. Shattering dishes splashed and sank to the kitchen floor, while pots and pans rumbled and floated everywhere. Spontaneously, the windowpanes blew out over the house. Clothes from the closets and dressers were everywhere. Pictures in frames fell from the walls and floated through the water over and around overturned furniture.

Finally, Lee Boy, Son and Dee Dee broke down the barricade they had worked so tirelessly to build. The waters rushed inside swiftly, bringing snakes, nutria rats, turtles, fish, crabs and all kinds of debris, logs, drift and seaweed with it. Lee Boy's clever plan to allow the waters to flow through proved to be very advantageous.

Once the house flooded throughout, the excess weight stabilized it in a stationary position. Though everyone had to battle the constant flow of waves rushing in—and the wild animals too—at least they didn't have to be wary of the house floating directly into the Mermentau. The river was only three quarters of a mile behind them, and could have brought on a major catastrophe.

After that incident Dee Dee triumphantly toddled the waves back to the barn. Several minutes later he decided to return to the house again, though, to lend his support, and the candle in the bedroom still burned and flickered from the overwhelming air current.

At approximately 9:00 A.M., the dark, tepid, overcast sky brought more torrential rains, and gale force winds of AUDREY struck the coastline with relentless reverberation. Out the window, Nita saw rooftops, shingles, branches, leaves, plants, and number three zinc tubs, hurling across the sky like sheets *of* paper, *all* sheeted in falling rain. Nearby trees had been blown down completely. An old car caught in a hurricane fence in the front yard to the west of the Vincent home stayed there for the longest time before it was finally released. Fortunately, floating away from the house. After he felt comfortable that the group was okay Dee Dee on a journey back to the barn, got tangled up in the howling forceful wind and rain. Things looked very dismal for him as he struggled to survive. The winds blew so hard, they actually lifted his body completely up from the water several times. Had it not been for the fence to which he clung for dear life, the first casualty of the day would have been witnessed right before Lee Boy and Son's eyes.

Dee Dee hung in there courageously and battled the gale winds and rustling waves. He managed to keep his head above water and eventually made it safely back to the barn. He was shaken so badly though he decided to stay put there for a long while.

In the midst of the forceful storm, Lee Boy and Son saw a large oil tank spinning over the waters out the front window, foregrounded by the marsh and headed straight for the house. Their eyes almost popped out, as they stared intently at the huge object aiming their way.

"There ain't no way none of us is gonna survive this one!" spoke Son in a whisper. "If it hits the house...."

"This is it!" shouted Lee Boy. "We're all gonna die...."

The huge tank continued on it's northerly course, rolling directly ahead, with the faint gray skies in the background. Nita and the others saw it coming too; the children were too young to comprehend the danger that was about to unfold. At that very moment, everyone put their heads down to await the inevitable, but something told Nita to pray out loud. So she bowed her head and said:

"Lord, please help us right now. We need you Lord. I beg you Jesus! Lord, let your Holy Spirit rain down upon us, Ol' Dear Master. You've got the power to conquer all. Save us right now Lord Jesus Christ, I pray to thee. Amen!" A split second later, Nita opened her eyes and looked out the window. The oil tank was in very close proximity to the house, but an infinite power from above had intervened. As it rolled over the hurricane fence at the edge of the front yard, the tank shifted its course to the west, abruptly spiraling to the left side of the house over the waves. It barely missed the home and the families inside.

When there was no immediate impact, everyone opened their eyes with confusion. Soon after, each person relinquished a sigh of relief, once they understood that the tank had passed them by. The group realized that it was only the grace of God that had truly spared their lives.

As if the tank wasn't oppressive enough to send everyone into a cardiac arrest, another dilemma quickly brought the families even more hysteria. Soon after the tank incident, a large black, water moccasin battling the waves tried it's best to gain entrance into the house. Greg and the other children wanted to get down off the bed to play in the water, but neither Nita nor Jeanette would allow such a thing fearing other snakes and animals could still be lodged under there. To divert the children's playful demeanor, Nita pointed out an interesting sight to them. A large nutria rat was approaching the window very gracefully, and riding on a log much resembling a kayaker. The animal appeared tranquil as it floated past the spectators. The kids became so excited over the amusing sight, they forgot all about wanting to play in the water below them.

Eventually, the waves swept the water moccasin away from the door and sent it on it's merry way, much to Lillie's relief. But at 11:30 A.M. came Nita's most grievous moment. The winds and rains still blew intensely, while the waters continued to fill up the interior of the home, rising to a level of about 18 inches. Nita picked up Greg and Marlon and walked over to the candle, which still brightly burned. All the other children, Jeanette and Lillie were in the living room with Lee Boy and Son, so that left the three of them alone.

"I wonder if I'm ever gonna see My family...My sisters...My cousins ever again?" She whispered and watched the flickering motion of the candle's flame that so gloriously illuminated the Blessed Mother" figure.

She continued to pray sincerely. Her meditation was interrupted, however, as she recollected the time when her father was caught in the 1918 storm. "I remember daddy said in the midst of a storm, never give up on God." Next, she thought about when as little girls she and Mary were trapped at sea on the sand pits out in the Gulf of Mexico. "That ol' Gulf has always been mean to us" she pondered. "Me and Mary both liked to drowned way back then.

And now look at what it's doing to us today! Mary, where ever you are, please don't give up hope. Please don't Mary!" she cried and sniffled softly. "What ever you do my dear sister, just hang in there for me. I hope all of you are okay. Please God, let my family make it through this storm. I beg you Jesus!"

Nita's cheeks were reddened from the flow of tears. Little Greg and Marlon sensed their mother's grief and wouldn't allow themselves to move an inch. They remained quiet, while she prayed and reminisced about all the anxieties of yesteryears. Greg stood on the bed next to her, his small consoling arms wrapped around her waist, and Marlon stayed close to her bosom, obedient and somber, staring directly into her glassy eyes. Nita stood next to the candle, praying in knee deep water; her two innocent, sympathetic children close by.

Marlon wanted to cry out himself because his raw, chafed bottom was beet red and irritated from the twice worn, urine-soiled diapers that clung to him. He withstood the pain like a little man, however he just kept his golden head of hair close to his mothers breast. Greg never once let his eyes wonder from Nita's face. The candle showed so brightly that three reflections of human life were imprinted large upon the wall, as the dull, mournful day provided a backdrop of despair.

Nita had to find a way to release some of the strife which tormented her bruised heart. She and her little ones looked out to the drumming sea from their vantage point at the window. She felt full. So full, another stream of tears poured down her face. "Please help us, Lord, to get through this storm...Please help my family where ever they might be. I really want to see them alive again, if it's not asking for too much...I beg you my heavenly father...From this day forth I promise I will serve you far better than I have in the past!"

Suddenly, a spiritual uplifting miraculously, overtook Nita's psyche, anointing her hurt and pain with a glorious calmness. She became zealously anointed, until she just couldn't help but to sing out:

"When the storms of life are ragin, stand by me.

When the storms of life are ragin, stand by me.

When the world is tossin me, like a ship upon the sea.

Thou who rulest the winds and waters. Come on Lord, and stand by me."

Greg and Marlon were speechless, though they maintained a stillness about themselves, allowing their mother to have her moment with God. Even as things appeared dismal for them all, Nita felt much better once she'd let the hurt and suffering out.

"Thank you Lord for standing by us thus far!" was Nita's joyful response after concluding a verse of "Stand by Me".

"Sometimes it's just good to praise God, even when your life is caught in the center of a vicious storm. Thank you my father."

In the midst of every storm, God shall and always will find a way to send the sun shining brightly through the dark clouds overhead. Again, the Lord heard Nita's call. In response, at twelve o'clock sharp, the sun lit up the darkness everywhere. The eye of AUDREY was passing over the Vincent home, bringing with it welcomed peacefulness. During that spectacular instance came the most beautiful view Nita and the boys had seen during the entire disoriented day: the sun's rays illuminating, magnificently, and sparkling over the Gulfs rough waters. The light was greeted as a glimmer of hope by everyone caught in this triangle of doom.

Nita and the boys joined the others in the living room, after her reverent moment, and a feeling of warm tranquillity covered the entire environment. Everyone rejoiced because they thought the storm was over.

The peacefulness, however lasted only a short time, for the audacious AUDREY had tricked them into believing she was finished with her treachery for the day. Instead, showing her ruthless spirit, she shifted her winds tremendously, and began blowing them again, forcefully, in the opposite direction. Each family member embraced one another, as she caught them off guard. They all just sat, sadly, awaiting the second half of dismay. For the eye of the storm had come and gone. "I wonder how Mary and the rest of my family are making out?" was Nita's somber, but sincere notion as the precarious skies, pulsating winds and pounding rains rolled in overhead one more time.

June 27, 1957, Bryant Bartie's Thursday morning had begun before daylight. He'd come home from the Swindell Pogy Plant late Wednesday night. The fish stench from the plant was embedded so deeply into his skin that he decided to sleep in the wash house out back to keep from disrupting his household with the foul odor. At about 5:00 A.M., Bryant heard something banging against the side of the little house. At first, he paid no attention to the noise, but it continued with the same rhythm, the wind disturbing his rest.

When he got up to see what the commotion was, darkness covered everything. He looked through a window and discovered that the noise was coming from a hanging bucket, swinging back and forth on a nearby tree. Bryant lay back down and tried to take another nap. however, the magnified noise was just too unbearable to go unnoticed. He jumped up again, longing to try and alleviate the clanging sound. As soon as he opened the door, though, he encountered a surprise.

"Plague-take-it" Bryant screamed loudly. "There's water everywhere out here!"

Bryant grabbed his same pair of soiled, fish smelling pants and shirt and put them back on. He threw on an old pair of work boots onto his feet, and rushed frantically out the door. The water came up to his ankles as AUDREY made her presence with debris flying across the sky, and winds that howled like a rampaging elephant. First, he ran around to the back yard where he noticed that most of his chickens had already drowned. Immediately, he dashed inside of the house, turned on several lights and screamed to the top of his lungs.

"Ya'll better git up from there!! They got water everywhere outside. Git up! Git up! Git up!"

Bean awakened first. Then Mary, Lil, Lo, Nip and Walter tumbled out of their bedrooms, startled.

Bean was half asleep. "What's the matter Bryant?"

"I believe that ol' Gulf done come up. They got water all over the place outside!"

"Oh Lord, Bryant! What we gon do?"

"Everybody hurry up and put some clothes on. We gotta go, as fast as we can. We ain't got no time to waste!"

Bean started running around picking up rugs, furniture and other things, trying to stack them at a point to where the water wouldn't damage the items, if it flowed to the interior. The entire house felt like it was going to blow off its blocks, as the Gulf raced towards it expeditiously.

"Bean!" shouted Bryant. "Leave that stuff alone. We ain't got no time for foolishness. Put your clothes on and let's go!"

Day break came in a flash soon after the family gathered themselves together in the front yard. The waves had come up to below their knees.

Bryant ran for his car parked in the garage, but he realized they'd get nowhere fast. Too much water had already rushed inland.

"Let's take the back marsh. Maybe we can make it to Momma's place before the water gets too high."

The Bartie family struck out, wading in the risen waters. They moved through the back marsh headed north like pilgrims under the somber, wailing skies. Although shabbily dressed, at least they had shoes on their feet. Mary, Lil and Lo were hand in hand, and Bryant held Bean's arm. Walter wore an ol' straw hat on top of his head, and he carried his dog with both arms. Nip walked besides him through the rushing waves. The journey would be a tough one because Big Momma lived approximately five miles away on the back ridge. In addition to the high waters, they would have to battle the marsh's boggy conditions, penetrate tall brush in some areas, plus cross over several barbed wire fences along the way. Bryant put forth a concerted effort to try and keep up the family's spirits because he realized the danger they faced as they trudged onward. Bean was the most pessimistic of the family.

"Lord, we ain't gon make it, Ya'll. We ain't gon make it!"

"Bean where's your faith in God?" responded Bryant, who appeared even-tempered. "Just keep walkin and don't look back."

At approximately 7:15 A.M., the water began to rise past their knees. Each one of them were fearful, as the waves rolled in rapidly from behind. The strong winds made it even more difficult to move ahead. Walter struggled desperately to carry his dog. Each of his steps continued to lag because of the extra weight.

"Walter," said Nip. "You gonna have to let that ol' dog go!"

"Yea Boy! Let that ol' thing go," said Mary.

"No! No! No!" he shouted. "I ain't gon let my dog go. Ya'll must be crazy."

Lil and Lo tried to remain at ease, but the waves were getting the best of them.

"Momma, you okay? Lil? Lo?" asked Mary.

"Yea!" They all responded in a huffy, exhausted tone.

"Just keep walkin and don't look back!" commanded Bryant. As the pilgrimage progressed, the family watched snakes, nutria rats, cows, horses, raccoons and other marsh inhabitants displaying fear, shock and confusion in their general vicinity. The animals appeared demented as they scrambled through the flooded marsh, trying to make sense out of all the water. When the family reached Joe LaSalle's place the water was so deep that Walter had fallen under several times, trying to save his dog's *life*.

"Walter!! Boy!!! Let that ol' dog go!" yelled Bryant.

"No Daddy. He can't make it by himself!" was the boy's tearful response. But Walter slid under the water again, this time losing his straw hat. Nip had to help his brother back onto his feet and, once up, the water was past the boy's waistline. AUDREY'S presence got worse as she blew debris in everyone's face. The wind blew so hard until it was difficult for them to keep their eyes open long enough to navigate through the surf.

"Where's my dog at Ya'll?" screamed Walter.

The dog somehow had drifted away and was struggling, hopelessly, to swim back to them. Walter in an effort to retrieve the animal tried his best to save its life, but the waves grew too overbearing.

"Come on boy. Leave that ol' dog along," yelled Bryant. "You can get another dog, but you can't get another life. Come back here, right now I said!!"

The surroundings got more intense with the coming of the turbulent rainfall and high winds. AUDREY'S rain beat the family unmercifully. Lil and Lo winded by now, Mary, in between the two girls tried to pull them along. The faster they walked, the further behind the dog remained. Everyone heard the dog howl for its life as he tried to battle the rolling waves. Walter kept looking back for his dear friend, but Nip dragged him along and tried to keep him content. "Ain't no time to worry about that ol' dog now, Walter. We got to save our own lives! Come on, boy! Let's keep going."

As the family got further and further away, the pet's whining cry diminished in the midst of the whistling winds, rain and rising waters.

Walter looked back one last time, and then the dog disappeared beneath the waves.

"I guess he died" sniffled the young boy, and a few bails of tears rolled down his face.

As each step progressed AUDREY'S waves and winds became more severe. So severe that Bean fell over into a large hole and slipped under the water herself. Once she surfaced, the trauma caused the poor woman to literally give up all hope for saving her own life.

"Oh Lord, Bryant! This is it," cried Bean. "I can't go no more. We ain't gon make it out of here alive! Not with all this water around us. I can't make it no more!! I just can't !!!"

The family stopped for a brief moment to catch their breath and Bryant encouraged his exhausted wife to push forward.

"Come on Bean, we almost to the Back Ridge Road," spoke Bryant encouragingly. "Just a few more miles to go and we'll be at Momma's house before you know it. Come on Bean. You can do it! I know you can."

"I can't Bryant. Ya'll go ahead and leave me here to die. I know I'm holding up everybody else. Just leave me, Bryant. Leave me here!" she cried.

"We ain't goin nowhere without you Bean. We going to make it together as a family. I know the Lord will see us through!!! Everybody just keep walkin."

The Barties seeing dead cows, coons, and nutrias floating around them were at the most gruesome point of the journey. They begun to fear for their own lives. Bryant tried not to think about the situation because the Back Ridge Road, where higher ground stood was just a few more steps ahead.

"Just hold on a little bit longer!" huffed Bryant. "Thank God we got this far, Ya'll."

He was so tired from having to literally carry himself and Bean, that he had to stop again for a well deserved break.

"Ya'll okay?" asked Bryant.

Everyone was too tired to answer. After a short pause, the family fought onward through more marshland and rough terrain. AUDREY, however, showed no mercy at all. She increased her wind's momentum and delivered a loud squalling sound all about them. Sheets of rain collided with their bodies making it more difficult for them to see two feet ahead. Thank God the water was not as deep for the last segment of the journey, which allowed them an opportunity to make better time.

After much strife, they reached Bryant's brother, Alcy's home. His wife, Stella, was canning some figs when they arrived. Each of the Barties were so tired and worn out until, they just fell down onto the floor once they got inside. Soon after, Bryant caught his breath and seeing that all of them were okay, ventured back out into the weather to go and check on his mother. Big Momma lived about a quarter of a mile east of Alcy's.

When Bryant stepped down onto the ground the water had already come up to his ankles. Hurriedly, he rushed to Big Momma's house, where he found his brother Pat and a house guest, Odelle Frank, with her. He didn't waste much time there after he felt comfortable knowing she wouldn't have to spend the storm alone. Bryant waded and sometimes swam back towards Alcy's place.

AUDREY'S rough waters, however kept on *pouring inland.* Bryant tried to run, but it did him no good because the waves and winds were too resistant. He wobbled through the water, as best he could. At Alcy's front yard, the waves had already risen up to his chest. There was no possible way for him to make it inside of the house because of the strong current.

Inside of the house the water had rushed in *everywhere. Alcy* and Stella were ecstatic as they witnessed AUDREYS surging waves overwhelming their belongings. Mary was worried stiff because she didn't see Bryant nowhere in sight. She didn't want to alarm Bean, but stayed at a front window and prayed to God for her father's safe deliverance.

"The water's gittin too deep in here," shouted Alcy, who became more desperate by the minute. "We gon have to knock a hole in the attic. That'll be the only way for us to save our lives!"

He worked quickly, and cleared a path through the ceiling for everyone to gain access into the loft. Mary remained, though, and continued to look out the window. The only thing she saw were rolling waves pouring into the house. Her heart throbbed, as she feared the worst for her father.

"Come on Mary! You gon have to climb up here with the rest of us," shouted Alcy, insanely. He literally went into a state of panic, so delirious over the high water. "Why you keep lookin out that window? Come on girl...Oh Lord, you better hurry up and git up here... Whooooo!!! That water is gittin real high down there...Look at it! Oh my God, Jesus!!! Please...Hurry up girl!!!! Whacha keep lookin out that window for? Whooooof!!! Come on and git on up here...Right now I said...Oh Lord! Help her Jesus!!!! Hurry up, Mary or you ain't gonna make it girl!!!"

"Wait a minute Alcy," Stella shouted. "I need to git back down there and put up my figs! I done worked too hard to loose all that fruit!!!"

"Stella...You crazy, woman? Leave them ol' figs alone and stay up in this attic before you go back down there and drown!!!!!"

As soon as the waves rolled over the stove the smell of figs mixed in with the gulfs stinky surf surfaced to the attic. The next thing everyone saw was the pot with figs all around it, floating on the water. Mary was having a difficult time trying to resist the raging waters. With water up to her breast she looked out the window one last time.

"Come on Mary. Git up here, girl!" shouted Alcy.

"I can't. I'm too scared of them ol' spiders and I know they got a lot of them up there."

"Girl, you better git on up here, right now!"

Mary knew she needed to move quickly or perish in the risen waters, but finally, she saw Bryant climbing up a tree in the front yard.

"Thank you Jesus" she screamed.

A big sigh of relief showed on her face.

"Daddy, you all right?" she yelled from the window.

"I'm okay. Tell Alcy to knock the front door open, so the water can go through the house!"

"Okay!" shouted Mary.

"And Mary, if the roof fly off, ya'll try to make it out here to this tree. Okay?"

"Okay Daddy" she responded loudly. I aint gittin back down in that deep water to do nothin!!" responded Alcy. "Lord have mercy... Bryant must be crazy if he thank I'm gon knock the front door down."

Mary was so relieved to see her father. In the nick of time, she climbed up into the attic and joined the rest of the family. Fortunately for her, she could still clearly see Bryant in the tree from the position where she sat.

Meanwhile, Bryant struggled to pull himself up to a higher point in the tree. During his exertion, he injured his arm, the task of climbing became even more difficult. The whole irony of his current situation was that when Bryant was fourteen, he saved his life during the 1918 storm by clutching the roots of a tree. Now, some 39 years later a tree became his means of salvation from the tempestuous winds of AUDREY, only this time, he clung to a tree's branches instead.

Bryant needed to climb up further still so he could pull his body out of the risen waters, but when he glanced up into the tree, much to his surprise, a huge black water moccasin snake was coiled around a branch directly overhead. The water moccasin opened its mouth widely, exposing the white interior of its throat obviously afraid of being threatened. Bryant got so scared he let half of his body stay in the whirling waters while he hung on tightly to a tree branch. Trembling with fear, he realized the snake was poisonous as he looked directly into it's mouth.

At about 9:00 A.M. the winds blew harder. Bryant's presence in the tree, along with the intermittent rain and the shifting of the branches, caused the snake's muscles to tighten. In reaction it raised upward, looked straight into Bryant's face and prepared to attack.

Realizing that he couldn't climb back down into the rough waters, Bryant remained in a stationary position, hoping and praying that the snake would eventually relax itself.

"What I'm gonna do now?" he pondered, petrified with fear. Below him the waters got rougher. He saw dead animals, debris, seaweed,

TV's and even a casket, which appeared to have been excavated from a nearby graveyard float past him.

"My Lord... And my God! Have mercy on me!!!" Bryant cried out.

To make matters even more bizarre, for the first time during this whole traumatic day, he witnessed two dead bodies wafting over the rolling waves, right past the tree. The presence of both corpses shocked him so that he let go of his firm grip and slipped down for a moment back into the water. "Ahhhhh!!!!" he gagged as he reached for a branch. Luckily, he caught hold of one and pulled himself up. He spat out a mouthful of the Gulfs salty, murky, waters. Reality sank into his mind, forcing him to comprehend just how uncertain his life stood at this point. As soon as he got back to the original point in the tree, the snake became arouse again, as if to dare him to move closer.

Mary through the window from the attic never took her eyes off of him and watched his every move. She had no inkling of the danger he faced. Bryant was in a no-win situation.

"In the midst of a storm, never give up" was his comforting speculation.

The winds velocity accelerated, and shook the snapping branches in every direction, but the snake never lowered its guard. The waves below swayed sporadically splashing water into Bryant's mouth. Determined not to be defeated, he took a deep breath and fought back with meditations:

"The Lord is my shepherd; I shall not want. He maketh me lie down in green pastures: he leadeth me beside the still waters. He restoreth my soul: he leadeth me in the paths of righteousness for his name's sake. Yea, though I walk through the valley of the shadow of death, I will fear no evil: for thou art with me; thy rod and thy staff they comfort me. Thou preparest a table before me in the presence of mine enemies: thou anoitest my head with oil; my cup runneth over. Surely goodness and mercy shall follow me all the days of my life: and I will dwell in the house of the Lord for ever."

But immediately after he'd finished reciting the 23rd Psalm, the winds only blew harder and harder and harder. AUDREY whipped, lacerated and beat him all over his face and body with the remaining branches of the tree, but he still hung in there bravely.

Leaves flew everywhere, and blinded him for brief moments. The Gulfs salty waves splashed high and the waters spurted over his bleeding, open lacerations causing him even more agony. The blood from these cuts dripped into the agitating waters below. To make matters worse, Bryant's dry mouth yearned eagerly for a glass of water. He could only quench his thirst by trying to grasp a few drops of the murky surf, as it splashed towards his head. Debris in the waves below continued to speed by, as death was about to envelop him. But he never once gave up hope.

"Please help me Lord!!!" was his mournful cry.

At about 11:00 A.M. things looked bad for the wounded Bryant, as AUDREY demanded his respect by bring him even more rigid punishment. As if retaliation to his profound courage, she shook the tree more vigorously than ever before. She rotated her rapid waves continuously below. Bryant lost his strong grip and slipped underneath the waters, again, but somehow managed to grab hold tightly to a nearby branch with one hand. After much agony and anguish he pulled himself upward to safety and slowly regained his composure. But through it all, he never gave up hope.

He knew that God was standing by his side. When Bryant looked up into the tree overhead and saw that the snake was no longer there, he let out a grateful cry.

"Whooooooof!!!!! Thank ya, my Lord!!! Thank ya for helpin me to make it through!"

Bryant, relieved over the disappearance of the serpent pulled himself up to an even higher point in the tree. That's when the sun came peeking through the dark clouds overhead at 12 o'clock noon.

The eye of the storm had finally come. Mary could see her father clearly as he sat high above in the tree. They kept communicating back and forth. Bean said very little during the whole ordeal. She just sat in the attic and mentally recited her rosary. Lil and Lo lay together in each other's arms. Nip and Walter slept through most of the agonizing weather. Finally, Alcy *and* Stella calmed down when they saw the sunlight shine brightly through the kitchen window. Nevertheless, no one knew the ordeal that Bryant had endured.

Bean stared up at the rafters as the sun pierced through a crack in the side of the house beaming a narrow path of light into her face.

"I wonder if Momma and Poppa made it out alive from that ol' beach?"

A small tear formed in Mary's eye, as her mind focused in on Nita, Lee and the boys. "In the midst of a storm, don't give up Nita. Don't give up!" she cried.

Lil sat up for a moment and looked a Lo. "Lo, I sure hope that Betty Jean is all right."

"I hope so Lil. And I hope that Bill, Susie and their kids are okay too. I thought about them as we passed near their home on our way here. Oh my God!! Please be with Nita, Lee and the babies, too" cried Lo.

Nip thought about his Uncle Joe, Aunt Alice, Annie and Vickie. Walter had Grandma Louisa, Grandpa Seedy and his dog on his mind.

The eye of the storm was a sad moment for the Barties as the reality of just how truly blessed they were to even still be alive began to sink in. The dark clouds moved in overhead once again.

Everyone in the attic remained motionless. Bryant prayed and thank the Lord for sparing his and the family's lives thus far. Then he braced himself for the second half of AUDREY'S treacherous invasion.

Being that the Gulf of Mexico was only a few yards away, the vibrant waters rose much quicker along the coastal beach than in other areas. At 4:00 A.M., Thursday morning, Bean's brother Harry (Jack) couldn't sleep for some disturbing reason. The harsh winds and dissonant rains had led him into a strange state of near panic.

He tossed and turned until finally concluding that this was not going to be a restful night, he jumped up, annoyed by the unusual climate.

Jack tried not to disturb Maw-Maw and Paw-Paw, who couldn't sleep themselves, as he walked slowly down the stair steps to the first level of the house. He was in search of some serenity there, but the bad weather made the same rumble as it did upstairs, providing little consolation. Heavy gusts of wind continued to blow the throbbing rain drops viciously against the rooftop of the house like torpedoes. With each blast of wind, Jack became more panic-stricken as he felt the entire house sway back and forth.

"Something just ain't right with this weather" he thought and stared out a living room window towards the Gulf.

Still weary over the high winds, and erratic rains, he opened the front door and stepped out onto the porch. That's when he noticed the Gulfs high tide rushing inland towards his parent's home. Jack's first reaction was to drive his car up on blocks, so that if the waters rose too high, it wouldn't be able to get inside. But soon after he accomplished that purpose and stepped back down onto the ground, the waves came rolling in at his ankles.

Jack sensed serious danger developing, so he rushed inside and awakened Maw-Maw and Paw-Paw. Jack and Paw-Paw merely had enough time to throw on a few pieces of clothes. Maw-Maw, however, moving a bit slower, was still in her nightgown and bare feet. Soon thereafter, the three of them made a mad, abrupt dash out of the house and towards the family car. Paw-Paw quickly started up the automobile and drove off, expeditiously, but Jack was so hysterical over the abnormal surf, that he forced Maw-Maw and Paw-Paw into a fearful state of excitement.

The three Bishops struck out eastward along the dirt road towards the "Swing Gate", with the waves splashing inside of the car. Paw-Paw tried to drive as fast as he could, hoping to make it to the Front Ridge Road before it was too late. However, too much water had already accumulated. Despite the fact Paw-Paw couldn't even see the dirt road ahead, he drove slowly onward, with the Gulfs water's coming up to each of their ankles inside of the car.

The vehicle putted and puttered, jerked and shook for as far as it could go through the rolling surf, but eventually, the engine died and the car's rigid, twitching motion came to a complete stop. The Bishops were trapped inside, as the waters eventually raised to their laps. That's when the pandemonium broke loose.

"Ahhhhhhhhhhhhhhhhhhhhh!!! Poppa what we gon do now? Look at all this water" screamed Jack. "We ain't gonna make it out of here alive if we don't do something quick!!!!" he cried.

Jack, desperate was vigorously attempting to shove open a back side passenger door, but the waves were too strong for him to even budge it. Each of the car's four doors were shut tight. Jack continued trying to muscle open the door.

"Ahhhhhh" he said, exasperated.

His efforts went in vain as the water kept seeping through. Maw Maw sat petrified in the front seat. The only thing she could do at this point was cry. Paw-Paw, quite apprehensive himself, let go of the steering wheel and cried out distressfully "Oh help us Lord, Jesus!!! Please!" His arms, hands, and legs shook as he tried to think of a quick way out.

In the meantime, the car continued to fill up with water as they lingered, until a sudden burst of adrenalin flowed through Paw-Paw's veins. He grabbed hold of the door handle and pushed it forcefully, with all his might. In an instant, the door sprang open.

"Hurry up. Let's get outta here, on my side" he huffed. Paw-Paw dragged Maw-Maw out of the car. Jack jumped completely over the front seat and crawled out to safety through the driver's side. Soon there after, the water engulfed the entire interior of the car.

"What we gon do now Poppa?" screamed Jack standing in knee deep water.

"Come on let's go" yelled Paw-Paw. He held tightly onto Maw-Maw's hand and never let it go.

Around them, the Gulfs murky surf covered all. As Jack looked back, the house and trees in the yard appeared to be sitting right in the middle of the roaring Gulf of Mexico. The Front Ridge Road near the "Swing Gate" already submerged was nowhere in sight.

Fortunately for them, the car had stalled out near a barbed wire fence, which stretched in a northerly direction.

The waves were so strong and fierce that each of them were plunged to their knees on several occasions. During the struggle, Paw-Paw spotted the top of a fence post, barely erect above the deep murky waters. He waded over to it, still holding tightly Maw-Maw's hand. Once there, he grabbed a strong hold and pulled himself along through the spewing waves. Maw-Maw still in a state of shock hung on to her husband's arm until she was able to grip the fence securely. Maw-Maw stayed between Paw-Paw and Jack for the start of their agonizing journey.

AUDREY'S winds picked up force, causing the waves to intrude more rigorously from behind. The Bishops remained clutching the razor sharp fence with their blood stained hands.

Slowly, they managed to make a little headway for higher ground. When the reality of the situation penetrated Maw-Maw's mind, she immediately set free the traumatic trance that had her so dispiritedly bound. The dear, petite, ol' soul walked along through the gyrating surf, with her main focus on God's deliverance. As she journeyed, her face looked upward towards the dark, tormenting skies and she began to recite:

"Hail Mary full of grace, the Lord is with thee. Blessed art thou amongst women and blessed is the fruit of thy womb Jesus. Holy Mary, mother of God pray of us sinners now and at the hour of our death. Amen!"

Death threatened the Bishops, but the more Maw-Maw recited her rosary, the more progress the three innocent victims were able to press forward. At one point, the water rose above Paw-Paw and Jack's waistline, and up to Maw-Maw's neck, being that she was much shorter. But she never gave up hope. Maw-Maw just continued to display adamant faith by praying her "Hail Mary's."

Their hands hurt from the open cuts acquired from the piercing fence, but through it all, their combined faith in God wouldn't allow them to let go of one another even though the pain was unbearable. The Bishops struggled together as a family with stabbed and bleeding hands and feet submersed under AUDREY'S salty surf which inflicted even more pain. In the midst of the waves, a trail of blood followed the trio along the fence as the gloomy clouds hung above, but the three relatives remained inseparable and pressed forward steadfast to save their dear beloved lives from AUDREY'S destruction.

As the morning progressed, the saga proceeded with the relatives battling more high waves, and winds and sporadic rain for the better part of the mile and a half expedition. Even though AUDREY, bruised, battered and beat them unmercifully, Maw-Maw's credence increased each step of the way, as she interceded to the "Blessed Mother." Finally, after a heart-rending fight, all three of them made it safely to the home of Sidney Van Dyke. Clad in tattered and torn clothes, they were welcomed in. There were deep wounds on their hands and feet. The Bishops stayed there for a very short moment, and then ventured on to the home of Mr. Ezeb LeBlanc at 12 o'clock noon. There, they waited out the rest of AUDREY'S traumatic anguish along with his family.

Paw-Paw felt more secure that the LeBlanc place could better withstand the rigorous winds. His decision would later prove to be a wise one.

Meanwhile, Maw-Maw spent the remainder of the storm praying continuously for her entire family, as she petitioned each individual's name out loud, unto the Lord.

All Wednesday nightlong before AUDREY struck, Betty Jane LeBlanc tossed and turned, rolled and quivered in bed, as she lay next to her husband Charles.

For some bizarre reason, her mature fetus, twisting and kicking its little body, thrashed wildly inside her stomach. The small unborn life had never carried on in such a peculiar manner before. The uneasiness got so overbearing that Betty Jane had to rise from her sleep to seek comfort in a chair beside the bed. The couple's 13 month old son Carl was sound asleep in a small crib.

"What's wrong? asked Betty Jane, while looking down and holding onto her stomach in a nurturing fashion. Her right side responded back with a hard kick.

"Maybe the weather's got you all shook up," Betty Jane said

"Well that's okay. Momma's gonna take good care of her baby. Now don't you worry yourself."

But her motherly jargon did nothing to soothe the little ones active movement. The small baby inside of her kept kicking and moving as the winds outside blew harder. The blows became so severe that Betty

Jane had to wake up Charles and tell him of her discomfort. Charles was experiencing a difficult time trying to sleep himself because of the disturbing weather. Immediately, he got up and held Betty Jane in his arms, while little Carl continued to rest through the bad weather.

"Charles, I'm so afraid something awful is about to happen outside. I mean with all this heavy wind and rain. I don't know! I've never seen the weather act this funny before."

"I think you're right, Betty Jane, but just try to relax. I don't want nothing to happen to you, Carl or this new baby."

"I'm trying to relax Charles, but I just can't. The baby is so upset and it just want let me sleep. It just keep on kicking me in the side. The funny thing is, it has never done nothing like this before."

"Shhhhhhhhh! You might wake up Carl," Charles whispered.

"I understand, Honey. But let's just try to lay back down and go to sleep. Maybe this weather will pass and tomorrow morning you'll feel a whole lot better."

"Okay, I'll try. But I don't think I'm gonna get too much rest, tonight."

Charles and Betty Jane lay back down together in bed. She took a longer time than Charles to fall asleep however, in the meantime, the fetus appeared to still have its days and nights confused, as it went on moving in a distressed manner. The wind outside picked up force, while the rain fell off and on throughout the night. When Charles, Betty Jane and Carl awaken, the waters had already risen rapidly inside of their house. The three of the them barely had enough time to wade through the ascending surf in search of higher ground.

"Quick Betty Jane!" raved Charles, with Carl in his arms. "We gotta get out of the house."

But there was nowhere to run or nowhere to hide from AUDREY'S treachery. Charles, thinking quickly decided a tree in the front yard would be the best means for his family to try and save their lives. Betty Jane was frightened by the presence of so much water and blustering wind. She moved herself fragilely through the waves because one wrong move could cost her and the baby their lives. When they both got to the small tree, Charles stooped down on all fours, so that Betty Jane could step onto his back. With little Carl in her arms, she attempted to climb. Charles almost drowning as he was so low to the ground, wrestling the oncoming waves. At one point, his head was totally submersed, but through it all he continued kneeling on his hands and knees, hoping his wife could pull herself up. To add to the confusion Betty Jane lost her balance several times. Still holding on to Carl, she tried desperately to get a strong hold onto a dangling branch in order to pull herself and the infant up into the tree. In a nick of time the poor feverish mother was able to ascend, but Betty Jane had to hand little Carl back to his father during the process to catch her breath, as the climb took every ounce of energy she had. In the meantime, the rough waters got too high for Charles, who was still holding onto Carl and trying to go up the tree. Charles became so disoriented over the deep water that he decided to wade back towards the house in hopes of saving himself and his infant son there. Betty Jane lost sight of the two, and from that moment on, she never saw them again. But that was only the beginning of the terror for the beautiful, young colored mother.

One might have expected AUDREY, a woman herself, after all, to be more compassionate towards an expecting mother.

Nevertheless, the insensitive Calamitress spared no mercy as she tested Betty Jane's fortitude to the utmost. Once in the tree, the clouds overhead became so dark and gloomy that the frightened girl almost gave up hope at that very moment, not knowing whether Charles or Carl were alive or dead. AUDREY, unblushing tormented her further by blowing the tree's branches violently over Betty Jane's face and body. As the wind rose in intensity, Betty Jane found it difficult to obtain a firm grasp anywhere on the shaking tree. Tears mounted up like a river and rolled down her delicate face. AUDREY was getting the best of her. Betty Jane was stuck in a treetop, pregnant, and scared to death in the midst of AUDREY'S betrayal, with no help obtainable from anyone in sight.

Betty Jane's fetus was having a fit as AUDREY pretentiously continued her deception. The pain in the young mother's stomach became so excruciating that she almost jumped into the whirling waters to end her suffering. Even though help, unfortunately, was nowhere to be found, her motherly instincts and religious upbringing would not permit such an unforgiving act as suicide to be carried through. The waves rolled higher, reaching her waistline as she stood in the tree. Betty Jane tried to climb a bit higher, but the pitiful, feeble young lady was too weak at this point to accomplish such a feat. So, she just remained helpless in a stationary position and watched the waves all around her rise higher and higher and higher. There was nothing humanly possible that she could do to stop the deadly water's ascension. The frail mother called out to Charles and little Carl, humbly, with a small bit of hope!

"Charles! Carl! Charles! Carl! Charles!" She yelled as loud as she could at first, but her weak voice merely faded beneath AUDREY'S earsplitting winds.

"Charles! Carl! Charles! Carl!" she yelled another desperate time, crying breathlessly.

Still, no response ever came from her husband nor Carl.

"Oh Lord, Please help me," she sniffled. "What am I gonna do now, up here in this tree all by myself?"

AUDREY'S presence in the area had caused a tremendous drop in the barometric pressure. It was this pressure change, occurring so rapidly, which had made the fetus jerk and jilt so keenly in response. Betty Jane's placenta that surrounded the baby's body unexpectedly, broke loose from the stress and strain. The young mother with child had no perception of the danger that stood before her, but felt only an immediate, unpleasant sensation. Once her amniotic sac erupted and the warm fluids oozed down her legs under the Gulfs salty waters the poor girl thought that she was having an uncontrollable bladder discharge. In an instant her uterus dilated several centimeters as contractions pushed the fetus into her vaginal canal. The baby's precious little head was positioned to enter the world. Betty Jane stood somberly, engulfed in the raging sea of doom. She began having contractions several minutes apart, delivering unbearable suffering. Debris flew overhead. The waves ascended to a higher level, and the lusty winds raced around the trees in the midst of the pale skies.

"Oh God...Please don't let me have my baby like this. Please! I beg you, my father...Charles! Carl! Charles! Please answer me. Where are ya'll? Why don't you answer me? Please answer me...Lord don't let them be dead...I need your help God, right now! Please help me Lord... Charles! Carl! I need your help."

But only the howling winds heard Betty Jane's dejected cry. Nevertheless, AUDREY answered back cruelly, blowing more gusts and leaves against the girl's face. Betty Jane grew weaker and weaker as the minutes rolled by. Finally, she just wept realizing there was no way on earth for this fetus to survive with the Gulfs water up to her shoulders. The mere thought of the unborn child's dilemma and her uncertainty over Charles and Carl's plight, dropped the young mother into a state of grief.

"Charles! Carl!" was Betty Jane's steadfast cry. "Where are you? Oh Lord, please help me. I've already lost my husband and my little son... Now I'm about to loose my baby, too. Please Lord, wherever you are, help me!!! I beg you Lord... You're the only one who can save me now."

The debilitated girl made another concerted effort to try and pull herself further up into the tree so that at least the lower half of her body would be out of the water once the baby arrived. No such chance came her way. AUDREY protracted the pain and suffering by swaying her waters and winds back and forth, similar to a brutal pendulum in the wake of this child's fatal birth. One last time Betty Jane petitioned the Lord, with both arms stretched broadly over two tree branches.

"Please God, I need you right now, to help me! Please help me! Help me! Please if you can...Help me, Lord."

At this point, the water was up to her neckline. She released a blaring, painful scream. The pain she felt was a familiar one, having experienced child birth previously with Carl. She knew the inevitable had come when she saw her own blood surface to the top of the salty, murky surf. Betty Jane found strength to pull one *of* her arms down from the branch. Slowly, she reached under the waters and felt the top of the baby's head protruding out of her birth canal. Fervidly, as she moved her hand about herself, Betty Jane touched the small head of thick, wet course hair with her fingertips. The girl's whole arm shook unmercifully, traumatized she wanted to cry, but was too weak even to do that. Bravely, the fatigued mother pulled her arm out of the water and placed it back onto the branch. She tried to hang on for dear life, with only an ounce of hope remaining, hoping that somehow, someone would possibly save her soon. Fortunately, a piece of her clothing got fastened onto a twig, which kept her frail body from otherwise drifting away in the waves.

She whispered delicately to herself, "Charles, honey! Little Carl! Wherever you both are, I had the baby... I had it ya'll." Afterwards, she wept a tearless cry. With arms still stretched wide, she hung her head down to where the rolling waves seeped into her dry mouth at irregular intervals. Soon after at 12 o'clock noon, the sun peeked its rays through the leaves and limbs down onto Betty Jane's bowed head and enervated body. The beaming rays sparkled radiantly over the waters that encircled the tree in which she stood. It was only for a short moment, however, the saddest part of all was that Betty Jane knew nothing of the most promising ray of light seen on this detrimental morning.

Late Wednesday evening the night before AUDREY struck found Bill, his wife Susie, their children Jimmy, Cheryl, Kathy, Harold, Marvin and Melvin, who had come down with a bout of pneumonia, at the St. Gabriel Hospital in Creole. While Dr. Dix examined the infant, the weather made up something terrible outside. The winds blew furiously throughout the evening, as the periodic rains fell. It got so bad the doctor suggested that the LaSalle family seek shelter at their own home and return early the next morning if Melvin's condition worsened.

Bill and Susie tossed and turned all night, unsettled over their child's precarious illness. Sounds from the unusual wind and rain continued invading their home as everyone tried to sleep. After an anxious night, Bill rose early the next morning and awakened the rest of the family so they could bring Melvin back to the hospital.

Susie's sister Katherine Holmes and her children Eve, Patty, Billie and Sandra were lodging with them, likewise. Bill loaded both families up into his car and ventured onward to St. Gabriel, struggling through the erratic atmospheric conditions.

Terror broke loose as soon as they got to the hospital. Water had risen rapidly inside of the building coming almost up to Bill's knees. About thirty people were trapped inside. By this time, everyone had already hurried to an area near the back of the wooden structure as the rising waves continued to inundate the building without hesitation.

Finally Bill grabbed hold of a 2 by 4 plank, then stood on top of a soft drink machine to knock a hole in the ceiling for everybody to climb up into the attic. Each person was frightened by AUDREY'S winds and water as they hastily clambered up onto the second level. However, during the process, the waters rose so quickly that Bill and the others feared for their lives if they were to remain in this particular area of the attic. He suggested everyone evacuate immediately and seek refuge on the second level, closer to the south end of the facility. The attic in this area was much higher than at the rear of the building. As the group of people returned to the floor, and waded through the high waters, a fatality took place. Mrs. Joe Nunez, an 80 year old white lady died on the spot during the transition. Mrs. Nunez's death created an immediate state of hysteria amongst everyone.

"We've got to move quickly, ya'll" yelled Bill, who despite this horrible tragedy kept the group propelled through the surf in an orderly fashion. Once at the south end of the building, Bill stood on top of a hospital bed and made another hole through the ceiling.

Quickly, he assisted each person up into the dark loft. Amongst this group were Willard "Yank" and Twila Savoie; Jack, Lorena and Jimmy Theriot; a husband and wife with the last name of Wainwright; August, Perlie and Lazeme LeBlanc; Raymond LeBlanc, his wife Anna—who had just given birth to two day old Raymond Jr.—and their two children Eve and Lula; Ferdinand and his sister Edith Bishop; Bill's wife Susie and their children; and his sister-in-law Katherine and her family.

As soon as the last person climbed up, Bill confronted Susie before he entered as well.

"Susie, where's the baby at?"

Oh my God, Bill I thought you had him" screamed *Susie*. "I don't have him," responded Bill, frantically.

"Oh Lord, where is my Baby?"

Somehow during the prompt evacuation up into the attic, Melvin had accidentally fallen into the water and floated around for a short while unnoticed by anyone.

Look Bill, there he is!" cried Susie.

Bill stood straight up on the bed, and glared down into the spiraling waters at his helpless, baby son. He jumped immediately down to the floor and tried to retrieve the infant, but the current was too intense for him. At that very moment, Little Melvin was about to float completely out of the hospital through an open window. Bill put forth an extreme effort to rescue him, but couldn't.

Susie, still in the attic, almost had a fit as she watched her youngest child whirling around in AUDREY'S rough surf.

Amazingly, a three foot plank with a nail embedded at the tip floated past Bill to the right of the hospital bed. He reached and grabbed hold of it as the baby struggled face down in the erupting waters to hold onto it's little life. Tears flowed down Susie's face as she observed with horror. Bill didn't have much time to waste.

After realizing that he couldn't get back down into the rushing waters, he took the plank and extended the end with the pointed nail as far as he could. Bill's skillful hand barely snagged a piece of Melvin's clothing, which enabled him to pull the infant slowly towards the bed. In a nick of time, he reached over and grabbed the baby before its little body went surging out of the window. Bill trembled as he handed the wet child to Susie, who shouted "Thank you Jesus. Thank you Lord for saving my baby's life!"

Eventually, Bill pulled himself up into the attic and joined the rest of the terrified victims. Once there, he turned Melvin over on his stomach and gently pressed his back to get the Gulfs water out of his little system. A portion of the attic's insulation was retrieved from the rafters and used as a blanket to keep the child warm. The other people appeared dazed as they had all presumed Melvin to be lost and dead, but Susie had never given up hope on her child's life however, now she just held him close to her breast for the time being because she knew deep in her heart he was still amongst the living.

A few seconds after that incident subsided the St. Grabriel Hospital began to rock and shift like a wild stallion. No one had any inkling as to what caused the jilting motion. Nevertheless, loud screams from the children and adults blared out, simultaneously, as the whole building shook and dipped. As soon after he felt the sharp twisting movement even Bill got frightened.

"I think this is it!" he pondered.

AUDREY'S winds had blustered, and the buoyant waves had lifted the entire hospital completely off its blocks. Then she sent the wooden structure sailing in a northerly route over the marshlands.

From Bill's viewpoint in the dark enclosed area, he could see clearly through a small window outside as the hospital rampaged onward over the waters. The walls, roof, and beams cracked and squeaked as the terrifying ride proceeded. Dead cattle, cars, trees, rooftops, TV's, appliances and other household items bustled on every side in the water below. Bill bowed his head during the grim moment, and thought deeply about his other family members. He hoped and prayed to God they were okay.

Meanwhile, Susie, still holding onto Melvin in a loving manner, reached over and whispered into her sister Katerine's ear,

"I sure hope Momma, Poppa, Viola and Emma are all right."

Katherine stared for a moment back into her sister's eyes, but then broke down sadly. She cried out when the reality of her family's predicament flashed through her mind.

"Katherine, let's pray for them," Susie said. "Don't cry."

She continued to rock her small infant to sleep while the scary ride went on. It was an intense moment for the two sisters, neither knowing where the hospital would finally end up as it slid over the charging waves. At least for the time being the two sisters sat contentedly in the attic of the hospital as it barreled along the rough waters.

Their mother Lucinda Mouton was not quite as fortunate. Lucinda's day started out on a very tragic accord. By the time she'd awakened Thursday morning the water had already taken over the entire interior of her house. She had very little time to prepare for the attack that caught her completely off guard. Once she concluded that the Gulfs waters had arrived, she went to the bedroom to awaken her husband John "Cass" Mouton.

He'd already expired from an apparent heart attack. Even though John's death grieved her so, Lucinda had to find enough courage to get her two daughters, Viola and Emma Lois, and her four year old grandson to the attic of the house before everything on the first level was engulfed by the hostile waters.

Lucinda's circumstance paralleled to that of her daughters Susie and Katherine, being that on the same morning each of them were up in an attic of a building trying to save their lives from the wrathful AUDREY.

But Lucinda, Emma Lois, Viola and John Darrell found very little security in the attic of the old house, as the structure began to totter and vibrate severely. All four relatives screamed for their lives as they lay inside the dark horrifying nook lodged below the roof. Each concluded shortly thereafter that there was no way for the house to withstand AUDREY'S turbulent winds and vigorous surf.

In a matter of minutes, the entire house detonated, and fell in, and each were lunged defenseless into the raging waters. The three women swam terrified, trying to save the life of little John Darrell. AUDREY negated their concerted efforts and in an instant snatched the small child under the waters. They lost sight of him for a short moment, then thereafter, they saw the four year old boy rolling over the waves in a direction opposite from where they stood. Little John Darrell sailed away quickly, and they never saw him again.

Horrified over the mishap, Viola and Emma barely made it to a group of trees in the front yard. Their distraught and weakened state over the loss of the small boy allowed AUDREY to sweep the two sisters away in a flash with her repugnant current.

Lucinda had now experienced the horror of losing her husband , both daughters and a grandchild right before her own eyes, all in the course of a single morning.

She knew, however, that there was no time to be saddened by the misfortune if she expected to save her own life. Lucinda glanced up at the dreary skies, and extended one of her hands unto the Lord.

"Lord Jesus Christ, have thine own way...Oh Lord!"

In a split second, a mattress floated close enough for her to reach out and obtain a stronghold. She jumped on and clung to the bedding as it glided swiftly across the waters. The further away she got from where her home once stood, the more her heart pained endlessly and she looked at the destruction all around her with no signs of any of her family members left in sight.

Katherine and Susie prayed for their mother, father and other family members as they continued to ride over the waves in the attic of the hospital.

Lucinda prayed for all her children's safe keeping as she ventured onward draped to the top of a full size mattress. At approximately 12 o'clock noon poor Lucinda had drifted well over thirty five miles past the Intracoastal Canal near Big lake, not far from a community known as Sweetlake. The dark clouds overhead were intermittently illuminated by the sun's radiant light as it shined brightly upon her. It was an unusual sight to witness: this worn, battered woman floating along the marsh over the surf, a tall white crane standing proudly by her side. Neither she nor the crane violated one another's space as they journeyed atop the mattress. As a matter of fact the ol' crane kept her company for the better part of the journey. During a short moment of sunshine, Lucinda thanked God intensely for helping her make it as far as she did on the makeshift raft.

Her devout meditation was suspended briefly when AUDREY brought back the barren skies and shifted her winds forcefully in the opposite direction. The ol' crane merely ruffled its feathers a bit once the wind began its debut all over again. The bird looked at Lucinda peculiarly, as if to say "Don't you worry my dear, I'm not gonna leave your side."

Lucinda glared back at the large white crane and spoke softly, "You know something, God has never left either one of us."

On Thursday morning as AUDREY ripped through the lower Cameron Parish coastline, Floyd and his wife Mae West Bargeman had awakened early at the home of a relative in Lake Charles. They had planned to drive back to Grand Chenier before the weather got to stormy. The Lake Charles vicinity was encountering the same intense gusty conditions as the coastal communities. Soon after Floyd and Mae ate their breakfast and dressed, he ran to put the luggage in the car as rains fell sporadically. The couple's family members tried sincerely to get them to delay the trip until the weather cleared up a bit, but Floyd had it in his head to get an early start. He had a list of chores to accomplish before going to work later on that afternoon.

Out the door he and Mae ventured, oblivious to the misfortune that awaited them. Before they were even out of the city limits of Lake Charles, Floyd experienced tremendous difficulty keeping his automobile on a steady path along the road. The constant attacks by the wind should have been forewarning enough for him that something unusual was in the making, but, he drove onward, thinking the harsh blowing rain was merely temporary and would subside the further southward he drove.

"Floyd, I think we should turn around and go back."

"Ah Mae, it's just a little wind and rain blowing. I gotta lot of things to do when I get home. I ain't got time to stay up here in Lake Charles all day!"

"But Floyd, I ain't never seent the weather act this funny before."

"It'll be all right Mae. I ain't scared."

"I am Floyd!"

Abruptly, the wind shifted the car's motion to the far right side of the road, almost thrusting it into a nearby ditch.

"Floyd, we better go back!" screamed Mae.

"Mae, I done told you once, I got to get home. I've got so much to do today until it's pitiful."

"Well be careful, then. You don't have to kill us both trying to rush home. Shoots! I'm scared to death as it is...And your driving...And this weather."

"Mae, why don't you just take a nap or something?

"Floyd, how am I suppose to sleep with all this rain and wind blowing outside? Huh!!! Watch out!!!"

"Mae you gonna have to be quiet! Whooof! You got me more nervous than the weather."

"I still say we should turn around and go back to Lake Charles, until things clear up."

"I done told you...I've got too much to do at home and I don't want to be tired when I go to work this afternoon.

"Tired at work! Ump!!! I hope we make it home first. The way you driving, I don't think we will!"

"Mae, please be quiet and go to sleep. Okay?"

Despite the poor visibility conditions on the road, Floyd drove on. Mae tried to lay her head back on the seat, but she kept one eye focused on the road while the other was closed. During brief moments when the rain wasn't falling so fiercely, Floyd picked up speed, only to be reduced later to a slow crawl as the powerful winds heaved the car over the road.

"Floyd, I can't take no more of this!" Mae shouted. "Let's turn around and go back. Just tell your boss the weather was too bad and you couldn't make it home safely."

"No Mae! We're going home and that's that!"

Mae said very little for the duration of the trip. Soon after they arrived in Creole, day break was upon them. The rains greeted the automobile with tremendous force. Heavy gusts of wind and layers of showers got so severe Floyd had to pull over to one side of the road for a brief moment. His visibility was limited to a mere foot in front of the car's windshield. As soon as the rain dwindled, momentarily, off he drove again racing to get to Grand Chenier before things got worse.

"See there Mae. We almost home, now."

"I don't care about that Floyd. You just don't know how much you done scared me to death already. It's a good thing I ain't got no bad heart, because you'd be driving a dead woman by now."

"Ah Mae quit talkin that foolishness. You sound like that ol' gypsy we seen in Cameron a few months ago at the carnival with that ol' crazy talk. Remember?" He laughed.

"Don't laugh Floyd, because that ol' gypsy might have known what she was talking about the way you been driving. Before it's all over we just might end up dead just like she said."

"Now why would you go and say a crazy thing like that for, Mae? I hope you didn't believe in none of that ol' mess she told us. Well...Do you?" he asked sarcastically, while waiting for her response.

"Well, you never know Floyd. This is June. And you know what she said about June. And the way you driving...Well? What can I say?"

"Say no more, Mae!"

By this time, Floyd and Mae had arrived at the Mermentau River in Grand Chenier, where they saw the enormous waves rolling across the wooden bridge. The river had already overflowed it's banks, being that the Gulf of Mexico was so close to the mouth.

"Oh my Lord, Floyd. Look!!! Where is all that water coming from? It's getting in the car!!! Stop this car fool, right now!!!!" screamed Mae.

Too afraid to speak at that moment Floyd, didn't respond. He held onto the steering wheel with all his might, as AUDREY shifted the car intensely, then blew the Mermentau's waters completely over the top. As the car approached the middle of the old wooden structure, the entire bridge shimmered and rock, cracked and swayed, as the callous calamitress made her presence known. The momentum became so profound that the car almost toppled over the right side and down into the rushing Mermentau.

Floyd and Mae's eyes got as big as marbles. They felt an earthshaking movement, heard the loud crackling sounds of the wooden piles swaying back and forth in conformance to AUDREY'S cannibalistic winds. The bridge almost gave way at one point, with the two victims still trapped at the center.

"Floyd as soon as we cross this bridge," Mae shouted, excitedly.

Floyd was speechless. "You better pull this car over or I'm gonna jump out. I mean that!"

"I should've listened to Mae and stayed in Lake Charles," he thought to himself. From that moment on, it wasn't *hard for him* to realize that they had stumbled into a vicious storm. Finally, after much agony, Floyd and Mae crept across the bridge over to the main road in Grand Chenier. There, the mighty Gulf of Mexico's waves were rumbling in from the south, and attacked their car abusively.

"Oh Lord have mercy Jesus. Look at all that water, Floyd," shouted Mae as her legs quivered.

"Mae it looks like the whole Gulf of Mexico done come over!" he responded with jittery teeth.

"Floyd ain't no way we can make it to Momma's house. Just pull the car over now!" cried Mae.

"No Mae, I believe we can make it there!!!!"

"You crazy fool? Ain't no way we can make it way over to Momma's house!!! Stop this car right now, I say!!! Stop!!! I mean stop!!! If you don't I'm gon jump out!!! Stop I said!!! Dog gone it!!!"

Floyd never had time to stop the vehicle because it drowned out on its own. Fortunately, the stranded couple was in walking distance of Mrs. Malize Miller's home. Hurriedly, he and Mae jumped out and waded through knee deep waters. As soon as they reached Mrs. Miller's home, frightened and trembling from the weather, Floyd banged on the door. He and Mae watched the surf rise higher and higher as the pouring rains fell from the desolate clouds overhead.

Complete chaos was going on inside of the house. Several people were insanely wandering around, trying to figure out a way to save their lives. Those included were Miss Malize Miller, her son Cleveland, his wife Nellie Mae, their two children Bonnie and Daniel; Rose Marie Quebodeaux, Evelyn and Doris Segura; seven oil field workers employed by Mack Truck lines, and now Floyd and Mae West Bargeman.

As soon as Floyd and Mae got inside, AUDREY began to show off her ferocious strength. She blew her winds majestically. Water instantly seeped in to cover the entire interior of the home. Floyd held onto Mae's hand the whole time, while the others ran around, frantic. Eventually, someone yelled "We all need to get of the house. It ain't gonna make it through this wind, Ya'll!!!"

Floyd still clutching Mae's hand looked dead into her face. A few tears rolled down as she stared back at his. Floyd told Mae "I really should've listened to you this time." However, no reply came from Mae.

Abruptly, an oil field worker yelled to Floyd and Mae "Ya'll need to go out through the back door! Hurry up!! Go!!! Right now!!! Before it's too late!" Floyd, by his wife's side, dragged her through the rushing waters. In a quick flash!!! A loud rumbling sound flashed around them. Soon after, the entire roof of the house came tumbling down on everyone inside.

Fortunately, Floyd and Mae's hands stayed intertwined, after they were thrown into AUDREY'S reverberating waves. The current was so forceful, however that it pulled them several times under the surf. They saw the distress on each other's face, submerged under the salty waters for that short moment. Still hand in hand Floyd and Mae rolled, turned, tumbled and then drifted a few feet away from the wreckage. When they surfaced each were choking from the murky waters that rushed down their throats. Mae and Floyd coughed and gagged amid the blowing winds, as they tried to survive AUDREY'S abuse. Floyd asked his wife if she was okay, while the waves continued running over their heads.

Then in an instant, AUDREY yanked Mae away from Floyd. She never had the opportunity to respond to her husband's question, everything happened so quickly. Later he saw her body hurling over the waters towards the Mermentau River.

"Oh no! Mae come back!!!! Please!!!! Come back to me, Mae!!!" was his disheartened cry. "Please don't leave me Honey!!!!! I'm sorry, I should've listened to you!!!"

Floyd ran through the waters with both arms extended to rescue his helpless wife, but his efforts went in vain, the current being too strong for him to master. Mae's body drifted further and further away from him.

"Mae, Honey don't leave me. Please don't leave me. I'm sorry, Honey" he cried out.

It was too late, however. Floyd looked over his right shoulder and saw another monstrous wave coming straight for him.

"Oh my God!!!"

Those were the last three words he spoke. In a matter of moments, AUDREY claimed his life too.

The sun light peeping out over the gruesome scene at twelve noon found Floyd and Mae's bodies dangling against each other, mysteriously, Floyd floated close to his wife's body, which was lodged under some oak trees in the back yard. They never left one another's side. Now Floyd and Mae were at eternal peace. Amongst them were included Mrs. Malize Miller, her two grandchildren Bonnie and Daniel, Evelyn Segura and A. P. Boudreaux, an oil field worker.

Talk about a sad sight to see, those two small children, Bonnie and Daniel floating along lifeless in the midst of the expired grownups. The barbaric AUDREY thought nothing of her ghastly feat, though, but only went about her business, shifting the motions of the winds accordingly. The dark, pale overcast clouds covered the atmosphere once again in preparation for the second half of terror.

If only Floyd had listened to Mae. Sometimes when the storms of life are raging, hindsight can be a deadly 20-20 vision!

CHAPTER 17

The second half of AUDREY'S devastation was not quite as alarming as it had been during the early morning hours, although gusty winds and torrential rain continued to inundate the area for the remainder of the afternoon. The shift in the wind's direction commanded the Gulf's high tide to recede just as quickly as it had previously ascended. Nita and the others sat around the Vincent home and thanked God for being alive. All of them were still in a state of shock as they watched the miraculous recession of the hostile water. Jeanette shared a sorrowful story with the group about an uncle, "Boot" Mayne, who was her father Henry's brother.

When the 1918 storm struck, Boot and his entire family were tragically killed. They lived near the coastal beach in Grand Chenier at the time of the atrocity. As Jeanette talked, Nita cringed thinking about Mary and the rest of her loved ones. She tried to brace herself for the worst. However, the pain of not knowing their plight tormented her. "Please my Father in heaven, let me see my family once again" was her firm plea to God.

As Nita prayed, and looked out of a nearby window, she realized just how mighty the power of God truly was. "What a little people we are" she thought. "But through the midst of the storm and rain, I know you can save us, Lord, if you really want to."

By 4:20 P.M. most of the Gulfs waters were gone. The candle in the Vincent's bedroom that had burned brightly all day at last reached its termination. The radiant light of the sun beamed through the living room. Lee and Son told the others to stay inside until they explored the surroundings thoroughly, making sure it was safe before anyone departed.

On every side of the house, remnants of AUDREY had been left behind by the insensitive calamitress. Lee Boy headed towards the barn to see how the Vincents withstood the storm. When he got there he found most of them bruised, battered, hungry, wet and beaten in torn, shredded clothes. The entire roof of the barn had been blown away. Mr. Curly told Lee that he'd made a very wise decision by staying in the house considering the traumatic bout his family had endured. After the roof had blown off, all of the Vincents were flogged by the harsh wind and rains for the duration of the storm. As Lee Boy and Mr. Curly continued conversing, Son saw a sack of money lying on the ground near where the general store once stood. He tried to pick it up, but it was too heavy for him to lift, so he dragged the ponderous bag of currency and coins closer to Mr. Curly's house.

"Mr. Curly" yelled Son, who was still in a state of shock.

"Whatcha won't my boy?" he responded back.

"I found your money, Mr. Curly."

"I don't want it! You keep it! It's your's...You found it...so keep it."

Son refused to honor Mr. Curly's request and left the sack exactly where he'd dragged it. Here was Son, without a dime left to his name, still choosing to abandon a whole bag of money after the owner gave him permission to keep it. Son knew, however, that Mr. Curly was irrational as a result of the onslaught of AUDREY.

Nita ran out the Vincent home with Marlon in her arms as Lee Boy and Son were walking back towards the house.

"Lee, Lee," she shouted, with a demented look. "I want to go and see about my house! I can't wait no longer."

"Okay, Honey...just calm down."

Immediately, Son assembled his family. Lee Boy carried Greg, while Nita toted Marlon along with a bag full of wet diapers. The miserable little infant was suffering terribly from a severe inflamed irritation on his bottom and genital area. Lillie walked in the midst of the two colored families, all of them barefoot, wet, rumpled, weary, hungry and dumfounded. They resembled nomads as they rambled along the ridge parallel to what was left of the washed out Grand Chenier road. Each person looked in amazement at the devastation, which increased dramatically the further they trudged westward over the barren land. Swollen surface water still overflowed the ditches. Marshlands and ridges were cluttered with cars, stoves, refrigerators, bathtubs, debris of all sorts, dead cows, horses, dogs, cats, nutria rats, fish and cranes. Rooftops, parts of rooftops, trucks, splintered wood, clothes, shoes, dishes and just about anything conceivable was scattered haphazardly, throughout along with pots, pans, parts of homes, driftwood, from the Gulf, fallen trees, broken branches, severed utility poles, washing machines, photograph albums, loose pictures and other irreplaceable items of sentimental value. From Grand Chenier to the Louisiana-Texas state line, the entire Cameron Parish coastline resembled a catastrophic war zone. The smell of fresh mud permeated much of the air. As the sun in the drab skies above slowly descended, the itinerant families continued westward finding very few houses left standing at the close of this unforgettable day.

Lillie's mother Frances caught a glimpse of them as soon as the wandering group of colored relatives reached Lionel Theriot's front yard. She ran out of the marred house overcome with joy.

"Oh thank you Lord Jesus...you spared my family," she cried and hugged Lillie gratefully. "Thank you, thank you, thank you, Thank you my Lord!"

It was both a happy and sad meeting between the mother and her daughter. Tears flowed from the eyes of every bystander as each realized just how truly blessed, they were to be alive on this day. Frances and Lillie embraced for a long moment, arm in arm. Then the families roamed onward over the rough terrain to see whether they had a home left in which to rest their weary feet.

The closer Nita, Lillie and Jeanette got to their property, the more their hearts pounded. Each saw the excavated sandy spaces where their homes had once stood. Nothing else was left except a bathtub and a few battered appliances on the desolate land. Nita was the first to break down and let out a big scream.

"Lee!" she cried. "It's gone. Our house is gone. It's gone Lee...it's gone."

Lee was so choked up, he couldn't even respond. He just stood speechless, with his mouth wide open, clutching at Greg in his arms.

"Oh Lord Son," was Jeanette's disheartened cry. "We ain't got no more house either. Our house is gone, too. It's gone!"

"Jeanette, I don't know whatcha cryin for," replied Son. "You better thank the Lord, you still alive."

"Lord have mercy Jesus!" screamed Lillie. "My poor house ain't there, Momma. We ain't got no more house left to go too!!!! What we gon do now?"

The moment was very intense for all three families, and they wept a river of tears. The only worthy things they owned were the ragged clothes that clung to their backs. Just a bathtub and a few other minimally worthless items were left in Lee Boy and Nita's yard. Son and Jeanette saw their stove, bathtub, washing machine, and a few dishes scattered here and there. The January's Ford was turned over on its side in a nearby field, not far away from the ruins. Lillie and Simon's old pink and blue Plymouth was parked in the same place where they'd left it. The vehicle was about the only reclaimable item of value still around. Only the rooftop of Lee Boy's neighbor Miss Allen's home remained in her front yard.

A closer look at the destruction revealed the severity of large pits embedded into the earth where each house had once stood. The churning of AUDREY'S waves had actually caused the natural gas pipelines to rupture. Pilot lights from hot water heaters must have ignited the escaping gas. The combustion had caused a chain reaction, completely detonating each home. It was a good thing the Harrisons and Januarys fled to the Vincent home when they did, or they might not have survived to give an account of their gruesome experience.

Soon after the emotional dialogue subsided, the reality of being homeless and penniless penetrated their uncomprehending minds. The outcast families had no other choice but to move onward and seek shelter elsewhere before the blackness of the night found them with no abode. It would take a while for all of their deep inner wounds to recover from such an extensive loss. Nita's already low spirits worsened after she saw the vacant lot, and the absence of her home. The perplexing sense of being homeless troubled the young colored girl enormously, and added more misery for her pysche to contend with.

In the midst of the deserted property, everybody could clearly see that the Immaculate Heart Catholic Church was still intact; however, as they walked past the graveyard, they received a shock.

Several caskets had been exhumed by AUDREY'S force and human remains lay exposed near a group of unearthed vaults and overturned headstones. What a morbid sensation for them to receive, especially, after all the grief they had already encountered.

However, maybe it was best that they came across this particular setting as a reminder to them of God's majestic grace, which had miraculously spared their lives.

Further west, down the washed out road from the church, the Miller Estate had endured the test of AUDREY, and stood undiminished in the same location. Ol' Dr. Miller must have had a premonition years ago when he'd solicited an architect to draw plans for the sturdy, storm proof home. Several white people were assembled inside talking about their dire experiences. Less than a foot of water had risen inside of the house, and it had only sustained two broken windows, along with a few other minor damages. Lillie was happy to know that Miss Annie and Miss Shutzie were still amongst the living.

From the Miller Estate, the group ventured next door to Lee Boy's employer Mr. Lee R. Nunez's home. Likewise, their place was fortunate enough to have withstood AUDREY'S forceful destruction. Mr. Lee's wife, Miss Emma gave Nita and Jeanette some milk for Marlon and Donald. She also shared what little food that was left in the refrigerator with the others. Soon after, evening rolled into a still, quiet, night and complete darkness blanketed the Grand Chenier area. There were no electric light poles with bugs swarming around them, nor could the sound of croaking bullfrogs be heard anywhere. The tranquillity of the night was incomparable, especially to the roar and thunder that AUDREY had brought with her earlier in the day. The only illumination for the region that night came from distant shining stars. A few gas lanterns could be spotted sporadically, in the aftermath of the most destructive June hurricane ever on record.

On this horrifying day, AUDREY went down in history as the worst Gulf coast disaster, since the 1918 storm that had completely annihilated the Galveston area more than a half century before. Though the residents of Cameron Parish lived in a aged of advanced communications, telephone and radio transmission had expired soon after the impact of the hurricane's winds commenced.

All of the roads leading into the parish were either blocked by water or completely washed out. It was going to take almost 24 hours before the outside world would know fully of AUDREY'S devastation. Likewise, most rescue efforts would encounter delays for the same reasons.

That night, the Harrisons and Januarys camped out on the kitchen floor of the Nunez's home. Nita was up practically the entire time with Marlon because of his painful diaper rash. The innocent little one couldn't seem to obtain any well-deserved rest.

After much frustration, he finally fell asleep in Nita's comforting arms. Before she positioned herself onto the warm, hard, floor, Nita thanked God immensely for saving each of their lives. Still, the thought of her mother, father, sisters, brothers and grandparents plagued her to no end. Throughout the night, she awakened intermittently, as the nightmares came and went. With tears rolling down her face, she cried softly "Please help me make it through this tough time, my Father. I don't know if any of my family members are dead or alive. But please, my Father, if they are—and if I'm not asking for too much-comfort them wherever they might be tonight. And let them know that me, Lee and the boys are all okay, too."

The poor distressed young mother lay there trying to find some peace of mind within her soul, and struggled desperately to hold onto a last bit of hope. Lee Boy and Lillie were restless as well, not knowing Simon's predicament. Jeanette was troubled over the plight of her parents Henry and Clara Mayne. The night brought with it one of the most ambiguous uncertainties of all, as no one had a clue of what tomorrow would bring. An unsettled feeling haunted everyone.

Friday morning couldn't come quickly enough for Nita, who awakened bright and early with an incredible numb feeling about herself. Eventually, Son and Lee Boy left everyone at the Nunez's to venture out over the area, to assist those in need and help recover some of the dead. By the minute all types of communications were coming in over a short-wave radio at the Miller Estate. Several white bodies had been recovered during the early morning hours and brought to the grounds of the estate for identification purposes.

The remains were lined up in the front yard under the oak trees in neat rows. The experience was a ghastly one for Lee Boy and Son, as they came across several inflated corpses. Some were dressed, others nude. Some were swollen as big as cattle, while others were beyond recognition. The chemicals and salt in the Gulfs waters had caused the hair of various bodies to shrivel and kink, and turned the skin on others to a pitch black color. Crab gnawing had severed the flesh of many. The parching bright sun above didn't ease the adversity much, because the area began to release a foul, rotting flesh odor, as the decomposition process started to occur.

The atrocious smell, similar to that of a refuse landfill, became unbearable as the day progressed. While more of the dead were being hauled onto the grounds of the Miller estate in groups of ten, the martial law sat up temporary quarters to patrol the area against looters. Once the news of the disaster surfaced, thieves roamed freely in search of jewelry, diamond rings and other items of value.

In some instances, when the bandits couldn't confiscate a ring easily, they merely cut off an entire finger in order to get the loot they desired.

When Lee Boy and Son made it back to the Nunez residence, they shared the shocking information with the others. In the process, Lee Boy had to break the first bit of dreadful news to Nita.

A white man in the area informed him that Nita's Aunt Alice Bishop was found about fifty miles north of her home at Boone's Corner in Grand Lake. A group of men were searching for survivors, when they discovered her body, and a money belt tied around her waist. Alice's valuables were given to Lee Boy to pass on to her family. Nita took the news sorrowfully, as Lillie and Jeanette tried to comfort her during the hour of heartbreak.

Once Nita pulled herself together, both the Harrisons and the Januarys started walking towards the Grand Chenier Bridge. Just before they got there, Son spotted an old cash register lying on top of the ground near the area where Mrs. Melaze Miller's cafe once stood. As he got closer to it, he saw it was full of money. In the interim, Mrs. Melaze's son, Cleveland "Blackbird," Miller was combing the area, salvaging whatever possessions he could find.

Son, still without a penny in his pocket nor a roof left over his head, was not tempted by the money. He directed Cleveland to its whereabouts. Cleveland later shared another bit of bad news with the group. He told them that Lillie's half-sister Irene "Pinee" West had experienced a fatality. Her daughter, Mae West, and husband Floyd Bargeman had also drowned on the property, along with his mother and two children. Lillie threw both arms up in the air, and shook her head, less hopeful than ever. In the meantime, the outlook appeared gloomier and gloomier for her husband Simon, whom no one had heard from since the day before the storm struck.

A large congregation of victims seeking assistance had gathered near the washed out Grand Chenier Bridge. The mood amongst everyone was one of warmth and love. Some of the people were naked, but nobody even gave them a second consideration.

Many were wrapped in grass sacks, sheets, or whatever attire they could find to cover their tired, worn, discolored, aching, bodies. Though this was the 50's, the color of one's skin caused no disunity on the particular day, as the white people comforted the colored, and the colored folks returned the same benevolence. The banks of the Mermentau were still swollen with water and appeared as a continuous river that flowed directly from the Gulf. At about 10:00 A.M., the loud sounds of helicopters dominated the airways overhead. These dropped all types of snacks, candies and first aid supplies to the victims below. People ran around in hysteria to gather food and supplies for themselves and their families. During the process Lillie bumped into a half sister Ida "Chink" Washington's daughter Rosie "Tee" LeBlanc.

"Tee! I'm so glad to see you."

"Thank you Jesus! Me too Lillie. We didn't know if ya'll made it."

"Thank the Lord, we did Tee. But I got some bad news for you. Poor Pinee's daughter Mae West and her husband Floyd both drowned."

"Oh NO!" screamed Tee. "You mean momma's poor sister, Aunt Pinee's Mae West?"

"I'm afraid so."

Tee broke down and cried. With tears in her eyes she said

"Lillie, what about Simon? Did he make it?"

Lillie got so full of emotion had to turn and walk away. She just couldn't talk about her husband at that moment. Tee watched her distressfully, and later rejoined her own family with some snacks in which she had recovered.

In the meantime, Thursday morning, June 27, 1957 found Simon Harrison on the True Friend, stuck out in a rice field near the Intracoastal Canal. Bombardment by AUDREY'S accelerated waves and winds had propelled the vessel completely out of the canal, and into the nearby field. Simon stayed stranded for the better part of the day. The True Friend reeled, rocked, and almost capsized on several occasions as the powerful motions of the waves pounced upon her hull, back and forth. Finally, when the winds subsided and the waters receded, Simon skillfully maneuvered the boat out of the rice field, and slowly back into the canal.

Miraculously, before the dawning of Friday morning, he was on his way home through the swollen waters. As soon as he'd entered the Calcasieu River and headed south towards the town of Cameron, Simon could detect chaos that had occurred by the erratic path of devastation along the banks. When he reached Cameron, he found the town was mutilated beyond recognition. His face perspired and his heart palpitated as he navigated the boat around all types of debris, logs, cars, appliances and a bobbing vault that had drifted into the river from the hurricane. He was flabbergasted.

"Oh Lord have mercy. I know they're dead" was his sincere thought about his family as he past through Cameron. "Ain't no way they gon be alive when I get home. Just ain't no way. Ump! They gon be gone!!! I know it!!" he said. At the same time, however, he refused to accept his own speculations. Once Simon got safely out of the Calcasieu River, he had to journey along the Gulf Coast all the way to Grand Chenier. The coastal beaches had been totally wiped out. Nothing was left standing as he passed along the seashore, except for a few salt cedar trees. The devastation continued for miles and miles. His only thoughts were "I hope Lillie, Lee Boy, Nita and my two grand children are still alive, when I get there." He tried to accelerate the True Friend as fast as it could go, but the boat was already tugging at top speed through the rigorous white caps of the Gulf of Mexico.

"Lord please don't let um be dead" he kept saying over and over.

Finally, after several hours of severe fretfulness, Simon reached the mouth of the Mermentau River in Grand Chenier, where the scene revealed the same damaging picture of despair. Once he approached where the bridge once stood, his whole heart dropped to the floor of the boat, seeing it was washed away and gone. On shore he saw a large assemblage of people standing around. Several "army ducks"—boats were transporting victims across the river over to "The District" where they boarded helicopters en route to Creole. Simon's breath choked in his throat when he saw no signs of his family anywhere. He halted the True Friend in the middle of the river to allow an army duck full of survivors to cross. Once it went by, he cruised slowly to shore. His heart was beating so fast, he almost went into a cardiac arrest, discontented over not knowing if he would ever see his family alive again.

When the boat pulled up to shore someone shouted "That's the ol' True Friend!"

Lillie, with Lee Boy, Nita and the others sitting, heard the announcement loud and clear. Immediately, Lillie and Lee Boy jumped up to their feet and ran as fast as they could towards the river, while Simon appeared on the deck of the True Friend, looking everywhere to see if he could spot any of his family.

"Simon! Simon!" screamed Lillie. "Honey! You're alive!" she yelled out of breath as she stood waving her hand vigorously in the air. "Oh thank God you're alive!" She panted and waved with Lee Boy right by her side.

Once Simon caught glimpse of Lillie and Lee Boy standing on the shore he shouted "THANK THE LORD!!!! WHOOOOOOF!!!! THERE THEY ARE...I SEE UM!!!! THANK YOU JESUS!!!"

Lillie danced a jig until she was completely out of breath then she stood there patiently in the sweltering heat for the man she so desperately loved to connect with her anxious arms. As soon as the boat was tied down, Simon jumped onto the shore and ran straight for Lillie and Lee Boy. It was a heart-moving reunion for the three Harrisons, as they locked arms over each other's shoulders. Simon, Lillie and Lee Boy cried happy tears of joy.

"Where's my little boys at, Lee?" asked Simon. "Are they both all right?"

"Look, they're over there with Nita!" he answered as Nita stood up and waved back, excitedly.

"Oh thank you Lordy!! Ya'll just don't know what I went through trying to get to you. I almost went crazy because I didn't think I was gonna find none of ya'll alive. Everything is torn up all the way from Big Lake to here. It's something to see. Ain't nothin left standing, hardly. Thank you Lord, I'm so glad ya'll alive."

"We almost went crazy too," Lillie responded, "wondering if you was gonna come home."

Lillie, Lee Boy, Nita and the boys said good bye to Simon when it was time for them to board the army ducks. For the time being, he was going to stay in Grand Chenier on the True Friend.

While riding across the Mermentau, Nita became a bit frightened because she had never ridden in such a contraption before. The seats were very low to the water and on a few occasions, she felt like she was going to fall right into the river as she held Marlon close in her arms. On the other side, the Harrisons and Januarys boarded the helicopter which would fly everyone to Creole. None of the family members had ever flown on a chopper before and the ride would be their first such experience. Soon after the helicopter was loaded with both colored and white people, it took off. The noise was so loud, no one inside could hear each other speak. The ride was probably Nita's most dreaded experience. Her whole chest felt like someone was standing on it. From this vantage above the earth, she could see precisely the disastrous footsteps AUDREY had left upon the land.

"Maybe I'll see my family when we land in Creole," she thought, optimistically.

However, as the helicopter flew onward, and Nita witnessed more destruction along the way, her optimism lessened. Lillie sensed something troubling her daughter-in-law, so she whispered softly "Honey, just put your faith in God. He's gonna bring your family to you!" Nita starred back at her with watery eyes. Lillie reached out and touched her hand. Nita broke down in a soft cry, under the loud chopping noise.

"Keep your faith in God" said Lillie as she rubbed Nita's hand. Lee Boy sat next to Nita and clutched Greg tightly, while she cuddled Marlon to her breasts. Once the helicopter began descending, the pressure on Nita's chest got heavier and heavier.

Her heart raced a hundred beats per minute and she took short deep breaths of air. When they landed at Creole, Nita had to make a concerted effort just to lift her own body off the floor of the aircraft. Once both feet touched the ground, she couldn't even comprehend how such a minor step had been accomplished. Her eyes wandered around endlessly through the crowd of people standing there, all of them daunted by the hostile behavior of AUDREY. She hesitated, and then stared at each colored person in sight hoping to find her family. Unfortunately, none of them was anywhere to be seen. Nita, expecting to be reunited with her loved ones, began to hyperventilate. She still knew nothing for certain, and there were too many people waiting to board the buses to search further for the Barties.

"Maybe a bus already took them to Lake Charles" she thought as the pressure mounted severely making her heart feel like a pile of rubble.

Again, Nita's hopes dwindled as both the Harrisons and Januarys climbed aboard the bus. For some strange reason on the ride to Lake Charles, her mind wandered back again to the time she and Mary were trapped in the Gulf as little girls. She just couldn't relinquish that memory, no matter how hard she tried. It came back to her on that day the same way it had during the storm. The memory of the white caps rolling over her and Mary, as they struggled to make it to shore was as clear as if it had occurred only that morning, rather than many, many, years ago.

"I remember Daddy telling us, in the midst of a storm, don't give up. Don't give up! Don't give up!"

Nita rose up and screamed. The shout was alarming, it frightened both Greg and Marlon.

"Honey! You all right?" asked Lee Boy.

"Yeah, yeah...I'm okay...I guess I just had a bad dream."

Nita looked around and hoped to still be dreaming, however reality brought her back amongst strangers on the bus. Lillie rubbed her back and said "It's good to let it out, Honey. Just trust God... Every thing's gonna work out after while. You'll see."

Once the ride concluded, the bus pulled up to the Arena at McNeese State College. Nita's heart accelerated once again as she set foot on the ground. Her body felt heavily sedated each step she took into the large facility. Nita looked in every direction, searching for any sign of her relatives. The shelter was too congested with hundreds of people for her to recognize anyone.

Little Marlon hung onto her arm tightly, but still she almost dropped him on a few instances as she walked. Inside the Arena, the noise in the building was loud amongst the colored and white people. Nita became stricken with a throbbing headache. Soon after they arrived, the Harrisons and Januarys were each assigned an army cot.

The first thing Nita and Lee Boy did after they settled in was to seek medical attention from the American Red Cross for Marlon's raw little bottom. The poor little hazel and green eyed infant screamed bloody murder when the nurse examined his thighs and buttocks. Greg watched and cringed in agony as real tears streamed down Marlon's face. It appeared as though he felt his baby brother's pain himself. Soon after his pain was soothed with Ammen's medical powder, Marlon felt a whole lot better. Lee Boy and the boys lay down and took themselves a nap, but Nita was too weary too sleep, so she wandered around the place to see if she could find her family. The first person she recognized was Bryant's brother Levion.

"Hello Uncle Levion!" she yelled over the loud noise.

He appeared demented, looking as though he didn't even know who she was.

"Have you seen daddy?" she asked in a low tone.

Levion stared straight through her, and nervously shook his head "no".

"You haven't?"

But not another word came from him. Nita later spoke to her Uncle Levion's son Rudolph, who told her that his father had dropped Rudolph Jr., in the rolling surf and almost lost him.

However, he was able to recover the toddler in the nick of time, which saved his life. Rudolph, Jr. was just a little older than Gregory. Nita asked Rudolph if he'd seen any of her family. His reply was "no I haven't seen any of them yet."

Nita wandered through the crowd of people, insanely searching for a clue. From a distance she saw the back of a colored girl's head which appeared familiar. She rushed towards the young lady. The faster she walked the more Nita believed that it was true. "Oh thank God, I see Mary. Thank you, Jesus that's got to be her. I know that's Mary!" Once Nita was close enough to the young lady, she reached out her arms and shouted "Mary! Mary! Mary" As soon as the girl turned around, Nita grabbed her excitedly, and extended a big hug. The unidentified female looked startled.

"I'm so sorry" said Nita under her breath. "I, I, thought...I mean, you looked like...I was hoping that you were my...I'm so sorry if I startled you."

As Nita apologized and tried to explain her behavior the girl was sympathetic. Nita gave up hope for a while and returned to Lee Boy and the boys. As the evening faded into the night, no sign of any of the Barties surfaced. Nita's heart bled as apprehension over her family's survival mounted. Before Nita lay down on the cot, she ate some sandwiches that Lee Boy had gotten for her. Then she prayed faithfully.

"Lord, I have not given up hope just yet. But it's so hard not knowing where my family is. I'm asking you Lord, one more time to please! Please! Please! let me see them again!"

Afterwards, Nita just rolled over and tried to go to sleep. June 28, 1957 turned out to be a sunny, hot Friday in downtown Houston, Texas. Mae Dozier had just gotten off from work at about 1:00 o'clock in the afternoon. The first bus dropped her off about two blocks away from Foley's Department Store. She needed to cross Lamar Street in order to transfer to another bus for the ride home. At the same time, a police officer was standing at the intersection of Lamar and Travis directing traffic. From out of nowhere strolled an attractive colored lady dressed in a fashionably white linen suit, with an arm full of shopping bags. She appeared to have just stepped out of a beauty shop, as she sported her very chic hairstyle. The elegant lady's face was perfectly made up and she also possessed an air of social grace. When the officer noticed the pretty female approaching the intersection, he halted the traffic and motioned for her to cross the street all by herself. Mae a few feet behind on the sidewalk saw the kind gesture that the policeman had rendered. Naturally, she desired the same courtesy.

"Oh no buddy!" said Mae. "You gon have to hold up the traffic for me too because she ain't got no walk like mines. Hum! Watch this."

Mae put it in high gear and wheeled around the other pedestrians standing patiently on the corner, awaiting their signal to cross. Mae was not dressed nearly as flashy as the other lady, but she showed off her million dollar walk and twisted by the officer in such a way that he couldn't help but to stop, look at her and comment.

"Lord, Lord, Lord…it ought to be a law for somebody to be that fine and walk like that…ump! ump! ump!" The officer said loud enough for Mae to hear him. She just smiled and said "Hi do," very feminine as she twisted over the pavement to the other side of Lamar Street. Not only did Mae turn the officer's head, but other men standing by gawked as they watched her pace down the street.

As Mae caught up to the attractive lady dressed in white, she gave her a "now that's how you supposed to do it" look and kept right on twisting her hips to the bus stop. The sophisticated lady paid no attention to Mae's triviality, and simply proceeded into Foley's with her head held high, her nose elevated directly into the air. Mae laughed to herself, and waited diligently for her designated bus to arrive. In the meantime, standing on the street amongst other transit riders, a paper boy selling the Houston Chronicle shouted out very loudly and clearly:

"EXTRA! EXTRA! EXTRA! READ ALL ABOUT IT! HURRICANE AUDREY KILLS OVER 525 PEOPLE DOWN IN CAMERON, LOUISIANA, YESTERDAY. READ ALL ABOUT IT...HERE!"

"OH NO!" screamed Mae at the top of her lungs. "ALL MY KIN PEOPLE LIVES DOWN IN CAMERON! THAT CAN'T BE TRUE!!!!!"

The unexpected announcement caused her to pass out momentarily. A crowd of people gathered quickly to see what the commotion was all about. The police officer abruptly left the intersection and ran over to investigate.

"Okay backup! Backup I say! Please backup and give the woman some air. Backup I said."

A few seconds later Mae came to and found herself draped in the arms of the policeman.

"Are you all right?" he asked.

"I, I, I, guess so, officer."

"I just saw you cross the street a few minutes ago. What happened to you?"

"I don't know. The only thing I remembered was when I heard that paperboy say over 525 people died in a storm down in Cameron, Louisiana...I guess I passed out."

"Oh yea! I heard about that this morning on my way in to work."

"Lord have mercy Jesus! Is it really true?"

"Um uh! They say it was the worst storm to ever hit the Gulf coast since the one tore up Galveston many years ago."

"Oh Lordy! My poor momma...my sisters...and my nephew with his lil family all live down in Cameron."

"Well Ma'me, I'm sorry to hear that," replied the officer as he assisted Mae up to her feet. "Are you sure you gon be all right?"

"Yes sir...I mean...I think so," she replied sort of staggering.

"Well take care now," said the officer, as he held onto Mae's arm, while she stepped onto the bus.

As soon as Mae got home she called her husband Tug at work. When he got home, he called his cousin, Jimmy Dozier, Mae's half sister Will's son, and together the three of them ventured to Lake Charles. The ride was a very intense one the entire way. At one point, a road block had been established and a patrolman told them that they would not be able to get through. Tug and Jimmy, however convinced the officer they were not going to return to Houston unless they found out the plight of their relatives.

Eventually, he let the trio through after giving them much aggravation. At approximately 11:00 o'clock that night, they arrived at the McNeese Arena. Mae and Tug found Frances bare-footed and damp, lying on a cot next to Lillie, Lee Boy, Nita and the boys. Mae was so glad to see that all of them were alive.

Eventually, Mae's two brothers Ben "Bobby" and Phillip "Ray" took Frances home with them to Port Arthur, Texas. Jimmy was relieved, after he saw his parents, Will and Lutchet Dozier, and his sister Annie Mae and husband Clem January, had all survived.

In the meantime, Nita still had not heard a word from her family. Once Mae and Tug got back to Houston, Mae's boss, Mrs. Eugene Shepherd, and Mrs. Shepherd's sister Catherine Johnson, heard about the catastrophe down in Cameron, they gave her several nice pieces of clothing for Frances, Lillie and Nita out of the goodness of their hearts.

Even though hundreds of volunteers such as the American Red Cross, the U. S. Army, the Coast Guard, Air Force, National Guard, Civil Defense and many other assistance agencies joined forces to provide aid to the survivors, Saturday morning June 29, 1957 brought with it much confusion and added bewilderment to say the least. The word circulating throughout the entire Arena was that well over 500 victims had lost their lives in the hurricane. The startling number sent Nita into a morose state for she still hadn't heard anything about her loved ones. Meanwhile, around the city of Lake Charles, the area funeral homes started receiving AUDREY'S fatalities by the truck loads. Unsurprisingly, the day after the storm, a mutual regard amongst colored and white people was established, even though both races lived in segregated communities. However, that sentiment changed considerable as plans for a mass burial got underway. Of course, the white victims would be buried at the Highland Memory Garden's Cemetery, while on the other hand the colored dead would be laid to rest at Combre Memorial Park. Most of the white citizens in the area had a definite concern over intermingling their relative's remains with the colored's fallen victims. In the midst of the confusion, several mistakes were made due to the fact that some of the white causalities had turned so dark. Funeral directors couldn't determine whether or not they were Negro or Caucasian. Those indeterminate white victims erroneously wound up either at Combre, Fondel or Winnfield colored funeral homes, while many fair complected Negro bodies were mistakenly taken to the designated white funeral parlors. Too much emphasis was placed on race, in the first place, especially after such a devastating catastrophe as AUDREY had claimed so many innocent lives. One would think that all of the dead corpses should have been buried together in one cemetery, however, that was not case. What difference did color make anyway? Everyone who lost a relative whether Negro or white shared the same unrelenting grief. Sadly to say, the color of one's skin did make a difference, even after death had claimed all those lives so tragically!

As Saturday morning progressed towards the noon hour, Nita's hopes of ever seeing her family alive again began to fade. She saw several people she knew from Cameron and Creole, however no one could provide her with any assured information about the Barties. Meanwhile, a relative had shared some very tragic news with her. She told Nita that nine bodies were discovered under the roof of Leon "Sinome" and Ida Moore's home west of St. Hubert's Catholic Church. Hearing about that tragedy caused things to look extremely dismal for Bryant and the rest of the family because Nita knew that the Moore's lived near her father's home. The cousin also told Nita that Bryant's brother Noah Bartie's son Lee lost his entire family as well. The dreadful news sent shock waves up and down her spine.

Nita returned to her cot and shared the horrifying information with Lee Boy. She couldn't keep calm. Her whole body shook as she tried patiently to wait out the dilemma, however, her patience was running very low by then. The only soothing solution that she could resort to was prayer.

"Dear God. It's me again. I know you're probably tired of me calling out your name so much. But, my Father, I'm left here with no other choice. You are the only friend that I've got in this whole world that will hear my call. Lord, my heart is full. I'm hurting, my Father, and I have no other place to turn to. I remember my daddy told me as a little girl, 'In the midst of a storm, don't give up on you.' And you know something, my heavenly Father, I can't give up on you now. No matter how tough this storm has been and still is now. I can't give up on you Lord. Even though I don't have a home to return too, and the only thing that I have left are my husband, my kids and the clothes on my back, I know that you are going to bring my family back to me. I'm tired, Lord, and I can no longer bear this burden all by myself. So I'm gonna give it up to you. But there is something that I must express in the meantime. Thank you, Lord. Thank you...Thank you.... Thank you...Thank you...Lord! Oh, Thank you Jesus. In the midst of my grief, I can never say thank you enough. For you have already blessed me tremendously, in more ways than I can ever think to repay. Oh, thank you my heavenly Father...Thank you so very much!

Soon after Nita had prayed devoutly, she felt an immediate serenity. Afterwards, she lay peacefully on her cot. Within a brief moment, she stared out over the hundreds of people and cots that lined the building from one end of the Arena to the other. As she stared, a young colored girl, shabbily dressed, bare footed, brown skinned, with beautiful coal black hair passed by her view at a distance. Nita couldn't see the girl's face from the viewpoint in which she lay. However, she recognize the back of the girl's head without a doubt. The colored girl appeared lost as she ventured through the crowd of people, looking as though she was searching for something or someone, desperately. All of a sudden, Nita jumped up onto her feet, stumbled and ran through several people in the process to get to the girl. The closer she got, the more familiar the young lady appeared. When Nita caught up to her, she yelled "MARY!"

The young lady recognized her familiar voice, turned and yelled "NITA!" at the top of her lungs. The two sisters grabbed each other like they hadn't seen one another for many years, and embraced for a very long moment. Then the tears rolled down both their faces. Finally, the glorious reuniting between Nita and Mary had come to pass, eliminating part of the enigma that had both of them tormented.

"OH THANK YOU JESUS FOR YOU HEARD MY CRY!" rejoiced Nita, as the tears kept flowing.

"THANK YOU JESUS, FOR BRING MY SISTER BACK TO ME!" responded Mary between loud sniffles.

"Mary! What about Momma?"

"She's okay, Nita!"

"Ahhh! Thank you Jesus!" screamed Nita. "Daddy?"

"He made it too!" cried Mary.

"Oh thank the Lord!" Nita screamed louder. "Lil? Lo? Nip? Bill? Walter? Maw-Maw? Paw-Paw? What about all of them?"

"Lil, Lo, Nip and Walter are all fine. But we haven't heard anything yet from Maw-Maw, Paw-Paw, nor Bill and his family."

"Oh Mary, I hope they are all okay. Oh thank you Lord!" cried Nita some more. "Mary you just don't know how I've been wondering if I was ever gonna see all of you again. You'll never know the grief I've suffered."

"How's my little fellows and Lee doing?" sniffled Mary.

"They're okay...thank God. Marlon's got a bad diaper rash, but other than that, everybody else is fine."

"We were so scared Nita. We didn't know if ya'll had made it out alive or what. Everything happened so quickly."

"I know Mary. Us too. I got so scared after we got here, and when I didn't see any of ya'll, I almost had a nervous breakdown," cried Nita. "I liked to lost my mind, girl."

Once the moving reunion between Nita and Mary settled down a bit, they sat around the Arena, talked and shared their gruesome experiences for hours. Nita was later reunited with Bryant, Lil and Walter, in exchange of some more happy tears of joy. Bean, Nip and Lo had been taken to Sulphur, Louisiana by helicopters, so Nita had not yet seen them. Just knowing they were alive and well was consolation enough for her. Mary, Bryant, Lil and Nip had been transported from Cameron by boat up the Calcasieu River to Lake Charles. Even though the plight of Maw-Maw, Paw-Paw, Bill and his family was not yet known, some of the pressure had lifted off of Nita's chest.

A few days later, Maw-Maw, Paw-Paw, Bill, Susie and their children were all joined with the Barties and Nita. When Bean met her mother, Maw-Maw they locked arms and sobbed together. This probably was the saddest reuniting of all. They both were extremely happy to see each other even though Maw-Maw's eyes were filled with tears. She had been crying extensively over the loss of her mother, Grandma Louisa, her step-father, Grandpa Seedy, and her half sister Lucille Moore. In addition to those tragedies, she and Paw-Paw also grieved over the loss of their son, Joe Bishop, his wife Alice—their daughter Annie and husband Dalton LeBlanc—and their little girl Vickie. Paw-Paw didn't have much to say as he sat overwhelmed with sorrow. He appeared to be still in a state of shock, staring vacantly into space. Bean took the death of her brother pretty hard, as well. So did Nita and Mary, and they wept loudly over the loss of their childhood cousin and friend, Annie. Another sad meeting occurred when Bill's wife Susie was reunited with her mother, Lucinda. That moment rendered another tear shedding ordeal, once Lucinda shared the grim news with Susie over the loss of her husband John Cass Mouton, two daughters Emma Lois Mouton and Viola Mouton Singleton, and her grandson John Darrell Ford. Susie's heart felt like it had stopped beating, as she tried to make sense of it all. After she'd gained her composure she reassured her mother that Katherine and her family had survived that awful day.

Once the burdensome news became well reported, many people arrived from far away places to identify their dead relatives. One family that was hit tremendously by AUDREY'S destruction was the Reed family. Lee Boy's uncle Frank Reed somehow survived the 1918 storm, however he was not quite as fortunate the second time around when AUDREY struck. Frank Reed was found dead near his home in Grand Chenier, clasping the body of his four year old grandson, Frank Reed, III. On the day of the vicious storm, Frank Reed's roomy house which stood on 80 acres of fertile land was overwhelmed by AUDREY'S rough surf. Four other grandchildren lost their lives Janet Reed, seven, Geraldine Guidry, three, Rebecca Guidry, seven, and Bobby Sims, nine. The bodies of his wife Jeanette "Aunt Duke", and little Rebecca were never found. In addition, Frank Reed's son Johnny lost his wife Leona and several children. Six out of the fifteen people who sought refuge at the Johnny Reed home in Cameron were fortunate enough to have survived. From Galveston, the Lake Charles area and as far away as California, the Reed relatives came home to mourn the losses.

Meanwhile, Bryant Bartie went from funeral home to funeral home, searching for family victims who were still missing. His mother Big Momma had survived along with his brother Pat. However, during the process, his heart ached immensely when he came across the body of his own son Raymond Bartie. Seeing the young man in such a decomposed state was a tough pill for him to swallow. Bryant later learned that Raymond's wife, Lula, also drowned. Before he left the funeral home, he whispered softly in the young man's ear, "May you rest in peace, son."

Son's wife, Jeanette January was elated over the news that her parents, Mr. and Mrs. Henry Mayne, had survived AUDREY. She later came to know they saved their lives by seeking refuge in an elevated portion of their home. The small house although it fell into a large hole, remained tilted upward out of the high water for the duration of the storm. Everyone in Jeanette's family was accounted for except a sister Bernice Payton. She and her husband Sidney lived on the Buster Sturlese property in Creole. Jeanette went from funeral home to funeral home in search of her sister's body, however she was never found amongst the hundreds of decomposed fallen victims.

The actual burial of AUDREY'S victims turned out to be one of the saddest days in the history of Cameron Parish. Two mass funerals were scheduled, one at Combre Memorial Park and the other at the Highland Memory Gardens Cemetery. Hundreds of people congregated at both locations to pay their final respects. Several lengthy six foot trenches were dug out by a huge drag line, and hastily built wooden coffins were lowered into the ground one by one. Lime had been sprinkled loosely over the victim's bodies to help suppress some of the smell, and the sun shined brightly on the men who assisted in the interment process. They wore masks draped across their entire face because of the odor, which was dispersed throughout the cemetery. Many Lake Charles area-colored residents had come to witness the service. A few of them made lewd comments over the unbearable smell. As Jeanette January watched sadly, an unknown woman commented, "Boy they sure do stink. I can't take this ol' smell no more! I'm going home!"

The comment infuriated Jeanette to no end. Here she was, already mourning over the fact that her sister's body was still missing, and that some of the dead being buried today were family and friends. To hear such insensitive remarks caused her to lash out at the anonymous bystander. Jeanette turned around and said "Hey Miss, you had no business coming out here today if you couldn't take the smell. Them poor people are dead, and they can't help the way they smell. And it ain't they fault, they had to die this way, neither. Maybe you should've just stayed home if the smell bothers you that much."

The woman realized only after it was too late that her comment was definitely out of order. She walked away very embarrassed over her insulting criticism. As the lengthy process went forward, many tears were shared on this day by everyone who had come. So many untold stories, dreams, and innocent lives would soon be buried six feet under the earth. One sad note was that somewhere embedded within the coffins of badly decomposed bodies lay 19 year old Betty Jane Leblanc, with her premature baby's head still projecting from her vaginal cavity. Also included amongst the dead was her 18 month old son, Carl. The body of Frank Reed was buried in the same wooden box with Frank Reed III, the grandfather clutching the grandson in the same manner in which they'd been found. Charlene Moore Galloway, along with her two children Delores and James; maternal grandparents Grandma Louisa and Grandpa Seedy Andrews; her parents Adam and Lucille Moore, and her paternal grandmother Susan Rose Moore were amongst the many bodies that lined the trench. Matilda "Big Momma" Bartie was there to grieve the loss of her daughter Sara VanDyke. The sweet old couple Ennis and Rosie Andrews, who Nita, as a young lady, had stayed many nights with while she worked for Mrs. Delia Rutherford were amongst the many inanimate casualties lying beneath the earth on that day.

On the other side of town, the same grief and sorrow' was experienced by the white survivors. They too had come from far away places to pay homage to their deceased family and friends. One interesting point was that even though a concerted effort had been made to keep the colored and white bodies separated that attempt was ultimately in vain. Frank Reed's half brother, Steve Sturlese, was a very fair complected gentleman who, as a matter of fact, resembled a white man. Though he was colored, somehow' his body was mistakenly buried along with the white victims. Many fair complected colored people whose bodies were never recovered or positively identified at the colored funeral homes were presumed to be buried at Highland Memory Gardens Cemetery, as well.

Remember the Eloi Conner's, a white family that lived near the Barties, while they were tenants on the Rutherford property? Those poor people certainly experienced tremendous heartache over their lifetime. First, their two sons Joseph Euclide and William Andrew' were tragically killed during wartime, many years before. Victimized by tragedy once again, the Conner's only surviving son, John Sidney, and his wife, Lou Elda Vincent, lay somewhere below the earth in a wooden box, as a result of AUDREY'S relentless onslaught.

As a gentle breeze blew over the midst of the colored people gathered at Combre Memorial Park, the sun slowly descended in the sky. Once the last wooden box was lowered into the trench, a huge pile of dirt was flattened over the massive hole. The repulsive smell dwindled soon thereafter. A feeling of sorrow lingered in every person's heart as they stood and watched the very last wooden box overcome with dirt. Not a dry eye remained, while an area Minister concluded a brief eulogy.

"Let us pause, please—for a moment of silence to remember the hundreds of fallen victims who lost their lives on a dreary, gloomy, shadowy, Thursday—June 27, 1957. This was an awful time for those who lived in the lower Cameron Parish area. One in which the survivors shall never forget, as long as they so live. My Father, we want to thank you for our past, give you the honor for the present, and we ask of your true mercies for the future. I pray for each innocent life, both colored and white, that was lost as a result of this mammoth hurricane. Remember them in the end with your precious grace. Please comfort the hearts of family and friends that are hurting during their hour of sorrow. Let them all know, that even through the storm, a brighter day is sure to come. And, my Father, in the midst of their grief and misery, we still want to lift up the glorious name of Jesus to the highest! For it has been your true mercies which has brought all of us thus far by faith. And faith, my Father will see each of us through this unforgettable tragedy that has pained our lives so immensely. Amen!"

Once the sun set into the evening, the picturesque sky turned to darkness with several beautiful floral wreaths prominently placed at both burial grounds. As the day came to a close, the mild wind blew a few decorative ribbons back and forth, and they fluttered gently. Nothing else could be seen over the large barren sites after the dirt had been leveled. Both mass graves shall endlessly depict the memories of AUDREY'S victims; Gone, But Not Forgotten." And God's true mercies shall endureth forever, and ever and ever! According to the Federal Emergency Management Agency (FEMA), AUDREY was the fifth most devastating hurricane of the twentieth century. As time went on, varied death tolls were reported between 525 to 600 people killed. Months after the disaster, many bodies continued to be found in Cameron Parish's isolated marshlands. Other storms greater than AUDREY on record included the 1918 Florida Keys and Texas Hurricane; the Okeechobee, Florida storm of 1828; the New England hurricane of 1938; and Hurricane Diane of 1955. AUDREY'S gale winds and high tides ranged well over several hundred miles to the east and west along the Gulf coastline at the time of the disaster. 30 additional lives were claimed along a 1,500 mile path after AUDREY left the Gulf of Mexico and made her way up to Ontario, Canada, where she finally dissipated. For most of the residents in the lower Cameron Parish area, Hurricane AUDREY became a milestone that chronicled events in their lives which occurred either "before the storm", or "after the storm."

Approximately 1,316 homes were completely destroyed, while another 1,206 were heavily damaged. About 640 farm buildings were totally beyond reconstruction, and an additional 1,227 required major repairs. However, the large beige courthouse built under President Franklin Delano Roosevelt's administration in the town square of Cameron majestically endured AUDREY'S gale forces. Several hundred lives were saved on the upper two floors of the courthouse, as droves of families sought refuge there. Sheriff O. B. Carter and Sheriff Henry

A. Reid of Cameron and Calcasieu Parishes, respectively, were praised highly for their outstanding work during the aftermath of the atrocity. So was the Cameron Parish Civil Defense for their tireless labor. Also recognized for their outstanding contributions were Dr. C. W. Clark, Dr. S. E. Carter, and Dr. G. W. Dix, who survived the storm in his house on top of a refrigerator, alongside his horse in the kitchen. The Cameron Consolidated School for Negro children was totally destroyed. A new school, Audrey Memorial High, was later reconstructed on the same property. It stood as a monument for those victims whose tears and blood were shed in the flood on June 27, 1957. The school's mascot became "the Hurricanes", a very befitting designation. The Ebenezer Baptist Church in Cameron was totally destroyed, and later rebuilt on the same property, as was the St. James Church of God in Christ in Grand Chenier. The St. Hubert Catholic Church in Creole was renamed St. Rose of Lima, after a new building had been assembled. A new modern facility, renamed the South Cameron Memorial Hospital in Creole, replaced the old St. Gabriel Hospital building in which AUDREY sent sliding over the surf during the flood.

Frank Reed's half sister. Agnes "Coot" Sturlese-Nash, became a very inspirational figure in the community as she strove earnestly year after year to recognize those victims who'd died as a result of AUDREY'S devastation. Mrs. Nash took it upon her own merits to go from door to door throughout the lower Cameron Parish area communities and collect money's for floral and wreaths to be placed annually at the monument erected in Combre Memorial Park commemorating the anniversary of the violent calamity. She also organized a memorial program which included orations, singing, and praying at the burial site rendered by local dignitaries, the clergy, area church choirs, and surviving relatives. Her diligent efforts were appreciated and remembered for many years to follow.

CHAPTER 18

As the months rolled forward, the residents of lower Cameron Parish were assigned rent houses in the Lake Charles area. They adjusted well to the temporary living conditions, until their new homes were later rebuilt. Many inhabitants, however decided not to rebuild in the Cameron area, fearing the same type of devastation would reoccur. Those skeptical citizens chose to stake their claims elsewhere, in other parts of the state. They hoped to find a more appealing lifestyle, and to forget about their traumatic experience.

However, Lee Boy, Nita and the boys decided that they would return to Grand Chenier, soon after they received their insurance reimbursements. The young colored couple didn't have much insight on a lot of things in life, but at least they still owned property there. Despite their tremendous loss, this was home for them, and Lee Boy felt that home was where they belonged, especially to raise a family. John "Son" January and his family shared the same sentiments as Lee Boy. "Why move somewhere else?" said he, "when we already gotta start in Grand Chenier? Jeanette, I say let's go back home." Simon and Lillie Harrison, and Frances January felt the same way. "We grew up down there, so why should we leave. This is home to us," spoke Simon from the heart. The Harrisons and Januarys returned to their original property, to start a new lease on life.

Bryant Bartie on the other hand encountered a bit of difficulty when he confronted Bean over the issue of returning home to Creole, Louisiana.

"Bryant, I ain't moving back to no Creole," said Bean. I mean it. Go back there for what? So the next time we all can drown in another storm...No Sir! Not me. I ain't going back down there. You can go if you want too, but I want be by your side. I say let's find us a place up here in Lake Charles. At least it will be safer here, than in Creole close to that ol' Gulf. And Bryant, you'll never know, when that ol' thing is gonna come over again, just like it did during AUDREY!"

"Na na na na Bean, I don't know why you talking crazy for in the first place. Creole is our home. You see Bean, the thing you've got to realize is, you can't run from LIFE'S RAGIN STORMS! Plague-take-it! No matter how hard you try, and it don't matter where you live at. You see, there's always gonna be some kind of storm going on in your life. Whether it's a flood... An earthquake...A fire...A tornado...or some other kind of natural disaster. And you know the bible speaks of earthquakes in diver's places. One day we might not even have enough food to eat on our table, and that's a tough storm to weather, because you know, we both done been there before in our lives. Other times, you might have a bad storm going on in your own mind. Playing all kind of ol' tricks on you. And them mind storms is the worst kind because they will drive you crazy if you let them. You might look good on the outside, but there's a whirlwind tearing your head up on the inside. Some of your storms might be other people trying to hurt ya and pull you down to the ground. While other storms just might be the Lord trying to get your attention to do what he wants you to do, and not what ya think you should be doing yourself. Dealing with the death of a loved one is a storm. Another storm may be having to deal with something your own children done, done that they ain't suppose to. Even though we know we ain't raised them like that—their behavior can cause a ragin storm in your heart that'll tear you to pieces. Another storm is gonna be dealing with these ol' white folks. And it don't matter where we live at in this country, either. You know how hard they can make things for us colored people. To some of um we's just like dirt anyways and the color of our skin sure don't help the situation.

Bean, I guess what I'm trying to say is, you gonna have all kind of storms going on in your life at some time or another to deal with. And just because AUDREY done came along and took everything away that we owned, don't mean it ain't gonna be something else, that will do the same thing all over again. Shoots, me and you both can get killed tomorrow in a car wreck or come down with some ol' sickness that can take our life that way. So you see, it's always gonna be a storm looking you dead in the face, no matter what! Now Bean, I know I ain't explaining myself too clearly to ya! But there's just one thing you've got to remember. In the midst of a storm don't give up on God. Because he will see you through every time. Remember, life is a storm, Bean. And at some point you're either entering one, in the middle of one or coming out of one! But through the wind and the rain, the Lord will always send the sun shining brightly through. You've got to let him have his own way, though. That's what's wrong with everybody in this world right now. When a storm comes...they just give up on God so quick. Just put your trust in the Lord, my dear."

"Well Bryant, you do make a lot of sense," responded Bean.

"We really can't run from the storms of life, can we?"

"No Ma'am, we sure can't. God spared us through AUDREY for a reason. So we must go on back home, and ask him to show us what he wants to do with our lives. Lee Boy, Nita, Bill and Susie are going to need us to help raise their kids. And we still got a big job to finish raising Mary, Lil, Lo, Nip and ol' Dad."

"Yeah, you're right again," sighed Bean. "Okay then, let's go on home to Creole, Bryant—and start all over again."

"Well Plague-take-it Bean, that sounds good enough to me," chuckled Bryant as he gave his wife a loving hug. "We done already got through a lot of storms in our lives before. And with the Lord and me, standing by your side," he laughed. "Together we gonna weather a many more!"

DENOUEMENT

Life's Ragin' Storms continued to terrorize the lives of many. There were physical, mental, ambiguous storms which were a constant ingredient of everyone's living; family members continued to transition, while new lives were welcomed to the world wholeheartedly. All the challenges life could bring were like a never-ending dream for my family and the people of lower Cameron Parish. Nevertheless, the citizens in that region of Louisiana were resilient. When the storms kept coming, they were able to somehow overcome so many obscurities and never gave up on the land they called home. "Cameron Strong" was a household metaphor that gave our people the strength to dream, to dream big and let nothing stand in their way of preserving that Cameron spirit.

Wanita B. Harrison was a stalwart trailblazer who never let much stand in the way of her personal goals. Eventually, she earned a Bachelor of Science in Secondary Education and a Master of Education and earned credits towards her 30 hours plus at McNeese State University in Lake Charles, Louisiana. She had hoped to become a nurse but was forced to change her major to secondary education because of the lack of opportunities in the nursing field for African Americans in lower Cameron Parish during the 1960s. For 33 years, Wanita was contented teaching biology, chemistry and physics at Audrey Memorial and South Cameron High Schools in Creole, Louisiana. Even though nursing was her first career choice, she found her niche and enjoyed every moment influencing the lives of her many students; in which she mentored, provided optimistic support and guidance during her tenure as a teacher. A poor sharecropper's daughter, Wanita, beat the odds and rose above the cotton fields of Creole. She was a self-taught, self-made lady, with a class and style of her own. For those that knew her one would have never comprehended her meager beginnings. Never pretentious. Just confident, soft spoken; a classic, well-polished, intellect, described her temperament profoundly.

Lee J. Harrison became a pumper on the Block 2 Well in the Gulf of Mexico. His recognition and eagerness to learn allowed him to master the skill in a short time frame. Sam L. Warren employed Lee in 1960, as a pumper and captain of the "Wanda B", which further enhanced his oil service expertise. In 1972 Lee took a leap of faith, resigned from Mr. Warren's company and became an independent contractor under the Harrison Oil Well Service Company. In 1983, his company was incorporated and became Harrison Production Services, Inc. in which Lee provided maintenance for inland oil wells to keep production flowing. Additional responsibilities included preparation of production and volumetric reporting. Wanita did an impeccable job keeping the financial records for the company which allowed him to remain in business for over 43 years as owner/operator. A milestone deserving of many accolades. In honor of his devotion to his work and corporation, he was named the 54th Louisiana Fur and Wildlife Festival King in 2011 which recognized a business owners' contribution to the oil industry; the first African American ever selected.

With all the storms Lee and Wanita had weathered during their lifetime God blessed them bountifully. Their complex located in Grand Chenier, Louisiana stood as a milestone in which the two had worked abundantly together to preserve their legacy.

Oh yes! Quite an accomplishment for two African Americans in which the odds for success was a barrier they overcame.

Lee and Wanita survived two major hurricanes in their lifetime, Audrey in 1957 and Rita in 2005. Even though Rita in September of that year annihilated the Cameron coastline leaving an eyesore of destruction in her path, Lee managed to keep his business operable by wading through high waters with the aim of getting the production to flow for his contracted wells expeditiously. Lee J. Harrison, quite a man to reckon with, will always be remembered for his passion, dedication, and irreconcilable work ethic.

After Hurricane Rita, Lee could not let go of the place he loved so much. However, the ragin' storm forced him and Wanita to relocate further inland to Lake Charles, Louisiana. After all the dialogue between family members who tried to convince him not to remodel the storm tattered home, he made the decision to invest funds to restore it. Once the home was finished, he and Wanita had to lease it to make the insurance payments which had become astronomical.

One thing's for sure catastrophic storms have no respect of persons. Even though a person may work profusely their entire life in the wink of an eye, mother nature will destroy your dreams as though they never existed. Your legacy gets washed away and the only memory that you must hold on too are those engraved in your psyche. Sometimes you may have salvaged pictures of the way things used to be. Nevertheless, your community will never be the same. Not as you remembered. So, you resort to live on as though it was a bad dream that never goes away. In the meantime, you thank God for all his blessings. Nothing is promised and we must come to the realization that material possessions can be here today and gone today. Like Lee and Wanita, you work hard to build your legacy, but life has no guarantees. Enjoy each day like it is your last and always know there is a higher being. The storms will come, and the storms will go. But do not fret because life is a multitude of storms. Hold on and continue to look up. And when the storms of life are Ragin' God will be standing by to see you through.

August 27, 2020, the Ragin Storms of Life once again was perceptible. Hurricane Laura made landfall with peak intensity riding on a 10-foot-high storm surge and 150 miles per hour sustained winds. The tenth strongest US hurricane on record made landfall near Cameron, Louisiana yet again. I could not sleep listening to the devastating forecast as Laura annihilated my birthplace in Grand Chenier, Louisiana. Anxiety set in a calamitous way. That treacherous day brought back so many memories. It took me back to 2005 when Mom and Dad's place took a palpitating beating. I reminisced the look on their faces when I arrived in Grand Chenier after Hurricane Rita.

All the news networks placed emphasis on the destruction Laura had so gruesomely plowed through the communities of Cameron, Creole and Grand Chenier. The news was unbearable. I saw what Rita had done years before and hoped for the worst. The only solace that I could comprehend was the fact that dad had passed away February 28, 2018, and Mom December 29, 2020, about 8 months prior to Laura's devastating trek through their homeplace. Their hearts and minds would never be prepared to face the wrath of Laura. God knew exactly, Mom and Dad would not be able to mentally deal with another tragic ending for everything they had so worked copiously for.

Finally, the citizens of lower Cameron Parish were given the thumbs up to go home and inspect the grievance Laura had capitulated. I planned my trip to inspect their property prudently. I had come to know the storm surge had not subsided and high water was still present during the aftermath. I decided to drive through Lake Arthur on to Kaplan and Pecan Island arriving in Grand Chenier from the east side. As I drove, I realized just how much God had spared the area even though there was very little left standing. I went alone. As I drove and saw the devastation it took my breath away. The further westward I drove the worse the landscape looked. Once I got to Grand Chenier there was a deputy check point that I had to go through. I came to a stop and introduced myself to him. "Hi, I'm Dexter Harrison. I came to inspect my parent's property, Lee and Wanita Harrison. He remembered me and knew my parents very well. I asked, "what does the road ahead look like?" He was very slow to answer. He was a cordial young man and didn't say much. I really wanted to know what my parents' place looked like. He just told me he knew Dad very well and let me through. "Drive safely" he replied. From what I can remember he was Officer Suire, and I remembered his relatives that lived in the area. I could tell the road ahead would be tragic. As I drove, it was very evident the Grand Chenier community was hit hard. "Oh my God, there was nothing left" I thought. I finally arrived at St. Eugene Catholic Church. The devastation was quite evident. The whole front of the church was blown out. Brush from the marsh line the road with a small pathway to drive in the center of the highway. There was brush all over the church and several graves had cracked open with a multitude of debris everywhere. I pulled over for a short moment and grasped for my breath. After seeing the devastation, I had no conceptual idea of what I would find when I reached my parent's home.

Next stop was the St. Martin DePorres Cemetery. "WOW". Several graves were cracked open. Caskets were disbursed in nearby fields. I went to check on my grandparents' gravesites Simon and Lillie Harrison. Everywhere the eye could see was pure devastation. Just about every headstone had been pulled away from the vaults and thrown haphazardly throughout the grounds. I started hyperventilating. I knew when I got to my parents' place it was not going to be good. I took pictures and videos with my camera.

The time had come for me to put my feelings aside and come to grips everything that I saw that day was the will of God. And I knew there was no questioning his works. No need to try and comprehend the works of the Lord. Not to say for a moment that it doesn't cut like a knife. What do you do? What do you say? How are you supposed to feel? The thought in my mind kept resonating "you are not alone." As I drove up to my parents' place I was in awe. And that's when it hit me God is enormous. He is real and his will be done regardless of my own convictions.

I drove up the driveway. Put the truck in the park. Got out. And walked towards the devastation. I took about 6 steps and fell to my knees. My head landed on my legs. I said, "Oh my God". While I was on my knees other citizens from the area passed on the road and blew their horns. At that very moment, I came to the decision "it was best that Mom and Dad had gone on home to be with the Lord. It would have been difficult for them to comprehend any good of what had occurred. Particularly, for the third time in their lifetime. And that thought helped me to cope with my own inhibitions. Because it wasn't about me and my feelings, instead it helped me to bring closure to the fact Mom and Dad was no longer with us and their place served its purpose and now God decided it is over. It is done, it is finished and it's time to move on. Even though the pain lingered plenteously. No one can comprehend the disappointment unless they have walked the same path. An indiscernible feeling of hopelessness, loss and despair. The place where you grew up is just a poignant memory of agony, anguish and sorrow.

As if Laura was not harsh enough for the people of lower Cameron Parish to overcome. Another storm Delta six weeks later finished obliterating the area October 9, 2020, as a category 2 hurricane. Delta came ashore near Creole, Louisiana packing winds over 100 mph with a 10-foot storm surge. Incredibly, both storms made landfall approximately 10 miles apart from each other.

For those who have experienced Life's Ragin Storms you must find a way to move on. You cannot become stagnant. It will tear your mind to pieces. You must find your own way to cope. No matter what anyone says, until they have walked in your shoes don't expect them to comprehend. I had to deal with all the misfortune in my own way. I realized I am only human, and you must take a new lease on life.

The day my parent's place was demolished. It brought closure as I looked onward when the last truck load of debris was hauled away. I turned and walked away. Grateful for the good, the bad, the ugly and unforgettable moments, me and my family shared. It's just stuff that God had placed in our lives for a short while. I knew there would be many more storms to weather. "Just keep living" I thought. Thou who rules the wind and water will always be standing nearby. And that's most important on this journey we call life. It is God that will get you through any type of storm inciting your faith.

THE END

www.ingramcontent.com/pod-product-compliance
Lightning Source LLC
Chambersburg PA
CBHW070903120626
46546CB00001B/113